Linda Mckie
Bradford
22nd November 87.

D0588745

INSTEAD OF THE DOLE

INSTEAD OF THE DOLE

An enquiry into integration
of the
tax and benefit systems

Hermione Parker

ROUTLEDGE
London and New York

First published in 1989 by
Routledge
11 New Fetter Lane, London EC4P 4EE
29 West 35th Street, New York NY 10001

Typeset by LaserScript Limited, Mitcham, Surrey
Printed in Great Britain

British Library Cataloguing in Publication Data
Parker, Hermione
   Instead of the dole: an enquiry into
   integration of the tax and benefit systems.
   1. Great Britain. Taxation. Law. Reform –
   Proposals 2. Great Britain. Married
   couples. Taxation law – Reform – Proposals.
   3. Great Britain. Social Security benefits.
   Law. Reform. Proposals.
   I. Title
   344.1034

ISBN 0–415–00961–8
ISBN 0–415–04266–6Pbk.

This book is dedicated to the memory of
Sir Brandon Rhys Williams,
but for whom it would not have been written.

"... it is from the champions of the impossible
rather than the slaves of the possible
that evolution draws its creative force."

(Wootton 1967)

Contents

Contents

List of figures

ix

List of tables

Acknowledgements

The research for this enquiry was funded by the Joseph Rowntree Social Service Trust and the Esmée Fairbairn Charitable Trust, and accommodated in the Suntory-Toyota International Centre for Economics and Related Disciplines, London School of Economics.

Of the many people who have helped me, I would especially like to thank Professor A.B. Atkinson, Professor Patrick Minford, Holly Sutherland and Philip Vince. Without Holly Sutherland's expert assistance, the final chapter would not have been possible.

The opinions expressed are, needless to say, entirely my own.

Introduction and summary

The new poor

In Europe they are called the new poor, and in most of the big cities you see them. Some put a brave face on it – they play music, or do whatever odd jobs are available. Others have given up. They sit on the pavements, sometimes behind cardboard notices explaining the nature of their predicament. They are the casualties of unemployment and broken marriages, the unmarried mothers, and worst of all the children. *Sans emploi. Ohne Arbeit.* Unemployed. The sight of the new poor outside shops piled high with luxuries is deeply shocking. It is the contrast that shocks first, and then the realisation that what you see is only the tip of a problem of immense proportions, a problem that is not going away despite economic growth, and despite expenditure on social security of unprecedented proportions.

This enquiry takes a fresh look at the dual systems of cash benefits and personal income taxation (including social insurance contributions) that have grown up during the past one hundred years, and concludes that the tax and social security systems now in operation are themselves partly to blame for the new poverty. A new initiative, based on integration of the tax and benefit systems and abolition of payroll taxes, would be much more effective. Integrated systems would help stave off poverty by removing the contributory principle. Abolition of payroll taxes would help reduce unemployment, by making labour more competitive with machinery.

By removal of the contributory principle everyone becomes entitled to the same basic protection against poverty, and the only criterion is need. The lower paid are included as well as the unemployed, and all earnings restrictions are abolished. For each person or family there is an income guarantee. With *social dividend* or *basic income*, the guarantee is credited automatically and recouped from those who do not need it through the tax system. With *negative* and *reverse income tax* the administration is more cumbersome. Benefit entitlement equals the difference between each family's income and the amount of the guarantee. It is paid in arrears and usually has to be applied for. It is still better than no entitlement at all.

1

Less of the same, or a new remedy?

Although the detail of this report refers to Britain, the implications go much wider. Change is in the air throughout the Western democracies. People are sick and tired of the constant benefit cuts, they know that the new type of society into which we are moving requires something much more fundamental. But they are up against the formidable opposition of those whose interests are rooted in the *status quo*.

Within the EEC reform of the systems of personal income tax and social security reform has acquired new urgency, because of the pressure for harmonisation. Harmonisation is premature so long as the fundamentals of existing systems are in disarray, but this is unlikely to deter the politicians and bureaucrats whose futures depend on the appearance of making progress. Unless national governments take action to prevent it, the mistakes of the past will be re-cast in Brussels stone, and those worst affected will be those most in need.

In Britain the post-World War 2 social security system has been dosed with palliatives and assorted quack remedies for at least twenty years and is steadily deteriorating. Symptoms include escalating expenditures (despite benefit cuts) on an ever-increasing number of claimants, labyrinthine complexity and the reappearance of grinding, hopeless poverty. Mr Norman Fowler's *Social Security Review* (SSR) was billed as "the most fundamental examination of our social security system since the Second World War" (DHSS June 1985, Vol.1). It offered a golden opportunity to make a fresh start. Instead all the patient received was a stern rebuke and a prescription for more of the same – but with a reduced dosage.

The SSR took all the fundamentals for granted and avoided the key questions, for instance:

(1) The extent to which financing and other problems, not least unemployment, are the result either of design faults in the original Beveridge Plan, or of the way in which the Beveridge Plan was implemented.
(2) The extent to which the system is out of line with contemporary life styles and contemporary requirements, as a result for instance of women's emancipation and of micro electronics.
(3) Any examination of alternative systems.

This enquiry takes up where the SSR left off. It is concerned with root causes not symptoms, with all cash benefits not just DHSS benefits, and with indirect assistance through income tax reliefs as well as direct assistance through cash benefits. It starts by showing why Britain's social security system is beyond repair. It then examines the feasibility and desirability of alternative systems based on new principles and involving full or partial integration of the systems of personal income taxation and cash benefits. Like the Beveridge Report it is not directly concerned with health, education, housing or employment. But the links are very close, because it is concerned to ensure that every person living on these islands has the resources necessary to purchase the requirements of everyday living, and to take full advantage of the health and education services provided and to buy access to decent housing.

The starting point is the gap between popular expectations of income maintenance and what the system in operation actually delivers. Regarding expectations, it is based on the following, closely linked assumptions:

(1) That a majority of the British electorate supports the concept of an adequate, easily accessible, non-stigma-tising safety net, below which no person or family should be allowed to fall.

(2) That a majority would also insist that the safety net should be a base on which to build, not a device that traps people into long-term dependence on the state.

(3) That a growing number of voters, perhaps a majority, would prefer a safety net that does not discriminate between men and women, married and single.

There are some, of course, who reject state-financed social security *per se*, and would make each family responsible for its own, with charity as the ultimate safety net. For them this enquiry is of little interest. Here we start from the assumption that Government should accept responsibility for the safety net, and the argument is about the most equitable and efficient way of going about it.

Is integration a realistic option?

Integrated systems change the basis of entitlement from contrib-ution record and contingency to citizenship (or legal residence) and assessed basic need. Basic income (BI), but not negative income tax

(NIT) , also changes the unit of assessment from the family to the individual. Either would be an improvement on the existing systems, but each on its own has major disadvantages. With NIT the income guarantees are withdrawn in much the same way as conventional means-tested benefits. Work incentives are undermined and families get more benefit by splitting up. A full BI (where the income guarantees are sufficient to permit abolition of all other benefits) is much too expensive. The tax rate necessary to finance it would itself undermine work incentives. Either way full integration is not a viable option

Most schemes on offer under the brand name integration involve at most partial integration, and some are no more than extensions of the existing system. For the purpose of this enquiry, partial integration is defined as a system with two components, one fully integrated and one not, and after close analysis of five schemes, the report concludes that partial integration is the best way forward. *Basic income 2000 (BI 2000)* combines fully integrated, fully automated partial basic incomes (not enough to live on) with BI supplements and a residual, income-tested housing benefit, operated locally along traditional lines.

BI 2000 is a target strategy for the twenty-first century. It offers the prospect of an easily accessible, easy to run safety net at a cost the country can afford. It avoids both the costliness of full BI, and the disincentive effects of a full NIT. It would be operated through a fully hypothecated Transfer Income Account, to which the average person would contribute the same amount as s/he took out, over the life-cycle. At 1988 prices and estimated 2000 incomes each adult would be entitled to a *partial basic income* (PBI) of about £28 a week, with less for children. Old age and invalidity pensioners would receive PBI supplements, bringing their full entitlement to £70. All the BIs would be non-contributory, non-withdrawable, tax-free, individually based and fully automated. They would replace almost all existing cash benefits and as many as possible of existing tax reliefs, but the first tranche of earned income would be tax-free. Employees' and self-employed NI contributions would be integrated in the new, hypothecated income tax. Employers' NI contribution would be replaced by an increased tax on profits (or similar) and would be used to fund general Government expenditure. *BI 2000* is estimated to require a flat rate income tax of around 38 percent.

For people with no income of their own, or very little, the BIs are cash benefits, but for most people they are fixed amount credits

4

against tax. The effect is like a huge increase in tax allowances. By lifting the lower paid out of tax and by increasing the amounts payable for children, pensioners and people with disabilities, poverty is substantially prevented and work incentives are increased.

BI 2000 would open the way to a huge transfer of resources into the pockets of lower paid families and low income pensioners. To do this savings have to made elsewhere. *BI 2000* would close off the *state earnings-related pension* (SERPS) and widen the income tax base by phasing out mortgage interest and private pension tax reliefs. It would also save several thousand million pounds worth of red tape and duplicated services.

Instead of earnings rules, cohabitation rules and fraud squads, *BI 2000* goes with the grain of human nature – decriminalising the black economy of welfare, setting the unemployed free to work, study and train without loss of benefit, and abolishing the cohabitation rule. It is not a blue-print, but it could be the foundation stone for a new, unifying strategy of poverty prevention – an alternative to the present divisive policies of tax beyond ability to pay, offset by soul-destroying poverty relief.

A Budget for 1990

BI 2000 would have to be introduced incrementally, on the basis of consensus. *BIG PHASE 1* has been costed as an alternative to Mr Nigel Lawson's 1988 "give-away" Budget, although it could not be implemented until the Inland Revenue can cope with independent taxation of husband and wife. *BIG PHASE 1* is therefore aimed at April 1990.

In his 1988 Budget Mr Lawson concentrated on improving incentives at the top, and left a black hole of disincentive at the bottom. *BIG PHASE 1* would improve incentives at all income levels, but the gains at the top would have been smaller than Mr Lawson's. The new top rate of income tax would have been 45 percent, and the basic rate 27 percent. In return there would be a partial basic income of £10.50 a week for every man, woman and child. By closing off SERPS, it is also possible to introduce BI supplements of £4 a week for every person aged 65 or over and every person claiming *invalidity benefit* (IVB), *severe disability allowance* (SDA) or *invalid care allowance* (ICA). All the BIs are tax-free and without means test.

The effect on incentives is striking. A family with two children would have a guaranteed income of £42 without any strings attached, plus residual *family credit* (FC) and *housing benefit* (HB) for those on low incomes. The guaranteed income is worth about half the *income support* (IS) entitlement. Additionally, everyone would be able to earn £20 a week tax-free, and mothers would be able to put their work-related childcare costs against their income tax. Unemployed people and lone parents would be able to choose between remaining on income support (with all the restrictions it imposes) and using their BIs plus tax reliefs as stepping stones to economic independence.

BIG PHASE 1 is a feasible alternative to income tax at 20 percent. It would have the following beneficial effects:

(1) Instead of Mr Lawson's marriage bonus, the tax system would become symmetrical between men and women, married and single, yet single-wage married couples would not lose out.
(2) Instead of Mr Fowler's and Mr Moore's new version of the poverty and unemployment traps, the benefit system would start to become a base on which people who are poor can build by their own efforts.
(3) Instead of the growing divide between rich and poor, there would be a significant shift of resources in favour of low income pensioners and families with children.

The obstacles are political

For nearly a decade the British public has been barraged with propaganda to woo them towards a residual welfare state. Debate about integration, even partial integration, has been stifled. The real (though seldom vouchsafed) reason for the opposition (at Government level) to basic income is its unconditionality, which is thought to encourage sloth. This fear is understandable, yet the protestant work-ethic, which developed in reponse to industrial-isation, is not necessarily suited to post-industrial societies. On the contrary, it almost certainly requires modification.

So it is that the reader, having battled with the technicalities, will gradually discover that the critical issues are ethical (and political), not technical at all. The technicalities must be confronted if the case for integration is to be fully understood, but the real argument concerns human relationships and human values. Do we want to live in a society where making money is all that matters, or are there other objectives that we hold more dear?

Part 1

SOCIAL SECURITY AT A CROSSROADS

1

No system can last forever

Social insurance, cornerstone of the social democratic state, is more than one hundred years old and is fast being overtaken by the effects of change. Some of those changes, especially in the labour market and including unemployment, are themselves partly the result of social insurance. Others, including breakdown of the traditional family, are not. Either way social insurance cannot stop the resulting poverty. On the contrary, insofar as it adds to unemployment, it has itself become an engine of poverty.

Social insurance was first launched on an unsuspecting world by Prussia's Iron Chancellor, Count Otto von Bismarck, in 1883. Bismarck was a titanic figure, who held, so it is said, that no man should die until he had smoked a hundred thousand cigars and drunk five thousand bottles of champagne. Yet his motive for introducing sickness and old age insurance (he avoided unemployment insurance) had less to do with benevolence than with a Machiavellian determination to beat the socialists at their own game. The results were astounding. For nearly a century, except during two World Wars, social insurance spread like wildfire, first in Europe and then throughout the world.

The enthusiasm of historian H.A.L. Fisher in 1936, half a century after Bismarck, is characteristic of public opinion at that time:

The German Insurance Acts constitute a landmark. Of all the political inventions of the nineteenth century none was so valuable a preservative of society as the discovery of a system of insurance, dependent on the contributions of the state, the employers, and the worker, and protecting the mass of the labouring population against the worst hazards of industrial life. (Fisher, H.A.L., 1944 edition, page 1052)

11

After World War 2 social insurance quickly established itself as one of the institutions no self-respecting social democracy could be without. In Europe there seemed no upper limit to the promised bounty, and as new gaps emerged new benefits were created, many of them non-contributory.

Millions of people benefited and millions still do. Then suddenly the bubble burst. Rising oil prices were the catalyst but not the cause. In this report I shall argue that there are three underlying causes for the persistence of welfare crisis despite economic recovery. The first is the long-term effect of social insurance on unit labour costs, the second (closely related) is the taxation of earnings below benefit entitlement levels, and the third is the inability of social insurance systems to cope with poverty caused by family breakdown.

Social insurance and unemployment

A high level of unemployment, provided the unemployed are quickly able to find new jobs, can be the outward sign of a healthy, growing economy. In the UK between 300,000 and 400,000 people

Figure 1.1: Long-term unemployment 1953-87

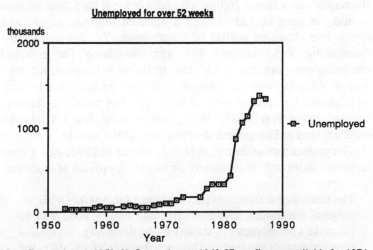

Unemployed for over 52 weeks

Note: Dec each year 1953-61; Jan each year 1963-87; no figures available for 1974 or 1975.

Sources: Hansard WA, 15 Feb 1984, cc 196-7, updated from Department of Employment Gazette.

12

join and leave the unemployment register each month. If that figure were to double it need not cause alarm, so long as the inward and outward flows remain in balance. What matters is when people stay on the register for month after month and year after year. In January 1988, despite 4.5 percent economic growth during 1987, there were 2.7 million registered unemployed in the UK, of whom 1.1 million had been out of work for over a year.

The return of mass, long-term unemployment in the UK is illustrated in Figure 1.1. Although it did not take off until 1980, there is clear evidence of a secular upward trend from the mid-1960s onwards.

Social insurance adds to unemployment by pushing up unit labour costs. Insured labour becomes uncompetitive with uninsured labour in the developing world, and uncompetitive with machinery. Unskilled labour is especially at risk. Far from "protecting the mass of the labouring population against the worst hazards of industrial life", social insurance has become Europe's greatest gift to the developing countries, enabling them to flood our markets with their products. It has also provided the biggest boost to technological advance since the invention of the wheel. The result, already, is to put millions of would-be workers on the scrap heap. The result in due course will be to deprive them of income security in old age, because they will not meet the contribution requirements.

Social insurance has led to a re-structuring of labour markets which was not foreseen. The traditional labour market has been fragmented. On the one hand is a relatively small core of highly skilled, well paid workers who work long hours, are fully insured and receive various assortments of fringe benefits. On the other is a growing army of peripheral workers, who have no job security, whose contribution records for social insurance are usually incomplete, and who as often as not are unemployed. This army includes many of Europe's new poor.

The upward pressures exerted by social insurance on unit labour costs are both direct and indirect. The direct pressures are through the employers' non-wage labour costs, that is to say the contributions made by employers to statutory social security funds, sick pay, redundancy fund contributions, training levies and so forth, and to non-statutory provisions like private pensions. The indirect pressures are through the benefits received by working age adults during sickness and unemployment. These benefits act as a floor for wages, because it is seldom worthwhile to work for less than the benefit amount.

Table 1.1: Non-wage labour costs as a percentage of total labour costs (wage earners in the manufacturing sector)

Country	1965	1983	Annual growth rate 1965-83
Austria	41.0	47.7	0.84
Belgium	32.5	44.9	1.82
Canada	—	21.7	2.20 (1970-83)
Denmark	14.1	22.0	2.53
Finland	21.6	36.7	2.98
France	40.2	44.4	0.56
Germany	29.7	44.4	2.25
Italy	44.9	46.3	0.17
Japan	—	15.5	0.44 (1970-83)
Netherlands	31.7	44.0	1.85
Norway	22.2	33.0	2.22
Sweden	19.0	40.6	4.32
United Kingdom	13.7	26.5	3.74
United States	17.1	26.7	2.51

Source: Tachibanaki 1987, Table 1.

Non-wage labour costs. In some countries total labour costs are increased by 40 percent or more on account of employers' contributions to social insurance. Non-statutory provision to private pension and insurance schemes, which is often an integral part of public policy and is encouraged by income tax reliefs, has a similar effect. Table 1.1, taken from a study by Professor Toshiaki Tachibanaki of Kyoto University, Japan, shows the effects of non-wage labour costs (statutory and non-statutory) in the manufacturing sectors of selected countries in 1965 and 1983. In Austria, France and Italy labour costs were already inflated by over 40 percent in 1965. Since then the gap between those countries with high and those with comparatively low non-wage labour costs has become narrower. In the UK the share of non-wage labour costs doubled in less than twenty years.

The wages floor. Unemployment benefits create a wages floor below which paid work is not financially worthwhile, or only marginally so. Sickness and disability benefits have similar effects. In countries like Britain where benefit is a flat rate amount regardless of former earnings, and is higher if the claimant has dependants, out-of-work benefits for families with children can be worth more than a lower paid job. In order to understand the full effects of unemployment and sickness benefits on the wages floor, it is also necessary to gross up benefit to allow for employees' social insurance contributions and income tax. Even in countries where unemployment benefit is earnings-related it is not unusual for benefit to exceed net earnings after deduction of social security contribution. In the UK income tax is charged on earnings well below benefit levels and without regard to work expenses.

In the UK the problem is compounded by *local authority domestic rates*. These resemble a property tax levied on all house-holders, but the unemployed receive 80 percent rebates. The lower paid may receive partial rate rebates, but the withdrawal of these rebates at the same time as income tax and NI contributions are being charged produces *poverty trap* effects that also, in due course, feed through into the labour market. After 1990, if the British Government's proposals for replacement of domestic rates by a *community charge* (or poll tax) are implemented, non-householders, including millions of young people, will be dragged into this cauldron of disincentive for the first time. For Londoners the weekly wage at which paid work becomes worthwhile could go up by more than £20, and twice that for married couples.

Most Western democracies face similar problems. Social insurance systems are helping those best able to help themselves, but do not reach those most in need. Governments rush in with scheme after scheme to fill the gaps, but it is like trying to fill a sieve with water. Each new scheme costs more money and the extra taxation makes the original problem worse, by pushing up unit labour costs still further.

Meanwhile in Brussels talk of harmonisation serves mainly to distract attention from the central issues, namely:

- Are payroll and income taxes still the best way to fund income maintenance?
- Are benefits based on labour market status (or former labour market status) still the best way to prevent poverty?

Social insurance and the family

Despite its obvious attractions, the idea that social insurance could prevent poverty was always over-optimistic. It never could reach those with inadequate contribution records, nor the lower paid, nor wives and mothers working in the home (except through the benefits of their husbands). Perhaps the most serious criticism of social insurance is its effect on values. If you start from the premise that only those people who have been in paid work deserve income security, you create a rat-race society in which people who work for nothing become second-class citizens.

A system that reserves all its goodies for those with a sufficient record in the labour market damages the family and weakens the sense of community. A woman who gives up paid work to look after her children is not only spurned, she also loses out financially. If her marriage breaks up she becomes a hole in the social insurance sieve. Even the most generous system of contribution credits cannot make up for the loss of a career. Similarly a woman who gives up paid work to look after an elderly relative puts her own income security on the line. In her own old age she too becomes a hole in the sieve.

Social insurance pre-dates women's emancipation and it pre-dates this century's increased life expectancy. It was devised by men, for men, with men in mind. It harks back to an era when "women knew their place", when divorce was frowned upon and when children born outside marriage were a term of abuse. Social insurance is about the deserving poor. Those who flout society's rules are not deserving. Widows' benefits were a useful addition because they strengthened the marriage bond. In Europe attitudes to divorce have been transformed, in Britain one in three marriages ends in divorce, but the casualties of family breakdown are beyond the pale of social insurance. Their situation is by no means the result of social insurance, but social insurance can do nothing for them. That is why divorced and separated women, lone parents and their children are the second largest contingent in the army of the new poor.

The incidence of poverty among lone parents is so high and the issue so emotive that they are a prime target for quick, easy remedies by governments eager to win votes. Each £ by which benefits for lone parents are increased costs only a fraction of similar increases for parents in general. The immediate cost of a new tax relief for lone parents is hardly noticeable to the taxpayer, and a sure vote-winner. But the long-term costs are much higher.

The cumulative effect over several decades of subsidy after subsidy for marriage breakdown has been to weaken the traditional family and to call in question the whole principle of benefit (or tax relief) according to marital status. In Britain where benefits and tax reliefs for married couples are considerably less generous than for two single people, this effect is very pronounced. Marriage break-up and *de facto* marriage are being subsidised at the expense of the traditional family. To say this is by no means to suggest that lone parents do not need help, or that common law marriage is somehow wrong, but as a reminder that any sort of preferential treatment tends to create its own demand. If the state treats lone parent families and unmarried couples more favourably than two-parent families and married couples, it is likely to end up with more lone parents and more unmarried couples.

Income maintenance in the UK

Throughout this report the term social security is used as a generic for all cash benefits, not just social insurance. The UK has a massive programme of non-contributory benefits. In 1988-89 planned expenditure on non-contributory benefits came to £21,000 million, compared with £26,000 million on national insurance benefits. Out of that £26,000 million, nearly £20,000 went on retirement pensions.

Table 1.2 summarises the figures, which include Northern Ireland. The year 1985-86 is included, because that is the year to which most of the comparative figures in this study will apply. Gaps in the figures for 1988-89 reflect abolition of certain benefits as a result of the 1986 Social Security Act. In April 1988 *supplementary benefit* (SB), which replaced Beveridge's *national assistance* (NA) in 1966, was itself replaced by income support. Similarly *family income supplement* (FIS), introduced in 1971, was replaced by *family credit* (FC).

The figures in Table 1.2 are not consistent with those in Appendix 1 because they refer only to Department of Health and Social Security (DHSS) benefits. Student grants and free school meals are excluded, as are Department of Employment allowances. Statutory sick pay and rate rebates are also excluded, because the Treasury counts them as *negative income*.

The figures show the extent to which the system in Britain has departed from the original Beveridge Plan. Beveridge recommended a system of social security based on contributory social insurance benefits plus non-contributory family allowances, with means-tested national assistance as a residual safety net.

17

Table 1.2: Social security expenditure in the UK, £m at current
prices

Benefit	1985-86 outturn	1988-89 plans
1. Contributory benefits (ie those paid from the National Insurance Fund)		
Retirement	17,057	19,845
Widows	829	902
Unemployment	1,638	1,527
Sickness	290	178
Invalidity	2,452	3,348
Death grant	19	—
Industrial injuries	484	517
Maternity allowance	169	45
Guardian's & child's special allowance	1	1
Total contributory benefits	22,939	26,363
2. Non-contributory benefits (ie those met from voted expenditure or paid by local authorities etc)		
Retirement including war pensions	632	646
Disability:		
Attendance allowance	715	948
Invalid care allowance	14	165
Non-contributory invalidity pension/severe disablement allowance	280	322
Mobility allowance	431	678
Supplementary benefit/income support and social fund:		
Supplementary pension*	1,044	—
Supplementary allowance (working age)*	6,707	—
Income support*	—	8,921
Social fund*	—	181
Family benefits:		
Child benefit	4,637	4,702
One-parent benefit	138	174
Family income supplement/family credit*	142	456
Maternity grant	17	—
Housing benefit:		
Rent rebates and allowances*	3,215	3,982
Total non-contributory benefits	17,972	21,175
TOTAL BENEFIT EXPENDITURE	40,911	47,538
Administration	1,850	2,450
TOTAL UK SOCIAL SECURITY EXPENDITURE	42,761	49,988

Source: Public Expenditure White Paper Cm 288-11, January 1988,
Tables 15.1 and 18.12.
Note: Benefits shown with an asterisk are means-tested or income-tested.

Today the holes left by social insurance and child benefit are so many and so large that expenditure on means-tested benefits accounts for nearly 30 percent of the total.

In addition to the direct costs of income maintenance through cash benefits there are the indirect costs of income tax reliefs. Income tax reliefs are important, because they prevent, or should prevent, the lower paid from being taxed on the incomes necessary to keep them out of poverty. In the UK each tax unit is allowed a personal income tax allowance which varies according to marital status. The amount of the tax allowance is deducted from taxable income before the tax rates are applied. Child benefit is shown in Table 1.2 as a cash benefit, because that is how it is presented in the national accounts. In fact it is not a benefit in the traditional sense, but a *convertible tax credit*. It tops up the incomes of lower paid families with children like a traditional cash benefit, but at earnings above the level where child benefit entitlement equals income tax liability it converts into a fixed-amount, child tax relief.

As well as the personal tax reliefs there are a growing number of non-personal tax reliefs, of which the most important are for mortgage interest and private pensions. A full list is included in Appendix 4. The cost of all these income tax reliefs, in terms of revenue foregone, is hard to quantify, but they are officially estimated to reduce the income tax base by over 50 percent. It is not far short of the direct expenditures through cash benefits.

A system overtaken by the effects of change

The maze of laws and regulations that passes for an income redistribution system produces the following perverse effects:

- It locks people into claimant roles.
- It adds to unemployment.
- It penalises marriage and weakens the family.
- It leaves much poverty unattended to.

Much has been written showing how these effects come about. The underlying causes can be summarised in terms of a combination of four factors: first, the existing, Beveridge-based, social security system no longer matches the economic and social conditions under which people actually live; second, the original Beveridge Plan was fundamentally flawed; third, the system introduced in 1948 was

19

even more flawed; fourth, what little coherence may have existed in 1948 has long since vanished under layer upon layer of patchwork change, the end result of which has been the creation of a huge, new underclass of welfare claimants, driven into dependency by a tax system that takes less and less account of ability to pay, and a benefit system that relies more and more on means-testing.

In one sense there is nothing unusual about the present situation. No system can last forever. In 1942 Beveridge set out to consolidate the piece-meal changes of the previous fifty years and the system instituted after World War 2, largely as a result of the Beveridge Report (Beveridge, 1942), is now itself forty years old. Thus under any circumstances the need for major reform was predictable. What makes today's circumstances so special is the scale and pace of change since World War 2, which is of a different order to that with which Beveridge had to contend in 1942.

Within less than a generation the world of Beveridge has disappeared. The micro electronic revolution has catapulted most western societies out of the industrial era into the post industrial era. In all the social states unprecedented increases in direct taxation and the maturing of pension systems have made the old distinction between taxpayer and beneficiary for all practical purposes irrelevant. Throughout the developed world modern science, through improved contraception, labour saving homes and fast foods, has freed women from unpaid work in the home and launched them *en masse* upon the labour market. Simultaneously modern medicine, by enabling people to live longer, has led to the emergence of a new generation of very old people and with it an ever-increasing, but in economic terms ineffective, demand for "carers" at the very time when women, the traditional providers of unpaid care, have become more interested in paid work.

These are tumultuous changes and the resulting confusion is more reminiscent of the social and economic turmoil of the sixteenth and late eighteenth centuries than the relative calm of the Beveridge era. Many of the changes taking place, especially increased life expectancy, drudgery-avoiding automation and women's emancipation, could add to the sum of human happiness, but only if we quickly adapt to the new conditions they impose. If we do not, if we cling to institutions handed down from the past, then there are dangers of accelerating relative economic decline, continuing mass unemployment, further destabilisation of family life and social discord.

20

The two institutions most overdue for reform are the systems of personal taxation (income tax, national insurance contributions and local authority domestic rates) and social security, and of these it is the first two that are the subject of this enquiry. Both operate through laws and regulations which originated in the distant past. One result of continuing to work through a legal framework based on archaic assumptions is to produce effects that are contrary to those intended. Thus the penalties for legal marriage, which government could impose with impunity so long as cohabitation and divorce were frowned upon, today result in more *de facto* marriages, more children born outside marriage, more separations and more divorce. Similarly the availability for work rule, which in nineteenth century terms followed logically from the doctrine of lesser eligibility, today adds to unemployment because it prevents the unskilled unemployed and those who need to acquire new skills from undergoing the necessary training or re-training.

Some of the changes now taking place are outside government control, but many are by-products of past government policies, especially the systems of personal taxation and social security. Whether or not any given change is exogenous, only governments can take the action necessary to help people adjust without jeopardising the living standards of low income families, and without adding to family break-up. Only governments can ensure that the tax and benefit systems match the economic and social conditions under which people actually live. And only governments can solve the paradox, which they themselves have created, of mass unemployment alongside mass unmet needs.

Somehow a social security system has to be found that will increase the *effective* demand for unskilled and semi-skilled labour by lowering unit labour costs, without reducing the living standards of those who are already at the bottom of the pile.

2

Flaws in the Beveridge Plan

Despite numerous changes, not least the 1986 Social Security Act, the fundamentals of the British social security system remain those advocated by Sir William Beveridge in 1942. Yet the Beveridge Plan was based on a mixture of explicit and implicit assumptions that do not withstand close scrutiny.

Explicit assumptions

Beveridge started from a very specific definition of social security and three key assumptions, which are worth quoting in full:

Scope of social security: The term "social security" is used here to denote the securing of an income to take the place of earnings when they are interrupted by unemployment, sickness or accident, to provide for retirement through age, to provide against loss of support by the death of another person, and to meet exceptional expenditures, such as those connected with birth, death and marriage. Primarily social security means security of income up to a minimum, but the provision of an income should be associated with treatment designed to bring the interruption of earnings to an end as soon as possible.

Three assumptions: No satisfactory scheme of social security can be devised except on the following assumptions:
(A) Children's allowances for children up to the age of 15 or
   if in full-time education up to the age of 16;
(B) Comprehensive health and re-habilitation services for

22

prevention and cure of disease and restoration of capacity
for work, available to all members of the community;
(C) Maintenance of employment, that is to say avoidance of
mass unemployment.
(Beveridge 1942, paras 300 and 301)

Beveridge's definition of social security and the assumptions that
followed from it are the key to the whole Beveridge Report.
Together they involved a series of implicit assumptions which
today are no longer valid, if indeed they ever were.

Implicit assumptions

*Assumption 1: that all poverty is due either to "interruption or
loss of earnings" or to "failure to relate income during
earning to the size of the family" (Beveridge 1942, para 11)*

Beveridge's "Plan for Social Security", and his decision to rely
largely on earnings-replacement benefits, started from a diagnosis
of the circumstances in which "families and individuals in Britain
might lack the means of healthy subsistence" (para 11). The
evidence from social surveys carried out during the 1930s showed
that from three-quarters to five-sixths of poverty was due to
interruption or loss of earning power, with most of the remaining
one-quarter to one-sixth due to failure to relate income during
earning to family size. On the basis of this evidence Beveridge
ruled out low pay as a cause of poverty and drew the general
conclusion that "abolition of want requires a double re-distribution
of income, through social insurance and by family needs" (para 11).

Starting from the proposition that earnings are always sufficient
to prevent poverty, given adequate family allowances, Beveridge
recommended that benefit be restricted to people who were not
working. To be eligible for any of the main benefits the claimant
must be unable to work on account of sickness or old age, or out of
work but available for work. Widows' NI benefits were the only
important exception to that rule. Widows would be able to build on
their benefit without restrictions. The availability for work rule
excluded and still excludes many students and trainees from
benefit, no matter how low their incomes. Likewise the *out of work*
requirement excluded the lower paid from benefit entitlement, no
matter how low their earnings.[1]

It is a system guaranteed to discourage people with low earnings potential from bothering to work at all. In a country without a national minimum wage it was also an unrealistic way to tackle poverty. "Very few men's wages," argued Beveridge, "are insufficient to cover at least two adults and one child " (para 417). On these grounds he also excluded first children of working parents from entitlement to the new family allowance. In the Family Allowances Bill Second Reading Debate he got cold feet and suggested the introduction of a national minimum wage (Hansard, 8 Mar 1945, c 2309) but by that time it was too late.

Even supposing that the pre-war survey evidence on which Beveridge based his case was accurate, his implicit assumption that the evidence had lasting validity has been proved false by the events of the past forty years. Low pay, especially the low pay of lone mothers, is a principal cause of poverty. And the tax-induced poverty which has crept into the system since the 1960s is a post-war novelty that Beveridge never envisaged.

Assumption 2: that society consists of happily married couples (no divorce), widows (no widowers) and heterosexual celibates living either alone or with their parents

Beveridge populated his visionary world with heterosexual celibates, widows and happily married, single-wage couples, where the wife's social security would depend on her husband, either through his contribution record or through his entitlement to means-tested national assistance. This middle class, essentially Victorian, image of society took no account of the minority of very disadvantaged families, whose lives have always been

Table 2.1: Proportion of marriages ended by divorce after selected years of marriage, England and Wales

| | *Proportion per thousand marriages* | | | | | |
| | *Duration of marriage (exact years)* | | | | | |
Year of marriage	*5*	*10*	*15*	*20*	*25*	*30*
1921	1	5	9	14	20	28
1926	1	5	12	19	32	40
1931	2	8	16	36	49	61
1936	1	10	42	57	69	82
1941	3	41	63	76	88	103

Source: *Social Trends*, 1973, Table VI, page 11.

characterised by change and uncertainty. By 1942 it was well on its way out for society at large. Divorce was on the increase long before World War 2, as is evident from the figures in Table 2.1, taken from an early edition of *Social Trends*.

For Beveridge the chief characteristic of a married woman, insofar as social insurance was concerned, was her status of dependency. Nor did this escape the notice of women's organisations, who campaigned throughout 1943 and 1944 for inclusion within the White Paper of independent insurance for married women and enforcement by the state of the husband's legal duty to maintain. In Appendix 5 to the Finer Report, Morris Finer and O.R. McGregor explain why Beveridge's approach to the insurance of married women made it impossible to develop a logical scheme of insurance in the case of marriage breakdown. (Finer and McGregor 1974). Questions of need were quickly overshadowed by questions of guilt. Women's groups were furious. Finer and McGregor quote the following extract from a pamphlet by Elizabeth Abbott and Katherine Bompass of the Women's Freedom League:

> the status given to the married woman in the report is not new,
> it is the reflection of her present status in law and insurance,
> that of a dependant without any right of her own person, by
> way of one penny of cash, though she doubtless can in both
> cases claim a legal right to subsistence. . .it is with the denial
> of any personal status to the woman because she is married,
> the denial of her independent personality within marriage,
> that everything goes wrong. (Abbott and Bompass 1943)

After much discussion the officials concerned with preparation of the White Paper that followed the Beveridge Report decided it was more important to implement "the grand design" than to get bogged down in the "subsidiary theme of provision against the risk of marriage breakdown" (Finer and McGregor Volume 2, para 109). The White Paper concluded that it was not feasible to introduce separation benefits, and the newly-fledged welfare state washed its hands of lone parents other than widows.

In the words of Finer and McGregor :

> the principles upon which the State made provision for
> lone-parent families remained after the Beveridge Report
> precisely what they had been before. Widows received

pensions with the possibility of supplementation, from the poor law or public assistance or, after 1948, from national assistance. But divorced, deserted or separated wives and unmarried mothers remained throughout dependent on the poor law or its substitutes, in the event of their receiving no support from their husbands. (Finer and McGregor, para 111)

Today, in a society where divorce and separation are commonplace, where far fewer adult children live with their parents and where people who are not married often share accommodation, in relationships which may be heterosexual, homosexual or Platonic, the Beveridge assumptions make no sense at all, and are the cause of countless anomalies. But always it is the very poor who are worst affected, because it is in poor families that marriage breakdown is most commonplace, and it is they who are most often in need of social security.

Assumption 3: that all married women are financially dependent on their husbands

"During marriage," Beveridge wrote, "most women will not be gainfully employed" (Beveridge 1942, para 111). He therefore divided the population into six classes, based on occupational status, marital status and sex: I– Employees; II – Others gainfully occupied; III – Housewives; IV – Others of working age; V – Below working age; VI – Retired above working age. The "marriage needs" of women were to be met by a *Housewives' Policy*, as recognition of their "vital unpaid service" (paras 309-311) although the recommended rates of the dependency benefits were less than 70 percent of the benefits payable to fully paid up contributors.

Table 2.2: Activity rates (%) of married women, Great Britain

Aged	1921	1931	1951	1961	1971	1981
20–24	12.5	18.5	36.5	41.8	45.8	57.6
25–34	9.4	13.2	24.4	29.5	38.4	58.0
35–44	8.9	10.1	25.7	36.4	54.2	
45–54	8.4	8.5	23.7	35.3	56.8	61.8
55–59	7.2*	7.0	15.6	26.0	45.1	

* Includes 60-64 age group.
Source: *Social Trends,* 1975 and 1983.

Beveridge based his assumption that married women would not be in paid work on the 1931 census, which showed that only about 12 percent of working-age, married women were gainfully occupied. By 1939 the proportion had increased but was still reckoned to be less than 15 percent. But this average figure concealed wide variations between different age groups. Figures in *Social Trends* No.6 show a steady increase in labour market participation by younger women from the 1920s onwards.

By 1983 approximately 60 percent of working-age, married women were economically active, just over half of them working part-time (OPCS, General Household Survey 1983), yet the benefit system is still based on a view of the labour market that is years out of date, and married men are still eligible for benefits equal to 160 percent of single person's benefit for the same rate of contribution.

Assumption 4: that it is within the power of governments to maintain full employment

Beveridge assumed maintenance of employment and the prevention of mass unemployment. This was one of his three, explicit, background assumptions, already noted, and he gave five reasons for including it. Again the original text is worth quoting in full, because it shows so clearly why the unemployment benefit system has become inoperable, and why reform within the existing system is fruitless:

ASSUMPTION C: MAINTENANCE OF EMPLOYMENT

There are five reasons for saying that a satisfactory scheme of social insurance assumes the maintenance of employment and the prevention of mass unemployment.

Three reasons are concerned with the details of social insurance; the fourth and most important is concerned with its principle; the fifth is concerned with the possibility of meeting its costs.

First, payment of unconditional cash benefits as of right during unemployment is satisfactory provision only for short periods of unemployment; after that, complete idleness even on an income demoralises. The proposal of the Report accordingly is to make unemployment benefit after a certain period conditional upon attendance at a work or training centre. But this proposal is impracticable if it has to be applied to men by the million or the hundred thousand.

Second, the only satisfactory test of unemployment is an offer of work. This test breaks down in mass unemployment and makes necessary recourse to elaborate contribution conditions...

Third, the state of the labour market has a direct bearing on rehabilitation and recovery of injured and sick persons and upon the possibility of giving to those suffering from partial infirmities, such as deafness, the chance of a happy and useful career. In time of mass unemployment those who are in receipt of compensation feel no urge to get well for idleness. On the other hand, in time of active demand for labour, as in war, the sick and the maimed are encouraged to recover, so that they may be useful.

Fourth, and most important, income security which is all that can be given by social insurance is so inadequate a provision for human happiness that to put it forward by itself as a sole or principal measure of reconstruction hardly seems worth doing...

Fifth, though it should be within the power of the community to bear the cost of the whole Plan for Social Security, the cost is heavy and, if to the necessary cost waste is added, it may become insupportable. Unemployment, both through increasing expenditure on benefit and through reducing the income to bear those costs, is the worst form of waste. (Beveridge 1942, para 440)

The explicit assumption is the maintenance of employment, and the argument is convincing. Benefits restricted to people who are not working are an open invitation to abuse unless either the benefit rate is below subsistence level, or the administrative authorities are able to offer every registered unemployed person a suitable job or training. The implicit assumption is that governments are capable of maintaining full employment and this is far more controversial. In *Full Employment in a Free Society* (Beveridge 1944), Beveridge set out the methods by which, in his view, there could always be "more vacant jobs than idle men". He relied on demand management, controlled location of industry and "organized mobility of labour", all highly controversial. Nor did he foresee that the unemployment benefit he proposed would act as a floor for wages and price British goods and British workers out of world markets.

Interestingly the Coalition Government's White Paper on *Employment Policy*, which was also published in 1944 (Cmd 6527,

HMSO 1944) and which formed the basis for much of post-war economic policy, aimed at "the maintenance of a high and stable level of employment", not full employment. Thus right from the start there was inconsistency between the employment and social security policies of post-war governments.

Today the 1944 White Paper is discredited, and the traditional Treasury view, that very little additional employment and no permanent additional employment can be created by increased government borrowing or expenditure, has reasserted itself. This view may or may not be correct, the point is that so long as it prevails the original inconsistency is greatly magnified. We bumble along with a benefit system based on a full employment assumption despite 2.5 million unemployed.

Assumption 5: that full employment means regular, full-time work for men, from age 15 to 65, with minimal job changes and minimal need for training or re-training

Beveridge's full employment assumption excluded women, who were supposed to be occupied in the home, or working for pin money. Full employment meant "more vacant jobs than idle men", and Beveridge took no account of the effects on employment opportunities if women started taking jobs previously held by men. Of course married women have always worked, the novelty that Beveridge failed to reckon with was that they should be paid for working and that marriage might become an equal partnership, with each spouse contributing essential cash and sharing the household duties.

For the very poor, at the edges of the job market, Beveridge's assumptions were always over-optimistic. Their jobs were seldom regular or full-time. It cannot be said too often that a social security system genuinely designed to assist the most disadvantaged families is one that helps them join the mainstream of economic life, by providing the sure income base they have always lacked. A system that starts by dividing the deserving from the undeserving poor cannot do this. The Beveridge system, based on replacement benefits for those with a steady record of regular work was, and is, a system of exclusion, because it puts beyond the pale all those in circumstances outside the specified contingencies and all those with incomplete contribution records. It is a system designed for relatively well-to-do men (fallen temporarily on hard times) rather than those most in need (Desai 1986 and Williams 1986).

Today it is not just housewives (or househusbands) and the traditional poor who are excluded. Due to mass unemployment, people from all walks of life are unable to meet the entitlement regulations. In 1985 only 26 percent of unemployed male claimants were in receipt of NI unemployment benefit (*Social Trends* 1987). Full employment in the Beveridge sense may never return. The traditional, male-dominated labour market has changed beyond recognition and is still changing. In the new labour markets there are few vacancies for workers who are illiterate or innumerate. Steady jobs require skills and the ability to acquire new skills. Income maintenance during further and/or vocational education, during skill training and re-training is fast becoming a pre-condition for the return of full employment. Beveridge recognised that it was better to pay young people to train than to pay them to do nothing, but he did not include trainees among his six occupational classes. On the contrary trainees were disqualified from benefit on the grounds that they would not be available for work. Most of them still are, the exception being those on Department of Employment programmes like the Youth Training Scheme.

3

Further flaws in the post World War Two legislation

The system introduced after World War 2 was more flawed than the Beveridge Plan, having lost the coherence of the original. Beveridge died a disappointed and disillusioned man. In *Shared Enthusiasm* his step-son Philip Beveridge Mair recounts how Beveridge returned to Oxford, shortly after the death of his wife, and one afternoon poured out his feelings to his life-long friend Hugh Bell, complaining that his ideas had been "mutilated, reversed, and taken completely out of his hands although given his name", and saying that he had "come to loathe both the caption 'Welfare State' and the title 'Beveridge Plan' which had become like advertising slogans" (Mair, P. 1982, pages 124-125).

Beveridge's disappointment was fully justified. Four "mutilations" stand out. The first was the failure to pay family allowance to working families at anything approaching subsistence level, the second the failure to pay NI benefits at rates high enough to lift claimants off the need for means-tested national assistance, the third the failure to introduce work or training centres for the unemployed and the fourth (which is closely allied to the other three) was the open-ended commitment to pay means-tested national assistance to single people and lone parents, regardless of the wealth of their families, and in preference to helping them to help themselves. Any one of these alterations would have weakened the Beveridge strategy. Together they acted like a slow, insidious poison.

Family allowances below subsistence level

The first of the three explicit assumptions underlying the Beveridge Plan was his scheme for children's allowances, and it rested on two connected arguments:

> First, it is unreasonable to seek to guarantee an income sufficient for subsistence, while earnings are interrupted by unemployment or disability, without ensuring sufficient income during earning. Social insurance should be part of a policy of a national minimum. But a national minimum for families of every size cannot in practice be secured by a wage system, which must be based on the product of a man's labour and not on the size of his family...
>
> Second, it is dangerous to allow benefit during unemployment or disability to equal or exceed earnings during work. But, without allowances for children, during earning and not-earning alike, this danger cannot be avoided. It has been experienced in an appreciable number of cases under unemployment benefit and unemployment assistance in the past. The maintenance of employment...will be impossible without greater fluidity of labour...than has been achieved in the past. To secure this the gap between income during earning and during interruption of earning should be as large as possible for every man. It cannot be kept large for men with large families, except either by making their benefit in unemployment and disability inadequate, or by giving allowances for children in time of earning and not-earning alike. (Beveridge 1942, paras 411-412)

Basing his argument on a combination of figures derived from pre-war sources, Beveridge advocated age-related family allowances, averaging 35 pence a week at 1938 prices. Unwisely he attempted as early as 1942 to revalue his 35 pence estimate at post-war prices and came up with a provisional post-war average rate of 45 pence, from which he deducted 5 pence to allow for provision of free school meals and milk. This rate he recommended as sufficient "to feed, clothe and board" each qualifying child. The Treasury seized on the notional figure of 40 pence in cash plus 5 pence in kind, and the Coalition government reduced the value of the cash benefit to 25 pence, promising to supplement it with "a great increase in meals and milk, which are to be free for all children in grant-aided schools" (Hansard 8 Mar 1945, c 2262). During the Family Allowances Bill Second Reading Debate many speakers questioned the adequacy of the 25 pence rate, the same amount having been proposed and passed by a resolution of the Labour Party as long ago as 1927. A rate of 60 pence (less the value of school meals) would have been nearer the mark to maintain the value of Beveridge's 35 pence estimate in line with price increases since 1938. The 25 pence family allowance nevertheless became law, only the "great increase in meals and milk" never materialised.

One result was continued hardship in large families, and in families with low earnings. Another result, as Beveridge had foreseen, was the need to introduce higher rates of child support for the children of parents dependent on the new national insurance and national assistance benefits than for children of parents in full-time work. In 1948 when the new legislation first took effect, family allowance for a working, two-child family was 25 pence, regardless of the age of the children, but an unemployed family was entitled to between 38 pence and 75 pence for each child, according to age. Thus both the relative poverty of today's families with children and the disincentive effects of the *unemployment trap* can be traced back to the Family Allowances Act of 1945.

National insurance benefits below subsistence level

The Beveridge Plan was "first and foremost a plan of insurance – of giving in return for contributions benefits up to subsistence level, as of right and without means test, so that individuals may build freely upon it" (Beveridge 1942, para 9). The importance which Beveridge attached to voluntary action was re-emphasised by the book of that name with which he completed his trilogy in 1948:

> It is clear that the State must in future do more things than it has attempted in the past. But it is equally clear, or should be equally clear, that room, opportunity, and encouragement must be kept for Voluntary Action, in seeking new ways of social advance. (Beveridge 1948, page 10)

The scope of voluntary insurance was to be two-fold. It would add to the subsistence level benefits provided by the state and it would provide cover against the less common risks not provided for by the state. Scope and encouragement for voluntary insurance must be provided, for instance, by avoiding so far as possible any test of means for the compulsory insurance benefits,and by limiting such benefits to "subsistence and primary needs" (Beveridge 1942, para 375). The need to minimise dependence on means-tested benefits was emphasised time and again:

> To give the fullest possible encouragement to voluntary insurance and saving, it is important to reduce to a minimum the cases in which assistance has to be given subject to consideration of means. *To do this is a central feature of the plan for Britain as set out in the Report.* (Beveridge 1942, Appendix F, para 16, my emphasis)

But when the new insurance benefits were introduced in 1948, they were below subsistence level. Right from the start fully paid up contributors to the new system of national insurance were forced to depend on means-tested national assistance. Instead of being "felt to be something less desirable than insurance benefit", national assistance was made part and parcel of the insurance package. Not surprisingly therefore, Beveridge's second tier of voluntary insurance, which was supposed to top up the subsistence level benefits, never materialised. It was not worthwhile. Instead voluntary savings were gradually syphoned off into tax-aided house purchase and tax-aided private pensions.

Instead of work and training centres, unemployment benefit limited to one year and no training allowance

Beveridge recommended that unemployment benefit be paid at the full rate indefinitely, subject to requirement of attendance at a work or training centre after a limited period of unemployment. Prolonged interruption of earnings, whether through unemployment or disability, was said to have two consequences:

(i) The income needs tend to increase rather than to decrease; the other means at the disposal of the insured person become exhausted; expenditures on clothing and equipment which he may have been able to postpone become unavoidable, since they cannot be postponed indefinitely.

(ii) Measures other than the provision of income become increasingly necessary, to prevent deterioration of morale and to encourage recovery. (Beveridge 1942, para 129)

But, argued Beveridge, it would nevertheless be unwise to make subsistence level unemployment benefit indefinite in duration without attaching some sort of conditions:

> 130...The danger of providing benefits, which are both adequate in amount and indefinite in duration, is that men, as creatures who adapt themselves to circumstances, may settle down to them...The correlative of the State's undertaking to ensure adequate benefit for unavoidable interruption of earnings, however long, is enforcement of the citizen's obligation to seek and accept all reasonable opportunities of work, to cooperate in measures designed to save him from habituation to idleness, and to take all proper measures to be well. The higher the benefits provided out of a common fund for unmerited misfortune, the higher must be the citizen's sense of obligation not to draw upon that fund unnecessarily.

> 131. This general principle leads to the following practical conclusions:
> (i) Men and women in receipt of unemployment benefit cannot be allowed to hold out indefinitely for work of the type to which they are used or in their present places of residence, if there is work which they could do available at the standard wage for that work.
> (ii) Men and women who have been unemployed for a certain period *should be required as a condition of continued benefit to attend a work or training centre...* The period after which attendance should be required need not be the same at all times or for all persons. It might be extended in times of high unemployment and reduced in times of good employment; six months for adults would perhaps be a reasonable average period for benefit without conditions. But for young persons who have not yet the habit of continuous work the period should be shorter; *for boys and girls there should ideally be no unconditional benefit at all; their enforced abstention from work should be made an occasion of further training.* (Beveridge 1942, paras 130 and 131, my emphasis)

None of these recommendations was put into effect, quite the reverse. Entitlement to NI unemployment benefit was limited to twelve months. But since national assistance was available indefinitely and since most claimants were forced to supplement their insurance benefit through national assistance from the start, the effect of the penalty was negligible.

Liability to maintain: a state take-over

For more than three and a half centuries, from the Poor Law Act of 1601, which consolidated earlier provisions, to the National Assistance Act of 1948, which abolished it, the state took responsibility for the relief of poverty, but only as agent of last resort. The twin pillars of the Poor Law were state responsibility for support of the poor at minimum cost to the public purse, the minimum cost principle being upheld by making every family responsible for its own. Not only were the better off expected to support their less fortunate relatives, they were also expected to repay any monies expended on behalf of those relatives by the Poor Law authorities. As late as 1928 the Poor Law Act of that year reiterated the old obligation:

...it shall be the duty of the father, grandfather, mother, grandmother, husband or child of a poor, old, blind, lame and impotent person, or other person not able to work, if possessed of sufficient means, to relieve and maintain such a person. (Section 41 (1))

Elsewhere in Europe, for instance in France and Germany, similar requirements are still in force and are referred to as the *subsidiarity principle*. The state moves in with assistance only in cases where relatives (first) and voluntary agencies (second) are unable to do so. In Germany federal law guarantees a minimum living standard to every citizen, but the bill for benefits paid out by the local agencies eventually lands up with the liable relatives, assuming they can be traced. Since most poor people do not like to sponge off their families, they tend not to claim so one result is hidden poverty. Another result is lower public expenditure on poverty relief than in the UK.

When national assistance replaced the remnants of poor relief in 1948 it removed some of the stigma from means-tested benefits. But that was not all. The "liable relative" obligation, which had been three generational, was henceforth restricted to husbands and wives (mutually) and to parents for their infant children (but not

children for their parents). For the unmarried poor, including many
lone parents, this meant that instead of being dependent on their
own parents they became dependent on the state.

Emancipation from family ties and the removal of stigma
effectively destroyed the second pillar of the Poor Law, namely
cost control. In theory this should not have mattered, because the
new social insurance system was going to abolish poverty. If the
Beveridge Plan had been implemented in full and if Beveridge's
assumptions had been correct, in other words if the 1948 provisions
had succeeded in preventing poverty, then only a tiny minority of
the population would have needed poverty relief and the risks taken
in abolishing the Poor Law would have been minimised.

But that is not what happened. The Beveridge Plan was not
implemented in full and even if it had been it was far from
water-tight. Right from the start fully paid up contributors to the
new NI scheme needed their benefits topped up by national
assistance, and right from the start unsupported lone parents had to
rely entirely on national assistance.

The result has been mounting chaos. A carefully targeted system
of poverty relief, which despite its manifest faults and limitations
had withstood the test of centuries, was exchanged for a virtually
open-ended Government commitment to support anyone on a low
income indefinitely, provided they were single and out of work but
available for work, or provided they were lone parents. With the
exception of cohabiting (but not separated) spouses, the traditional
system of family responsibilities and family-imposed disciplines
was replaced by a gigantic but largely ineffectual bureaucracy.

4
1948-88: Genesis of an underclass[1]

Tax-induced poverty

The Family Allowances Act (1945) together with the National Insurance Act (1946) and the National Assistance Act (1948) constituted the main framework of social security measures designed to abolish want and establish the foundations of the welfare state. They were primarily a victory of principle, and those who supported the principle but had reservations about the legislation hoped that in due course the more obvious inadequacies would be rectified. But this was not to be.

The history of the welfare state in Britain is one of mounting expenditures; increasing welfare dependency among people of working age; increasing direct taxation of the lower paid, especially families with children; mind-boggling complexity; and a series of *ad hoc* responses by successive governments which have usually been worse than useless. Today there are signs of strategic, revolutionary change. That change has been going on, often unnoticed, since Mrs Thatcher's first administration took office in 1979. It is a strategy based on the premise that "welfare is bad for you" and its goal is a society in which a means-tested safety net looks after the minority who are in demonstrable need, while the rest look after themselves, paying less tax and encouraged to save voluntarily by income tax reliefs. This is the neo-liberal dream. Unfortunately those who proclaim its virtues overlook one vital fact. If you want a residual welfare state, and are also genuinely committed to a safety net that is adequate, the first priority must be to stop taxing people into poverty. Otherwise the scale of dependence on the safety net can never be reduced to manageable proportions.

Excessive taxation of people on low incomes, especially families with children, is the single most important reason for the increase in welfare dependency since the 1960s. It is no new phenomenon. Two hundred years ago the great Scottish economist Adam Smith warned that it would lead to poverty, wage inflation and unemployment. In the excerpt that follows Smith was referring to "the inferior classes of workmen", not labour in general:

...a direct tax upon the wages of labour can have no other effect than to raise them somewhat higher than the tax...in order to enable him to pay a tax of one-fifth, his wages must necessarily soon rise, not one-fifth part only, but one-fourth. Whatever was the proportion of the tax, the wages of labour must in all cases rise, not only in that proportion, but in a higher proportion...If direct taxes upon the wages of labour have not always occasioned a proportionable rise in those wages, it is because they have generally occasioned a considerable fall in the demand for labour. *The declension of industry, the decrease of employment for the poor, the diminution of the annual produce of the land and labour of the country, have generally been the effects of such taxes...* (Smith, A., Everyman Edition 1947, Vol 2, page 346, my emphasis)

Adam Smith's warning goes unheeded. The old principle of taxation according to ability to pay has been replaced by a new-fangled delusion that taxation beyond ability to pay can be rendered harmless, provided "the really poor" (unquantified and undefined) are able to claim rebates.

Britain's over-taxation problem is not restricted to income tax. NI contributions and local authority domestic rates are also charged on incomes well below the poverty lines laid down by Parliament. The proposed *community charge* (or poll tax), will take no account of ability to pay (except through incentive-destroying rebates) and will have the same effects on the labour market as any other tax on the "labouring poor". Those effects are not removed by rebates. Once again we can go back for counsel to Adam Smith:

Capitation taxes, so far as they are levied upon the lower ranks of people, are direct taxes upon the wages of labour, and are attended with all the inconveniences of such taxes. (Smith, A., Everyman Edition 1947, Vol 2, page 351)

One result of Britain's new, tax-induced poverty is that the social security system has acquired a second function. Its original function was to prevent poverty due to unemployment, sickness or old age. But now it is also required to top up the incomes of those whose poverty is due to tax. A further consequence of the new, tax-induced poverty, and more specifically of the rebates that offset it, has been the creation of a huge, American-style underclass of individuals and families whose living standards depend more on government handouts than on their own efforts.

By 1986 an estimated 30 percent of the population were living in families receiving means-tested or income-tested benefits, and a further 10 percent were probably entitled but not claiming (page 57). The politicians' answer to this extraordinary state of affairs is to say it is the result of kindly governments, anxious to target benefits on "the poor". But most of the working families receiving benefit top-ups are paying more in tax than they are receiving in benefit, and most of the families receiving income support are trapped into welfare dependency by a tax system that cuts in on poverty incomes and make no allowance for the costs of working.

Figure 4.1 illustrates the problem. The horizontal axis represents gross income and the vertical axis net income. The 45° line tracks net incomes assuming there are no benefits and no income taxes. It is not necessary to put figures to the poverty line. It can be at subsistence level (however defined) or it can be extended to include social necessities.

The traditional aim of social security was to fill the gap between the 45° line and the poverty line, the PAO triangle in the first diagram. In the second diagram the line PA is the line of disposable income, after adding in benefit and assuming a benefit withdrawal rate of 70 percent. Tax does not come into it, because poor people

Figure 4.1: Tax-induced poverty

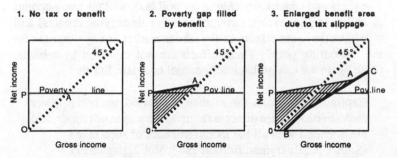

are assumed not to pay tax. Now look at the third diagram, which illustrates the situation once poll tax is introduced. Income tax, NI contributions and poll tax cut in on incomes well below the poverty line. The poll tax will be charged at nil income and a rebate will have to be claimed. The line BC in the third diagram shows how net incomes are dragged below the 45° line, as a result of which the poverty gap is greatly enlarged. The number of people entitled to welfare benefits grows disproportionately, partly because the 70 percent taper causes benefit leakage to people with incomes above the poverty line, and partly because point A (where benefit ceases to be payable) is pushed into more thickly populated areas of income distribution.

The early years

During the 1950s all went reasonably well. Jobs were plentiful and growth was steady. Some of this growth was used to finance increased social benefits, but increases in industrial production kept

Figure 4.2: Economic growth compared with benefit expenditure, 1950-85

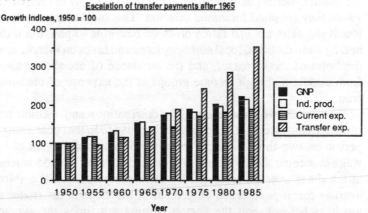

Notes: GNP = Gross National Product at constant factor cost, 1980 prices.
Ind. production = Index of industrial production. Current exp. = General
Government consumption, at constant 1980 prices.
Transfer exp. = General Government transfer payments, deflated by GDP deflator
at 1980 market prices. Figures include current grants and subsidies, capital
transfers and debt interest payments, but not net lending.
Sources: 1950-74: Hansard WA 17 Oct 1975, c 831, and 3 Nov 1975, c 3.
    1975-85: *Economic Trends* Annual Supplement 1986, and Treasury.

well ahead of increases in public expenditure. Social security expenditure would have been higher if more of those entitled to national assistance had claimed it (Atkinson, Maynard and Trinder 1981), nevertheless it was not until the 1960s that things started to go visibly wrong. Industrial production and GNP grew faster than during the previous decade, but not fast enough to keep up with ever-increasing expenditure on transfer payments, much of it on benefits and pensions of one sort or another. The year 1966 marked a watershed, after which expenditure on benefits came to bear less and less relation to wealth creation.

Illustrative figures, all in volume terms, are shown in Figure 4.2. In 1967 expenditure on transfer payments increased faster than industrial production for the first time since 1950. By the mid-1970s the system had fallen apart, with benefit expenditure soaring uncontrollably ahead. Nor did the first two Thatcher administrations make any noticeable difference.

Increasing taxation of the lower paid

The effects were devastating. Whereas during the 1950s the increased benefits could be paid for out of growth, by the end of the 1960s they required increased taxation. This might have mattered less if the extra tax had fallen on those best able to pay, but it did not. NI contributions, local authority rates and taxes on income bore the brunt of the increases, and the incidence of tax shifted away from middle and high income groups at the expense of the lower paid.

Figure 4.3, which refers to NI contributions and income tax, illustrates the effects of tax changes since 1956. In that year a single person on two-thirds average earnings forfeited 14 percent of his wage in income tax and NI contribution, compared with 55 percent at ten times average earnings. By 1978 the person on two-thirds average earnings forfeited 28 percent of his wage in tax (twice as much as before), and the person earning ten times the average forfeited 68 percent – a much smaller increase. Since 1978 direct taxes at the bottom have fallen slightly, but the main beneficiaries of Mrs Thatcher's tax cuts have been those with more than twice average earnings. By 1988-89 tax liability at the bottom was still an incredible 26 percent of gross earnings, but at the top it had gone down to 38 percent (considerably less than in 1956). Married couples have been affected similarly.[2]

Figure 4.3: Changes in tax incidence since 1956

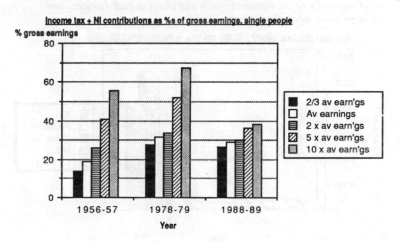

Income tax + NI contributions as %s of gross earnings, single people

Source: Hansard WA 29 Apr 1988, c 318

The changed incidence of taxation, at the expense of the lower paid, can be accounted for in several ways, including removal of the lower rate tax bands and earned-income tax relief, greatly increased NI contributions, and erosion of the income tax base by the non-personal income tax allowances. In their evidence to the House of Commons Treasury and Civil Service Select Committee *Enquiry into the Structure of Personal Income Taxation and Income Support* (henceforth to be referred to as the Meacher Committee) in 1982-83 the Inland Revenue estimated that theoretical tax rates at the top were reduced by 4-5 percent on account of mortgage interest and private pension tax reliefs. By 1987-88 less than 1.2 million out of 21 million tax units were paying higher rate income tax, and only 140,000 paid at the top rate of 60 percent (Hansard WA 15 Feb 1988, c 419).

NI contributions hit the lower paid relatively harder than the well-to-do. So do local authority rates. Yet both have grown faster than income tax. Figure 4.4 shows that during the period 1950-84 revenue from taxes on income increased by a factor of 26, whereas NI contributions went up by a factor of 51, and revenue from local authority rates by a factor of 39. Prices went up 11 times, much more slowly than taxes. Average earnings of male manual workers went up nearly twice as fast as prices, but not fast enough to keep up with tax.

*Figure 4.4: Increased revenues from income taxes, NI contributions and
local authority rates, compared with increases in retail prices, and
average male manual earnings: 1950-84*

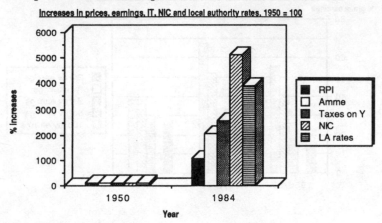

Notes: RPI = Retail prices index.
Amme = Index of average male manual earnings.
Taxes on Y = Taxes on income.
NIC = National insurance etc contributions.
LA rates = Local authority rates.
Source: *National Income and Expenditure* (Blue Books), CSO.

Diminishing child support for working families

Alongside the changing incidence of tax at the expense of the lower
paid other developments have weakened the relative position of
working families with children at all income levels, especially
families dependent on a single wage. One way to show what has
happened is by looking at *tax break-even points* . In Figure 4.5 the
tax break-even point is defined as the point on the income scale at
which net liability to income tax begins, after deducting family
allowance/child benefit. This is the definition used by the Inland
Revenue (Inland Revenue 1980, 2A, page 71).

The decline in tax break-even points, right across the board, is
clearly shown in the graph, but it is working families with children
who have been worst affected. Lower paid working families with
children have therefore been hit four times over: by the
disproportionate increases in income tax, NI contributions and local
authority rates explained above, and by the failure of successive
governments to uprate family allowances and child benefit in line
with the adult tax allowances.

Figure 4.5: Tax break-even points 1950-85 as percentages of average male manual earnings (amme)

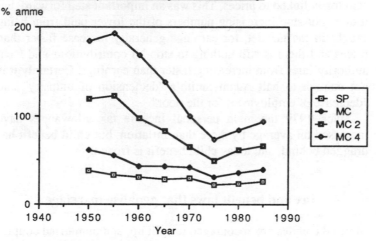

Source: *Inland Revenue Statistics*

No coherent strategy on benefit upratings

While tax break-even points kept going down, all the main social security benefits except family allowance/child benefit kept going up. During the 1950s and 1960s the main out-of-work benefits (but not family allowance) were moved up more or less in line with earnings. In 1972 the introduction of long-term supplementary benefit rates added approximately 25 percent to the SB scale rates for adults over pension age. By the mid-1970s long-term benefits were indexed to earnings and short-term benefits to prices, although family allowance, paid to working families, was never indexed to anything, and was allowed to drag further and further behind the child additions payable to out-of-work families. In 1980 the link between pensions and earnings was broken and today all the main social security benefits are indexed to prices, but child benefit is not indexed to anything, and is under constant attack.

Only the children of working parents are unprotected against inflation

For thirty years after World War 2 there was nothing in law to prevent income tax allowances, like family allowance, from dragging behind prices as well as earnings. It was not until 1977, as a result of the Rooker/Lawson/Wise amendment to the Finance Bill of that year, that the personal income tax allowances were statutorily linked to prices. This was an important step forward, but it does not stop increasing numbers of the lower paid from being caught in the tax net, for earnings generally increase faster than prices and there is still nothing to stop NI contributions and local authority rates from increasing faster than earnings. Certainly it is not enough to halt Adam Smith's "declension of industry" and "decrease of employment for the poor".

Since 1979 the main personal income tax allowances have increased on average by more than inflation, but child benefit has dragged behind, and today child benefit is frozen.

Tax and benefit laws that penalise marriage

Married couples are encouraged to split up, and unmarried couples are discouraged from entering into legal marriage, by tax and benefit laws that treat unmarried couples and lone parents more generously than married couples and parents who live together.

Despite women's emancipation and despite changes in the divorce laws, the tax treatment of married couples has remained virtually unchanged since income tax was introduced in 1799. The income of a married woman living with her husband (but not otherwise) is deemed for income tax purposes to be his income and not her income. So long as they stay together they are taxed as a single unit, the husband is reponsible for his wife's tax affairs, they may claim only one lot of *mortgage interest tax relief* (MITR) and one lot of capital gains tax relief. But if they stop living together the wife regains her status as an equal citizen. The wife becomes once again responsible for her own tax affairs and if she has a child she can claim the *additional personal allowance* (APA) as well as the *single person's allowance* (SPA), which together sum to the *married man's allowance* (MMA). Not only that, if she chooses a new partner, who also has a child, they may each claim the equivalent of MMA, and they may each claim mortgage interest tax relief. If one of them does not have the income to set against the tax allowance, the other can covenant the necessary amount on their behalf.

Much of this is due to change. In his 1988 Budget Mr Lawson announced independent taxation of husband and wife from April

1990, and he restricted APA to one per family from April 1989. He also ended tax relief on non-charitable covenants between individuals and restricted mortgage interest tax relief to £30,000 per residence, regardless of the number of borrowers. Although most of the penalties for marriage will be removed, the system due to take effect in April 1990 remains asymmetrical, and this is discussed in Chapter 5.

The growth since World War 2 in the number of lone-parent families is by no means unique to Britain. It is a part of social change throughout the developed world. But in Britain it is encouraged by the social security system. Couples who might otherwise have stayed together break up, and unmarried mothers who might otherwise have married the father of their child choose not to do so. In the 1986 Social Security Act and in the new income support regulations a "married couple" is defined as "a man and a woman who are married to each other *and are members of the same household* " (my emphasis). So for social security purposes the life-long commitment that used to be part of the marriage contract is almost completely done away with.

In 1960 expenditure through the social security system on lone parents was £20 million, at 1985 prices. By 1985-86 it had reached nearly £2000 million at 1985 prices (Hansard WA 16 Jul 1986), with no signs of slowing down.

The price of shelter has shot ahead of earnings

Like income tax and NI contribution, rent and rates are a budget component over which most low income families have little control. In Britain they have soared. Between 1950 and 1984 the average rent paid by low income householders went up by a factor of 34, compared with an eleven-fold increase in retail prices and a twenty-one-fold increase in average male manual earnings (DHSS Aug 1986). Most of this increase has taken place since the mid 1960s, coinciding with the doctrine that governments should subsidise "people not bricks". Between 1965 and 1984 average rents and rates paid by local authority tenants increased about twelve-fold, compared with a less than nine-fold increase in average male manual earnings. Some of the biggest increases have occurred since Mrs Thatcher took office, and more are planned.

Figure 4.6 shows what happened to rents and rates during the first two Thatcher administrations. The figures refer to average, unrebated local authority rents and average, unrebated domestic rate bills in England. Those unable to afford the increases are in theory given rebates. By the mid 1980s about a third of all households depended on housing benefit, and in Northern Ireland the figure was about 40 percent.

Figure 4.6: Rent and rate increases 1979-87

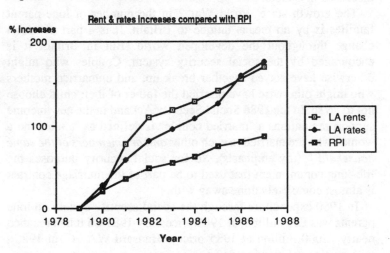

Source: Hansard WA 29 Jun 1987, cc 41-46.

The unemployment and poverty traps

Those who have been dragged into long-term welfare dependency are increasingly held to blame, but the situation is not of their making, they are its victims. They are being shoved from pillar to post by a system that is excessively doctrinaire, and has lost touch with reality.

Given that people wholly dependent on social security benefits are exempt from income tax, NI contribution, 80 percent of their local authority rate bill, rents and mortgage interest, one of the effects of excessive tax and escalating housing costs has been to narrow the gap between incomes in and out of work, and to make lower paid work financially unattractive . This effect is called the *unemployment trap.* Already by the mid 1960s there was growing awareness that lower paid families with children could be better off on the dole. But instead of tackling the problem at its roots (by lifting them out of tax) it was decided to introduce a national scheme of income-tested rent and rate rebates for the lower paid, and family income supplement (FIS) for families with children. This helped to widen the gap between incomes in and out of work, but it also narrowed the gap between living standards at different levels of earnings. Out of each extra £ earned the wage earner had to pay income tax and NI contribution at the same time as his benefits were being withdrawn, producing marginal tax rates of more than 100 percent. This effect is known as the *poverty trap*.

The theoretical effects of the traps on the disposable incomes of single householders, single-wage married couples and single wage couples with two children, in the period between November 1985 (when benefits were uprated) and March 1986 (before the 1985 Budget tax changes took effect), are illustrated in Figure 4.7. For explanation of the abbreviations used here and in later diagrams, please refer to the Glossary.

Figure 4.7 assumes full take-up of all benefits to which there is entitlement. At nil earnings the families are assumed to be on supplementary benefit (SB), including passport benefits like free school meals, but excluding SB single payments and income disregards.

Figure 4.7: Unemployment and poverty traps, November 1985

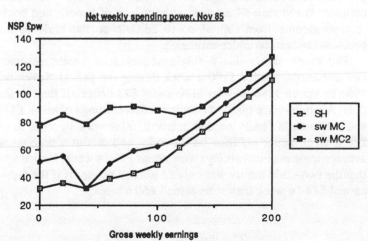

Source: Appendix 2, Table (1), less work expenses £6 pw.

The type of analysis used for Figure 4.7 is called *model family analysis*. The circumstances of the families in the graph are hypothetical, and the figures apply only within the assumptions made. These assumptions are set out in Appendix 2. Model family analysis will be used many times in this report, but it has to be interpreted carefully. Looking at the graph it is tempting to conclude that all two-child families needed £140 a week in November 1985 to March 1986 in order to be £20 better off than on the dole. But that is not so. The position varies according to the age of the children, housing costs and housing tenure, fares to work, whether or not both parents are in paid work, and many other factors. Figure 4.7 assumes fares to work of £6 a week except where the wage earner was working part-time for £20 a week, in which case work expenses are assumed to be nil. In practice a person earning £50 or £60 a week would be unlikely to pay £6 a week travel costs. The job would not be worth taking. On the other hand a person earning £200 a week might well be paying more than £6. The rent and rate figures used are taken from the DHSS *Tax Benefit Model Tables* for November 1985, and are low compared with what many people have to pay. With housing costs higher than those assumed, or if the unemployed person is receiving mortgage interest as part of SB, then the disincentive effects of the system become more pronounced. Conversely, with lower housing costs, the disincentive effects are smaller. In November 1985 each claimant could earn £4 a week without loss of benefit and could receive income from capital up to £3,000, so the scale of the problem tends to be under-estimated.

The graph shows that a single householder, in the assumed circumstances, needed £100 a week during the period November 1985 to March 1986 in order to be about £23 better off than on the dole. A single-wage married couple needed earnings of about £130 and a two-child family needed nearly £160 a week in order to be £30 a week better off than on the dole, and this at a time when average male manual earnings were about £170 a week. Notice also that the two-child family was only £1 a week better off if the father earned £140 a week than if he earned £60 a week.

The lone-parent trap

For lone parents, especially lone mothers, the position is generally worse that for two-parent families. This is partly because SB entitlement for lone parents was relatively more generous than for two-parent families, partly because of the childcare costs that most lone parents incur if they go out to work, and partly because of the lower earnings potential of women than men. Appendix 5 shows the extent to which lone parents in paid work are concentrated at the bottom end of the income distribution. In 1985 about half of those (the minority) who were in paid work were earning less than £150 a week.

Figure 4.8: Lone-parent trap, November 1985

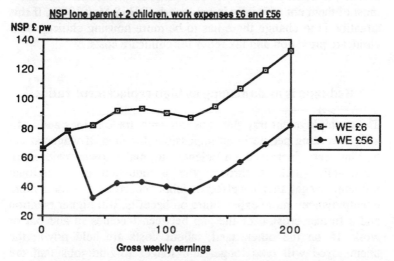

Source: Appendix 2, Table (1), less work expenses of (a) £6 and (b) £56.

In Figure 4.8, I have assumed that the out-of-work lone mother was in receipt of the long-term SB (payable after one year on benefit), and the in-work mother had work expenses either of £6 a week (as in the DHSS Tax Benefit Model Tables), or £56 a week. The second figure includes £50 a week for childcare costs. The average weekly charge reported to the National Childminding Association in 1985 was £30 a week, but I have assumed a reduction for the second child. The graph shows that the mother could improve her position slightly by going out to work, but only provided she did not have childcare costs. Otherwise paid work in the formal economy was unlikely to be worthwhile. The necessary wage was about £200 a week.

Of course, if the lone mother were living with her own parents, or with another lone parent, or with a friend, her position would be much better. She would still qualify for the additional tax allowance available to lone parents, and so long as the person with whom she shared accommodation was not a man, she would also be eligible for *one-parent benefit* and family income supplement. This is an area where lone parents can end up substantially better off than parents who stay together. For the poverty experienced by lone parents has at least as much to do with household status (living alone) as with lone-parent status. Either way welfare dependency is an integral part of the system. In 1985 nearly 60 percent of lone parents in Great Britain were receiving supplementary benefit – most of them not officially in paid work (DHSS May 1988). If this situation is to change there has to be more housing choice, more childcare provision and tax relief for childcare costs.

Red tape is as damaging as high replacement ratios

The unemployment trap puts governments, trade unions and individual working people in an impossible dilemma. If wages at the bottom were increased sufficiently to make lower paid work worthwhile (perhaps through the introduction of a national minimum wage), then the effect on labour costs could result in more unemployment, more expenditure on benefits, still higher taxation and a further erosion of the gap between incomes in and out of work. If, on the other hand, labour costs are held down, the unemployed will take longer and longer to find jobs that are competitive with the dole.

In such circumstances it is futile to talk about "scroungers", or to accuse people of "choosing not to work". The key issue is the price at which it is financially worthwhile for individuals in different circumstances to sell their labour. Changes are needed that will bring that price down (especially for unskilled labour), without causing hardship and without destroying the dignity of working people. By far the most obvious way to do this, which has yet to be tried, is by lifting the lower paid out of direct tax entirely, and by increasing the amount of non means-tested income support for families with children.

A change of that sort would be a major step forward, but it would not be enough. Excessive red tape is as likely to create welfare dependency as high replacement ratios, but it gets less publicity because its effects are more difficult to quantify. Most computer models still take standard families in the most straightforward circumstances, for instance the "typical" two-child family where the father is unemployed. But the actual circumstances of actual families are not that simple. Those affected are not just the registered unemployed, nor just those on SBIS. Many , as we have seen, are lone parents. Others are people with physical or mental handicaps who are in receipt of invalidity benefit, or who have forfeited invalidity benefit because they tried unsuccessfully to get back into the regular labour market, or whose living costs (as a result of their disabilities) are so high that they cannot earn enough to escape the unemployment trap, although they could do regular part-time work if the system allowed it. Others are unskilled workers in need of training or education, which they do not take because they would forfeit benefit on the grounds that they were not "available for work". Others are seasonal or part-time workers avoiding the hassle of signing on and off; wives with unemployed husbands who would lose their dependency addition; students during vacation, topping up non-existent or inadequate grants; or people with very high housing or travel-to-work costs.

Such people are locked into benefit dependency by a system that assumes they can *either* do nothing at all *or* they can be in regular, full-time work. People with disabilities get the roughest ride of all. They need to be allowed to work part-time, within their capabilities. It is part of the rehabilitation process. Instead, if they earn more than the therapeutic earnings disregard, they lose all their benefit.

Those who have not been through the claiming rigmarole have difficulty understanding its ramifications. The tangle of red tape itself defeats analysis. Yet the results are straightforward. Claimants who could earn money from time to time do not do so, or they do it on the sly.

The pensioner poverty trap

Retirement pensioners suffer their own versions of the unemployment and poverty traps. The young old who would like to add to their NI pensions through paid work, are allowed to earn up to a certain amount (£75 a week in 1988-89), after which the NI pension starts to be withdrawn (by 5p for every 10p earned between £75 and £79 a week, and by 10p for every 10p thereafter). Investment income or occupational pension does not affect entitlement to the NI pension in this way, only earned income.

By contrast, income from all sources can affect entitlement to SB/IS and housing benefit. Figure 4.9 shows the effect of tax plus benefit withdrawal on the disposable incomes of pensioners in the same November 1985 to March 1986 period as before. The figures assume entitlement to full Category A pension for the single pensioner, and, in the case of the married couple, Category A pension for the husband and Category B pension (through the husband's contributions) for the wife. Category A and B pensions constitute benefit income, to which are then added varying amounts of *original income*, defined here as allowable earnings and/or additional, earnings-related or occupational pension. Investment income is not included, because SB was subject to a capital limit of £3,000 – another complexity.

At £0 per week on the horizontal axis the pensioner has his/her basic state pension of £38.30 (single) and £61.30 (married), but no other pension. Disposable income is defined as the basic NI pension, plus the varying amounts of original income, plus means-tested benefits (taken up in full), less income tax, rent and rates. The figures understate the disincentive effects of the situation, because they leave out the single and special needs payments which until April 1988 were available to supplementary pensioners.

Figure 4.9: Pensioner poverty trap, November 1985

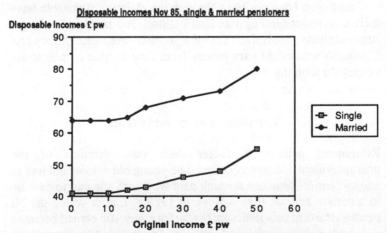

Disposable Incomes Nov 85, single & married pensioners

Source: Appendix 2 and DHSS.

The graph highlights the *poverty plateau* effect of the pre-Fowler system. With rent and rates higher than those assumed the curve of disposable income would be flatter still, for instance a single pensioner with an occupational pension of £50 a week, paying rent of £30 and rates of £10, was only about £3 a week better off than the poorest supplementary pensioner. Although these income amounts are small by comparison with earnings, they are not small by pensioner standards. Appendix 5 shows that in 1985 about 80 percent of single pensioners and about 55 percent of married pensioners had gross incomes excluding state basic pension of less than £40 a week.

Scale of the problem

Some people regard the unemployment and poverty traps as a problem of equity, more theoretical than real. Yet by 1983 an estimated 14 million persons (some 25 percent of the population) were living in families dependent on family income supplement, housing benefit or supplementary benefit (Hansard WA 14 Apr 1986, c 271).

Until 1988 the DHSS published regular analyses of the distribution of low income families, based on the Supplementary Benefit Annual Statistical Enquiry and the Family Expenditure Survey. The figures distinguished between families in receipt of SB and families not in receipt of SB but with *relative net resources* either below the appropriate SB level, or less than 40 percent above it. The DHSS defined relative net resources as net income less housing costs net of housing benefit, less £5.85 for fares to work, divided by the appropriate SB scale rate. The scale rate used was the ordinary rate for families with the head under pension age, and the long-term rate (25 percent higher) for families with the head over pension age, although there is no reason to suppose that working age families need 25 percent less than pensioners in order to reach the same living standard.[3]

From the 1981, 1983 and 1985 enquiries, three main features emerge. First, the large numbers of people with net resources *below* the SB entitlement levels laid down by Parliament, indicating failure to reach all those in need. Second, the ever-increasing number of working-age families dependent on SB, and locked into economic inactivity. Third, the number of families with incomes so close to SB levels that they are probably caught in the poverty trap. The figures are summarised in Table 4.1. They refer only to Great

Table 4.1: Low income families, 1981, 1983 and 1985, Great Britain, millions

	Families			Persons in families		
	1981	1983	1985	1981	1983	1985
1. Not receiving SB or HB supplement, but with relative net resources below SB level	1.6	1.9	1.6	3.6	2.8	2.4
2. Receiving SB or HB supplement	3.0	3.6	4.1	4.8	6.1	7.0
3. Not receiving SB or HB supplement, but with relative net resources below 140% SB levels	5.2	5.7	4.9	9.8	10.3	8.5
4. Total "low" income" (2.+3.)	8.2	9.3	9.0	14.6	16.4	15.5

Source: *Low Income Families 1985* (DHSS May 1988).

Britain. In Northern Ireland the proportions affected would be higher. The figures should be read bearing in mind that the SB reference points have increased more slowly than earnings since 1981. This should automatically reduce the number of wage earners with relative net resources below 140 percent of SB levels. In fact the number slipping through the safety net (line 1) is remarkably stable.

The figures in Table 4.2 show the proportions in 1985 of different client groups (by family composition, employment status and so forth) who were dependent on low incomes. Over 20 percent of large families (defined as having three or more children) were dependent on SB. Nearly 60 percent of lone parents depended on SB (compared with 48 percent in 1983) and a further 11 percent had net resources below 140 percent of their SB scale rate. An estimated 15 percent of all children were living in families dependent on SB (compared with 13 percent in 1983), and nearly a third of all children were living in low income families.

Since 1985 the situation has got worse. In November 1987, in reply to a Parliamentary Written Question, the Minister estimated that about 4.9 million families with 3.3 million dependants were receiving SB in 1986, and a further 3.7 million families were receiving standard housing benefit (Hansard WA 30 Nov 1987, cc 471-2). No estimate of the number of persons (as opposed to claimants) dependent on housing benefit was given, but assuming an unchanged ratio since 1983, then the total number of persons dependent on FIS, SB and housing benefit in 1986 must have been

Table 4.2: Low income families, 1985, Great Britain. Incidence of disadvantage by family type and client group

Family type or client group	Total families	% of family type or client group			
		(a)	(b)	(c)	(b)+(c)
		Below	On	Below	Low
	thousands	SB	SB	140% SB	income
		%	%	%	%
All families	28,630	6	14	17	32
Over pension age:	6,680	12	24	41	65
Married couple	2,360	8	11	41	52
Single people	4,320	13	31	41	72
Under pension age:	21,960	4	11	10	22
Married couples with children	5,940	3	7	12	19
Single people with children	910	3	59	11	70
Married couples, no children	4,770	2	4	5	11
Single people, no children	10,340	5	12	11	23
Large families (3 or more children)	1,120	4	21	20	40
Full-time work or self-employed	15,690	2	0	6	6
Sick/disabled	770	6	29	27	56
Unemployed	2,300	14	67	21	88
Others	3,200	7	23	16	39
	Persons				
Children	12,440	3	15	13	29

Note: The low income total in column (c) includes those in column (a).
Source: DHSS May 1988.

in the region of 17 million – or about 31 percent of the population. Assuming no change in take-up ratios since 1983 and 1984, a further 3 million families (about 5 million persons, or nearly 10 percent of the population) may have been eligible but not claiming. Thus by 1986 an incredible 40 percent of the population would have been in receipt of withdrawable benefits, if take-up had been 100 percent.

Response by the Thatcher administrations.

The Conservative Party returned to office in 1979 with reform of the systems of social security, income tax and local authority rates high on its agenda. From the evidence available it was clear that nothing but harm would be achieved by further tinkering. The whole of income maintenance (cash benefits and income tax reliefs) must be tackled together, and the changes introduced must be on a grand scale, even though it might take several years to put the whole strategy into effect.

Nothing like this happened. During her first two administrations Mrs Thatcher chose to stay within the existing (spuriously Beveridge) social security system, watering it down with increasing reliance on means-tested benefits. The expected tax reform did not materialise. At first there was an attempt to help low income taxpayers by raising income tax thresholds faster than inflation, but the emphasis then switched to cutting the standard rate of income tax to 25 percent. *Child benefit* (CB), which replaced child tax allowances as well as family allowance in 1979, was not allowed to keep pace with the adult tax allowances, and the cuts in income tax were offset for the lower paid by increased NI contributions and by the increases in rents and rates already referred to.

Mr Norman Fowler's Social Security Review

By early 1984 the situation was so clearly out of control (requiring nearly 100 million manual entries a week for administration of supplementary benefit alone), that the announcement by Secretary of State for Social Services Mr Norman Fowler of a full-scale review was generally welcomed. Instead his efforts were a fiasco. The review process was marred throughout by excessive haste. It took the fundamentals of the existing system for granted, avoiding the most difficult questions, and it excluded from its terms of reference any examination of alternative systems.

The Green Paper *Reform of Social Security* (DHSS Jun 1985), was followed by a truncated consultation period from June to September, and publication of a White Paper before the end of the year (DHSS Dec 1985) . The ensuing Bill, which was like three major Bills in one (pensions, housing and supplementary benefit), was presented to Parliament in January 1986 and made subject to guillotine during its final committee stages and on return from the

House of Lords. It reached the statute book, despite concern on all sides and in both Houses of Parliament, two days before the 1986 summer recess. A quite separate consultation paper on *The Reform of Personal Taxation* (Treasury March 1986) was not published until the following spring, as though to emphasise the Government's basic position that taxation and benefits should not be confused.

Mr Fowler's review nevertheless served two useful purposes. It showed that reform of social security in the 1980s cannot succeed without coordinated reform of personal taxation. It also showed the technical difficulties of moving to a system based on the means-test, without exacerbating the poverty trap. Throughout the review process DHSS ministers emphasised the attractions of means-tested benefits, which they re-named targeted or *income-related* benefits. The Green Paper included a beautiful, gently-rising curve, showing the "illustrative effect of the family credit scheme, taking account of changes in other benefits including supplementary benefit and housing benefit" (DHSS Jun 1985, Fig 6, page 30). The poverty trap had vanished, but there were no figures on either axis. It took months for the unfortunate DHSS statisticians to put acceptable figures to that graph. In the end the only way to do so was by *cutting* disposable incomes at the bottom, both in and out of work. Anything else would have added to the cost of the scheme, or would have dragged more families into welfare dependency.

Figure 4.10 shows net spending power for the same two-child family as in Figure 4.7, before and after Fowler. The figures for the new system refer to 1987-88. The new spending power figures were calculated using the April 1988 benefit rates announced by Mr John Moore in October 1987, reduced by just over 4 percent to make them comparable with 1987-88 benefit rates. Rents and rates were taken from the DHSS *Tax/Benefit Model Tables* for November 1987. All the figures are comparable, and the results are astonishing. Far from targeting more resources on the lower paid, the peaks and troughs of the poverty trap have been straightened out by undercutting the troughs. The children in Figure 4.10 are assumed to be aged 4 and 6. Most low income families, including pensioners, have been treated similarly. The only families who made worthwhile gains are those with children aged over 11, or lone parents living with friends or relatives (Parker, H. Jan 1988).

Today, as a result of the 1986 Act, very few working families face marginal tax rates of more than 100 percent. But those drawing both family credit and housing benefit still forfeit between 90 and

Figure 4.10: Poverty trap in 1987-88, compared with poverty trap assuming April 1988 benefit changes

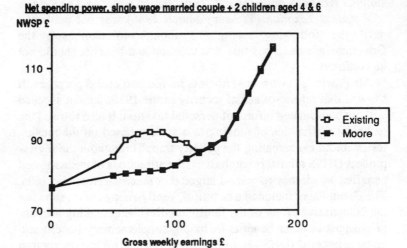

Net spending power, single wage married couple + 2 children aged 4 & 6
NWSP £

Gross weekly earnings £

Assumptions: rent £18.35, rates £7.70, water rates £1.70, fares to work £5.60.

100 pence out of each extra £ earned. Already, as a result of freezing child benefit in April 1988, some 15,000 more families may have become entitled to family credit (Hansard WA 27 Oct 87); and the new community charge seems likely to add at least 1.5 million to the number of people claiming means-tested rebates (Hansard WA 10 Nov 87 c 153)[4] Decontrol of rents will have a similar effect.

Thus a government that set out to help the poor and encourage self-reliance has managed to cut living standards at the bottom and reduce work incentives simultaneously.

5
New concepts

The Beveridge Plan was out of date before the ink was dry on the paper, because Beveridge did not take account of the changing role of women. If there is to be thorough-going reform of income maintenance in the 1990s, we must ensure that the new system is in line with social, economic and technological change since World War 2 and we must also take into consideration changes now taking place, the effects of which are still not fully understood. We must recognise the effects of new technologies on the labour market and the urgent need for an income support system that helps people move with the tide of change, instead of leaving them stranded and helpless. We must also recognise the effects of better health and longer life expectancy on attitudes to retirement and on family life, for instance the need to give elderly people (especially the "young old") the chance to build on their pensions by doing paid work, and the need to compensate those who give up paid work to care for disabled or very elderly relatives.

Government is out of touch

In his book *Blind Victory* former Cabinet Minister David Howell accused the Government of concentrating on old problems that have been overtaken by new, larger questions (Howell, D. 1986). Nowhere could this accusation be more appropriate than in connection with income maintenance. The debate is being focused on issues that have lost their relevance whilst others are being side-tracked.

One such question is integration. Can the tax and benefit systems be merged? If so, what should be the *basis of entitlement* and the *unit of assessment*? These are critical questions, yet they were excluded from the 1985 Social Security Review. Instead Government has concentrated unrelentingly on the time-worn and increasingly sterile debate between universalists and selectivists, and public opinion is being manipulated by the use of euphemisms like 'targeted' and 'income-related' to refer to common or garden means-testing.

Taxpayer or beneficiary?

The continuing preoccupation with means-tested as opposed to universal benefits, and with what has come to be known as "churning" (when the same person both pays tax and receives benefit), shows how easy it is when dealing with a complex subject to distract attention from the real issues. For the true purpose of improved targeting is not to help the poor, but to cut benefit expenditure, and the real issue is whether to accentuate the fast-disappearing division between taxpayers and beneficiaries or allow them to merge.

During the past few decades a social and technological revolution has swept through Britain, but it came so quickly that most people do not realise what has happened. For centuries the dichotomy between taxpayers and beneficiaries, rich and poor, was absolute. Then, within a generation it became obsolete. Suddenly millions of people found themselves receiving benefit *and* paying tax. The old divisions started to melt away and the Inland Revenue acquired a second role as automatic, non-stigmatising benefit withdrawal system. Technological innovation made it possible to credit benefit and debit tax in a single, split-second, tax/benefit calculation. The GIRO cheque replaced cash handouts, but that was only the start. Today the expertise exists to replace perhaps £2,500 million worth of administrative paperwork by an automated tax/benefit system that would determine the *net* tax liability or *net* benefit entitlement of every citizen.

The obstacles to further advance are almost entirely political. They include the philosophical objections of a government committed to accentuating the differences between taxpayer and beneficiary, and the practical objections of civil servants who see their jobs at risk. By 1985-86 this formidable alliance was costing every British household an average of £2.50 a week to pay one army of DHSS officials to distribute benefits and a second army of tax collectors to gather it up again. It cost each household a further 30 pence a week to finance the administrative costs alone of civil servants employed by the Manpower Services Commission (Whitehall's fastest growing army) so they could pay out an ever-changing, ever-increasing flood of grants and allowances, most of them carefully tailored to exclude. Additionally, and here the figures are unobtainable, the taxpayer must finance the pay and pensions of countless smaller units throughout the country – local government officials responsible for housing benefits, student grants, free school meals and educational maintenance allowances, as well as social workers and health visitors caught up increasingly in welfare rights counselling instead of the work for which they were trained.

Government ministers complain about churning, but the churning is of their making. If advantage were taken of the new technologies, there need be no armies of officials – just a single calculation showing net tax liability or net benefit entitlement and requiring perhaps a few seconds of computer time.

Benign churning and malignant churning

Computerisation and national insurance have had two effects. First, the old dichotomies between taxpayers and beneficiaries, tax reliefs and cash benefits, have become wasteful of resources and largely meaningless, as have the traditional Treasury accounting procedures. Instead of the old distinctions between cash expenditures and tax expenditures, what matters now is that *net* tax in the aggregate and *net* benefit should balance, and that the tax rates necessary to achieve this balance should not discourage effort or diminish the tax base. Second, the debate between universalists and selectivists has lost its edge. For once benefits credited to the rich can be simultaneously recouped through the tax system, the problem becomes arithmetical (that is to say a question of *marginal tax rates* -MTRs), and above all political (who will lose and who will gain), rather than administrative.

Most churning is benign, or could be, but there is one sort of churning that is deadly. This occurs when tax is charged beyond ability to pay, and low income taxpayers are expected to claim means-tested benefits in order to bring their net incomes up to the accepted poverty levels. The figures in Table 5.1 refer to 1988-89. Benign churning, when benefits are withdrawn through the tax

New concepts

Table 5.1: Benign and malignant churning, April 1988
Single-wage married couple with two children, rent
£19.12, rates £9.80

1. BENIGN CHURNING	£
(a) Earnings	150.00
+ (b) Child benefit	14.50
− (c) Income tax and NIC	31.31
− (d) Local authority rates	9.80
= (e) Net income	123.39
Net tax: (c + d − b)	26.61
2. MALIGNANT CHURNING	
(a) Earnings	120.00
+ (b) Child benefit	14.50
− (c) Income tax and NIC	21.11
− (d) Rates	9.80
+ (e) Family credit	16.34
+ (f) Housing benefit	0.00
= (g) Total resources	119.93
Net tax: (c + d) = (b + e)	0.07

Source: Hansard WA 17 May 1988, cc 402-406.

system, is illustrated in the first part of the table. In order to
understand what is going on all that is necessary is to think in terms
of *net* benefit and *net* tax. The family earning £150 a week pays
£26.61 a week more in income tax, NI contribution and rates than
it receives in child benefit. The system is easy to operate and
incentive neutral. Child benefit operates exactly like a tax credit,
reducing the family's net tax bill by £14.50.

By contrast malignant churning (illustrated in the second part of
the table), has a pauperisation effect, destroying the family's
economic independence. Even at this low level of earnings (£120 a
week was about half average earnings in April 1988) the family
must pay £16.41 more in tax than it receives in child benefit, and is
then expected to top its income up again by claiming family credit.
At the end of the day, it receives 7 pence less in child benefit and
family credit than it pays out in tax. But the penalty for claiming
family credit is a marginal tax rate over 80 percent, which is why
the family earning £150 is only £3 a week better off than the family
on £120.

New concepts

Tax break-even points and tax progressivity

The tax break-even point, or income level at which people become net taxpayers, is one of the most useful indicators of changing tax incidence and income distribution, and will be referred to many times in this report. When tax break-even points at the bottom of the income distribution (or for families with children) go up, it is a sign that income is being redistributed downwards (*vertically*) in favour of people on low incomes, or sideways (*horizontally*) in favour of families with children. Conversely when tax break-even points at the bottom (or for families with children) go down it is a sign that people on low incomes (or families with children) are paying more in net tax by comparison with better-off taxpayers (or taxpayers without children). Either their relative living standards are going down, or they become more dependent on means-tested benefits, or there is a mixture of both effects.

Tax break-even points can be measured taking into account just income tax, or income tax plus NI contribution, or both of these plus local authority rates/poll tax. Under the existing tax and benefit systems, the tax break-even point (second definition) is the same for non-householders without children as the lower earnings level at which NI contribution starts to be payable. From that point on they are net taxpayers. For families with children the starting point for tax has to be grossed up to allow for child benefit. For NI pensioners it has to be grossed up to allow for retirement or invalidity pension.

In 1987-88, and assuming local authority rates of £7.70, the tax break-even point (using the widest definition) for a couple with two children was £78 a week. In other words families with two children in the assumed circumstances became net taxpayers once their earnings reached about 40 percent of the national average for male manual workers. If one excludes local authority rates then the break-even point in 1987-88 was about £100, or about half average male manual earnings, and if one takes income tax only then it becomes £127 a week or about 69 percent of average male manual earnings. During the early 1950s it was over 100 percent on this narrowest of definitions (Figure 4.5).

When tax break-even points come down welfare dependency goes up, and those at the bottom are caught in the poverty trap. Figure 5.1 compares proportional and progressive tax schedules with the marginal tax rates implied in the existing (1988-89) tax/benefit system. At the bottom of the earnings distribution the comb-

65

Figure 5.1: Proportional, progressive and declining tax rates

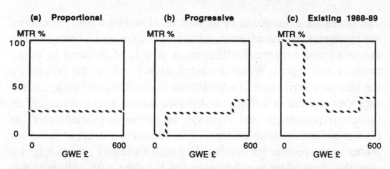

ination of benefit withdrawal plus income tax and NI contribution produces declining marginal tax rates. The example refers to a married couple with two children in 1988-89. The benefit withdrawal rate once earnings exceed £5 per spouse is 100 percent. Full-time work brings entitlement to family credit and housing benefit, and a marginal tax rate of just under 100 percent. Over the band of income between withdrawal of means-tested benefits and the upper earnings limit for NI contribution, the rate falls to 34 percent, and this is the band in which most wage earners are congregated. Then, on earnings above £305 a week it drops to 25 percent, because NI contribution is no longer payable. On earnings around £500 a week (depending on the amount of mortgage interest and superannuation tax reliefs that can be claimed) it rises to 40 percent, where it remains.

Low tax break-even points combined with steeply withdrawable benefits increase tax revenues and reduce public expenditure, because only the very poorest are net beneficiaries. Consequently the tax rate for the majority can be lower than would otherwise be possible. From the evidence submitted to the Meacher Committee of Enquiry (House of Commons 1983), the need to make the system more progressive by lifting more of the lower paid out of tax, was abundantly clear. Instead, when Mrs Thatcher or her ministers recommend cuts in child benefit, or a 20 percent standard rate of income tax in preference to higher tax allowances, they risk making the system less progressive.

Targeting to help the rich

As explained there will soon be no technical reason why benefit credited to all families with children, or to all pensioners, cannot be recouped from the rich through tax in a single, tax/benefit calculation. The rich need not lay their hands on any extra money, it need not even reduce their tax bill. On the contrary it is much more likely to increase it. Figure 18.1 will show that an integrated system can be much more progressive than the existing, dual system. But that is not what the advocates of improved targeting are after. By increasing the net tax liability of the millions congregated just above the new poverty lines, the rich and the well-to-do can see their tax liability reduced. For the rich high tax rates are said to be bad, but for the poor they seem not to matter.

One of the paradoxes in the campaign for improved targeting is the way it is directed almost exclusively at families with children (child benefit), although some of the worst targeting in the system concerns national insurance pensions. NI invalidity pensions are not even taxable. In 1987-88 an invalidity pensioner could have £73 a week tax-free income in addition to his invalidity pension, and his wife could earn £47 tax-free, before IVB started to be recouped. Yet the problem is not even discussed. Retirement pensions are taxable and are recouped through the tax system faster than IVB, but not nearly so fast as child benefit, because pensioners do not have to pay NI contribution. In 1987-88 the tax break-even point for a single pensioner was about £150 a week, compared with £100 for a man, wife and two children. A 20 percent tax rate will push pensioner tax break-even points still higher.

The basis of entitlement and the unit of assessment

Instead of prolonging ancient arguments, it is time to move on. New concepts are needed, new words through which to express them, new ways of presenting official statistics and new national accounting techniques. Interwoven with the debate about integration is the fast-emerging debate about the basis of entitlement and the unit of assessment.

The basis of entitlement. The right to benefit can be based on need, contingency, contribution record or citizenship/legal residence, or on several of these attributes. Most UK benefits are based on mixtures of contingency plus contribution record, or contingency plus need. They are expensive to administer, they lock people into claimant roles, and they leave a substantial minority uncatered for. Child benefit is a citizenship benefit, extended to all legal residents.

It has the advantages of nearly 100 percent take-up and low administrative costs. It is withdrawn from high income families through the tax system. Citizenship pensions and citizenship basic incomes could operate in similar fashion.

The assessment unit. For tax purposes the unit of assessment is the single person or legally married couple. A married couple counts as one person (the husband), and an unmarried, cohabiting couple counts as two. From April 1990 the married couple also will count as two people. For benefit purposes the rules are different. Each spouse can build up an independent right to the contributory benefits, but for means-tested benefits they count as a single unit. Married and unmarried (heterosexual) couples have a mutual liability to maintain. They also have a liability to maintain their own and each others' children under age 16. The anomalies in this system are obvious. The increasingly favoured alternative is to make the individual the assessment unit for both tax and benefit purposes, regardless of sex or marital status. This would ensure neutrality between the sexes and between married and single, but it nevertheless raises complex issues. Few people would countenance an independent right to means-tested benefits, regardless of the income or wealth of the other spouse.

The arguments in favour of individual tax/benefit units with entitlement based on citizenship revolve round six major issues, with some overlap between them. As set out below each new concept is put forward as replacement for an older one. In each case the older concept is rejected on the grounds that it is ineffective, slows down adjustment to change and produces undesirable side effects. The new concepts are in no way an attempt to question traditional moral values. They should strengthen them. What the new concepts do question are the traditional ways of applying those values:

(1) Poverty prevention, not poverty relief.
(2) Citizenship, not contribution record.
(3) Need, not status.
(4) Income security, not social security.
(5) Individuals, not couples.
(6) Equivalent incomes, not pot luck.

Each new concept will now be examined in turn.

First new concept:
Poverty prevention, not poverty relief

For centuries the Church, public and private charities, wealthy individuals and governments have tried to tackle poverty through programmes of poor relief, or support for the destitute. The introduction of free, compulsory education, free health care and social insurance are conspicuous exceptions. Generally speaking the poverty relief ethic still prevails. Poverty relief is included as a charitable activity by the Charity Commissioners, whereas poverty prevention is excluded. Many grant-making trusts specify that the monies they provide may only be used for poverty relief, not poverty prevention. Indeed the bias towards poverty relief is so deep-seated that some writers use the terms poverty relief and poverty prevention as though they were synonymous. In a way the confusion is not surprising, since both require the guarantee of an income sufficient for physical and social functioning. But in most respects they are as different as chalk and cheese.

Poverty relief is concerned with symptoms not causes and it is concerned to remove them as inexpensively as possible. In order to do this the relief must be restricted to those in greatest need, and in order to sort out the sheep from the goats it has to be tough, it has to involve case work and it almost certainly has to involve stigma. The new vogue for computerised poverty relief on a mass scale, as envisaged by the Government, by the Institute for Fiscal Studies (Dilnot, Kay and Morris 1984) and the Social Democrats (SDP 1986), is almost certainly inoperable. For computers cannot decide who is genuinely poor and who is "playing the system".

Poverty prevention tackles the causes of poverty. It is concerned with the dignity and right to economic independence and freedom from an intrusive bureaucracy of each human being, and with the contribution that each can make to the welfare of all. It requires strong action by government to help people stand on their own feet, including guarantees to ensure that the incomes they need to keep them out of poverty are not whittled away by tax. Poverty prevention means helping people to become and remain economically independent. The success or failure of a poverty prevention programme can be judged by the numbers who continue to need assistance. Large-scale or increasing dependence on means-tested benefits is a sign that poverty prevention programmes are not working.

At national level a switch away from poverty prevention in favour of poverty relief provides governments with tempting opportunities for quick tax cuts. But it builds up problems for the future. It can only work so long as politicians turn a blind eye to the minority at the bottom, and in democracies this tends not to happen. With the approach of each election governments seek to win votes by making their poverty relief programmes more generous. This is the road to disaster. For it produces an ever-growing underclass of means-tested benefit recipients, and the now famous Charles Murray dilemma:

> We tried to provide more for the poor and produced more poor instead. We tried to remove the barriers to escape from poverty, and inadvertently built a trap. (Murray 1984)

Poverty prevention is investment in human capital, a process that enriches and unifies the nation. In the early stages it is expensive, like all investment. It costs more than poverty relief. The rich have to pay more tax. But in the longterm it costs less than poverty relief, and everybody stands to gain. In Britain the vogue for greater selectivity has been much influenced by studies from the United States like George Gilder's *Wealth and Poverty* (Gilder 1981/1982) and Charles Murray's *Losing Ground*. Both books shed light on the snowballing, disincentive effects of benefit payments. Yet the primary concern of both authors was the disincentive effects of means-tested benefits (which is what Americans mean by welfare), especially *aid to families with dependent children* (AFDC) and *aid to families with dependent children – unemployed fathers* (AFDC-U). In his book Gilder criticised welfare for eroding work and family life, and keeping people poor, and recommended introduction of child benefit in the United States, as a means of overcoming poverty without undermining wealth creation:

> Child allowances succeed because they are not means-tested. Because they do not create an incentive to stay poor, they avoid the moral hazards of the war on poverty... (Gilder 1982, page 128)

Poverty prevention, keeping everybody in the mainstream of economic life and keeping the poor out of tax and out of welfare dependency, is the only way to overcome poverty and create wealth. That is the central message of Gilder's book and that is why some (though not all) of the recently introduced workfare programmes in the United States are supported by Democrats as well as Republicans. If workfare can provide good quality vocational training and good childcare facilities, then there is a real chance for families to escape the cycle of deprivation.

Second new concept:
Citizenship, not contribution record

The *sine qua non* for poverty prevention is replacement of social insurance and its attendant contribution conditions by a simple test of citizenship or legal residence, as is already the case with child benefit. Social insurance is a system of exclusion, because those who are not insured, or who have not paid sufficient contributions, or who fail any of the other manifold requirements, are ineligible or receive substandard amounts. Despite its clear achievements, social insurance is not, never has been and never can be a sufficient guarantee against poverty.

Social insurance protects the strong and not-so-strong but leaves the weak dependent on means-tested social assistance or poor relief, and in some countries nothing at all. Today social insurance is getting to look more and more like a select club, from which millions of would-be workers are excluded. Millions more, who do unpaid work in the home or the community, have always been excluded. In the dual labour markets now emerging core workers still stand to benefit from old-style social insurance. But increasing numbers of peripheral workers will be left in the cold and this will affect their future pensions as well as their current living standards.

Social insurance protects people against specified contingencies, but it cannot cover every risk. Being a woman carries an above-average risk. If a woman is black, single and a mother the chances are high that she and her children will be poor. Yet there is no social insurance system that covers the risk of being black, or of being a single mother (widows excepted). Nor is there any system that covers children against the risk of having poor parents. Nor is there any system that covers the unborn child against the risk of being born with a physical or mental handicap, or of developing a disability during childhood, which is one reason why deprivation is transmitted from generation on to generation.

Only an actuary could unravel the maze of subsidies and cross subsidies between men and women, rich and poor, black and white in the social security systems of the Western democracies. But almost certainly it is the most disadvantaged who stand to gain most from a switch to benefits based on citizenship.

Third new concept:
Need, not status

We live in a society that worships the God of money and hence of paid work. As a result our culture is debased, there is not enough paid work to go round and people who do unpaid work are second-class citizens. To say this is not to denigrate paid work, nor to underrate its importance. It is to stress the value and importance of unpaid work, and to question the effectiveness of work (or out-of-work) status as a condition for benefit.

For reasons that are largely historical, almost the whole of our social security system is tied to work status and its benefits restricted to those who have been regularly and successfully in the labour market. Child benefit is a conspicuous exception. Yet if poverty is to be prevented work status (or previous work status) is an inadequate criterion. What matters is how much people need, not why they need it, or how much they earned thirty years ago. If nothing is done to right the imbalance between paid and unpaid work, one day there will be nobody left who is prepared to do the unpaid work. Children will be brought up by other children's mothers, in return for a wage, education will degenerate into preparation for the labour market and old people will be hived off into institutions. Indeed this is already happening.

So long as married women were tied to the home by their responsibilities as mothers of large families, it was possible for society to under-value their unpaid work with impunity. But that time is past. Women today are caught up in the same cash nexus as their husbands. They bear one or two children and return to the paid labour market as soon as possible. For many families the second wage of the mother pays for the mortgage, for others it is an essential barrier against poverty. Moreover with one marriage in three ending in divorce women are coming to realise that the main prerequisite for security in old age is an independent right to retirement pension, and the bigger the better. In a society where the devil looks after the hindmost (in the form of latter-day poor relief) women, like men, are fighting their way to the front.

Social security systems worldwide pay far more attention to work status than to need, and they cover a far narrower range of contingencies than is generally supposed. The sectarianism of most systems can be explained (but not justified) by the background of trade union and friendly society insurance schemes against which they emerged, by the close links that developed between the state as prime mover of social insurance on the one hand and the trade unions and employers' associations on the other, and above all by the (paid) work ethic handed down from earlier generations. This explains why children's allowances (and child poverty) were never strictly speaking a part of social security. In most countries they were added at a much later date than the original social security legislation, and at first they were part of the employment contract. In some countries, for instance, Belgium, they still are.

Poverty due to low pay was never within the ambit of social security. It was left to the trade unions, or to minimum wage legislation. Failing all else it was left to families to look after their own.

Poverty prevention, in the sense used in this report, has nothing to do with work status. Poverty prevention requires an income safety net based on systematic assessment of individual and family needs, and the abolition of all earnings restrictions. Questions of previous work status or of how, when or where a disability occurred, or of how long some one has been unemployed, may be important for other purposes, but they have almost no bearing on the amounts of money people need to keep them out of poverty.

Fourth new concept:
Income security, not social security

Social security in 1988 is like a game of snakes and ladders played at the Mad Hatter's tea party. Instead of a common starting point some people are not allowed to play at all, some start at the bottom of ladders and others at the top of snakes. The rules change as the game proceeds, snakes turn into ladders and ladders into snakes, and once on a snake it is impossible to escape, because the Mad Hatter keeps increasing the penalties. The people running the party love the game. But Alice (and most claimants) long to escape.

Income security applies the same rules to all. It encompasses every man, woman and child as equal citizens, it gives protection against every sort of poverty and it is a base on which to build, not a trap.

The case for income security rests on three connected arguments: first, the theoretical limitations of social insurance as a system of exclusion; second, its practical disadvantages, its failure to meet expectations, its effects on the labour market and its effects on family life; and finally the need to provide a safety net that is proof against tax. So long as the poor did not have to pay tax society was concerned, quite rightly, with gross incomes. Today it is net incomes that matter, so it is time to consolidate cash benefits and tax reliefs into a single programme which we can call *income security*.

The concept of income security is easily misunderstood, because it involves ideas to which people are not accustomed. Certainly it does not imply, as is often suggested, the introduction of some grand universal benefit payable by the state at the same uniform rate to every man, woman and child week after week or month after month. And there are two reasons for this. First, the amount of the guarantee cannot be uniform, because some people need more than others in order to achieve the same living standard. Second, and more significantly, most people in paid work, and others with investment income, do not need any subvention from the state. All they require is a surety that the income needed to achieve the basic living standard is free of tax. It is only the minority with incomes that are less than the guarantee levels who need them topped up through cash benefits. For everyone else the guarantee can be a tax credit.

Table 5.2 provides a very simplified example of something quite new, something that is neither a traditional cash benefit, nor an income tax allowance, both of which it replaces. Instead it is a

Table 5.2: Income security.
Net tax/net benefit position, single person, integrated tax/benefit regime. £ pw

Earnings	−Tax @ 35%	+ Guarantee	= Net income	Net tax/net benefit position
£	£	£	£	£
150	52.50	25.00	122.50	−27.50
100	35.00	25.00	90.00	−10.00
50	17.50	25.00	57.50	+ 7.50
10	3.50	25.00	31.50	+21.50
0	0.00	25.00	25.00	+25.00

hybrid, which converts between the two – a *convertible tax credit* or basic income, similar to the tax credits proposed by Mr Edward Heath's Government in 1972 (Treasury and DHSS 1972).

Because it is neither a conventional cash benefit nor a conventional tax relief, basic income does not suit the Treasury's accounting methods. Each year the Treasury publishes (in the Public Expenditure White Paper) detailed figures of benefit expenditures. A quite separate table, tucked away as unobtrusively as possible, gives the approximate costs of each separate income tax relief, and warns the reader not to try and add the costs together to reach an overall total. This makes it impossible to find out the aggregate cost in any one year of income support (cash benefits plus income tax reliefs). It also creates a permanent bias in favour of income tax reliefs (which help the rich) by comparison with cash benefits (which help the poor).

A Transfer Income Account (TIA). Time and again, when introduced to the idea of income security through basic income, politicians ask how much it will cost. And to this there is no easy answer, because income security and social security plus tax reliefs are two different concepts and the balance sheets would have to be drawn up differently. We can imagine the introduction of a consolidated income security or transfer income account, to which the average person would contribute as much, over the life cycle, as s/he took out. The TIA would be separate from the rest of the current account and from the capital account, it would be fully automated, and divided into three main sections:

> *Section one: tax expenditures*, would set out the costs (in terms of revenue foregone) of the tax credits or BIs received by those who had paid more in tax than the value of their tax credit or BI. Since they are net contributors to the system there can be no logical reason for showing their BIs as a cash expenditure.
>
> *Section two: cash expenditures*, would set out the cash expenditure costs of the BIs received by those net beneficiaries who had paid less in tax than the value of their BIs. This section would include some of the lower paid, most pensioners, the sick, people with disabilities and so on.
>
> *Section three: tax break-even points*, would set out the tax break-even points (taking into account any remaining income tax reliefs) of individuals and families in different circumstances throughout the life cycle.

The Treasury would hate this table, but for voters it would be like sunshine after fog. At last they would be able to see who really are the gainers and who the losers from income redistribution processes that involve a third of Gross National Product and yet leave about 5 percent of the population below the poverty levels laid down by Parliament.

Fifth new concept:
Individuals, not couples

Most governments want to support "the family", but they go about it in odd ways. There is little or no symmetry in either the tax or benefit systems, nor much concern about it.

By refusing to acknowledge the existence of married women within the tax system, by restricting married couples to the same width of income tax bands, the same mortgage interest and capital gains tax relief as single people, and by providing more generous levels of income support to couples who split up than to couples who stay together, successive governments have promoted *de facto* as opposed to legal marriage, and subsidised marriage break-up. In similar fashion they subsidise the birth of children outside legal marriage, and they force the taxpayer to take over the maintenance responsibilities of the absent parent when marriages finish. This is not just a problem of equity. Too many people are involved and each year the number of lone parents goes up. The £2,000 million they cost the taxpayer is enough to raise child benefit by £4 a week.

For those who believe that stable family relationships are important for the well-being of children in particular and of society in general, whilst recognising that individuals have the right to order their lives without outside interference, the question must be how to help married couples without being unfair to single people, how to prevent poverty in lone-parent families without encouraging more of them, and how to assist the victims of family break-up without penalising those who stay together. Almost certainly the most widely acceptable solution is a system where sex and/or marital status are irrelevant.

Sex and marriage neutrality in the benefit system. For benefit purposes, one way is to move as far as possible to individual assessment units, if necessary using householder status instead of marital status to take account of the economies of scale that result

Table 5.3: Penalties for marriage in the benefit system

	SB 1987 %	IS 1988 %	Marriage-neutral system %
	Relativities, excluding housing *Married/unmarried couple = 100*		
1. Working age couples			
– Married or unmarried couple	100	100	100
– Any other 2 adults sharing accommodation (age 25 & over)	111	130	100
2. Working age families with children			
– Married couple + 2 children, aged 3 and 6	100	100	100
– Two lone parents, each 1 child, one aged 3, one aged 6	107/128	137	100
3. Pensioners			
– Married or unmarried pensioner couple	100	100	100
– Any other 2 pensioners sharing accommodation	113	130	100

when any two or more people share accommodation. The old saying that "two can live for the price of one" is as true today as ever it was, but the two do not have to be man and wife. Table 5.3 shows how former supplementary benefit and income support, penalise married couples and those deemed by the DHSS to be living as husband and wife. The third column shows what a marriage neutral benefit system might look like in terms of relativities, with married couples as the reference point.

Sex and marriage neutrality in the tax system. Here too symmetry and equity require individual assessment units, and for tax this is more widely accepted than for benefits. The difficulty is that a tax allowance is valueless to people without the money to set against it, so a conflict develops between the criteria of equity and poverty prevention.

(1) **Reform within the existing system.** Almost nobody likes the existing system. There is no earned income tax relief, a single wage married couple gets only 157 percent of the allowance of a single person, yet a two wage married couple gets 257 percent, and an unmarried couple with two or more children can get 315 percent. The effect on tax-free incomes, for single people and couples

Figure 5.2: Tax-free incomes, six alternative tax regimes

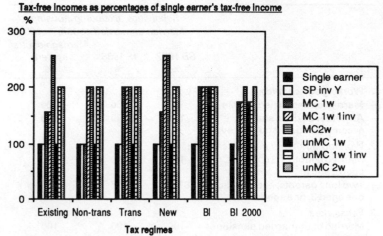

Notes: Existing = existing system, Non-trans = non-transferable allowances, Trans = fully transferable allowances, New = post 1990 system, BI = a full BI, BI 2000 = Basic Income 2000.

without children, is illustrated in Figure 5.2, with the single earner as the reference point. The figures for the existing system are based on tax allowance relativities in 1988-89. Figures for the other systems are based on proposed relativities, not cash amounts.

Most poverty lobby organisations have long campaigned for married man's tax allowance (MMA) to be replaced by a *non-transferable* income tax allowance, with the revenue gain redirected into child benefit. This would be symmetrical, but would mean that couples where one spouse had no income would forfeit the value of the second tax allowance. They would be taxed on the same basis as single people, and some would be forced into welfare dependency.

The Government's Green Paper *The Reform of Personal Taxation* (Treasury 1986) recommended replacement of MMA by a *fully transferable* allowance, which would have been equal to half MMA plus *wife's earned income allowance* (WEIA). This would have raised tax allowances generally and would have helped prevent poverty in single earner families, but transferability would have been restricted to legally married couples, so it lacked symmetry. It would also have been difficult to administer.

After consultation, the Chancellor announced in his 1988 Budget that husbands and wives will be taxed independently from

1990. This is the new system in Figure 5.2. Every taxpayer will get a personal allowance equivalent to existing single person's allowance, but husbands will also get a *married couple's allowance* (MCA), which will be transferable to the wife if the husband does not have enough money to set against it. The new personal allowance plus the married couple's allowance together sum to existing MMA. The new system is less symmetrical, although easier to administer, than the Green Paper proposal. In terms of relativities, and for families without children, it is almost the same as the existing system, the exception being that wives will be able to put their investment income against their own allowance.

By restricting unmarried parents to one additional personal allowance instead of two, the new system will be symmetrical between all two-parent families with children, whether or not they are married. But it will not be symmetrical between married and unmarried couples without children, nor between married couples and single people. It also seems likely to remain assymmetrical between one- and two-parent families with children. That will be so if (as seems likely) lone parents who live alone are allowed to keep the APA. This would give a lone parent the same tax allowance as a single-wage, two-parent family, and could encourage two-parent families (married or unmarried) to split up. In Figure 5.2 the effect of MCA stands out like a sore thumb. Why should married couples get 257 percent of the tax-free income of a single earner?

(2) **Basic income.** One of the advantages of integration is that each individual can have the same tax-free amount, which converts from tax credit to cash benefit if there is no income to set against it. In Figure 5.2 the BI solution is symmetrical between married and single, and it helps to prevent poverty. But it still makes no distinction between earned and unearned income. That is why *Basic Income 2000*, which is the target system recommended in this report, has an earned-income tax discount as well as the BIs. The tax-free income of a single person with unearned income falls to 73 percent of the tax-free income of a single earner. The amounts available for couples depend on whether or not both are earning. The reasons for this refinement will be explained in Chapter 19.

Sixth new concept:
Family budget standards, not pot luck

If poverty is to be prevented, and if public expenditure is to be targeted efficiently, the first essential is to produce systematically based and regularly updated estimates of the needs and costs of men, women and children, at low to moderate living standards, and at different stages of the life cycle. Such calculations, called *family budget standards*, are not easy, but without them government is targeting blindfold.

Budget standards help ensure that benefit rates are adequate and fair between different families. Large families need more than small families. The amounts needed also vary according to the age and activity of the household members, and according to economies of scale. The incomes necessary to produce living standard equivalence are called *equivalent incomes*. Using the *equivalence ratios* derived from the equivalent incomes it is theoretically possible to estimate the incidence of poverty between different groups in the low income population.

In North America and in other European countries family budget standards, based on a mixture of normative information (how much people need) and empirical information (how people spend the money they have) are well known, but the last time they were attempted in Britain was by Beveridge in 1942. Beveridge relied partly on consumer expenditure enquiries undertaken by the Ministry of Labour in 1937-38 and partly on two pre-war scales of nutritional requirements, one produced by the BMA, and the other by the League of Nations. In the event, as we have seen, the benefit rates introduced in 1948 were not those recommended by Beveridge. The failure, over a period of more than forty years, to update Beveridge's budget standards is even more significant.

Gradually the income maintenance policies of successive governments have come to rest on two, dangerously complacent, assumptions: first, that poverty in the sense of absolute deprivation has been largely eliminated, and second, that poverty can be kept indefinitely at bay so long as benefits are indexed to inflation. Needs, unlike costs, are assumed not to change with time.

Mr Fowler's Social Security Review was a golden opportunity to update Beveridge's budget standard in line with forty years of economic and social change, but it was dismissed in one sentence: "It is doubtful whether an attempt to establish an objective standard of adequacy would be fruitful" (DHSS Jun 1985, Vol 2, page 21).

His reform strategy rested on the proposition that working-age families with children have overtaken pensioners as the new poor, but that want in the sense of absolute deprivation has been largely eliminated. The statistical back-up is tucked away in volume three, paper one of DHSS June 1985, where low incomes are defined as the bottom quintile of equivalent income distribution. It required a Parliamentary Question to elicit the equivalence scale used for the calculations (Hansard 25 Jul 1985, col 751), and it turned out to be a slightly amended version of two scales (with and without housing) first published in *Social Trends* 1977 (Van Slooten and Coverdale 1977). Those scales were based on analyses of the 1971 and 1972 Family Expenditure Surveys. There was no input of normative data, nor any updating of Beveridge's dietary standards.

Since families cannot spend money they do not have, benefit scales based exclusively on survey data underestimate the needs of families on low incomes, especially families with children. For simplicity I shall call the earlier scales the EAO 77 (with and without housing) scales and the scale used by Mr Fowler for his background analysis the SSR 85 scale. The differences between the EAO with-housing scale and the SSR 85 scale concern adults only. Whereas the EAO authors stressed the extra costs of householder status, the SSR 85 scale emphasised marital status. This emphasis was carried over into the April 1988 income support scale. The IS 88 scale is even less generous to children and married couples than the EAO 77 or SSR 85 scales. It also differentiates (for the first time) between people below and above age 25. Single people above age 25 qualify for the equivalent of the former SB single householder rate, whether or not they are householders, but single people below age 25 get a lower rate, whether or not they are householders. This new, lower rate is nevertheless more than half the rate for married couples.

Table 5.4 compares the IS 88 scale with the EAO 77 scale and with the equivalence scales implied in the original Beveridge scale, the West German social assistance scale and the lower of two scales produced by the Montreal Diet Dispensary for welfare purposes. This last scale is thought to be reasonably representative of North American scales in general. All the scales exclude housing. No allowance is made for the premiums for families with children available with income support, since these replace single and additional needs payments, the equivalent of which are still payable with German social assistance.

Table 5.4: Family budget standards: equivalence ratios

Household type	Budget standards (excluding housing)				
	Bev 42	*EAO 77*	*IS 88*[1]	*Ger 85*	*MDD 84*[2]
Single householder	1.00	1.00	1.00/0.78[3]	1.00	1.00
Married couple	1.77	1.82	1.54	1.79	1.61
Non-householder aged					
16-17	0.96	0.69	0.58	0.89	0.85
18	0.96	0.82	0.78	0.89	0.85
19-20	0.96	0.82	0.78	0.89	0.81
21-24	—	0.82	0.78	0.79	0.79
15 and over	—	0.82	1.00	0.79	0.79
Children aged					
0-1	0.42	0.13	0.32	0.45	0.55
2-3	0.42	0.33	0.32	0.45	0.55
4	0.42	0.33	0.32	0.45	0.60
5-6	0.56	0.38	0.32	0.45	0.60
7	0.56	0.38	0.32	0.64	0.69
8-9	0.56	0.42	0.32	0.64	0.69
10	0.66	0.42	0.32	0.64	0.74
11-12	0.66	0.47	0.48	0.75	0.77
13	0.66	0.51	0.48	0.75	0.79
14	0.72	0.51	0.48	0.75	0.79
15	0.72	0.51	0.48	0.89	0.79

Notes:
1. Excluding family and lone parent premiums, which replace SB heating additions, single payments etc.
2 Montreal Diet Dispensary averages of rates for men and women, boys and girls – children assumed to be in two-parent, two-child families; single-wage families.
3. Higher rate from age 25 only.
Sources: Beveridge 1942, paras 217-232; *Social Trends* No. 8, 1977, Table B1, page 28; Schedule of main proposed social security benefit rates from April 1988, DHSS October 1987; *Nachrichtendienst des Deutschen Vereins für öffentliche und private Fürsorge,* August 1985, page 245; Montreal Diet Dispensary *Budgeting for Basic Needs,* June 1984.

The EAO 77 and IS 88 scales are significantly less generous to children and juveniles than any of the others. That is because the other scales use normative as well as empirical data. For single non-householders the IS scale stands out as being more generous than any of the others, whereas for couples, especially couples with children, it is much less generous.

The figures in Table 5.4 can be translated into cash equivalents. In Table 5.5, the 1988-89 income support scale rate for a single non-householder has been taken as the reference point, in order to convert the equivalence ratios implied in Table 5.4 into weekly

Table 5.5: Family budget standards: equivalent net incomes

Household type	Implied equivalent net incomes excluding housing:			
	Bev 42 £	IS 88 £	Ger 85 £	MDD 84 £
Single householder	33.40	33.40	33.40	33.40
MC + 2 children aged 1 and 4	86.50	72.95*	89.84	92.18
MC + 2 children aged 12, 14	105.21	83.65*	109.89	105.88
MC + 3 children aged 9, 14, 16	133.93	97.70*	135.93	131.60

Note: *Add £6.15 in each case for family premium.

benefit entitlements. In cash terms none of the scales is particularly generous, but the argument here is about relativities. The figures show that the larger the family the further the IS rates drag behind, even if one includes £6 for the new family premium. The three other scales are surprisingly consistent.

In Britain anyone concerned about the safety net must question the validity of the equivalence ratios implied in the IS scales. Almost certainly the amounts for spouses and children are too low.

They must also question the validity of the DHSS's new publication, *Households below Average Income: A Statistical Analysis, 1981-85* (DHSS May 1988), which has replaced the *Low Income Families* series referred to in Chapter 4. Although, like its predecessor, the new series relies on data from the Family Expenditure Survey, it no longer takes the SB/IS scale rates as the reference points for "poverty" or "low income". Instead, all the members of each household responding to the Survey are taken to have the "same income level reflected by the equivalised household income" (page 28), and are graded on the overall income distribution accordingly. It follows that the value of the new series depends first on whether or not all household members do in fact share out their incomes according to the equivalence scales used by the DHSS, and second on whether or not those scales are accurate.

Since the scales used are the same EAO 77 scales referred to above, the official estimates of living standards at the bottom (including the alleged improvement since the early 1980s) lack credibility. Children under age two, for example, are assumed to need only 13 percent of the income of a single householder (excluding housing costs) in order to achieve living standard equivalence, mothers during pregnancy and lactation are assumed to need the same as any other adult, and non-earners are assumed to need the same as earners.

New concepts

Take a simple illustration. The 1988-89 income support rate for a single person aged 25+ is £33.40. We know that an adult can subsist on £33.40, because they do, but is it realistic to suppose that a one-year-old can survive on 13 percent of £33.40, which is only £4.34?

Part 2

INTEGRATION

INTEGRATION

6

Forwards or backwards?

One consequence of welfare crisis is that it enables those who dislike state-financed social security in principle to discredit the whole idea, when all that is needed is thorough-going reform. There is a danger that governments of the right will allow the different institutions of the welfare state, including social security, to deteriorate to the point where almost any alternative would seem an improvement.

In the UK integration is only one of three main reform options, which can be summarised as follows:

(1) *Back to Beveridge*, or coordinated reform within the existing dual systems of mainly categorical benefits and income tax reliefs.

(2) *Back to the Poor Law*, or privatisation of social security alongside increased emphasis on income tax reliefs.

(3) *Forward to the twenty-first century*, through integration of income tax reliefs and social security benefits, and the introduction of a guaranteed basic income.

Each of these options requires careful evaluation, using empirical as well as theoretical evidence, and taking into account the dynamic effects of change on the tax base, the labour market, family life and social cohesion as well as the immediate effects on public expenditure and living standards. Some introductory studies by individuals have already been attempted (Parker Jul 1984; Atkinson Dec 1984; Barr Jan 1987, see also Toynbee Hall 1985), but there has been no systematic evaluation by Government, and none is planned.

The purpose of this study is to examine the desirability and feasibility of the integration option in detail. But it is helpful to look quickly at the other two approaches first, for there is no single integration option and the same issues cut across the boundaries between integrated and dual systems time and again. Indeed the most intractable differences are not those between advocates and opponents of integration, but the far older ones between universalists and selectivists, libertarians and authoritarians, and devotees of the protestant work-ethic *versus* those who think society should now put a monetary value on unpaid work.

Option No. 1: Back to Beveridge

Within this option there is a wide variety of proposals, but all retain the existing dual system of largely categorical benefits and income tax reliefs. For some it would involve a return to the original Beveridge Plan, with increased benefit levels, and with coordinated changes to income tax and NI contribution, including mandatory independent taxation of husband and wife, but joint assessment for means-tested and income-tested benefits. For the radical left it would involve abolition of the contributory principle, individualisation of tax and benefit units, and the introduction of a national minimum wage. Most proposals retain some means-tested benefits, but on a much smaller scale than at present.

The first approach is typified by the proposals considered by Professor A.B. Atkinson in a paper prepared for the National Consumer Council in 1984 (Atkinson Mar 1984), and the NCC's own proposals published later that year (NCC 1984). Atkinson envisaged retention of the existing benefit structure, but with big increases in benefit rates, especially child benefit, which would become taxable. NI contribution for employees would be abolished. All personal income tax allowances would be replaced by a single non-transferable tax allowance, mortgage interest tax relief would be reduced to a 15 percent credit, and the structure of income tax rates would be more progressive, starting at 18 percent and moving steeply upwards, to reach 63 percent at just above average earnings. The scheme was designed to be revenue neutral.

The National Consumer Council also recommended reform within the existing structure. Their scheme would cost very much more than the present system, and would involve non-contributory, flat-rate benefits for children, people with disabilities and careers, alongside contributory earnings-related benefits during sickness, unemployment and old age. Child benefit would be raised and the equivalent of widowed mother's allowance would be extended to all lone parents. Most means-tested benefits would disappear, but housing benefit would remain. NI contribution would remain, but the lower and upper earnings levels would be abolished. Married man's tax allowance would be replaced by a non-transferable allowance for all adults, and there would be reduced income tax reliefs for occupational pensions. The scheme had a substantial net cost.

The objective of a 1985 book written by three London-based welfare rights workers was to "tear away" the convention that income maintenance policies are "apolitical" and to set out the principles of a radical socialist approach. In *Who's to Benefit?* Peter Esam, Robert Good and Rick Middleton (1985) recommended abolition of the existing systems of contributory NI and means-tested supplementary benefit in favour of non-contributory, non-means-tested *positional benefits*. There would be a national minimum wage at a "socially determined level" and greatly increased child benefits. The unit of assessment would be the individual, regardless of marital status and regardless of the income or wealth of the other spouse or partner. Their proposals were not costed.

Out of a wealth of similar proposals that have emerged during the past two to three years (for instance, Lister 1987), two points stand out. The first concerns the basis of entitlement and the second the work test.

Citizenship as the basis of entitlement. Traditionally the basis of entitlement has been contribution record or demonstrable need. Entitlement based on contributions paid was supposed to remove all vestiges of stigma and almost all need. But it did not work out that way. Consequently even those writers who prefer reform within the existing system show a growing preference for citizenship (or legal residence over a specified period) instead of contribution record as the main basis of entitlement. For instance the NCC, who would retain NI contribution, proposed gradual abolition of contribution conditions for basic retirement pension.

Work guarantees and workfare. Very few of those who seek to retain categorical benefits are prepared to face up to the problem of how to ensure that all those in receipt of unemployment benefit are fit for work, trained for work, actively looking for work, and have a genuine chance of finding suitable work. The tougher parts of Beveridge (including his work and training centres) are steadfastly ignored.

One exception to the general indifference is Ralph Howell (Conservative Member of Parliament for North Norfolk), who has long advocated that "after a period of six months every able-bodied adult should have a statutory right to work – meaning work or training", and that "failure of employable adults to take advantage of the opportunities offered would result in total disqualification of benefit" (Howell 1985, pages 26-27). Another exception is Professor Patrick Minford of Liverpool University, whose workfare proposals will be discussed in Chapter 13. Partly at Howell's instigation, the Employment Research Centre at the University of Buckingham commissioned a study into the feasibility, costs and operating requirements of a workfare system in the UK. *Would Workfare Work?* by John Burton was published in 1987.

Ideas similar to those of workfare also emanate from the left, by way of a work guarantee or last-ditch attempt to tackle unemployment. At the end of 1986 Peter Mitchell, formerly head of research at the Royal Association for Disability and Rehabilitation, recommended that "every adult citizen should be entitled to a basic, non-contributory, non-means-tested, earnings-replacement benefit (ERB), unless they are in paid employment or refuse specific available paid employment of which they are capable without good cause" (Mitchell 1986, para 8.2). This proposal amounts to a full basic income for all, subject to a work condition. In March 1988 a three-day seminar at St George's House Windsor was held to discuss the possibility of an income and work guarantee. The proposal amounts to an unconditional partial BI, topped up by a guarantee of part-time work (Ashby 1988). It got a luke-warm response.

All these writers include a work test, and they all put responsibility for finding suitable work onto the state. Within the parameters of a system where benefit is a replacement for earnings, some sort of workfare is probably inevitable (J. Rhys Williams 1943), but it has major disadvantages. These include widespread dislike of anything that smacks of direction of labour, the operational limitations for government of finding suitable jobs for a constantly moving target, and the costs of guaranteeing paid work for anyone who wants it. There is also Charles Murray's objection that workfare would never turn out as intended, because administrators would pursue their own agendas (Murray 1987).

Option No. 2: Back to the Poor Law

This is Richard Titmuss's "residual welfare state". The safety net is restricted to those who are demonstrably unable to help themselves, there is Howell-style make-work to sort out the sheep from the goats, and tighter laws of liability to maintain, as protection against creeping universalism. For there is little doubt that without strict liability to maintain laws, benefit systems that are means-tested can be taken over by middle income groups, who rearrange their affairs in order to qualify (Goodwin and Le Grand 1986).

In Britain disillusion with the welfare state has produced a renaissance of nineteenth-century liberalism and the emergence at Westminster of a new breed of politician, well versed in the writings of the Poor Law reformers, of contemporary anarchists and libertarians, of public choice economists Gordon Tullock and J.M.Buchanan and other writers from the New Right. Many of the ideas now taking root have wafted across the Atlantic from the United States, where individualism has always taken precedence over sense of community. Charles Murray questions the ability of people operating in a public capacity ever to get things right. The minimal state advocated by libertarian Robert Nozick (Nozick 1974) forbids taxation for welfare or social security purposes. Murray Rothbard argues that the best way to increase living standards generally, and especially for the poor, is for governments to "get out of the way" (Rothbard 1978, page 162).

Many hard-pressed taxpayers echo (or used to echo) those sentiments, but there is another view. Public choice theory rightly draws attention to the propensity of governments to extend their activities above the socially optimal level, but overlooks the fact, as Atkinson has pointed out, that the reverse may also be true, in other words that governments cutbacks may result in activities below the optimal level (Atkinson Oct 1986, page 24). Considerably more research into the economic and social effects of a residual welfare state is required before one can judge the underlying assumption that all benefits are bad and all tax reliefs good.

Option No. 3: Forward to the twenty-first century

This is the integration option, with which the rest of this enquiry will be concerned. Although the word "integration" is used increasingly, it is ill-defined and the source of much confusion. At one extreme it refers to any sort of knitting together of the tax and benefit systems, at the other it becomes the gateway to paradise.

The interest in integration stems from realisation that poverty has many causes, hence the best way to tackle it is by filling the gaps between what people have and what they need, not by trying to fit people who are poor into pre-defined, rigid categories, and least of all by using the power of the law to keep them in those categories. One reason for the confusion is media enthusiasm for anything that sounds like a panacea. In Britain integration has become a media "buzz-word", a sure way to attract attention. It is used to refer to proposals that are no more than glorified extensions of the existing system, but it sounds good.

In order to reduce the confusion the first requirement is a clear definition of integration, and the second is to distinguish the different categories. For the purposes of this report a narrow definition has been chosen, with two main criteria. Very few of the schemes currently on offer under the integration label meet those criteria, but they help to highlight the issues.

The first criterion of a fully integrated tax and benefit system is replacement of all existing cash benefits and all income tax reliefs by a single, unified structure of non-contributory, guaranteed minimum incomes, the levels of which would be related to family size and composition, entitlement to which would depend on legal residence, and the operation of which would be the responsibility of a single government agency. This definition breaks the traditional link between benefit and out-of-work status. Benefit can be made conditional on participation in voluntary work or in the labour market, but it is never conditional on *not* working. Also ruled out are benefits related in value to former earnings, or to the circumstances surrounding the origin of a disability. Integration does not rule out a work test, provided there is a work guarantee, and it does not rule out variations according to age, family size, household status, or anything else that has a direct bearing on needs and costs. But it does rule out all earnings restrictions, and it should rule out the accretion of *ad hoc* vote-winning additional benefits. In practice the requirement that all other cash benefits be abolished is almost certainly impracticable, since there must always be a residual, locally operated safety net, for use in exceptional circumstance. The danger is that the safety net would grow bigger year by year, in which case the system would cease to be fully integrated.

The second criterion of a fully integrated tax and benefit system is complete harmonisation of all administrative regulations below and above the income break-even levels at which people become net taxpayers. This is the *sine qua non* without which full integration does not exist. It is an intrinsic part of the simplification process and the very essence of a system that treats everybody according to the same ground rules. It is also the most radical ingredient of integration, because it closes the distinction between taxpayers and beneficiaries, sheep and goats, deserving and undeserving. It is also the criterion on which most allegedly integrated schemes slip up.

These are the essential elements of integration, without which it does not exist. Other characteristics are many and variable. The basis of entitlement is need, but it can be demonstrable or non-demonstrable. Where it is demonstrable a work condition is imposed and workfare has to be included. Where it is unconditional, the labour market can be left to sort itself out. The income guarantee can be universal or selective, or a mixture of both, but only provided the regulations can be harmonised above and below the break-even levels. Selectivity based on age or other exogenous characteristics can be introduced fairly easily, but selectivity on the basis of income quickly snarls up the harmonisation process. The unit of assessment can be the individual, the family or the household, but again only provided there is consistency below and above the break-even levels. A national minimum wage is by no means incompatible with integration, nor is it essential.

So far the discussion has referred to *full integration,* but for those prepared to venture further it is possible to devise an income support system with two components, one integrated and the other not. This variant is called *partial integration.* Partial integration does not mean mixing together the characteristics of dual and integrated systems within a single component. For the purposes of this enquiry, a system that is partially integrated is defined as a system with two or more components, of which at least one is fully integrated.

Having accepted the possibility of partial integration, it follows that there is no single, integrated tax/benefit model. On the contrary, there are potentially as many variants within the integrated approach to income maintenance as there are within the conventional, dual approach. These variants fall into three main categories:

(1) *Social dividend or basic income*, which rests on the universalist, or "one nation", approach to welfare. At nil income each person is entitled to a basic income "sufficient to meet basic living costs" , which is withdrawn through the tax system, using flat-rate or progressive tax schedules. Full integration possible.

(2) *Negative income tax*, which rests on the selectivist, or "residual", approach to welfare. At nil income each family (or household) is entitled to a *guaranteed minimum income* (GMI), but benefit withdrawal rates below the break-even levels are generally higher than the rates of positive taxation above them, thus retaining the traditional distinction between taxpayers and beneficiaries, and making integration virtually impossible.

(3) *Hybrid schemes*, which rest on a pragmatic or compromise approach to welfare, using various mixtures of BI, NIT and the existing system. Integration is at most partial. Partial integration lacks the quick, easy appeal of the full model, but is probably the best way forward.

For the sake of simplicity BI is henceforth taken to be synonymous with social dividend, social wage, national dividend and tax credit in the English speaking countries, with *l' allocation universelle* in France and Belgium, and *Bürgergeld* or *Grundeinkommen* in Germany and Austria. NIT is taken to be synonymous with reverse income tax. In each case the reference will be to basic income (BI) or negative income tax (NIT).

7

Moves towards integration

Integration is the preferred solution of those who believe that the limitations and deficiencies of social insurance and other categorical schemes are inherent and incurable. Some have seen it as an end in itself (J. Rhys Williams 1943), others see it as a transitional system towards a residual welfare state (M. and R. Friedman 1981, pages 149-50), but all recognise the need to improve the safety net by introducing some sort of guaranteed minimum income. Some also recommend a second layer of earnings-related provision, and here there is a further division between those who recommend that the second layer should be statutory, and those who would leave it to voluntary action.

The interest in integration dates largely from the 1960s, although Lady Rhys Williams's costed programme for a conditional social dividend was put forward in 1943, and Titmuss drew attention to the similarity, in terms of cash in hand, between social, fiscal and occupational benefits, in his now famous Eleanor Rathbone Lecture of 1955:

> Under separately administered social security systems, like family allowances and retirement pensions, direct cash payments are made in discharging collective responsibilities for particular dependencies. In the relevant accounts, these are treated as 'social service' expenditure since they represent flows of payments through the central government account. Allowances and reliefs from income tax, though providing similar benefits and expressing a similar social purpose in the recognition of dependent needs, are not, however, treated as social service expenditure. The first is a cash transaction; the second an accounting convenience. Despite this difference in

95

administrative method, the tax saving that accrues to the individual is, in effect, a transfer payment. In their primary objectives and their effects on individual purchasing power there are no differences in these two ways by which collective provision is made for dependencies. (Titmuss 1955, in Titmuss 1958, page 44)

Discussion of negative income taxation is conventionally dated from Milton and Rose Friedman's *Capitalism and Freedom* in 1962, but it was not until a few years later that Milton Friedman set out the proposals in detail (Friedman 1966 and 1968). The Friedmans recommended a NIT that would replace all existing welfare provisions, including old age pensions, disability benefits and benefits in kind. Their proposals coincided with the "rediscovery of poverty" in the early 1960s and with President Lyndon Johnson's declaration of a war on poverty in 1964. By 1965 we find James Tobin proposing a "basic income" of $400 a year (Tobin 1965), and in 1967 Brookings published Christopher Green's *Negative Taxes and the Poverty Problem*, in which he referred to the work of Lady Rhys Williams.

Among the proponents of integration there quickly developed two opposing camps, firstly those, like the Friedmans, who saw NIT as part of a revenue neutral (or cost-cutting) transition to privatisation, with benefit levels low enough to preserve work incentives, and secondly those who saw a guaranteed minimum income, at a "decent" level, as an end in itself. Equally important was the political opposition from those who disliked the unconditionality of most NIT proposals. Here the division of opinion is between libertarians and authoritarians rather than between left and right. For although integration has supporters across most of the political spectrum, one of its main appeals is to those wishing to enhance the autonomy of the individual (Jordan 1985).

In 1965 Robert Theobald, described by Martin Anderson as "the father of the guaranteed income concept in the United States" (Anderson 1978 page 72), summarised the case for a guaranteed income:

We will need to adopt the concept of an absolute constitutional right to an income. This would guarantee to every citizen of the United States, and to every person who has resided within the United States for a period of five consecutive years, the right to an income from the federal government sufficient to enable him to live with dignity. No government agency, judicial body, or other organization whatsoever should have the power to suspend or limit any payment assured by these guarantees. (Theobald ed. 1965, page 229).

Coming from a country without even a child benefit, these were strong words indeed. From the end of the 1960s, for the best part of a decade, interest in the possibility of radical welfare reform in the United States along NIT lines was considerable. Between 1967 and 1970 six major experiments were undertaken, in New Jersey, in North Carolina and Iowa, in Gary, Indiana, and in Seattle and Denver, designed to test the effects of a NIT on work incentives and family stability. The Nixon Administration's abortive Family Assistance Plan was effectively a variant of NIT which would have provided income support for all families with children. So was the 1974 Income Supplement Program (ISP). During the 1972 presidential elections Senator McGovern proposed what would have amounted to a social dividend, and it was an electoral fiasco.

It was the unconditionality of NIT that chiefly annoyed its opponents, and much of the opposition was political. "The clamor for radical welfare reform comes essentially from a small group of committed ideologues who want to institute a guaranteed income under the guise of welfare reform," wrote Martin Anderson in 1978, in his influential book *Welfare: The Political Economy of Welfare Reform in the United States*, as if guaranteed income were a dirty word (Anderson 1978, page 67). Anderson, who advised Presidents Nixon and Ford during the development of the Family Assistance Plan in 1969 and the ISP in 1974, and who was Ronald Reagan's social welfare adviser during the 1976 election, used the results of the NIT experiments to kill off the whole idea. They suffered, he said, from a number of methodological biases , as a result of which they greatly underestimated the potential reduction in work effort among low-income workers, which, according to his calculations, could be as much as 50 percent. Strangely he seems not to have found bias in the opposite direction.

By the end of the 1970s interest in NIT in the United States began to wane. Anderson wrote about "The Impossibility of Radical Welfare Reform" and his key paragraphs apply to Britain as well as the US:

All radical welfare reform schemes have three basic parts that are politically sensitive to a high degree. The first is the basic benefit level provided, for example, to a family of four on welfare. The second is the degree to which the program affects the incentive of a person on welfare to find work or to earn more. The third is the additional cost to the taxpayers.

...To become a political reality the plan must provide a decent level of support for those on welfare, it must contain strong incentives to work, and it must have a reasonable cost. *And it must do all three at the same time.* If any one of these parts is missing or deficient the reform plan is nakedly vulnerable to anyone who wishes to attack and condemn it. (Anderson 1978, page 135)

In *Free to Choose,* the Friedmans concluded that NIT, or rather the version of it they had proposed originally, was not "currently feasible politically", although it could one day become so. They quoted Anderson (Friedman 1981, page 157). Since then a swing to the right in politics has led to a reaffirmation of the conventional distinction between taxpayer and beneficiary. By the mid-1980s the order of the day became tax cuts for the taxpaying majority and workfare for the welfare minority.

Times have changed since first publication of *Capitalism and Freedom,* and the debate has acquired new dimensions. During the 1960s integration offered the possibility of worthwhile change both to those whose concern was poverty, and to those whose concern was escalating government expenditures. Neither concern has gone away, on the contrary both have been accentuated, but today the main issues are mass unemployment and escalating family breakdown. So the emphasis has switched to helping the unemployed into the world of work, and protecting the casualties of broken marriages and unstable relationships, without encouraging more of them. That explains the continuing interest in integrated tax and benefit schemes, especially in Europe, and it also explains the growing interest in individual assessment units.

In Britain integration has been on the political agenda since Mr Edward Heath's Government produced their *Proposals for a Tax-Credit System* (Treasury and DHSS 1972). At the time of the 1987 general election both Alliance parties were committed in principle to integrated reform of tax and social security, and their solutions will be discussed in Chapters 12 and 15. As yet there is no official support for any sort of integration from the British Labour

Party, but within the voluntary sector there is considerable, though guarded, interest in BI (Ashby 1984; BIRG Bulletins 1985-88).

Within the Tory Party integration has many advocates, both inside and outside Parliament. Negative or reverse income tax has been recommended in studies published by the Institute for Economic Affairs (Christopher, Polanyi, Seldon and Shenfield, 1970; Clark 1977; Minford 1984), and by the Adam Smith Institute (ASI 1984). Basic income was recommended for many years by Sir Brandon Rhys Williams, Member of Parliament for Kensington (B. Rhys Williams 1967, 1969, 1972, 1982), and in 1986 it was was the subject of a study by Stephen Davies of Manchester Polytechnic, published by the right-wing Centre for Policy Studies (Davies 1986).

Given the scale of change which any move towards integration would involve, it is nevertheless wishful thinking to suppose that it could happen without broad-based support across all the main political parties. This is the significance of the last principal conclusion to the Meacher Committee of Enquiry (House of Commons 1983), whose members were drawn from all the political parties. Although the Subcommittee's draft report was never approved by the main Treasury and Civil Service Committee, due to the earlier than expected dissolution of Parliament in 1983, it had nevertheless been approved by the Subcommittee, who had this to say about integration:

> We are not attracted by schemes of the reverse income tax kind with their high rates of tax on low incomes. In principle, we prefer schemes like the Basic Income Guarantee Scheme and the combined benefit and tax scheme submitted by Mr Philip Vince. On the other hand, it is clear to us that a good deal more work needs to be done on such schemes before it can be said with confidence that they are feasible. Bearing in mind the considerable problems associated with the present system and the difficulty of doing more than ameliorate them by piecemeal reform, *we recommend that the Government should put such work in hand*. It is necessary to establish the costings in detail and to ensure that the poorest in the community do not suffer financially from the change and that the necessary administrative changes are practicable to make. If the feasibility of a scheme can be demonstrated, there can then be political argument about the precise degree of redistribution it should involve and the alternative modes of

finance. *Meanwhile, it is desirable that changes to the present system should be compatible with an eventual move to an integrated structure of tax and social security.* (House of Commons 1983, para 13.35, my emphasis)

Despite the considerable interest, the official Conservative Party line on integration during Mrs Thatcher's premiership has been lukewarm, veering on hostile, doubtless a reflection of the feedback on NIT from the United States during the late 1970s, plus Mrs Thatcher's own aversion to anything that smacks of "money through the post".

The early background to the integration debate, together with an assessment of the NIT experiments in the United States and Canada was usefully summarised in a Research Paper published by the Department of Social Security, Government of Australia in 1981 (Whiteford 1981). In 1975 an Australian Government Commission of Inquiry into Poverty recommended the introduction of a social dividend scheme (AGPS 1975), and in the same year the Australian Priorities Review Staff Report argued for introduction of a tax credit scheme:

...in simplifying the welfare system, such a scheme would ensure that most of the needy would get help. To the extent that it incorporated existing means-tested benefits, a minimum income scheme integrated with the personal income tax system would avoid sharp jumps in the effective tax rate sometimes faced by welfare recipients. (*Possibilities for Social Welfare in Australia,* Priorities Review Staff, Canberra: AGPS 1975, page 20)

More recently, in Canada, the Government of Quebec published a White Paper in 1984 recommending integration of its tax and transfer systems (Quebec White Paper 1984). In 1985 the Royal Commission on the Economic Union and Development prospects for Canada (The Macdonald Report) recommended introduction of a "universally available income guarantee", but these recommendations have not been taken up by the new government.

In the Netherlands the idea of a BI has been circulating at least since the mid-1970s, and in 1985 the Netherlands Scientific Council for Government Policy produced proposals for an individualised, partial basic income (PBI) worth just under 450 guilders, or about £25 a week, at that time. In the Social Affairs

Committee of the European Parliament there has been continuing interest in BI and, more recently, in a NIT (BIRG Bulletins Nos. 6 and 7). The pressure for change is due partly to low and uncertain benefit levels in some member states for people without entitlement to social insurance benefit. But for many Europeans a guaranteed minimum income means an *additional* layer of social security provision (somewhat along the lines of British supplementary benefit/income support) and integration need not come into it (Cantillon and Deleeck 1985; Schulte 1985).

Despite the interest there is as yet no country that operates an integrated tax and benefit system. It cannot happen until support is much more broad-based than at present. There are however many countries where taxable child allowances and child tax reliefs have been integrated to form tax-free child benefits, which are in effect BIs for children. Generally speaking, the experience has not been encouraging. There is also the beginnings of a move towards citizenship-based old age pensions. In Britain further advance is blocked partly by the speed with which we are being carried towards a residual welfare state, and partly by confusion about the issues. In the next chapters we shall try to sort out that confusion.

8
Mechanics of integration

In Chapter 6 the criteria for a fully integrated tax and benefit system were explained. Distinctions were drawn between full integration and partial integration, and between basic income, negative income tax and hybrid schemes composed of several ingredients. In this chapter we will take a closer look at what the full integration criteria involve and at the obstacles to full integration. We will enlarge on the distinction between full and partial integration and warn against spurious integration. First, a reminder about technicalities.

Direct and indirect assistance, convertible and non-convertible tax credits. One of the main characteristics of existing tax and benefit systems is the sharp distinction drawn between cash benefits (*direct assistance*) and income tax reliefs (*indirect assistance*). Each performs a different function. The purpose of cash benefits is to provide income where none would otherwise be available, or to boost incomes which would otherwise be insufficient. The purpose of income tax reliefs, especially the personal income tax allowances, is to prevent people being taxed on the income necessary to keep them out of poverty. The difference is the crucial one between giving and not taking away, but it produces two major problems.

The first is the well-known difficulty that income tax reliefs are of no value to people without the income to set against them, which was the main reason why in several countries child tax allowances and family allowances were integrated to produce tax-free child benefits. Child benefit is a basic income or convertible tax credit for children. Every family gets the same and nobody loses out. For rich families child benefit cuts the net tax bill by comparison with non-parents at the same income level. For families who pay no tax child benefit converts automatically into a cash benefit.

The second difficulty comes about because of the way in which British income tax is calculated. In addition to being worth nothing at all to people without the income to set against them, British income tax allowances are worth 60 percent more to people paying 40 percent income tax than to people paying tax at 25 percent. This is because the income tax rates are applied to taxable income *after* deducting the income tax allowances. An alternative system is to apply the tax rates to the whole of taxable income, and deduct the value of the income tax allowances (calculated at the starting rate of tax) from the resulting tax bill. The income tax allowances then become fixed-amount tax deductions, called *tax credits*. These are the tax credits referred to in OECD comparative tax tables, by the Institute for Fiscal Studies in their proposals for the reform of social security (IFS 1984), and by the Social Democrats in their proposals discussed in Chapter 15 (SDP 1986). They are not to be confused with the convertible tax credits referred to in the preceding paragraph, because they do not convert into cash.

A basic income is a convertible tax credit. With negative income tax the principles involved are similar insofar as tax can be negative or positive, but the administration is different and the value of the tax allowance to those paying positive tax can still go up with the marginal tax rate of the taxpayer.

Tax break-even point. The key to understanding the mechanics of integration is the tax break-even point. As already explained this is the level of income (earned or unearned) at which the tax unit neither pays tax nor receives benefit. With conventional, dual systems taxpayers and beneficiaries are treated differently, but with an integrated system the break-even point becomes part of a continuum. A single calculation determines whether the assessment unit pays net tax or receives net benefit. With BI net tax means tax payable after deducting the BI credit, and net benefit means the amount by which the BI received exceeds the income tax paid. With NIT the situation is much closer to the existing system, because NIT retains a conceptual distinction between negative and positive tax, and there are administrative and tax rate distinctions as well. Net benefit for NIT purposes is best defined as the amount of *guaranteed minimum income* (GMI) remaining after benefit withdrawal, and net tax as the amount of tax paid on incomes above the tax thresholds – as with conventional, dual systems.

Mechanics of integration

Marginal tax rates, average tax rates and benefit withdrawal rates. In this context it is also helpful to distinguish between *marginal tax rates* (MTRs) and *benefit withdrawal rates*; and between *marginal tax rates* and *average tax rates* (ATRs). The MTR is the percentage paid in income tax out of each extra £ earned, and sometimes MTR is also used to refer to the rate of benefit withdrawal. ATRs are quite different. ATR is the percentage of original income (earned or unearned) which the assessment unit has to pay out in net tax, after taking into account BI or GMI received.

Table 8.1: Net taxpayers and net beneficiaries
Basic income system, BI £60 a week, tax rate 70%

Gross earnings/ Investment income	Tax @ 70%	BI	Net tax (−) net benefit(+)	Marginal tax rate	Average tax rate
£	£	£	£	%	%
0	0	60	+60	0	0
30	21	60	+39	70	0
60	42	60	+18	70	0
Break-even point					
86	60	60	0	70	0
100	70	60	−10	70	10
160	112	60	−52	70	33
200	140	60	−80	70	40
500	350	60	−290	70	58
1000	700	60	−640	70	64

Table 8.1 illustrates these concepts, assuming introduction of a BI of £60 per person per week, and a marginal tax rate on all other income of 70 percent. The tax break-even point is £86. Although MTR is 70 percent, ATR (which takes into account the £60 BI) is much lower. Even on earnings of £1,000 a week ATR is under 70 percent.

Full integration

The main characteristics of a fully integrated tax and benefit system are summarised in Table 8.2. They fall into two main categories, corresponding to the criteria for a fully integrated income support system explained in Chapter 6.

104

Table 8.2: Characteristics of a fully integrated tax and benefit system

1. The basis of benefit entitlement is citizenship or legal residence, and sometimes work status, but never contribution record.
2. The amounts of entitlement depend on assessed basic need, not contribution record, previous earnings or circumstances surrounding disability.
3. Abolition of all, or virtually all, other cash benefits.
4. Abolition of all earnings rules.
5. The income guarantee is neither a conventional benefit nor a conventional IT relief, but a hybrid that converts between the two, according to the income of the assessment unit.
6. The same administrative regulations are applied below and above the income break-even levels.
7. The guarantee levels and the tax rate become the responsibility of a single government agency and the tax/benefit calculation is fully automated.

First criterion: Consolidation of all income support systems

With a fully integrated system *all* existing income tax reliefs and state cash benefits are replaced by income guarantees that vary according to the age and perhaps other characteristics of the assessment unit, but not according to contribution record or contingency. These income guarantees also replace benefits in kind, like British free school meals and United States food stamps. Although the income guarantees are tax-free, they are closely related to income (and therefore to need) either through the system of benefit withdrawal (NIT) or through the taxation of all other income (BI). The rate at which they are withdrawn depends either on the benefit taper or on the marginal tax rate.

Because the income guarantees are not paid as compensation for loss of earnings, they carry no earnings restrictions. The black economy of welfare (working while claiming) is decriminalised, and the natural desire of most people to do paid work is harnessed to the common good. Since each pound earned is liable either to tax or benefit withdrawal, even part-time earnings reduce the amounts by which people on low incomes are net beneficiaries, and hence the overall cost of the scheme. This is one of the dynamics of integration which are hard to cost, but important.

A fully integrated income guarantee is neither a cash benefit in the conventional sense nor a tax relief, but a hybrid. For people with incomes above the guarantee level, it is a tax offset. For people

Figure 8.1 Elements of an integrated tax and benefit system

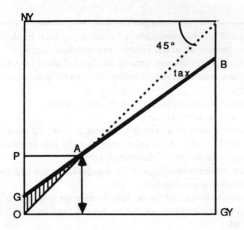

without any income of their own it converts into a cash benefit. For people with incomes that are less than the guarantee level, it tops them up. This process can be seen in Table 8.1. For national accounting purposes, and assuming that the scheme were financed by a personal income tax, aggregate benefit expenditure equals the sum of the amounts of net benefit received. The rest are tax expenditures.

Figure 8.1 is the conventional way of illustrating the elements of an integrated tax and benefit system. The 45° line shows the relationship between gross income (GY) and net income (NY) assuming no tax or cash transfers. The line OAB shows the relationship between gross and net income under the existing system. Net income starts off on the 45° line, because no tax is payable, but above the tax threshold at point A it starts to diverge, as the taxman takes his cut, total tax being equal to the vertical distance between OAB and the 45° line. Under the existing system, and assuming no entitlement to child benefit, the tax threshold and the tax break-even level A are one and the same.

Figure 8.1 is the first of a series that will be used throughout this report. The poverty line (P) is always marked as either a horizontal line or a square box. All the diagrams refer to a single person (unless otherwise specified), all are approximately to scale and all assume a poverty line in 1985-86 of £60 a week, £60 being approximately 30 per cent of average earnings in April 1985. The maximum gross income shown on the horizontal axis is £200 a week.

Another consistent feature is the tax break-even point (A), which

106

is always marked with double arrows. When point A moves over to the right this indicates income redistribution from rich to poor, through increased benefit expenditure and/or higher tax thresholds. When point A moves over to the left more low income families have to depend on income-tested benefits, or are left in poverty, but the tax rate for middle and high income groups can come down.

With the simplest form of guaranteed minimum income the line OAB is replaced by the line GAB, and the triangle OAG represents the amount of negative taxation or benefit payable. At nil income each tax/benefit unit receives the income guarantee OG, which is then gradually withdrawn until the break-even income is reached at point A. By using a rate of benefit withdrawal below the break-even point which is the same as the rate of positive taxation above it, the income redistribution process can be unified and the processes of benefit withdrawal and income tax payment, although conceptually different, become almost indistinguishable. The tax payable, shown as the difference between the 45° line and the line AB, refers to *net* tax, in this case tax at 30 percent of all income *less* the tax offset of the BI or GMI.

In practice the introduction of a GMI is far less straightforward than Figure 8.1 suggests. In Figure 8.1 the tax threshold in the existing system (point A) is assumed to be the same as the poverty line (P), but in real life this need not be the case, and in Britain it has not been the case for many years, hence the starting position for any reform proposal looks more like Figure 8.2

Figure 8.2 shows the position of a single person in April 1985. Net income starts off up the 45° line, but income tax cuts in on

Figure 8.2 Existing system

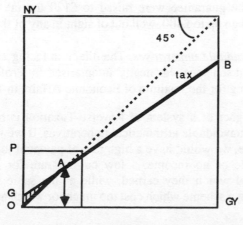

earnings above £42.40 (point A), and NI contribution (not shown) cuts in on earnings above £35.50. To reach the position illustrated in Figure 8.1, the tax threshold for a single person would have to be raised to £60. Moreover some of the people who would have their incomes topped up by the new GMI at present receive nothing. Other things being equal, the tax rate on all other income would have to be increased, which means that line AB would have to be tilted downwards.

Nor is that all. The systems illustrated so far do not constitute full integration, because full integration requires abolition of all other benefits and the GMIs shown here are far too small to make this a realistic option. Even assuming a tax threshold of £60 (as in Figure 8.1) the GMI is only £18, and in Figure 8.2 it is £13, whereas ordinary supplementary benefit for a single householder in April 1985 was £28 a week (plus housing costs in full), and the long-term rate was £36 (plus housing). Unless voters were prepared to see large numbers of people marooned on poverty incomes, it would be unrealistic for government to try and abolish all benefits except a GMI at those levels.

All these problems are greatly intensified for families with children. Figure 8.3 makes the same assumptions as Figure 8.1, but this time it illustrates the position of a family with two small children, and the family is assumed to need about twice as much as a single person in order to reach approximate living standard equivalence. Immediately the square representing poverty incomes doubles in size, and the break-even point is pushed over to the right. Yet the GMI, which is the amount the family would receive if they had no income of their own, is still only £36 a week (30 per cent of the assumed poverty level), which is far too small to be a realistic option. If the guarantee were raised to £120 the tax break-even point would go up to £400, well out of sight in any of the diagrams.

Three unavoidable imperatives. The dilemma facing all designers of integrated schemes was neatly summarised by Professor Colin Clark, writing for the Institute of Economic Affairs in 1977:

> The designer of a system of Reverse Taxation is bound by certain unavoidable arithmetical imperatives. If we were free to choose, we would have a high rate of payment to families with little or no income, a low cut-out rate for anything additional which they earned, while at the same time not designing a scheme which cost too much, or which applied to

Figure 8.3 Integrated system, couple + 2 children

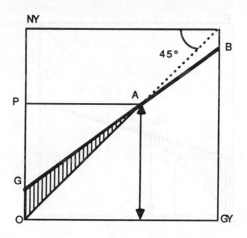

too large a proportion of the population.

These objectives are irreconcilable. (Clark 1977, page 37)

All integrated schemes are subject to three variables, and the relationship between those variables is such that once any two are decided upon, the third follows automatically, regardless of whether or not it is desirable. The first of these variables is the *income guarantee*, which may or may not be set at the poverty line, but, as explained above, if it is below the poverty line then other provision is likely to continue. The second variable is the *break-even level* at which net benefit is reduced to zero and where liability to positive income tax begins. The third variable is the *marginal tax rate*, or more accurately the rate of benefit withdrawal below the break-even level and the rate of positive income tax above it.

Assume, for example, that the income guarantee is £25 a week and the marginal tax rate 50 percent. In that case the break-even point becomes

$$\frac{25}{50} \times 100 = £50.$$

Push up the marginal tax rate to 100 percent and the break-even point becomes £25. Conversely, if the guarantee level were £100 a week and the government wanted to keep the break-even level down to £120 a week, then the benefit withdrawal rate would have to be

$$\frac{100}{120} \times 100 = 83.3\%.$$

Figure 8.4 Full basic income

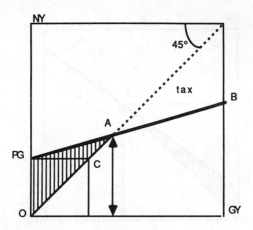

Two main policy options. Within the full integration criteria the two main policy options are full basic income and full negative income tax, and we will start with basic income.

A full BI is illustrated in Figure 8.4. Point G has gone up to the poverty level and the line GAB is tilted so that it starts at point P and finishes well below existing point B. The break-even point (A) is pushed over to the right and large numbers of people receive net benefit who do not need it, because their incomes are already above the poverty line. These are the people in the triangle GAC. Assuming an income guarantee of £60, this option would require a tax rate on all other income of at least 70 percent, which is the rate illustrated in the diagram, and which would almost certainly produce unwanted side effects. It is nevertheless important to remember that the tax shown in the diagram is net tax (after deducting the BI credit). At the maximum earnings level shown, which is £200 a week, the redistributive effects of a full BI are not fully apparent. On earnings of £200, the £60 BI credit cuts the 70 percent tax bill by nearly half (from £140 to £80). But on earnings of £1,000 a week it cuts the 70 percent tax bill by less than 10 percent (from £700 to £640).

Negative income tax, the second policy option, is illustrated in Figure 8.5. Here the net income curve GAB is kinked, the rate of benefit withdrawal below the break-even level being significantly higher than the rate of positive tax above it. This cuts the cost of the scheme by reducing the numbers of people who are net beneficiaries. Point A moves back over to the left. Figure 8.5

Figure 8.5 Negative income tax

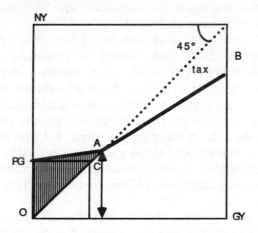

suggests that with a benefit withdrawal rate of 90 percent the break-even level can be held down to only a few £s above the poverty line. This is not necessarily the case, but it helps to get the point across. Note also how NIT reduces the amount of benefit leakage. The triangle GAC is much smaller than in Figure 8.4.

A full NIT is less expensive than a full BI, but is more expensive than is commonly supposed, for two reasons. First, in order to ensure a smooth transition at the break-even point, and to avoid any disincentive effects, the new income tax threshold must be raised not just to the poverty line, but to the break-even point above it. Otherwise people would be charged income tax at the same time as their GMI was being withdrawn, producing marginal tax rates above 100 percent. This refinement adds considerably to the costs of NIT. For instance, in 1985-86, single person's tax allowance would have had to be raised by 60 percent (from £42.40 to £67 a week). Of course the increase could be less if the guarantee were less, but the principle remains.

It is only with a benefit withdrawal rate of 100 percent that the break-even point can be held to the poverty line. With a 70 percent withdrawal rate point A moves over to the right, exactly as in Figure 8.4, and at this point the mechanics of BI and NIT look so alike that many people confuse them.

The second reason why a NIT is more expensive than is commonly supposed is the "moral hazard" effect when unconditional benefits are combined with very high benefit withdrawal rates. The higher the rate of benefit withdrawal the lower the cost in year one of any given scheme, but the greater the likelihood that employers and employees will "re-arrange" their affairs in order to maximise benefit.

The NIT break-even points could well fall in thickly populated areas of income distribution. Almost all pensioners could be affected, 30-40 percent of families with children, and an even higher percentage of large families. If the self-reliance of so large a proportion of the population were undermined, integration could start to look more like poverty creation than poverty prevention. Very much depends on the guarantee levels, but with an income guarantee for single people of £60 a week and equivalent rates for families with children, it would probably be only a matter of time before some sort of direction of labour would be necessary.

Limitations on the amount of means-tested income support that a system can absorb. The pattern of income distribution is a major constraint. In the UK about two-thirds of all income is concentrated in the range between one-half and twice the average, and this exerts as powerful a strait-jacket effect on policy-making as the three variables discussed earlier. Not only does it determine the number of people affected by any combination of those variables, it also imposes a strict operational limit on the amount of means-tested income support that the system can absorb. Depending on the claimant group (pensioners for instance, or families with children), there are points of no return on the scale of original incomes above which huge numbers of people start to be congregated. If entitlement to benefit extends beyond these points then the number of claimants takes off uncontrollably.

The bottom two-thirds of income distribution includes not only the majority of old age pensioners and people with disabilities, most lone-parent families and most of the unemployed, but also large numbers of working families with children.

Take retirement pensioners first. If NI retirement pension were replaced by a NIT, most pensioners would be entitled to it, because their original incomes are so low. A NIT guarantee for a single pensioner of £60 a week, withdrawn by 70 pence in the £, would produce a break-even level of £86 a week. But Appendix 5 (based on the 1985 Family Expenditure Survey) shows that only 315,000 single pensioners, out of a total of 4 million, had gross incomes excluding basic pension of more than £85 a week. Even with a 90 percent taper only 10 percent of single pensioners would have been free of the NIT poverty trap. Married pensioners have higher original incomes than single pensioners, but the effect is similar, because the NIT guarantee has to be higher for two people than one. Assuming unisex pensions of £60 a week (£120 for a couple) and a 70 percent taper, the break-even level becomes £171. In 1985 only about 200,000 married pensioners (out of a total of 2.5 million) would have been free of the NIT poverty trap. Even with a lower pension of £100 for a couple and a taper of 90 percent, there would still have been only about 14 percent of married pensioners above the NIT break-even level. In those circumstances very few people would bother to save for their old age, because the savings would serve merely to lift them off entitlement to the NIT.

Millions of families with children could be similarly affected. People in paid work have higher original incomes than pensioners, but if they have children their guarantees too would be higher. Appendix 5 shows that in 1985 there were in Great Britain (excluding Northern Ireland) nearly 7 million families with children, of whom nearly 5.5 million were in paid work and 1.5 million were out of work (unemployed, sick, lone parents and so forth). During most of 1985 supplementary benefit (including rent addition and free school meals) for a family with two children averaged between £90 and £100 a week (depending on the age of the children), and this was barely adequate. For families with one child SB was £12-£16 less, depending on the age of the child, and for larger families it was higher by similar amounts. If we assume that an average NIT guarantee of £100 a week would have been sufficient for a-one child family in 1985, with £15 extra per child per week, and if we also assume a NIT withdrawal rate of 70 percent, then the break-even levels become £143 for the one-child family, £164 for the two-child family, £186 for a three-child family, and so on.

Of the working families in Appendix 5, there were nearly 400,000 one-child families with gross weekly incomes excluding state benefits below £143 a week, there were nearly 500,000 two-child families whose incomes were less than £165 a week, and there were some 200,000 families with three or more children whose earnings were less than £185 a week. These figures include one-parent as well as two-parent families. So a NIT at the proposed levels, and with a 70 percent taper, would have affected nearly 1.1 working families as well as the 1.5 million out of work families – about 2.5 million families in all, or about 38 percent of all families with children in Great Britain. The percentage in Northern Ireland would almost certainly be higher.

Suppose that the break-even levels had been just £20 a week higher, either because of a lower taper, or because of higher guarantee levels. Then the number of working families affected would have gone up by another 400,000, bringing the total to around 3 million, or more than 40 percent of all families.

Second criterion: Harmonisation of all administrative procedures

With full integration the same standard regulations and procedures are applied to all. This aspect of integration is frequently over-looked, but is essential. Nor should it be confused with improved departmental coordination. Coordination means rules and regulations that do not clash, integration means the same rules and regulations applied to all. With different rules above and below the break-even points the likelihood of achieving the smooth transition illustrated in Figure 8.1 is negligible.

If full administrative integration of the tax and benefit systems were introduced, the effect in Whitehall would be like removing centuries of whitewash from an old cow byre, and starting again with washable emulsion. For the Treasury it would be a moment of truth they prefer to avoid. For centuries the edifice of government has been built around the premise that discrimination, both positive and negative, is in the public interest. Integration not only questions that assumption, it cannot operate unless discrimination within the income support system (cash benefits and income tax reliefs) is removed. Below are just some of the changes that the removal of discrimination would involve.

The unit of assessment. Under existing law the unit of assessment depends on a variety of circumstances, and is largely the product of history. It is incompatible with full integration. If there is to be smooth transition across the break-even levels, the assessment unit can be the individual, the married couple, the nuclear family, the extended family, or even the household, but it must be consistent. A system that treats people independently for tax purposes but jointly for benefit purposes (or *vice versa*) is not an integrated system.

The obstacles to reform of the assessment unit are largely political, and have already been discussed. Although there is a strong body of opinion in favour of change there is no agreement on an alternative system. Most NIT proposals in the UK take for granted that the family (undefined, but probably meaning the married couple and infant children) would be the assessment unit. They do not mention the problem of unmarried couples, or of homosexual couples, or of men and women sharing a household where there is no commitment to mutual support. Most BI proposals take the individual as the assessment unit, in which case there is no harmonisation problem. Each individual would receive the same BI, regardless of marital status, and the BI would be recouped through the tax system afterwards.

Definition of income. With a fully integrated system the definition of income must be the same throughout. With BI this is not problematical. The BI is withdrawn through income tax in the same way as existing child benefit. Income is defined for tax purposes in the same way as for existing income tax, except that the number of tax reliefs would be substantially reduced, thus simplifying the assessment process.

With NIT, the definition of income below and above the cross-over points tends to differ, in much the same way as under existing dual systems. Positive tax systems start with the concept of gross income and after allowing for various reliefs and allowances arrive at taxable income. Negative tax systems use a different concept of gross income, which includes money from gifts and the imputed value of wealth, as with existing means-tested benefit systems.

Cumulative and non-cumulative systems. A fully integrated tax and benefit system can be either cumulative or non-cumulative, but not both. In the UK income tax is cumulative in respect of both *liability* and *payment*. Tax liability is based on annual income, and each weekly or monthly tax deduction (depending on how often wages are paid) takes account of the income and tax allowances received during the previous weeks or months. Most NI contributions, on the other hand, and most benefits are non-cumulative, which means that income during the rest of the tax year is not counted. Consequently a person who earns irregularly pays the same amount of income tax during each tax year as a person who earns the same amount each week, but the amount of NI contribution payable varies according to individual circumstances. Moreover a person who earns nothing during the first six months of the benefit year and claims income support, is not expected to repay it, even though his earnings during the second six months of the same year may bring him well above the annual IS entitlement level.

The case for and against cumulation was very clearly explained by the Institute for Fiscal Studies in Appendix A to Chapter 4 of *The Reform of Social Security* (IFS 1984, pages 106-109). Here the issue is primarily one of consistency. Differences like those described above are incompatible with integration. There would have to be changes. Once again a full BI presents no serious problems. The BIs are tax-free and would be credited automatically each week or month, regardless of the other income of the taxpayer. Liability for the new income tax would be cumulative within each tax year, as at present, and payment could be cumulative or non-cumulative, integration does not affect the issues.

With NIT there are serious problems. A fully integrated NIT would almost certainly involve a switch to cumulative benefit liability, although payment could be non-cumulative. Benefit received during the course of the tax year would be included in the annual tax return, and some people would find themselves having to repay benefit received when they were out of work or on low earnings, on the grounds that their annual income put them above the accumulated, annual entitlement level.

Accounting period. Harmonisation of the accounting period presents similar problems. For benefit purposes the accounting period needs to be quite short, a month at most, because people in financial difficulties need assistance quickly. It is no good telling someone who loses his job during the last three months of the tax/benefit year that he must wait until next April for benefit, because his earnings during the previous nine months were above his annual benefit entitlement. He has probably spent them. For tax purposes, on the other hand, a year is short enough.

With BI this apparent divergence need not present any difficulties, because the BI is credited automatically and withdrawn through the tax system in the light of each person's other income. Difficulties could emerge if the tax rates were progressive, and this is an argument in favour of flat rate tax, or of higher rate tax bands that affect only a tiny minority of the population. NIT, on the other hand, produces serious difficulties. Again this is the result of discontinuity at the break-even levels. So long as the rate of positive tax above the break-even point is lower than the rate of benefit withdrawal below it, the accounting period for net taxpayers and net beneficiaries must be the same. Otherwise the discontinuity produces arbitrary variations in net income that have nothing to do with need. Provided that the number of people affected in this way were small, it might not matter, but this is unlikely. It is more likely that the break-even levels would be at income levels where large numbers of people were affected.

Partial integration

In the following chapters it will be argued that full integration (whether through BI or NIT) is an impossible dream, for two main reasons. The first is the economic impossibility of paying for it without undermining work incentives, and the second the political unlikelihood of being able to treat taxpayers and beneficiaries alike. Although at first sight the barriers to administrative harmonisation look technical, the reality has more to do with politics, especially public prejudice against claimants and the self-interest of those whose jobs depend on preservation of the *status quo*.

A full BI is too costly to be feasible, although it would be easy to administer. A full NIT is less costly than full BI, but still very expensive, and it is unlikely to meet the harmonisation criteria, even if the problem of cost could be overcome. In administrative terms most NIT schemes are little more than extensions and rationalisations of existing, dual systems. NIT preserves the dichotomy between taxpayers and beneficiaries, which is why it has more supporters in high places than BI.

Given the difficulties, it is not surprising that most costed proposals for integrated reform of tax and social security amount at most to partial integration and often to no more than improved inter-departmental coordination. None meets the criteria set out in Table 19.2. Some try to combine the best elements of both BI and NIT, some also retain parts of the existing system.

With partial integration the integrated component can be made to meet most of the criteria in Table 8.2, the exception being that the income guarantee is never sufficient to allow abolition of all other benefits. The non-integrated component picks up the pieces left behind, and can be left to operate along conventional lines. Ideally the integrated component would be dominant and the non-integrated component would be the residual safety net, but during the initial stages the integrated component is bound to be quite small. This approach has much to commend it and is the subject of the last three parts of this report.

Spurious integration

Sometimes it is difficult to distinguish between partial integration and systems that are said to be integrated, but are really no more than extensions of existing, dual systems. Many proposals have more to do with improved coordination than with integration. Processes not dissimilar to a NIT already operate through family credit in the UK, and similar benefits elsewhere. In many proposals the principal new features are the extension of coverage (to include all legal residents instead of just families with children) and the new administrative processes involved. The new administrative processes usually involve large-scale rationalisation, quite substantial cuts in bureaucracy and greatly increased automation, all of which may well be worthwhile, but do not constitute integration. A great deal is made of automation, which is itself sometimes confused with integration.

In 1983 Britain's Social Democrats put forward reform proposals which included "integration of the benefits and tax systems". It turned out that all they meant by integration was "adding to the information which is required for the tax return, to include family circumstances...and housing expenditure... " in order to make possible payment of a fully automated, income-tested *basic benefit* (BB). The final aim was "to eliminate claiming by making the payment of tax benefits automatic for those families who are entitled to them" (SDP 1983, page 4). There was no mention of administrative harmonisation. On the contrary the tax unit was to be the individual, whereas the benefit unit was to be the family (undefined).

Some proposals marketed under the integration label meet virtually none of the criteria listed in Table 8.2. Mr Fowler's family credit was originally billed as a step towards integration, but everybody knows it is just another means-tested benefit, replacing family income supplement. The reform proposals put forward in 1984 by the Institute for Fiscal Studies (IFS 1984) were heavily marketed as integration, but met hardly any of the criteria in Table 8.2, and bore little resemblance to the situation illustrated in Figure 8.1.

The IFS scheme was one of those that would count husbands and wives as independent units for tax, but jointly for benefit purposes. Although it is hard to tell from the book, it seems the authors had in mind a multi-tier administrative system, with non-integrated, local advisory offices to deal with the benefit claims of people on

Figure 8.6 NIT, tax threshold below poverty line

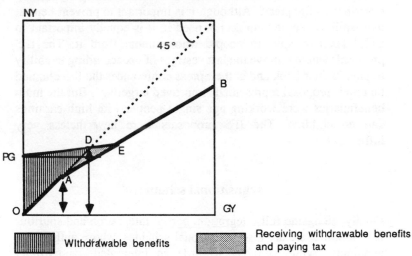

low incomes, and an annual, cumulative tax/benefit return. Tax relief for non-earning spouses would be removed, as would child benefit. Nor would there be any child tax relief. Consequently the proposed tax thresholds are well below the new poverty lines and well below the new tax break-even points. An IFS-style proposal is illustrated in Figure 8.6. The line OAB represents after-tax income. Tax starts to be payable on incomes above point A, which is the tax threshold and the tax break-even point for people not in receipt of withdrawable benefits.

The IFS scheme would add to the number of people in need of benefit, by taxing them beyond ability to pay. These are the people in the bottom part of the triangle DAE. This triangle does not appear in any other diagram in this chapter. The line GEB represents net income, after deducting tax and then adding in the *benefit credit*. Notice the second tax break-even point (D) (for people receiving withdrawable benefits), to the left of the kink in the tax curve at point E. Some people are paying more in income tax than they are receiving in income-tested benefit.

The diagram refers to a single person. For families with children the poverty line is considerably higher, but the tax threshold (point A) remains the same. Consequently the amount of benefit credit payable is much, much higher, and for families with four or more children the second tax break-even point (D) moves far over to the right, or even out of sight.

Figure 8.6 is an extreme example of the malign churning described in Chapter 5. Although it is important to prevent benefit over-spill to people who do not need it, it is equally important to avoid tax over-spill to people who cannot afford it. The IFS proposals would remove the last vestiges of tax according to ability to pay. In their book and at their press conferences the IFS claimed that their proposal represented "improved targeting". But the main beneficiaries were working-age single people with high earnings and no children. The IFS proposals were nevertheless very influential.

Transitional schemes

Finally, alongside full integration, partial integration and spurious integration, there are also transitional schemes, whose authors are genuinely trying to move towards an integrated, or partially integrated, system in the long run. *BIG PHASE 1* (Chapter 20) is one such scheme. Since integration would take a number of years to implement, some characteristics of the existing dual systems are bound to remain during the initial stages. In such cases it is only by looking at the target system, that it is possible to judge the likely extent of integration in the long term.

Basic income and negative income tax will now be examined in turn.

9

Basic income

From "New Social Contract" to "Basic Income Guarantee"

In Britain the idea of a guaranteed basic income that is automatic, that replaces all existing cash benefits and income tax reliefs and that takes the individual as the unit of assessment, descends directly from the *New Social Contract* advocated during the second World War by Lady (Juliet) Rhys Williams DBE (J. Rhys Williams 1943 and 1953). Starting from the premise that "hope of gain", as opposed to fear of starvation or state compulsion, is the only acceptable motive for wage labour in a free society, Lady Rhys Williams argued against the Beveridge Plan, partly because it would leave large sections of the population unprotected against poverty, and partly because it would destroy the will to work and in due course necessitate direction of labour:

> There can be little doubt that the Beveridge Plan...will have the effect of under-mining the will to work of the lower-paid workers to a probably serious and possibly dangerous degree. Not only will the idle get as much from the State as will the industrious workers, they will get a great deal more. Indeed, the whole basis of the Scheme rests upon the conception that those who serve the community by working and producing wealth must not on any account receive any State assistance or reward, but must be heavily taxed instead. (J. Rhys Williams 1943, page 141)

Unless we recognise this fundamental fact and adjust our ideas accordingly, it will be impossible to continue to utilise the desire for gain as the motive for labour, and we shall find ourselves obliged to revert to some form of State compulsion in order to keep the wheels of industry turning. (J. Rhys Williams 1943, page 148, original italics)

Her solution was straightforward:

*The prevention of want must be regarded as being the duty of the State to all its citizens, and not merely to a favoured few...*The new relationship would be expressed by the actual signature of a contract between the individual man or woman of eighteen and over, and the State, whereby the State would acknowledge the duty to maintain the individual and his children at all times, and to ensure for them all the necessities of a healthy life. The individual, in his turn, would acknowledge it to be his duty to devote his best efforts to the production of the wealth whereby alone the welfare of the community can be maintained...The idea of issuing any form of State grants to individuals who are not poor or sick has been introduced and accepted in respect of Family Allowances...Children's allowances are not a species of charity, as are other forms of assistance, but rather a kind of wages paid by the State to the parents of the next generation in return for services rendered to its future citizens. *They form, in short, a social contract, not a dole.* (J. Rhys Williams 1943, pages 145 and 147)

The practical result of the contract was to be the weekly payment of £1.05 for each man, £0.95 for each woman (*"paid in her own right and not merely as a dependant"*), and £0.50 for each child up to age eighteen (payable to the mother). The amounts for adults were close to Beveridge's recommended amounts for single people, but considerably more for married couples. The amounts for children were also more than Beveridge, and were to be paid for each child including the first. All the rates were close to subsistence level, allowing almost nothing for non-essentials. The scheme was designed to be revenue neutral assuming a social security tax, on all other income, at a flat-rate 45 percent.

The war-time coalition Government did not take up Lady Rhys Williams's proposals, which were over-shadowed by those of Beveridge, but her ideas were influential. In the United States they reappeared in amended form as negative income tax. In Britain they were worked on by Nobel prize-winner Professor James Meade in books and papers published during the ensuing thirty-five years (for instance Meade 1948 pages 42 ff, and Meade 1972 and1978), and by Lady Rhys Williams's son, Sir Brandon Rhys Williams. They also fitted admirably with Sir Arthur (now Lord) Cockfield's plan for convertible tax-credits (Treasury and DHSS 1972).

As Member of Parliament for Kensington from 1968 until his death in 1988, Sir Brandon Rhys Williams was an indefatigable supporter of his mother's ideas, at the same time amending them in the light of changing circumstances and changing social attitudes. For both of them the motivation always rested on ethics as well as economics and as the years passed the case in favour was accentuated by events. At the end of the 1960s Conservative Central Office was taking an active interest in integration, and in 1967 the Conservative Political Centre published Sir Brandon's pamphlet *The New Social Contract* (B. Rhys Williams 1967). Two other pamphlets were published at about this time (B. Rhys Williams 1969 and 1972), but his later ideas are to be found only in private papers, in Parliamentary and other speeches, and in the evidence he submitted to the Meacher Committee of Enquiry (House of Commons 1983, Minutes of Evidence 21 Jul 1982). That occasion marks the first official use in Britain of the terms *basic income* and *Basic Income Guarantee* (BIG).

There are two fundamental differences between Lady Rhys Williams's new social contract and the Basic Income Guarantee proposals put forward by her son. Lady Rhys Williams included an obligation to take paid work, whereas BIG is unconditional, which from the standpoint of the 1980s is one of its main attractions, the purpose being to encourage work-sharing and unpaid work. On the other hand, Lady Rhys Williams's income guarantee was supposed to be enough to live on, whereas for able-bodied adults of working age BIG is never more than a stepping stone to independence.

The term basic income was adopted in 1981, soon after Sir Brandon had invited me to produce updated costings. We chose the words basic income partly to emphasise that this was a new initiative by comparison with the somewhat discredited 1972 Tax-Credit proposals, and partly to indicate a shift away from the traditional subsistence approach in favour of something more generous.

In 1984 a small group of individuals interested in the possibility of integrating the tax and benefit systems along social dividend lines, came together under the auspices of the National Council for

Voluntary Organisations and set up the Basic Income Research Group (BIRG). One of their first decisions was to adopt the term basic income in preference to social dividend, social wage, national dividend or any other. BIRG publishes its own Bulletin and runs regular seminars. In 1986, BIRG affiliated to the Basic Income European Network (BIEN), which was founded at the first international conference on basic income, at the university of Louvain-la-Neuve, Belgium, in September 1986.

As a result of these initiatives the term basic income is gradually becoming part of the English language. It is easier to understand than the older, virtually synonymous term tax credit, and a partial BI is slowly coming to be regarded as a realistic reform option.

The 1972 Tax-Credit Green Paper

The convertible tax credits proposed by the Conservative Government of Mr Edward Heath were similar to partial BIs, but the assessment unit would have been the single person or married couple, as under existing law. If these proposals had been put into effect, a large part of the UK personal taxation and social security systems would by now be integrated. The Green Paper proposed replacement of the main IT allowances by convertible tax credits of £4 for a single person, £6 for a married couple and £2 for each child. Despite its limitations the scheme was a radical departure, too much so for many. After extensive debate a Select Committee of the House of Commons recommended that the scheme be adopted, without "endorsing any particular level of tax, or credit or relativity", but with a split along party political lines, Tories voting in favour and Labour against (House of Commons 1973, Vol 1, page 7).

After the Heath Government went (in 1974) the new Labour government let the matter drop. In theory the Conservative Party remained committed to tax credits, but in practice, under Mrs Thatcher's leadership, the attitude was at first luke-warm and then hostile. On receipt of adverse reports on NIT from America, and on the untested assumption that NIT and tax-credit (or BI) are synonymous, the Tory leadership decided to forget the whole idea. Thus the only tangible result of Mr Heath's tax-credit proposal so far has been the introduction in 1977-79 of child benefit, which is a partial BI for children.

Origins of basic income: the three rights

The basic income concept is by no means unique to Britain, or to the present time. But it is in Britain, as a result largely of Sir Brandon Rhys Williams's initiative, that the idea of a BI financed by integrating the tax and benefit systems is most firmly established. Elsewhere in Europe the term basic income often means a minimum guaranteed income which may or may not replace existing benefits, and which would be additional to tax reliefs (Euzéby 1987).

Three strands of thought come together in BI. The first and oldest, with roots that go back at least to the early nineteenth century, concerns the right of every individual to a minimum of existence. The second, of much more recent origin, concerns the uncoupling of income from work. The third concerns individual freedom, which today links in with freedom from an overpowering bureaucracy and women's emancipation. For the sake of simplicity we can call these the three rights: the right to a means of existence, the right to work, and the right to individual freedom.

The right to a means of existence. "You exist, therefore you have a right to the means of existence" is one of the key slogans of the Voedingsbond, a Dutch trade union for workers in agriculture and the food industry, which has been campaigning since the 1970s for BI in the Netherlands. The dream of enough to live on for all is as old as history, but it is only now, and still only in the richest countries, that society has perhaps the means to turn that dream into reality.

Starting with the industrial revolution it is possible to identify a chain of writers, most of them visionaries, all representing what may be called the "solidarity" tradition of political science (Charles Fourier, Jean-Baptiste Godin and Léon Bourgeois in France, Thomas Paine and Edward Bellamy in the United States of America, John Stuart Mill and Bertrand Russell in Great Britain, Theodor Hertzka, Peter Kropotkin, Atlanticus and Joseph Popper-Lynkeus in Germany, even Sun Yat Sen in China) and all of whom advocated, in one way or another, that just as every human being owes a debt to society, so society in return owes a minimum of existence to all its members (for historical accounts see: Morley-Fletcher 1980-81, Van Parijs 1985, Vobruba 1986). Since few, if any, of the early advocates of BI put figures to their proposals, nobody can say if they were feasible. But it is unlikely. Even today the amounts available for distribution are much smaller than is generally supposed.

The right to work. Some leading advocates of BI are individuals working in institutions concerned with the labour market and the effects of new technologies on employment. When Riccardo Petrella (Director of the European Commission's FAST-11 programme)[1] or Gabriel Fragnière (director of the European Centre for Work and Society in Maastricht) or Guy Standing of the International Labour Organisation at Geneva speak about the need to uncouple incomes and work they are not advocating mass idleness. They are looking for ways to bring the demand for paid work into line with job supply, without causing unacceptable poverty and without resort to Luddism (Fragnière 1987; Standing 1986). For the unemployment with which BI in the 1980s is concerned goes far beyond the "voluntary" unemployment that troubled Lady Rhys Williams in 1942. It includes the frictional and structural unemployment that results from rapid technological and industrial change, and the involuntary, Keynesian-style unemployment that results from imbalances between demand and supply.

It was the speed of industrial and technological development during the first World War that caused two former soldiers, one French and one British, to question the viability of old-style labour markets based on long working hours put in by unskilled or semi-skilled labour. In France, Verdun veteran Jacques Duboin, who had watched the newly manufactured tanks succeed where echelon after echelon of men had died, argued passionately for institutional change that would completely uncouple income from work. In order to prevent mass unemployment and to take advantage of the material abundance made possible by new technologies, he proposed that each country's national income should be shared out equally between its citizens, with a tax of 100 percent on all their other income.[2]

In Britain, Scottish engineer and accountant Major C.H.Douglas had similar fears. The Douglas *social credit* scheme proposed that Government should increase consumer demand by paying a *national dividend* of £5 a month (equal to about 30 percent of average earnings at that time) to every householder, financing it by increasing the money supply (Douglas 1920 and 1922).

The right to individual freedom. As civilisation progresses freedom is found to be elusive. Abolition of slavery turned out to be no more than a step in the right direction, as did the right to vote. In Britain the next stage after universal adult suffrage was to be economic freedom through the guarantee of "a national minimum", but that too turned out to be an illusion. Forty years after Beveridge there is still no real economic independence for millions of people dependent on social security benefits, nor for millions of married women dependent on their husbands. For libertarians therefore, the next stage is to remove the bureaucratic excesses of the welfare state and to enhance autonomy by giving every individual the right to an automatic national minimum.

A change of this sort could transform family life. Dependency within the family is the traditional lot of married women, and because it is not always a happy one, increasing numbers of women seek independence through the labour market. Others go out to work because their families need the extra money. Either way the decision can be a hard one, for women, unlike men, have to fit their paid work in with their family responsibilities. BI would soften this dilemma by giving a modicum of financial independence to every woman (and every man), whether or not they were in paid work. BI does not take away the right to work outside the home, but it does increase freedom of choice. It does not take away the responsibility of spouses for each other above the minimum, but it does increase the autonomy of the non-earning spouse or partner.

In some Western countries there already is a national minimum, but it is never unconditional and it always takes the couple (sometimes the three-generational family and sometimes the household) as the unit of assessment. The conditions imposed can amount to infringements of personal liberty – Britain's much detested *cohabitation rule* is one example. The *earnings rules* to which most benefit claimants are subject cut a swathe through personal freedom.

Since the mid-1970s, as a result of crisis in the welfare state, crisis in the labour market and crisis in the family, each of the strands that come together in basic income has been accentuated, and the micro chip looks as though it could be the *deus ex machina* to bring it all about.

Characteristics of basic income

A full basic income meets all the criteria listed in Table 8.2, but it also has distinctive features, and these are summarised in Table 9.1.

127

Table 9.1: Distinctive features of full basic income

> 1. The BI is sufficient to meet all basic living costs and replaces all existing benefits.
> 2. The BI is without means-test (or income-test) and is tax-free.
> 3. The BI is credited automatically and withdrawn through the tax system.
> 4. The tax rate is flat-rate or progressive, but not regressive.
> 5. The unit of assessment is the individual.
> 6. Tax is payable on all other income.

With a full BI each individual would be guaranteed enough to live on and each would be taxed separately on all their other income. The BIs would replace all existing cash benefits, including state earnings-related pensions. One of the aims of BI is to have benefit categories that are exogenous, therefore most schemes distinguish on grounds of age alone, although supplements for people with disabilities are generally recognised to be essential.

A partial basic income is based on the same principles as full BI, but the income guarantee is smaller, necessitating retention of some proof-of-need benefits and perhaps some income tax reliefs. In the rest of this chapter we shall discuss full BI. Partial BI will be examined in Parts Three to Five of this report.

Imagine that £40 is considered adequate for an able-bodied, working-age adult, plus £20 for a teenage child, these amounts being arbitrary. Imagine also that the tax rate on all other income is 50 percent. If we take a couple with two teenage children where the father earns £200 a week and the mother £80, then each spouse's net income and the BIs for the children would be calculated as in Table 9.2. Despite the 50 percent tax rate the family is £32 a week better off than under the system in January 1988. There is also a considerable redistribution of income within the family, from wallet to purse. The husband's net tax is £60, compared with income tax and NI contribution of £52 in January 1988, but the wife's net tax bill goes down from £15 to nil. Child benefit goes up from £7.25 to £20, but older children would have to pay tax at 50 percent on any earnings, and tax would also be payable on income from savings or trust income on their behalf.

An important feature of BI is that it is credited automatically in the light of each person's circumstances, and recouped through the tax system afterwards, in the light of each person's income. This makes the system easy to understand, easy to operate and easily

Table 9.2: Calculation of tax liability, full BI, £ week

		£	£	Net tax (−) Net benefit (+) £
1. Father	gross earnings	200.00		
	− income tax @ 50%	100.00		
	+ BI	40.00		
	= net income		140.00	− £60.00
2. Mother	gross earnings	80.00		
	− income tax @ 50%	40.00		
	+ BI	40.00		
	= net income		80.00	£0.00
3. First child	BI		20.00	+ £20.00
4. Second child	BI		20.00	+ £20.00
5. Family's net income			260.00	
6. Net tax/benefit of family				− £20.00

accessible. It is money on which people can depend, and involves the minimum of red tape. There is no need for benefit entitlement to be reassessed at the end of each year, and no need for different assessment units above and below the income guarantee levels. With full BI the tax is proportional, and the marginal rate is never more than the rate of the new income tax, since all means-tested benefits are removed. In theory this bolsters work incentives, but in practice full BI is so expensive it creates its own disincentives. In the example above, each spouse stands to gain 50 pence out of each extra £ earned, but those figures were only illustrative. In practice a full BI, at a level sufficient to make possible abolition of housing benefit, would have to be at least £60 a week, and the tax rate at least 70 percent.

A further distinctive feature of BI is that it is unaffected by changes in marital status. Since the BI is so much per adult and so much per child, and since the tax/benefit unit is the individual it makes no difference in terms of net benefit entitlement or net tax liability whether a person is male or female, married, single, divorced, or anything else. The cohabitation rule can be abolished.

In order to reduce the cost of BI, some proposed systems have a smaller BI per adult and a BI addition for householders. This preserves marriage neutrality, but it introduces an endogenous element which might encourage household formation. In effect it amounts to a subsidy for people who live alone. It would also reintroduce administrative complexity.

Another important feature is that all income except the BI would be taxable. Theoretically this requires abolition of all the personal and non-personal income tax reliefs listed in Appendix 4, the aim being to increase the income tax base, simplify tax assessment, and remove discrimination.

The arithmetic of full basic income

The idea of BI has immediate appeal to many people. It seems to offer a real chance of achieving objectives that have eluded governments in the past. But the stumbling block is expense. Administratively a BI looks good, but in terms of cost and incentives a full BI is not feasible.

By full basic income I mean an income sufficient to meet all basic living costs, and therefore to make possible the abolition of all other cash benefits. This immediately raises three questions:

- How much is enough?
- What tax rate would be necessary?
- What would be the redistributive effects?

How much is enough? Ideally one would start from family budget standards. Unfortunately, as was shown in Chapter 5, Britain has none. Generally speaking all we have to go on are income support (which almost certainly under-estimates the costs of children), and the long-standing target of 30 percent average earnings for single pensioners and 50 percent for couples.

Additionally we have to work within the following BI criteria:

(1) No differences on account of sex.
(2) No differences on account of marital status.
(3) No differences on account of origin of disability.
(4) No differences on account of contribution record.
(5) No differences on account of work status.

The differences to be avoided are, needless to say, the arbitrary differences that do not affect a person's basic needs. If a woman incurs extra expenses during pregnancy these should be allowed for, as should the expenses incurred as a result of disability, or doing paid work.

How much for adults? All the figures refer to the UK and the period between November 1985 and April 1986. Average weekly earnings in the April 1985 New Earnings Survey were £208 for full-time men (all occupations), £137 for women (all occupations), and £185 for full-time men and women on adult rates. On the assumption that adults of working age need at least as much as the elderly to reach an equivalent basic living standard, the politically acceptable target BI lies somewhere between £55.50, which was 30 percent of average earnings for men and women, and £62.40, which was 30 percent of the men only figure. We will settle for £60.

A major difficulty is that full BI is supposed to cover housing costs. Although £60 a week (which is just £21.70 more than the standard NI pension in November 1985) would be enough for people with low housing costs it would not be enough for others. Retired households with incomes under £100 a week are reported in the 1985 Family Expenditure Survey (FES 1985, Table 9) as having gross housing costs averaging £19-£25 a week. Non-retired households with gross normal weekly incomes of under £200 are reported as paying £19-£22 a week on rent, rates and water charges. These average figures conceal wide variations, and take no account of mortgage payments.

Housing, without major reform of housing finance, is the Achilles heel of full BI. If the amount allowed for housing is small (or even average) the result will be a residue of housing poverty, but if it allows for people with above average housing costs, it will be poorly targeted. There remains the alternative option of a lower universal BI, perhaps £50 per person, plus a BI housing supplement of £20. Both would cost about the same in year one, and neither is particularly generous. But why subsidise people for living alone?

How much for children? For children there is nothing equivalent to the TUC target for pensioners. If the children's additions with long-term NI benefit had been moved up since 1979 in line with inflation, the full amount payable in April 1985 for each child of a recipient of long-term NI benefit would have been about £16, not age-related. Some people say the rates should be age-related. On the other hand the amount for very small children should perhaps include an element for childcare costs. Child BIs should also include an element for housing, and once again the housing component presents problems, because in the privately rented sector the presence of a child can easily double the rent.

Starting from a full BI for adults of £60 a week, age-related child BIs might be as shown below. To reach these amounts, it is assumed that £20 of the adult BI is for housing and the children's equivalence ratios are close to Beveridge's scale in Table 5.4, adjusted to include extra housing, which Beveridge excluded. All the figures are approximate.

Possible full BIs for children, 1985-86

Age 0-4:   45% of £40 = £18   + £2   for housing = £20
Age 5-10:   55% of £40 = £22   + £3   for housing = £25
Age 11-15: 70% of £40 = £28   + £4   for housing = £32
Age 16-17: 100% of £40 = £40   + £4   for housing = £44

How much for people with disabilities? The extra costs incurred as a result of disability cannot be estimated until publication of the 1986 survey by the Office of Population Censuses and Surveys (OPCS). In 1987 the Disability Alliance put forward proposals for a *disability costs allowance* (DCA) which would have cost £4.2 billion at 1985-86 prices, and this is the estimate used throughout this report (DA 1987).

The figures in Table 9.3 are the income guarantee figures that, throughout the rest of this report, are assumed to constitute a full BI in 1985-86. No allowance is made for people with above average housing costs, but local provision for emergencies is retained.

Table 9.3: Suggested values for a full basic income, 1985-86

Demogrant	£ per week
Each adult, from age 18	60.00
Each child aged 0 – 4	20.00
5 – 10	25.00
11 – 15	32.00
16 – 17	44.00
Disability costs allowance	variable

Costing basic income

A full BI would be fearfully expensive. Even those who do recommend full BI usually make significant provisos. In Denmark, for instance, physicist Niels Meyer, whose 1978 book *Revolt from the Center* (Meyer, Petersen, and Sorensen 1978) sold over 100,000 copies, recognises that "it is very difficult to introduce a basic income in a society with large unemployment and a high degree of economic inequality". He proposes to reduce inequality by paying the same wage rate for all, although he says this is not essential (Meyer 1986(a), page 1). Elsewhere he accepts that a full BI might make too many people want to quit paid work, but argues that since the level of BI is a "politically adjustable parameter", it could easily be reduced at times of labour shortage (Meyer 1986(b), page 2). Thus at a stroke, the citizen's "full" BI becomes a political football, and a threat to living standards instead of a boost.

Appendix 1 describes the costing techniques used in this study, first the NA/SPI method, which relies on statistics from the annual *National Income and Expenditure Blue Book*, the Family Expenditure Survey and the Survey of Personal Incomes, and second TAXMOD, which is a computer model based on the 1982 Family Expenditure Survey, and produced by Professor A.B. Atkinson and Holly Sutherland at the Suntory Toyota/International Centre for Economics and Related Disciplines (ST/ICERD), London School of Economics (Atkinson and Sutherland 1988). TAXMOD is not used for costing full BI, because it cannot take into account all the changes that would be involved, for instance abolition of the non-personal tax reliefs. Instead we shall use the first of the three NA/SPI formulae described in Appendix 1, and the outcome will depend very much on the assumptions made about the new income tax (IT) base.

$$\text{Tax rate} = \frac{\text{BI} + \text{IT,ACT \& NIC} - \text{S}}{\text{New IT base}} \times 100$$

The aim is to ascertain the rate of income tax (or BI contribution) necessary to finance a full BI during 1985-86, assuming no other major tax changes (for instance no switch from income to expenditure taxes) and no change in the income tax base as a result of the proposed changes. This is a rather unrealistic exercise, since it takes no account of demographic changes during the period of transition, nor of behavioural effects. It is sufficient nevertheless to show that a full BI is not feasible – certainly not in the UK.

Table 9.4, at the end of this chapter, sets out the different stages of the calculation. All the figures are from Appendix 1, and it is emphasised that they are only approximate. Stage (1) calculates the costs of the BIs, including disability costs allowance, administration, and emergency provision. Total cost is £159,000 million. Stage (2) adds in the costs of abolishing existing income tax, advance corporation tax and NI contributions (IT, ACT and NIC), which comes to £65,000 million. Stage (3) then subtracts the estimated savings (S) on benefits and subsidies that the BIs should replace. These include student grants, free school meals, Manpower Services Commission (MSC) grants and allowances, rate rebates, some expenditure on personal social services, abolition of state earnings-related pension (SERPS), agricultural subsidies and statutory sick pay, as well as DHSS benefits. Total savings come to £60,000 million, which is less than 40 percent of the cost of the BIs, so the tax rate depends crucially on the extent to which the tax base can be extended. Stage (4) shows that this involves a very large measure of uncertainty. Assuming that the Inland Revenue can collect tax on every single £ of personal income other than the BIs, the maximum tax base becomes £239,000 million. At the other extreme, assuming retention of mortgage interest and all the private pension tax reliefs, it becomes £191,000 million. Stage (5) shows the tax rates necessary to fund the net cost of the programme, according to which tax base is thought most likely. The answer lies somewhere between 68 and 86 percent. In practice it would be so difficult for the Inland Revenue to raise a tax at any of these rates on virtually all income other than the BIs, that it seems wise to assume a minimum tax rate of 70 percent, bearing in mind that it could be much higher.

Thus the poverty trap would be institutionalised and the whole population caught in a stunted version of Edward Bellamy's Utopian fantasy of the year 2000, quoted by Milton Friedman in *Free to Choose:*

> No man any more has any care for the morrow, either for himself or his children, for the nation guarantees the nurture, education, and comfortable maintenance of every citizen from the cradle to the grave.
> (*Looking Backward*, Edward Bellamy 1887, New York, Modern Library 1917, page 70)

Who gains and who loses?

A full BI is highly redistributive from rich to poor, from full-time workers to part-time workers, and from families without to families with dependent children. Yet the full BI of £60 a week assumed here is not particularly generous to people who cannot work. Despite the high tax rate, poverty would remain because there is no housing benefit. In order to prevent housing poverty, there would have to be large-scale construction of readily available, subsidised housing at a rent of £20 a week or less. Nor is the system cost efficient, it is too inflexible. Many people would receive net benefit who did not need it, and because of the high tax rate the incentive to do paid work in the formal economy would be seriously at risk.

Figure 9.1 illustrates those effects, using data from Appendix 2. The figures refer to net incomes, because there would be no means-tested benefits. The scale of change is enormous. Only a few people would be within £10 of their current net incomes. A single person earning £52,000 a year would lose over £10,000 a year, or £200 a week, before taking into account loss of private pension tax reliefs. Even on earnings of £500 a week, the weekly loss is £110.

Figure 9.1: Full BI, net incomes, March 1986

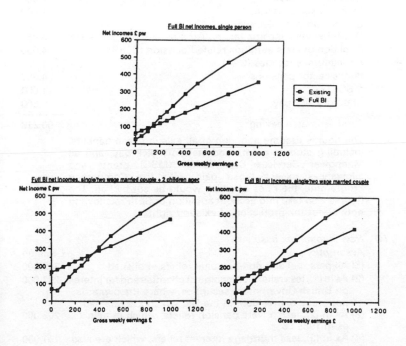

Table 9.4: Costing full Basic Income, 1985-86

(1)	Cost of the basic incomes	£ million
	43,054,900 adults @ £60 a week	134,332
	3,610,400 children @ £20 a week	3,754
	4,093,700 children @ £25 a week	5,322
	4,058,200 children @ £32 a week	6,753
	1,800,700 young people @ £44 a week	4,121
	Disability costs allowance	4,200
	Administration	500
	Residual cash and care benefits	200
	Total cost of BIs	**159,182**

(2) *Cost of abolishing income tax, employees' NI contributions and advance corporation tax*
£64,707 million

(3)	Savings on existing public expenditure	£ million
	Social security benefits, excluding administration	40,969
	Maintenance element of student grants	717
	Free school meals	270
	MSC grants and allowances	1,156
	Cost of rate rebates	1,550
	Personal social services	1,000
	Savings on administration:	
	DHSS benefits, income tax, housing benefit and some MSC	3,057
	Abolition of state earnings related pension (SERPS)	4,000
	Agricultural subsidies (CAP)	1,857
	Public sector pensions	4,082
	MSC	1,000
	Statutory sick pay	560
	Total estimated savings	**60,218**

The figures assume abolition of all existing cash benefits, including student grants and statutory sick pay, and all Manpower Services Commission (MSC) grants and allowances except those paid with the Community Programme, the rates of which would be cut by half. The figures also take into account abolition of SERPS, allowing nothing for the protection of existing rights.

(4) *New income tax base*
Assumptions   £ million
(1) All personal and non-personal reliefs abolished   239,000
(2) As in (1), less reliefs for income of charities and for interest 237,000
    on British Government securities, where the owner is
    not ordinarily resident in the UK, which are retained
(3) As in (2), less private pension reliefs, which remain   206,000
    as in 1985-86
(4) As in (3), less mortgage interest reliefs, which are also 191,000
    retained

(5) Rate of the new income tax or BI contribution

$$t = \frac{159.18 + 64.71 - 60.22}{239} = 68\%$$

$$t = \frac{159.18 + 64.71 - 60.22}{237} = 69\%$$

$$t = \frac{159.18 + 64.71 - 60.22}{206} = 79\%$$

$$t = \frac{159.18 + 64.71 - 60.22}{191} = 86\%$$

10

Negative income tax

Negative income tax tries to overcome the problem of excessive cost associated with BI, by reducing the amount of benefit leakage to people with incomes above the poverty line. One way to do this is by using benefit withdrawal rates below the break-even levels that are higher than the rates of positive taxation above them. This produces the "kinked" net income curve in Figure 8.5. Another way is by making the family, or household, the unit of assessment, instead of the individual. In Britain this could mean resurrection of the household means test. A third way is by keeping the guarantee levels below the poverty line, in which case the NIT is only partial, and is unlikely to replace all existing benefits.

NIT experiments in North America

As with BI there is no country that operates a negative income tax. But the labour market and family stability effects of NIT were tested in a series of pilot projects in the United States and Canada (see Table 10.1). The US experiments reflected growing concern during the 1960s that "the mushrooming welfare system was an ill-coordinated and inefficient means for helping the poor" (SRI International 1983, page 3). There is no equivalent of child benefit in the United States, and the high tax rates (nominally between 76 and 100 percent) imposed on AFDC and AFDC-U families were thought to discourage work effort and perpetuate welfare dependency. Likewise the fact that entitlement to welfare was restricted to lone-parent families and to families where the father was unemployed was thought to encourage family breakdown and idleness.

The purpose of the US experiments was to ascertain the work incentive effects of extending an income guarantee to able-bodied heads of low income, two-parent working families. Any family whose income during the accounting period came to less than the appropriate guaranteed amount would have it topped up. Guarantee levels representing different proportions of the poverty level were tried out in each of the experiments and the benefit withdrawal rates varied between 30 and 80 percent. Of these experiments by far the largest and most influential was the Seattle-Denver experiment (SIME-DIME), which lasted from 1970 to 78 and which also examined the effects of the guarantee on marital stability. A similar experiment in Canada, known as the Canadian Basic Annual Income Experiment, or Mincome Manitoba, was conducted between 1975 and 1978. All the experiments are important, not just for the conclusions drawn regarding work incentives and family stability, but also for the light they throw on the administrative complexities of a NIT.

Table 10.1: US negative income tax experiments

Title of experiment	Date	Sample size (families)	Family types	Races	Guarantee levels $[1]	Tax rates[2] %	Years on program
New Jersey	1968-72	1,357	Mainly dual-headed families	White, black, Spanish speaking	1,650 2.457 3,300 4,125	30,50,80	3
Rural	1969-73	809	Dual & single-headed families	White, black	1,741 2,612 3,482	30,50,70	3
Gary	1971-75	1,780	Dual & single-headed families	Black	3,300 4,300	40,60	3
Seattle/ Denver (SIME/DIME)	1970-78	2,042 2,758	Dual & single headed-families	White, black, chicanos	3,800 4,800 5,600	50,70,80[3]	3,5,20

Notes: (1) Family of four. The New Jersey figures refer to year 1968. Rural to 1969. Gary to 1971 and Seattle/Denver to 1971.
(2) Average.
(3) With average rates of decline of zero and 0.25/$1,000.
Source: Derived from SRI International 1983, Volume 1, Table 1.1.

Negative income tax and basic income: points of resemblance

NIT and BI are similar in a number of respects, of which the most important is the basis of entitlement, which becomes citizenship (or legal residence) and need, instead of contribution record and contingency. Both involve abolition of NI contributions and all earnings restrictions. Usually the NIT is payable to any assessment unit where the combined income of all its members is less than the guaranteed minimum income (GMI). If the GMI is tied to a work test, then suitable work or training is provided. Either way a single Government agency should be responsible for payment of net benefit or collection of net tax.

Negative income tax and basic income: main differences

Some economists take the view that there is no difference between NIT and basic income. In *Public Finance,* Prest and Barr were categorical:

> What we have shown is that there is an *exact equivalence* between social dividend schemes and negative income taxes. Such schemes have been given a variety of other names such as minimum income guarantees, reverse income tax, and guaranteed income schemes. Analytically, they are all identical...All have three crucial parameters, the size of the payment to an individual with no other income...the breakdown level of income at which an individual's net tax liability is zero...and the tax structure applied to any income which the individual receives. In the case of a system with a single tax rate...any two of these parameters *completely* characterise the scheme.
> (Prest and Barr 1986, page 382, my emphasis)

This conclusion seems to stem from the very simplified model used by Prest and Barr, which refers only to a single person and takes no account of administration. Although it is correct to say that NIT and BI are both governed by the same "crucial parameters", those parameters do not "completely characterise" the different schemes, because the administration is different and because NIT takes the family as the assessment unit whereas BI takes the individual. It is also misleading to assume a single rate of tax, since more than one tax rate, or more accurately a benefit withdrawal rate below the break-even point that is higher than the rate of positive taxation above it, is one of the main characteristics of NIT.

Some of the most significant differences between NIT and BI derive from the different importance attached by different system designers to the three parameters. With NIT, which tends to be the right-wing solution, the main priority is to hold down costs, and the key variable is the break-even level. Keeping the break-even level at its pre-NIT level (or below it) is reckoned to be more important than having a guarantee level at the poverty line (however defined), and more important than avoiding a "kinked" tax curve, even though the result may be to leave some people in poverty, and despite the disincentive effects of high benefit withdrawal rates. At the other extreme, for advocates of full BI, the key variable is the income guarantee and the emphasis is on benefit adequacy. Much less attention is paid to the break-even level, indeed some people would regard a higher break-even level as a positive advantage, since the result would be increased redistribution from rich to poor. Thus almost by definition a system with an income guarantee at the poverty line and a single rate of tax is a BI system, not a negative income tax, and *vice versa.*

"No radical welfare reform plan can be devised," wrote Martin Anderson in *Welfare, "* that will simultaneously yield minimum levels of welfare benefits, financial incentives to work and an overall cost to the taxpayers that are politically acceptable" (Anderson 1978, page 133). Within the integration camp NIT and BI represent two distinct answers to this conflict of interests, with a partial NIT at one end of the spectrum and full BI at the other.

Table 10.2: Distinctive features of a full negative income tax

> 1. The income guarantee replaces all existing benefits, but not all income tax reliefs.
> 2. The unit of assessment is the nuclear or extended family, or the household.
> 3. The rate of benefit withdrawal below the break-even level is generally higher than the rate of positive income tax above it.
> 4. The income guarantee is credited after it has been adjusted for changes in the income of the different family members.
> 5. The income guarantee takes into account economies of scale.
> 6. The income guarantee is generally credited to the head of the family, or chief breadwinner.

Professor James Meade drew attention to some of the dissimilarities between BI (which he referred to as social dividend) and NIT in his 1972 paper *Poverty in the Welfare State*, although he did not mention the unit of assessment, which he seems to have assumed to be the family throughout (Meade 1972). Although the redistributive effects of BI and NIT can in theory be identical, this happens only in the unlikely event that the GMIs are the same, that the benefit withdrawal/tax rates are the same, that the unit of assessment is the same, that benefit take-up (despite different administrative systems) is the same, and that the post-NIT tax thresholds are raised to the break-even levels at which entitlement to negative tax is phased out – point A in Figure 8.5.

The model used by Prest and Barr, and reproduced in Figure 10.1, is a standard NIT model. Point A, representing both the tax threshold and the tax break-even point, is taken to be £2,000 a year and the tax rate is assumed to be 30 percent. Under the existing system each single person is allowed to earn OA, or £2,000, before being liable to tax. With a NIT he continues to pay tax at 30 percent on the excess of his income above the guarantee level, but if his income falls below £2,000 he receives either 30 or 50 percent of the shortfall (line GA or the dotted line respectively). Since with NIT (unlike BI) there is nothing in principle against regressive tax schedules, the benefit withdrawal rate below A can be higher than the tax rate above it. Indeed the higher the rate of benefit with-

Figure 10.1: Prest and Barr's NIT

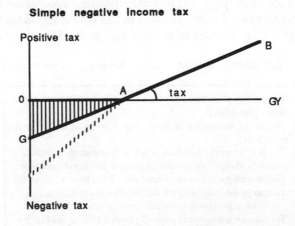

Simple negative income tax

Source: *Public Finance*, Prest and Barr, Weidenfeld & Nicolson 1986, page 381.

drawal the higher the maximum amount of benefit that can be paid without affecting the break-even level. Thus with a 50 percent rate of benefit withdrawal the income guarantee becomes £1,000, whereas with a 30 percent rate of benefit withdrawal it is only £600.

As Prest and Barr point out, it makes no difference in terms of net incomes whether you pay someone on a low income 30 percent of the shortfall of their income below £2,000 (the NIT approach) or pay everybody £600 and tax all their other income at 30 percent (the BI approach). Similarly it makes no difference whether you pay people on low incomes 50 percent of the shortfall, or pay everybody £1,000 and tax all other income at 50 percent. In each case the first is the NIT approach and the second the BI approach, and both look identical.

But the model used by Prest and Barr is only a partial NIT. With either option the individuals involved are left in poverty, since they need a minimum of £2,000, not some percentage of it. However if the GMI were raised to £2,000, then the tax threshold would have to be raised to £4,000 assuming a 50 percent benefit withdrawal rate, and to £6,666 if the rate of withdrawal is to be 30 percent. If it were less, people in receipt of GMI would be better off than people with gross incomes above the tax threshold but below the break-even level.

It is at this point that NIT and BIT start to diverge.

First main difference: NIT is less redistributive from rich to poor

BI uses proportionate or progressive marginal tax rates, whereas the NIT marginal tax rate goes down rather than up. The preference for "kinked line" tax schedules is only partly in order to reduce costs. Although the terms benefit withdrawal rate and income tax rate are used interchangeably, this is not strictly accurate. Having one's benefit reduced is not at all the same as paying tax to finance someone else's benefit, and most NIT advocates prefer to keep the distinction. Colin Clark made the point in *Poverty before Politics:*

> There may also be some complaints about the supposed comparison between the 50 per cent maximum marginal rate of taxation proposed for higher incomes and the 70 per cent tax on additional earnings of low-income families. But people who reason in this manner do not see the fundamental

143

difference between a tax imposed on a person's own earnings and a partial withdrawal of benefit from those claiming to live on other people's earnings.
(Colin Clark 1977, page 37)

Because of the importance attached by NIT advocates to keeping down the rate of tax paid by the bulk of the population, many NIT proposals, for instance those of Milton Friedman, go further and recommend an income guarantee that is below the poverty line. In *Free to Choose* the Friedmans proposed a NIT at 50 percent of the poverty line, with a 50 percent withdrawal rate, on the grounds that 50 percent would be just about low enough to preserve some work incentive. They rejected suggestions that the withdrawal rate should be reduced and the break-even point allowed to go higher, on the grounds that this would add to the number of people entitled to negative tax payments and would increase the cost of the scheme. Despite the theoretical merits of a move to negative income tax, they argued against it unless the GMIs were below many existing welfare scales, as well as replacing all existing benefits:

> This (negative income tax) is a fine dream, but unfortunately it has no chance whatsoever of being enacted at present. Three Presidents – Presidents Nixon, Ford, and Carter – have considered or recommended a program including elements of a negative income tax. In each case political pressures have led them to offer the program as an addition to many existing programs, rather than as a substitute for them. In each case the subsidy rate was so high that the program gave little if any incentive to recipients to earn income. These misshapen programs would have made the whole system worse, not better. Despite our having been the first to have proposed a negative income tax as a replacement for our present welfare system, one of us testified before Congress against the version that President Nixon offered as the Family Assistance Plan.
> (Friedman 1981, page 155)

With NIT the curve of net income starts off almost flat and falls behind net income from BI, but above the break-even level it shoots ahead. Although NIT is less redistributive from rich to poor than BI, a full NIT could still be very much more redistributive than the existing system.

Second main difference: NIT uses a family or household means test, BI takes the individual

Economists have an annoying habit of assuming (without saying so) that money within the family flows equitably between its different members as though guided by an invisible hand, hence that living standards within families are homogeneous. This may be logically convenient, but is often not true. On the contrary there is reason to suppose that mal-distribution of income *within* families is a common cause of poverty. The repercussions of NIT on the living standards of low income families, especially of the individuals within those families, would depend on the unit of assessment, and on the member (or members) of the assessment unit to whom the benefit cheques were payable.

With BI the situation is clear-cut. The assessment unit is the individual, and the BI is credited to each family member, although the child credits would normally be drawn by the mother. With NIT the assessment unit can be the nuclear family, the extended family, or the household, but is seldom if ever the individual. With NIT everything therefore depends on the detail of the regulations, which are seldom spelt out. Many people under-estimate the importance of who gets the benefit. In a report on *Negative Income Tax* published in 1974, the OECD summarised the accepted position:

> There is a general agreement that the family should be the basic unit of any NIT plan, as the extent of any individual's economic welfare depends on the joint income of the economic unit to which he belongs. If the individual members of a family are allowed to file separate tax returns, some members may qualify for a net benefit whereas, when taken as a unit, the family's joint income would be deemed adequate. *The family is probably the closest approximation to an ideal welfare unit.* (OECD 1974, page 29, my emphasis)

Yet the main finding from a series of enquiries in the UK and Australia is that money received by individual family members is not necessarily shared with other members of the immediate family. Mothers and children in low income families, and more particularly the mothers, tend to have lower living standards than the male breadwinners. Even in families where the husband hands over the "whole wage" to his wife, he still keeps some personal spending money (Pahl 1980, 1983, 1984, 1986; Edwards 1984). That is one reason why child benefit is so popular. In families where the mother cannot rely on money from the father, child benefit may be the only way she can keep the family going. Paying extra benefit to the father, or charging him less tax, is generally recognised to be a less effective way of combating family poverty than a cash benefit paid to the person who has day to day responsibility for the care of the children, who is usually the mother.

There is also evidence to suggest a correlation between money distribution within the family and marriage breakdown. In a series of studies in the UK, between a fifth and a third of women whose marriages had broken down, and who were living on supplementary benefit, are reported as saying that they were "better off" on SB than when living with their husbands. In one study most of the women had come from households where the men were earning wages well above SB levels, therefore the poverty of the wives was due solely to non-transference of money within the family (DHSS 1973). That is one reason why organisations in Britain concerned with child welfare have consistently recommended payment of child benefit to the mother.

Some NIT proposals take the household as the assessment unit. According to SIME-DIME rules, if two family units shared a household (for instance where an older daughter with her own child lived with the primary family) the family size index of each family unit was adjusted downwards. This was in order to "reflect the presumption that living expenses for families sharing a household would be lower than for families living separately" (Christophersen

Table 10.3: SIME/DIME support levels adjusted for family size*

Family size	Family size index	Annual income guarantee		
		$3,800	$4,800	$5,600
		$	$	$
1	—	1,000	1,000	1,000
2	0.62	2,356	2,976	3,472
3	0.83	3,154	3,984	4,648
4	1.00	3,800	4,800	5,600
5	1.12	4,256	5,376	6,272
6	1.23	4,674	5,904	6,888
7	1.32	5,016	6,336	7,392
8	1.38	5,244	6,624	7,728

* 1970 dollars

Source: *Final Report of the Seattle-Denver Income Maintenance Experiment, Volume 2: Administration,* Gary Christophersen, Mathematica Policy Research May 1983, Table IV-1.

1983, page 41). Table 10.3 reproduces the income support levels, in 1970 dollars, used in SIME-DIME. Instead of exogenous, age-related BIs, the guarantee allows for economies of scale. There is nothing extra for household members beyond eight.

Who gets the benefit cheque is as important to the recipients as the assessment unit. The SIME-DIME benefit cheque was made payable to both parents as joint heads of household, but with many NIT proposals it goes to the "main breadwinner". In the words of the OECD again:

> A problem which is related to the definition of a family unit is that of deciding to which members of the family unit the NIT allowances or credits should be paid, particularly the child allowances or credit. From the administrative and incentive viewpoint it is preferable to have these benefits paid to the main wage earner – usually the father. The father will generally be the recipient of the tax allowances relating to the family and, if these are replaced by child allowances or credits which are paid to the mother, his take-home pay may be adversely affected. Also it is administratively more convenient to pay the whole of the NIT benefits to one member of the family. Against this is the argument that, on social grounds, it is preferable to pay these benefits to the mother, who is the person usually most directly responsible for the welfare of the children. (OECD 1974, page 31)

If a NIT were introduced in the UK it would almost certainly involve a redistribution of money from mothers to fathers (purse to wallet), thereby undoing the progress made towards "incomes for wives" since World War 2. It could also signal a return to the household means test and smaller *de facto* benefit payments than with the existing social security arrangements or with BI, even if the guarantee levels were ostensibly the same.

Table 10.4 compares the impact of a NIT and a BI on income distribution *within* the family. In each case the GMI is assumed to be £110 a week, and in each case the benefit withdrawal/ tax rate is 50 percent. These assumptions are improbable but they help to isolate the distributional effects of each system. With NIT it is assumed that benefit is paid to the male head of household, and that the new tax threshold is £220 (ie the tax break-even level). This figure is roughly equivalent (in relation to average earnings) to the UK tax threshold for a two-child family during the early 1950s.

Table 10.4: Income distribution within the family, NIT and BI compared, £ week.
Married couple with son aged 13, daughter aged 16.

Family member	Earnings	Net income	
		NIT	BI
Father	0	110	40
Mother	0	0	40
Son	0	0	10 (paid to mother)
Daughter	0	0	20
		110	110
Father	0	85	40
Mother	50	50	65
Son	0	0	10 (paid to mother)
Daughter	0	0	20
		135	135
Father	0	0	40
Mother	250	235	165
Son	0	0	10 (paid to mother)
Daughter	20	10	30
		245	245
Father	250	235	165
Mother	50	25	65
Son	0	0	10 (paid to mother)
Daughter	20	10	30
		270	270

Assumptions: Guarantees £110 pw, 50% withdrawal rate and tax rate, break-even points £220.

The table shows that the effects of NIT need not always be to the advantage of the family head, whose benefit income could go up and down like a yo-yo. The example in Table 10.4 assumes a small, nuclear family, but if Grandma joined the household, the situation could change dramatically. With some schemes, if Grandma's pension pushed household income above the GMI (which would be increased a little on account of Grandma's presence), then Dad would quickly find himself with nothing to call his own. Likewise if a lone mother moved in with her own parents, she would forfeit her right to separate assessment.

Third main difference: NIT is less accessible and more difficult to administer

This point was emphasised by Meade in 1972. Social dividend (or BI) would be credited automatically each week, or month, and it would then be up to the tax authorities to extract revenue according to the other income of the citizens concerned. But with NIT a single tax authority has to pay out negative tax, or levy positive income tax, according to the exact amount by which the income of each tax/benefit unit falls below or above the predetermined level. This severely reduces the efficacy of the income guarantee as a tool for preventing poverty, because, as Meade explained:

> With the Social Dividend schemes a minimum-standard allowance is paid out weekly to everybody rich or poor through the Post Office or other similar administrative arrangements; and it is then the job of the tax authorities to extract revenue according to the level of the other income of the citizens concerned. With the Negative Income Tax... a single tax authority has to pay out in income subsidy, or to levy in income tax, a given net amount according as the citizen's income falls below or above a pre-determined level. The Social Dividend type of administrative arrangement involves a much larger gross turnover of funds. . .In spite of this, however, the Social Dividend type of administrative arrangement is, in my opinion, to be preferred. Citizens' needs and cash receipts may vary from week to week; and with self-employed, or part-time workers, or casual workers, or persons with small incomes from property, it may be very difficult to make a prompt weekly adjustment of any net income subsidy or tax under an income-tax administrative machine. With the Social Dividend type of arrangement everyone is guaranteed the minimum-standard income every week; there is no problem of people not taking up their rights, and the means-tested adjustment is then carried out solely by the taxation of their other income through the accepted machinery of the income tax authorities on a basis which does not require the same degree of precise, prompt response to meet a sudden or irregular change of income flow.
> (Meade 1972, pages 311-313)

Today as a result of computers, even the "larger gross turnover of funds" to which Meade drew attention need not be a problem.

Benign churning, as we have seen, has been rendered harmless. It is malignant churning that causes problems.

The only major administrative difficulty with BI is the taxation of all other income. NIT is much more complex. The designers of the US experiments left it to individual assessment units to file their returns within the appointed period, or forfeit entitlement. But a national programme that put the onus for claiming onto the citizen would be unlikely to reach all those in need. In order to ensure full and accurate coverage, a NIT system would require computer files showing the income and family composition of every assessment unit throughout the country and throughout the whole of the current accounting period. Assuming cumulative liability there would have to be re-assessments at the end of each accounting period, to recoup money over-paid and to make good under-payments.

The need for constant re-assessment would not only reduce the efficacy of NIT as a method of poverty prevention, it would also add to the costs of administration, to the likelihood of errors, and to the opportunities for fraud. With a BI the income-test is through the new income tax, which could operate approximately as at present. With NIT the new "integrated" tax/benefit authority would have to carry out two distinct functions. The first would be that of tax collection, and the second would resemble the most labour-intensive parts of the existing social security system, but on a much more grandiose scale, because it would subsume existing NI as well as supplementary benefits. Experience during the NIT experiments in North America quickly highlighted the administrative complexities involved in the definition of apparently straight-forward concepts like "the family", or "family income".

Perhaps the best way to grasp the complexity of a NIT is by looking at the administration of SIME-DIME. The SIME-DIME families were selected largely on account of their extreme poverty, indeed the researchers had difficulty in contacting families who were poor enough to meet the criteria laid down. The families were nevertheless expected to fill in each month an *Income Report Form* (IRF) running to seven pages. On the last working day of each month a blank IRF was sent to each family, together with any payment due for the previous filing period. The IRF was stamped with the dates of the period to be covered and the date by which it had to be returned, which was within fourteen days. If the IRF was submitted on time, the family would receive the benefit cheque on the regularly scheduled payment date. If the IRF was submitted within two weeks of the due date, payment would be delayed by two weeks. If the return was more than two weeks late, the family forfeited their benefit (Christophersen 1983, Chapter VI).

Given that NIT is supposed to reach out to the poorest families, many of whom have difficulties with reading and writing, it is inconceivable that those forms were filled in accurately. The information required includes all changes in "family" composition during the relevant period, full details of all earnings by every "family" member (including pay stubs and hours worked), full details of any other income received during the previous month (including income from prizes, inheritances, earnings of children under sixteen and odd jobs), all childcare and medical expenses, and full details of income from business or self-employment, including proceeds from the sale of any "property, buildings, equipment, stocks or bonds".

Effects of negative income tax on work incentives

In theory NIT is more cost-efficient than BI. It cuts costs by keeping down the break-even level and by taking the family or household instead of the individual as the assessment unit. But there are only two ways to keep down the break-even level. Either the guarantee levels must be below the poverty line, or the benefit withdrawal rate must be high.

This is the dilemma noted by Milton Friedman, Martin Anderson and others. The most obvious effects of high benefit withdrawal rates are to reduce work incentives and discourage small savings. The effect of taking the family or household as the unit of assessment is to encourage family break-up and the formation of small households, because that is the only way for individuals to retain, or acquire, some sort of independence. There is also a danger of abuse, both by employers seeking to save on wages and by claimants seeking to maximise their benefits.

The extent to which a NIT would discourage self-reliance (within the regular economy) depends on the guarantee levels, the rate of benefit withdrawal, the threshold for positive tax, the unit of assessment and the member(s) of the assessment unit to whom the benefit is payable. In Britain benefit withdrawal rates of between 70 percent and 100 percent have been suggested. A withdrawal rate of 100 percent, as recommended by Polanyi, Seldon and Shonfield in 1971, reduces the number of people to whom benefit is payable, but has maximum disincentive impact on those who are affected. A 90 percent withdrawal rate, as recommended by the Adam Smith

Institute (ASI 1984), is fractionally better, but still takes insufficient account of the disutilities of work. A withdrawal rate of 70 per cent, as proposed by Professor Patrick Minford (Minford *et al*.1983, 1984, 1985) is more expensive in the first instance, but the impact on incentives is much less harsh.

As already noted, the only way to have a GMI that is adequate and avoids trapping unacceptably high proportions of families with children and pensioners in a NIT-style poverty trap is by using a taper of at least 90 percent. This is because of the large numbers of pensioners and families with children whose original incomes are either below or only slightly above the likely GMI levels. Minford tries to overcome this problem by retaining child benefit, and by imposing a 100 percent NIT withdrawal rate on families with children. His pensioners are not even eligible for NIT. The proposals by the Institute for Fiscal Studies (IFS 1984) would have left about a third of families with children subject to marginal tax rates of above 80 percent, and almost all pensioners with marginal tax rates of 55 percent. The SDP proposals, discussed in Chapter 15, would have similar effects.

Some NIT schemes produce marginal tax rates of over 100 percent, even though the taper is below 100 percent. This happens if the tax threshold is below the break-even level. Table 10.5 assumes a GMI of £100 a week, a taper of 70 percent and a 40 percent starting rate of tax. Where the tax threshold is also £100, the marginal tax rate goes up to 110 percent, just as it used to with family income supplement, because tax is being charged at the same time as benefit is being withdrawn. In order to ensure that the

Table 10.5: NIT, the notch problem.
Married man with two children. Guarantee £100, benefit withdrawal rate 70%, income tax rate 40%.

Gross earnings	NIT	Tax threshold £100		Tax threshold £142.85	
		IT	Net Y	IT	Net Y
£	£	£	£	£	£
0.00	100.00	0.00	100.00	0.00	100.00
50.00	65.00	0.00	115.00	0.00	115.00
100.00	30.00	0.00	130.00	0.00	130.00
120.00	16.00	8.00	128.00	0.00	136.00
140.00	2.00	16.00	126.00	0.00	142.00
145.00	0.00	18.00	127.00	0.86	144.14
150.00	0.00	20.00	130.00	2.86	147.14

marginal tax rate never exceeds 70 percent, the tax threshold has to be £142.85.

Similar effects would occur if a partial NIT did not replace all existing benefits. In Britain, for instance, there would be problems if free school meals for low income families were retained, unless the entitlement ceilings were above the NIT break-even level.

Family stability

One of the most worrying characteristics of negative income tax is its impact on family life. Unlike BI, NIT payments are not exogenous. They are reserved for the poor and they would affect low income families with children disproportionately. Most of the working families affected would be dependent on a single wage, and although lone parents would be disproportionately affected, many families with young children would be at risk. Appendix 5 shows that in 1985 there were over 7 times as many two-parent families as one-parent families earning less than £150 a week, and most of them were dependent on a single wage. In many countries a new pattern is emerging in the life cycle. In Britain it starts with the "Dinkys",[1] who until August 1988 were able to claim mortgage interest tax relief on two times £30,000. On marriage they forfeit half the mortgage interest tax relief, and on arrival of the first child the wife gives up paid work. There follows a period of acute financial stress before the wife is able to return to paid work. The families affected in this way are not just the "traditional poor", they include middle grade professionals, including many civil servants. With a NIT, they and their children would be dragged into dependence on poverty relief, and for many of the children the experience would be repeated when they in turn became parents. Although only 30 percent of families might be affected at any one time, far more would be affected over the life cycle.

The children in these families would be brought up in an atmosphere of frustration and disrespect for the law. Often the only way for the family to take a holiday would be by breaking the law – or for the parents to split up. Almost all NIT schemes pay bonuses for marriage break-up, because families who split up qualify for independent benefit status (and more benefit) than families who stay together.

When the results of SIME-DIME were published, people were shocked at its destabilising effects on family life. Marital dissolution rates went up by over 40 percent for blacks and whites and by up to 19 percent for Chicanos. As a result of marriage break-up and remarriage (counting *de facto* marriages on the same basis as legal marriages), 12,000 new family units were created out of the original 4,800 units, all during the period of the experiment (Christophersen 1983, page 39). Having warned the reader against the dangers of extrapolating the effects of SIME/DIME for a national programme, the analysts concluded that any NIT programme would have similar, though less pronounced, effects:

> Given the magnitude of these findings, it is unlikely that any national NIT program would be neutral with respect to marital stability. Although the effects of a national NIT program are unlikely to be as dramatic as the experimental effects, the potential for such effects must not be ignored.
> (SRI International 1983, page 365)

This conclusion was one reason why NIT got too hot to handle. Politicians were terrified that any sort of income guarantee (including BI as well as NIT) would undermine the traditional family.

Any tax/benefit system that treats spouses who stay together less favourably than those who live apart encourages marriage break-up. It already happens in the UK, and the British experience is by no means unique. When SIME-DIME was designed there was no generally accepted theory as to how a NIT should or would affect family composition (SRI International 1983, page 17). As it turned out, the chosen design loaded all the dice in favour of marriage break-up and a string of sexual partners, which is exactly what occurred. The amount paid to an enrolled family unit depended on the combined "net income" of all members of that unit (Christophersen 1983, page 163), and the guarantee levels had more to do with alleged economies of scale than with individual needs and aspirations. On the other hand there was nothing in the regulations to stop individual family members from setting up their own households. By doing so they counted as independent assessment units, but the award for single people was disproportionately low, hence the incentive to find a new partner. The figures are set out in Table 10.2: $1,000 for a single-member family, compared with $2,356, $2,976 or $3,472, for two-member families, depending on the support level.

The following excerpt describes the detail of the SIME/DIME regulations:

To observe what family unit changes would occur under national program conditions, individuals who were originally enrolled in the experiment were allowed to maintain their eligibility if they left the original family unit. Furthermore, if the individuals formed their own family units, they were allowed to transfer their eligibility to other individuals even if the other individuals were not previously enrolled in the experiment. For example, if an individual enrolled in family unit No. 1 left the original family and acquired a spouse, family unit No. 2 would have been created. If during the course of the experiment, family unit No. 2 dissolved and both spouses acquired new spouses, family units No. 3 and No. 4 would be created. The originally enrolled members would have created units 2 and 3 because of their ability to maintain eligibility after leaving the original unit...All the units, when active, were eligible to receive the same treatment as the originally enrolled family unit.

This ability to subdivide and create new family units was limited by eligibility waiting periods. For example, if an enrolled individual was married, the new spouse would be eligible to participate in the experiment 1 month later. If an enrollee decided to cohabit, the waiting period for eligibility was 3 months after establishing residence by affidavit. Additionally, the couple had to remain together at least 6 months for the newly acquired spouse to retain eligibility if they split up. Even with these waiting periods, 12,000 new family units were created during the experiment from the 4,800 original families.
(Christophersen 1983, page 39)

It is unlikely that all NIT systems would have as damaging effects on family life as SIME-DIME. An obvious improvement would be to make the guarantee amounts the same for all adults, regardless of marital status. Nevertheless it would be extremely difficult to design a NIT that was as "family-friendly" as an individually assessed BI.

Part 3

PARTIAL INTEGRATION

11

Hybrid schemes

As yet we have looked only at full basic income and full negative income tax, in other words at systems where the income guarantees are sufficiently generous to enable all other state-financed cash benefits to be abolished. Full BI can be ruled out on grounds of expense, and a big question mark put over the alleged greater cost-effectiveness of NIT, but there is still the possibility that either or both might be useful in small doses. A partial BI, combined with a partial NIT, or with elements of the existing system, might well be a step forward compared with present arrangements.

This approach, bringing together elements of several different systems, is the logic behind a number of proposals in the UK and elsewhere, all of which aim to combine the simplicity and effectiveness of BI with the lesser costs of a NIT, or *vice versa*. I know of no one who has taken the trouble to calculate the costs and redistributive effects of integrated reform options in detail and who has not concluded that one system on its own cannot meet all requirements. Instead they end up trying to mesh together the advantages of several systems, and to avoid the disadvantages. Even proposals publicised under one or other brand name tend to include foreign elements. Patrick Minford's proposals for a NIT, discussed in Chapter 13, retain a non-withdrawable child benefit, and all Basic Income Guarantee schemes retain income-tested housing benefit.

In the next chapters four such hybrid schemes will be examined. Afterwards we shall look at the core issues that divide them, and compare their effects in terms of income redistribution and work incentives. Despite differences, all the schemes' designers are basically trying to do the same thing. They are all searching for a

159

way out of the George Gilder dilemma (Gilder 1982), a solution that will prevent poverty without undermining wealth creation.

Summary of the basic ingredients

To some extent the *pros* and *cons* of BI, NIT and the existing system are in the eye of the beholder. Those with an aversion to universal benefits automatically dislike BI, and those with an aversion to anything that smacks of the means-test automatically dislike NIT. Those with bitter experiences of the existing system may wish to throw it out entirely, whereas others, who have benefited from it, may wonder what all the fuss is about. On close inspection the results of any particular system may not be those expected. An unconditional BI that allowed people to take whatever work was available might be better for wealth creation than a conditional NIT that unleashed miles of red tape in order to catch the solitary "scrounger". The purpose of the analysis that follows is to get beyond partisanship, and find a solution that capitalises on the advantages of each system and minimises the disadvantages.

Take first the basic ingredients, and look again at the main differences between them:

(1) **A full basic income** has the advantages of simplicity, ease of access, marriage and sex neutrality, improved labour market flexibility, and the removal of all stigma, *but* it is too expensive. In the UK a full BI would require an income tax rate of at least 70 percent. Moreover it is no good hoping that economic growth will resolve the problem, for economic growth leads to higher expectations, and in any case a tax rate of 70 percent is more likely to produce economic decline.

(2) **A full negative income tax** would be difficult to administer, and is poverty relief rather than poverty prevention. Introduction of a NIT in the UK would institutionalise and extend the existing system of means-tested benefits, and halt the trend towards independent tax and benefit units. The number of people subject to high marginal tax rates would go up, especially among pensioners and families with children. *But* the

principle of avoiding benefit leakage is an essential part of any reform package.

(3) **The existing tax and benefit systems** have themselves become an engine of poverty. Marriage is penalised and administration a nightmare. *But* the system has its good points. Child benefit is a partial BI for children, and by international standards, comparatively few people are left with nothing at all. At local level the structures exist to provide a quick, efficient response to need. Those structures need to be improved, not replaced by computers.

Hybrid schemes

The schemes selected for this part of the report have the rare advantage that all were designed to be revenue neutral. They all seek abolition of the contributory principle, but in most other respects they are surprisingly unalike. Nor are these distinctions semantic, as is sometime alleged (Brittan 1987). On the contrary, in terms of income distribution, work incentives and family life, the differences between them are as important as the differences between integrated and dual systems:

(1) **The Liberal Party Tax-Credit proposals.** The tax-credit system designed by Philip Vince for the British Liberal Party aims at full integration, using a mixture of unisex, partial BIs topped up with a *non-earner's credit* reminiscent of Beveridge, and a NIT style *low income credit*. The administrative details are not spelt out, but integration looks improbable. Assessment unit is the individual for the BI, otherwise the family or household.

(2) **Patrick Minford's "Efficient Relief of Poverty"** is costed on the assumption of substantial expenditure cuts in Government spending programmes other than social security. Minford combines privatisation of health, old age pensions and education with a conditional NIT, a "capped" subsistence income (SI), and compulsory workfare. Child benefit retained. Administration complex. Assessment unit as at present. Integration most improbable.

(3) *BIG 1(a)* is a *Basic Income Guarantee (BIG)* strategy with two administrative components, first an individualised, partial BI system operated through a fully automated, fully integrated Transfer Income Account (TIA), and second a locally operated Cash and Care service, operated along traditional lines, and including a new, unified housing benefit. Partial BIs for children and people of working age. Full BIs for pensioners and people with disabilities. Disability costs allowance. Partial integration.

(4) **SDP** *Basic Benefit* **proposals.** The third of three major policy documents published by Britain's Social Democrats, recommended a mixture of non-contributory positional benefits, taxable child benefit, non-transferable non-convertible tax credits and replacement of existing means-tested benefits by a new "unified", income-tested basic benefit. Assessment unit various. Spurious integration.

Method and assumptions

Reference date. First, the schemes will be explained, then compared with the existing tax and benefit systems, and with each other. All the figure-work refers to the financial year 1985-86. Until April 1987 benefits were uprated each November whereas taxes were changed each April. In order to be able compare the effects of the different reform options with the pre- and post-Fowler social security systems, the five-month period between the November 1985 benefit uprating and the start of the new tax year in early April 1986 was chosen as the reference point. The tables and graphs are dated March 1986, that being the latest full month to which they can be applied.

Pre-Fowler and Fowler TA. For the existing system, the benefit figures used refer either to the system operating in 1985-86 (*pre-Fowler*), or to the illustrative figures in the Technical Annex to the December 1985 Social Security White Paper (DHSS Dec 1985). The latter are referred to as Fowler TA. The most important changes since the Technical Annex are the increased housing benefit taper for rent rebates (from 60 to 65 percent), and the

162

adjustments made in the April 1988 income support scales as compensation for the 20 percent rates contribution. The figures in the Technical Annex gave no indication of what that compensation would be. For my Fowler TA calculations it was therefore assumed that rates were still being rebated in full. As implemented the reformed system is less generous to householders than was expected. At nil earnings some of the gains in my graphs have turned into losses, and the disposable income curve has become even flatter. These changes strengthen rather than invalidate the conclusions drawn here.

Model family analysis

At this stage the comparison involves six systems: the four reform options, the system in operation in November 1985 and Fowler TA, with the latter very close to the system in operation in 1988. Some of the differences between these systems are unquantifiable. They have more to do with quality of life and human relationships than with money, or they concern the dynamic effects about which nobody can be certain. The differences that can be quantified are measured here using two techniques: first model family analysis, which shows how the incomes of selected hypothetical families would be affected in a series of closely defined circumstances, and second actual family analysis, which shows how the incomes of families participating in the Family Expenditure Survey would have been affected in a given year in the past.

Model family analysis was used in Chapter 4 to illustrate the effects on disposable incomes of the existing tax and benefit systems, pre- and post-Fowler. Those calculations were done using a computer model written by Atkinson, Sutherland and Warren (TAXEXP) and the illustrative rent and rate figures in the November 1985 DHSS *Tax Benefit Model Tables*. Model family analysis is an invaluable tool for showing the effects of change on different client groups. It is also relatively straightforward. All that is necessary is to take a sample of typical families, specify the assumptions made (married or single, number and age of children, housing tenure and housing costs) and compare their incomes before and after any proposed change. Model family analysis will be used in the chapters that follow to show how each new system would work, to compare the redistributive and incentive effects of each new system with those of the existing system (Fowler TA), and afterwards (in Part 4) to make comparisons between all the systems.

To do this, distinctions are drawn between net incomes, disposable incomes and net spending power. *Net incomes* are defined as gross income (earned and unearned) plus non-withdrawable state cash benefits, less income tax and NI contribution (or equivalent). Unearned income includes occupational pensions and retirement annuities. NIT and other withdrawable benefits are excluded because some of them involve assumptions about housing costs, hours worked or work status. *Disposable incomes* are defined as net incomes plus withdrawable benefits, less the assumed rent and rates, but water rates are not deducted. *Net spending power* is defined as disposable income less travel-to-work and childcare costs.

Net spending power is included because of the importance of work expenses for people on low incomes, especially lone parents. It is nevertheless fraught with difficulties. Travel-to-work costs are not shown separately in the Family Expenditure Survey and childcare costs are no easier. For their November 1985 *Tax/Benefit Model Tables*, the DHSS assumed fares to work of £5.95 a week (DHSS Nov 1985). This was described as the average paid by householders using public transport and making at least seven journeys a week. It therefore excludes those who use private vehicles. In practice the costs of getting to work play a big part in the decision whether or not to take a particular job, and people who earn more are able to pay more. The costs assumed here are arbitrary but credible. Extra earnings are assumed to involve extra travel costs, either because the job is further from home or because more journeys have to be made:

Travel to work costs assumed:

Earnings £ pw Travel costs £ pw

Earnings £ pw	Travel costs £ pw
0.00 – 40.00	0.00
60.00 – 100.00	5.00
120.00 – 160.00	10.00
180.00 – 200.00	15.00

The DHSS model tables make no allowance for childcare costs, but in 1985 the average weekly charge reported to the National Association of Childminders was £25 for 40 hours of care and £12.50 for 20 hours (Owen 1986). In the net spending power graphs that follow, work expenses for the lone parent with two children are assumed to be as follows:

Lone parents' assumed travel to work and childcare costs

Earnings £ pw	Travel and childcare costs £ pw
0.00 – 40.00	0.00
60.00 – 100.00	42.50
120.00 – 160.00	47.50
180.00 – 200.00	52.50

The term original income also requires explanation. It is used here to mean gross income from all sources except flat rate (but not earnings related) state benefits, but in the tables and graphs showing pensioner incomes in the existing system, earnings and investment income also have to be excluded. This is because the NI basic pension is withdrawn if earnings exceed £75 a week, and supplementary pension/income support is withdrawn or reduced if the claimant has income from capital above £3,000.

At the end of each new-scheme chapter there is a set of tables showing how disposable incomes for nine model families should be calculated. For reasons of space there are no families with more than two children, and no families with older children, which is somewhat misleading. Fowler's family credit and the SDP's basic benefit are more generous to older children, whereas the other schemes do not differentiate on account of age. If the children in the two-child model families were aged 11-15 instead of 0-10, the family's disposable income could be nearly £10 a week higher with Fowler TA, and £7 higher with the SDP scheme at certain earnings levels than the amounts shown. This would bring Fowler TA closer to the Minford amounts, and it would take the SDP above them, but it would still leave the Vince and BIG schemes looking more generous than the others.

Model family analysis gives only the narrowest glimpse of the total effects of each package, for instance there is no table that shows how people with disabilities would be affected. A glimpse is nevertheless better than nothing, and the tables in Appendix 2 provide the data for the assessment in Chapters 17 and 18. Used carefully, model family analysis can guide the reader to the likely long-term effects of change. If a new system improves the relative position of lower paid families by comparison with unemployed families (replacement ratios), or of two-parent families by comparison with lone parents (symmetry), it is reasonable to assume that (other things being equal) the number of unemployed families will go down and family stability will be strengthened. Conversely if replacement ratios go up, or if there is redistribution in favour of lone-parent families relative to two-parent families, then the unemployed are likely to take longer to find jobs, and there may well be more one-parent families.

The assumptions to the model family analysis are set out in Appendix 2.

Actual family analysis

Despite its attractions, model family analysis has important limitations. It gives an over-simplified impression of the circumstances in which people actually live, and the conclusions drawn from it cannot be extended to cover families whose circumstances are in any way different to those assumed. This is especially true where the figures refer to disposable incomes, which depend on housing costs and housing tenure. It is less true where the figures refer to net incomes, but even here there are differences on account of mortgage interest and superannuation.

Model family analysis can illuminate the structure of a system, but it cannot be used to quantify the overall impact of change, for instance the numbers of gainers and losers. In order to do this we need data showing the actual circumstances of actual families. These are far more diverse than is generally supposed, indeed, as Professor Atkinson and Holly Sutherland have pointed out, figures based on hypothetical examples tend to suggest a preponderance of gainers, and hence a revenue deficit, which may not be correct (Atkinson and Sutherland 1984, page 3). Fortunately the raw data showing the income and expenditure of actual families is available in the tapes of the annual Family Expenditure Survey (FES). Using a computer model it is possible, by simulating any given set of reform proposals, to find out how the net incomes and marginal tax rates of each family participating in the survey would have been affected. The results can then be grossed up to produce estimates for the entire population.

For this report I have used various, specially prepared, versions of a computer model (TAXMOD) written by Professor A.B. Atkinson and Holly Sutherland at the London School of Economics, as part of the ESRC Programme on Taxation Incentives and Distribution. A similar model (IGOTM) is used by Government. The Institute for Fiscal Studies also have a similar model. Although conceptually straightforward, preparation of this type of programme is extremely difficult. It requires detailed knowledge and time-consuming programming of every tax and benefit regulation both before and after any given change, not just the more obvious changes, but also the nitty gritty of administrative regulation that most authors forget to specify. Because it calculates the disposable incomes of real families before and after every change, there is no way of avoiding the complexity of real-life situations. That is part of its value. The technical background to TAXMOD, together with the uses to which it can be put, are described in Appendix 1 and in *Tax-Benefit Models* , edited by A.B. Atkinson and Holly Sutherland, and available from ST/ICERD, London School of Economics (Atkinson and Sutherland 1988).

TAXMOD too has its limitations. It does not measure behavioural change, it requires more administrative detail than most authors provide, policy proposals that involve changes in administrative regulations are hard to programme, and it can only measure changes that directly affect personal incomes and that are accessible through the FES. Minford's proposals could not be put through TAXMOD because some (like privatisation of health, pensions and education) would not show through. With BIG schemes there are similar problems. When BIG schemes are put through TAXMOD, or the rather similar IFS tax-benefit model, they show revenue losses which then have to be set against expenditure savings (for instance on administration) or revenue gains (as a result of extending the tax base) calculated by other means. These problems are discussed in greater detail in Appendix 1. For similar reasons, TAXMOD has to be used with great care when measuring the redistributive effects of change. It can be misleading. Minford's proposals were not put through TAXMOD to find the number of losers and gainers, because the all-important effects of his health and education cuts would not show up. BIG 1(a) was not put through TAXMOD because most of the effects of removing private pension tax reliefs would not show up.

TAXMOD, especially used in conjunction with TAXEXP, is nevertheless an invaluable tool. The two most important messages that come out of TAXMOD are the complexity of real life situations, and the huge scale of change that a move to integration, even partial integration, would involve. Even the Vince scheme, which is only a partial BI, involves redistribution on so large a scale that it could not possibly be implemented within the life-span of a single Parliament.

12

The Liberal Party Tax-Credit Scheme

It is the long-term policy of the British Liberal Party to replace all existing social security benefits with tax-free credits, some withdrawn through the income tax system in the same way as BIs, some withdrawn as other income rises in the same way as NIT, and some conditioned on labour market status as with the existing system. This is a typical hybrid scheme, an attempt to capitalise on the advantages of several approaches and to avoid their disadvantages.

Details of the proposals are to be found in a short booklet written on behalf of the Liberal Party by computer systems manager Philip Vince, and published under the title ...*To each according... Tax Credit – Liberal plan for Tax and Social Security* (Vince 1983). Its aim was to replace the existing "confused and confusing" arrangements with a unified system which would be easier to understand and administer, improve take-up and increase the amount of support available to people on low incomes, especially the lower paid, "take the edge off" the poverty trap, and treat men and women alike, irrespective of marital status (Vince 1983, page 7). It has not been updated. In an article written for the Basic Income Research Group in 1986, Vince described the scheme "as an integrated replacement for personal income tax reliefs and social security benefits " (Vince 1986).

The non-withdrawable *tax credits* (TCs) recommended by Vince are like the convertible tax credits (or partial BIs) proposed in the 1972 Tax-Credit Green Paper. For most people they would be no more than offsets against tax, but for people with no money of their own, or with very little, they would automatically convert into cash benefits. They would then be topped up by the withdrawable credits.

Figure 12.1 : Liberal Tax-Credit proposals

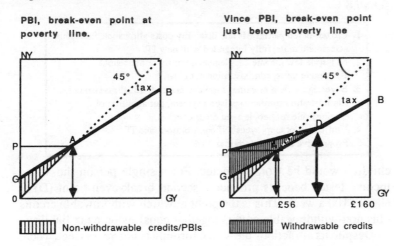

PBI, break-even point at poverty line.

Vince PBI, break-even point just below poverty line

|||||||| Non-withdrawable credits/PBIs |||||||| Withdrawable credits

Returning to our diagram series, we can bring back Figure 8.1 and re-name it partial basic income (PBI). This is the first diagram in Figure 12.1. The triangle OAG represents the partial BI, net income follows the line GAB, and the tax break-even point A (defined as earnings plus non-withdrawable credits less income tax) is at the poverty line P. But with the Vince scheme, illustrated in the second diagram, the tax break-even point A is slightly below the poverty line. Despite the fact that Vince's poverty line is £56.15 a week, by comparison with the £60 assumed elsewhere in this report, there is still a small amount of tax spillage. The diagram refers to a single person, and is approximately to scale. Net income (before adding in the withdrawable credits) follows the line GADB. Using Vince's income tax rate of 44 percent, his proposed universal credit of £23.95 is withdrawn by the time earnings reach £54.43, compared with a non-earner credit of £56.15. The difference is so small that it hardly shows up, but it is there all the same.

The question becomes how best to top up net incomes below the poverty line P (the GAP triangle in the first diagram), without producing the sort of benefit leakage to people with incomes above the poverty line, which makes full BI so expensive, and which was illustrated in Figure 8.4. With Vince the area to be filled is enlarged on account of tax spillage. Some people will need income-tested benefit in order to bring their net of tax incomes back up to the poverty line. Moreover the diagram understates the scale of the problem because it refers to a single person, and families with

Table 12.1: Essential characteristics of the Liberal Tax-Credit scheme

> 1. Citizen-based partial BIs and disability costs allowance, individual assessment units, fully integrated with new IT.
> 2. NIT style low income supplements, family or household assessment units, administration not clear.
> 3. Beveridge style non-earner supplements, individual assessment, administration similar to existing system, but abolition of earnings rule for people aged 65 or over.
> 4. Unification of employees' NI contributions and IT.
> 5. Progressive IT, starting rate is 44%.

children would be worse affected. For a single person the Vince income-tested benefits produce a second break-even point (D) at about £100 a week. This is the point at which withdrawable credits plus non-withdrawable credits together equal income tax liability.

Despite its attractions the Vince formula is not yet perfect. There remains an element of malignant churning, it requires a starting rate of tax on all other income of at least 44 percent, and the administration is extremely complicated. Because of the high cost, there would always be pressures to reduce the universal PBIs. This could increase the amount of malignant churning in the system, and there is nothing in the scheme's structure to prevent it.

The proposals are designed to be revenue neutral assuming a 44 percent starting rate of income tax, which in 1985-86 was 5 percent higher than income tax at 30 percent plus contracted-in NI contribution at 9 percent, and 14 percent higher than income tax on its own (for pensioners and others not liable to NI contributions). Pensioner tax break-even points would come down and people with investment income would tend to lose. Employees' NI contributions would be abolished and any employee currently paying contracted-out NI contributions would pay a reduced rate of the new income tax. The withdrawal rates for the proposed NIT-style credits would vary, but the top rate would be 40 percent, producing a maximum tax plus benefit withdrawal rate of 84 percent. Employers' NI contributions would continue as a payroll tax.

The credits

All existing social security benefits except SERPS, and all personal income tax allowances would be replaced. There are three main types of credit:

(1) Age-related *personal credits*, or PBIs, for everyone.
(2) A larger, *non-earner's credit*, replacing the personal credit for everyone aged 65 or over (subject to residential qualifications), and for those prevented from earning by sickness, disability or unemployment.
(3) An additional, *low income credit,* including a *householder credit*, which is progressively withdrawn, rather like a NIT.

There are special credits for children of lone parents and of mothers with disabilities, and for people with impaired ability to earn. And there are credit supplements for those who are partially disabled (according to degree of disability) and for carers (according to degree of attendance).

All the credits are tax-free, most other income would be taxable, but taxpayers would continue to be able to set their mortgage interest and superannuation against tax. It is not clear what would happen to the other non-personal income tax reliefs. Presumably they would stay.

Vince emphasises that the credits are not intended to provide a subsistence income for everyone. He also emphasises the need for revenue neutrality and political realism:

> It is necessary to produce basic income proposals which are revenue neutral and which do not assume tax increases or expenditure cuts outside the area of personal taxation and social security benefits, because ultimately a change of this magnitude can only be implemented if accepted by people with widely divergent views on other policies. This means that the total benefit to those who gain from the reform must equal the total loss to those who suffer reduction in their net income...

> It is in order to limit the area of change that Liberal tax credit policy does not include any change in the State earnings related pension (SERPS), nor in the tax treatment of private and occupational pensions and mortgage interest, nor any reform of local government finance. There are separate Liberal policies in each of these areas. Thus we have advocated the abolition of SERPS in order to finance an immediate 25% increase in the basic State pension and we are now revising this proposal in the light of the Social Security Bill, which modifies SERPS.

(Vince 1986, page 6)

It is for reasons of cost that Vince uses a combination of universal, selective and withdrawable credits. Although every legal resident would be entitled to the personal credit, eligibility for the other credits would depend on status (old age, disability, unemployment) or proof of need.

(1) The personal credit would be paid to every legal resident aged over 18 but under 65, regardless of sex or marital status. The rate in 1985-86 would have been £23.95, which is just over half the supplementary benefit (SB) scale rate for a married couple under 65 in November 1985. For young people aged 16-17 the personal credit is £18.20, which is equal to the SB scale rate for that age group. Vince sees this as the "basis for a policy of providing all those who remain in education or training with a uniform income" (Vince 1983, page 20). For children up to age 16 the credit is £10.10, which is equal to the SB scale rate (excluding passport benefits) for children under 11 in November 1985, but £5 less than SB for children aged 11-15. Higher rates of child credit, the same as for juveniles, would be payable for children of people with disabilities, and of lone parents, but only lone parents living in a household without another adult (of either sex).

Table 12.2: Liberal Tax-Credit Scheme, main credits and withdrawal rates, 1985-86

	£ per week
1. *Personal credits* (withdrawn through the income tax system)	
Each adult aged 16-64	23.95
Each juvenile aged 16-17, and each child of lone parents	18.20
Each child aged 0-15	10.10
2. *Non earner's credit* (withdrawn through the income tax system)	
Each person normally resident aged 65 years or over	56.15
Each person who is sick, disabled or unemployed and seeking work	56.15
3. *Low income credit*	
Maximum equals the difference between the non-earner's and the personal credits, ie £32.20, withdrawn by 40 pence in the £, to reach nil at £80.50	32.20 max
4. *Householder's additional low income credit*	
Varying amounts according to marital status, number of children, and income level, but not according to actual housing costs. Taper is 40 pence in the £ above £80.50. On incomes below £34.40 (single) and £34.35 (married) the householder's credit operates like a NIT, cutting the high marginal tax rate produced by withdrawal of the low income credit	8.60 max SP 17.20 max MC +4.20 per child

(2) A non-earner's credit of £56.15 would be paid to all men and women aged 65 or over, subject only to a test of residence. Women aged 60-65 who had been contributing to NI retirement pension, would receive the credit from age 60 on a transitional basis. It would also be payable to anyone aged 18 or over who was completely prevented from earning on account of sickness or disablement, and who was completely unemployed but seeking work. It does not carry any dependency additions, nor is it payable to anyone under age 18. The rate is set at one-third of median male earnings. Entitlement to the credit for reasons of ill-health or disability would be decided solely on medical grounds, regardless of whether or not the person had been in paid work. All women would be entitled to the credit for 18 weeks around the birth of a child. It would also be payable to widows during the first six months of bereavement, but not to widowers.

(3) The low income credit is intended as a replacement for family income supplement and housing benefit, and as a means of smoothing the withdrawal of the non-earner's credit from those who have been sick or unemployed. It would not be payable to those low earners who had not previously been entitled to the non-earner's credit because they had not been seeking work. So a married woman who wanted to work part-time would not qualify, even if her husband was also on low earnings, unless she first registered for work. Presumably this would have to be full-time work. At this point the administrative detail is far from clear.

The rates and operation of the low income and householder credits are very complicated. For those earning less than about half of median male earnings (and previously sick or unemployed) the low income credit is gradually withdrawn at a rate of 40 percent, in addition to income tax at 44 percent. In 1985-86 the threshold above which only a standard personal credit would have been given is £80.50 for single-wage families and double that for two-wage families. Low income householders would receive a householder credit in addition to the low income credit. The effect of this credit is to counteract tax slippage at the bottom of the income scale. The householder credit does not start to be withdrawn until all the low income credit has been withdrawn. Thus in 1985-86 single householders with original incomes below £34.40 would have received credits equal to 25 percent of original income. Married and lone-parent householders would have received credits of £6.90, plus £4.60 for each child, and the former would have gone up by 30 pence for each extra £ of income, to reach a maximum of £17.20 per week when original income was £34.35. These credits are reduced by 40 percent of earnings above £80.50, with the break-even level depending on family size. The tables at the end of the chapter show how the system would have worked in 1985-86.

How much would it cost?

The scheme is designed to be revenue neutral assuming a 44 percent starting rate of tax. For his costings Vince used a technique similar to Formula No. 1 in Appendix 1, and he relied for his input figures on national accounts statistics from the annual *National Income and Expenditure Blue Book,* and the Public Expenditure White Paper. As explained in Appendix 1, this is the method used by Professor Meade in 1972, but found wanting by Professor A.B. Atkinson (Atkinson 1984) because the tax base figures derived from the Blue Book were higher than the income actually taxed at that time (as recorded in the Inland Revenue *Survey of Personal Incomes*).

Table 12.3 compares the Vince and Atkinson figures, starting from the following formula:

$$t = \frac{A - B + C + D - E}{F}$$

where:
A is the cost of the tax credits,
B is the saving on existing expenditure,
C is the cost of abolishing existing income tax and employees' NI contributions,
D is the cost of retaining mortgage interest and private pension tax reliefs,
E is the revenue from the new higher rate tax and the investment income surcharge,
F is the new income tax base.

Some of the discrepancies between the Vince and Atkinson estimates are the result of technicalities or minor omissions. Atkinson used updated figures, and Vince's estimate of savings on existing expenditure did not include Northern Ireland, likewise his estimate of the cost of abolishing existing income tax omitted Advance Corporation Tax and self-employed NI contributions. Neither column makes any allowance for the future cost of SERPS, which Vince retains, although costs will increase rapidly after the turn of the century. But by far the most important discrepancy is in

Table 12.3: Cost of Liberal Tax-Credit scheme, 1982-83

Elements of the calculation	Vince estimates £ b	Atkinson estimates £ b
Cost of tax credits	65.6	65.6
Savings of existing expenditure	29.7	31.1 – 33.3
Cost of existing IT and NIC	39.2	41.5
Cost of IT reliefs retained	5.8	4.7
Revenue from new higher rate IT and inv Y surcharge	1.2	1.5
New IT base	180.0	159.0 – 167.0
Starting rate of new IT	44.0	47.5 – 51.3

Source: Atkinson 1984, page 27.

the calculation of the income tax base, for which Vince relied largely on the Blue Book and Atkinson on the Survey of Personal Incomes (SPI). The Vince formula runs as follows, and produces a starting rate of tax of about 44 percent:

$$t = \frac{65.6 - 29.7 + 39.2 + 5.8 - 1.2}{180.00} \times 100 = 44.28$$

This calculation was then qualified by Vince, in order to allow for the "black economy", the costs of administration and the cost of the low income credit, which he reckoned would together add between £3 and £7 billion. This extra cost would have to be met either by increased economic activity as a result of other policies, or by reducing the rates of tax credit.

By contrast the Atkinson calculation, which allows £3 billion for the low income credits (the bottom end of the range given by Vince), produces a tax rate in the range of 47.5 percent to 51.3 percent, depending on the costs of administering the new scheme and on the new income tax base:

$$t = \frac{65.6 - \{31.1 + 41.5 + 4.1 + 1.5}{\{167.0 \atop \{159.0}} \quad \text{(Atkinson April 1984, page 28)}$$

These discrepancies are important. Any reduction in the credits would reduce the numbers gaining as a result of the scheme, and any increase in the starting rate of tax would exacerbate the poverty trap effect of the low income credit. Elsewhere Atkinson and Sutherland have calculated that an increase in the rate of income tax from 44 percent to 48 percent would reduce the proportion of working families gaining from the scheme from 55 percent to 33 percent (Atkinson and Sutherland 1984, page 17).

How easy is it to administer?

As explained, the scheme is a mixture of partial BI, partial NIT and benefits conditioned on work status. The formulation of the NIT style credits is too complex for most people to be able to understand, which can only be to the disadvantage of claimants and administrators alike.

A major problem with all income-tested benefits (which is all that the Vince low income credits really are) is the need to keep tabs on all the changes to family incomes and family composition that affect entitlement, and to ensure that employers and employees, and low to middle income families generally, do not re-arrange their affairs in order to maximise benefit entitlement (either legally or illegally). It is important not to underestimate the frequency with which family incomes and family composition change, especially in low income families. Far from offering simplification, the Vince mixture of universal and selective benefits could be even more difficult to administer than the existing system, it could result in more run-away expenditure, and there is no guarantee that access (except for the non-withdrawable credits) would be improved.

The only credits that are natural candidates for integration with the new income tax are the personal credits and the non-earner credits for people aged 65 or over. The latter are effectively BIs for pensioners. They take the individual as the unit of assessment, require very little case-work, and could be automated using the latest technologies.

Vince proposes that the personal credits should be paid either through employers (in cash or as offsets against Schedule D tax liability), or at post offices, depending on whether or not the person was in paid work. Those for children would normally be paid to the mother through the post offices. Employers would be responsible for calculating the PAYE tax liability or cash entitlements of their employees. Most tax liability would be calculated at the standard 44 percent rate, tax at the higher rates being collected in arrears at the end of each tax year, as surtax used to be. This makes it possible to make payment of PAYE non-cumulative. Employers would have to compare tax liability with credit entitlement and deduct tax, or pay any excess of credit over tax liability, accordingly. For each pay period employers would be expected to produce and send to the Inland Revenue one total of net tax deducted and another total of net excess credit paid out, together with individual pay records and the amount by which net tax had exceeded net excess credits. If net excess credits exceeded net tax, the balance could be claimed from the Inland Revenue.

Although this part of the system looks straightforward, problems arise as soon as the individual has several employers, or works irregularly or part-time. The regulations affecting the low income credit, and for that matter some of the non-earner credits, would be different to those affecting the personal credit, for instance the low income credit would take the family or household, not the individual, as the unit of assessment. Although the calculations might all be the responsibility of one government department, different regulations would apply, some of which would require individual case-work. In practice it is much more likely that the low income and householder credits would be dealt with separately, much as family credit and housing benefit are dealt with today.

For similar reasons the non-earner credit for unemployed people could not be included within the integrated part of the system. This credit, based on "compensation for interruption or loss of earnings", looks sadly out of place in a scheme that otherwise stands on the principle of benefit according to need, not work status. Vince anticipates that the Department of Employment would pay the non-earner credits for unemployed people, "so that they can verify that applicants are seeking work" (Vince 1983), although it is not clear how this would be arranged. But people who were unable to work on account of sickness would receive their non-earner credits first from their employers, and then from the DHSS.

Assessment units. The assessment unit presents considerable problems. For the personal credits, some of the non-earner credits, and the new income tax, it is the individual, but for the low income and householder credits it is intended to be the family or the household. This is not made clear in any of the written sources available, but Vince has no intention of allowing a spouse to draw income-tested benefits regardless of the income of the other spouse.

Access and control of expenditure. One of the main disadvantages of the existing social security system is the low take-up of means-tested benefits alongside benefit leakage to people who do not need it. Although take-up of Vince's personal credits presents no problems, there is no guarantee of prompt and efficient delivery of the income-tested credits, nor of the non-earner credits for the sick and the unemployed. Nor does there appear to be any machinery to prevent over-payment of benefit to those who do not need it. The only protection is an annual income report declaration, which each person would be required to sign. Even for the most honest taxpayer a year is too long. Moreover, unless income were defined on the same basis for the low income credit as for tax purposes, the forms would be extremely complicated.

Collection of income tax from the first pound. Another fundamental weakness, common to most BI schemes, is the need to collect income tax from the first £ of income other than the credits. Under existing arrangements each single person and each married woman can earn up to £50 a week free of income tax, and a married man can earn £79 (1988-89 figures). Large numbers of part-time workers, predominantly married women, remain outside the income tax system quite legally, and their employers are spared the chore of acting as unpaid tax-collectors. Arguably this system is not in the long-term interest of part-time workers because it encourages employers to keep their wages below the tax threshold. But it does make life easier for the Inland Revenue, and it has the added advantage of realism. There can be few people who seriously believe the tax authorities could levy tax on income from the first pound, and it seems unwise to recommend reforms based on that assumption. Moreover insofar as the new law could be made effective, it would discourage unemployed people and people with disabilities from taking part-time work, thus undoing one of the main attractions of a switch to basic income.

Who gains and who loses?

The scheme is generally redistributive from rich to poor and in favour of families with children, people with disabilities and the unemployed. There are nevertheless some strange discrepancies. The non-earner credit produces very large gains for single non-householders, and the low income credit produces anomalies between one- and two-earner couples. The idea is to limit eligibility for the low income credit to people who were previously unemployed and seeking work, but the figures at the end of this chapter show that it produces variations in net income of over £20 a week in low income families, depending on whether or not the second earner was previously registered as unemployed.

178

The householder's additional low income credit varies according to family size, but it does not vary according to the housing costs incurred. In Britain this would be a new departure. With SB housing costs were always payable in full. Even with income support, the amount payable is a proportion of the actual rent and rates paid. Vince justifies introduction of a fixed amount subsidy on the following grounds:

> Different amounts of credit could be defined for each region in order to reflect varying housing costs from one part of the country to another. This would be preferable to the present practice of reimbursing to those with little or no income the actual cost of rent and rates or a means-tested proportion of it, so that people in similar financial circumstances in the same area receive different amounts of income support according to the type of accommodation in which they choose to live.(Vince 1983, page 22)

Vince's argument is close to that of Minford in Chapter 13. Each assumes that people can economise on housing in the same way as they can economise on food. Others argue that people who are poor tend not to choose their housing, they take what they can get and move house only if they have to. Although Vince's housing credit looks generous, it offers less protection against housing poverty than SB or income support. This shows up in Table 12.4, where about a third of tenants lose out as a result of the change. These are families where the head was in work. If the analysis had included out-of-work families, the proportion of losers would probably be higher. Most of the losses were less than £5 a week, but nearly 2 percent would have lost £15 a week or more.

Model family analysis: net incomes, disposable incomes and net spending power

Figure 12.2 *net incomes* shows how Vince changes the angle of the net income curve – reducing net tax liability at the bottom. For single people the amounts involved are smaller, and for families with children they are larger, even without taking into account the withdrawable credits. Single wage couples earning £100 gain £23 a week, and with two children they gain £29 a week. Two-wage couples gain less, and the cross-over point is also lower.

Figure 12.2: Vince net incomes, March 1986

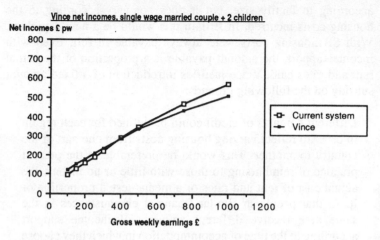

Source: Appendix 2.

Figure 12.3 *disposable incomes* shows the effects of the scheme on out-of-work families and the lower paid, by comparison with the existing system. Although the figures on the vertical axis vary according to family type, scale is maintained. As explained, the Fowler TA figures refer to the illustrative benefit rates published in the Technical Annex to the Social Security White Paper (DHSS, December 1985). Vince tries to redistribute income to people with

Figure 12.3: Vince disposable incomes, March 1986

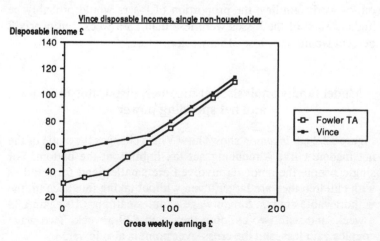

The Liberal Party Tax-Credit Scheme

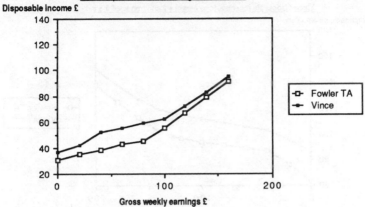

Vince disposable incomes, single householder

Fowler TA age 25+, Vince age 18-64.

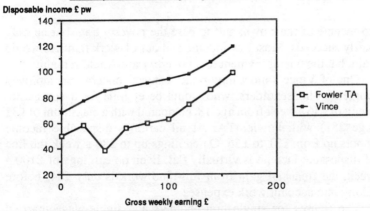

Vince disposable incomes, single wage married couple

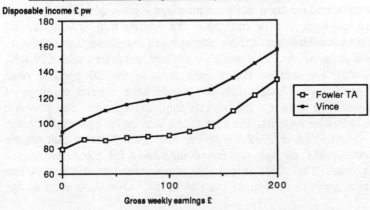

Vince disposable incomes, single wage married couple + 2 children aged 4 & 6

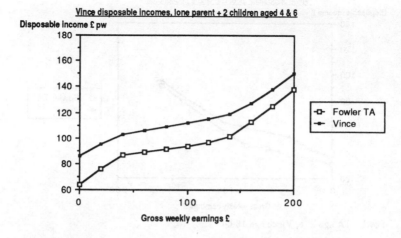

Source: Appendix 2

no income of their own, and to ease the poverty trap, but he only partly succeeds. Most low income and out-of-work families would gain, but the unemployment and poverty traps would remain.

One of Vince's most important changes concerns unemployed single non-householders, who would be eligible for a non-earner credit of £56 a week from age 18, compared with a maximum of £31 (age 25+) with Fowler TA. At nil earnings disposable income shoots up from £31 to £56. On earnings up to £80 a week the line of disposable income is virtually flat. Even on earnings of £100 a week, the financial gain from full-time work is only £24, before taking into account work expenses.

The figures for single householders and single-wage married couples look much better. There are worthwhile gains at the bottom, and the tax penalty for marriage is gone. Marginal tax rates are still high, but the troughs of the poverty trap have gone, and living standards are up. An unemployed single-wage couple with two children has £93 a week with Vince, compared with £79 with Fowler TA (before taking into account the 20 percent rates contribution). Vince's families would have needed earnings of about £150 to escape the poverty trap, about the same as pre- and post-Fowler systems. The curve for a lone parent also looks better.

Figure 12.4 *net spending power* shows that Vince's changes are nothing like enough to restore incentives for those with work expenses. The effect of including the assumed travel-to-work and childcare costs is to make the Fowler TA curves look even worse,

Figure 12.4: Vince net spending power, March 1986

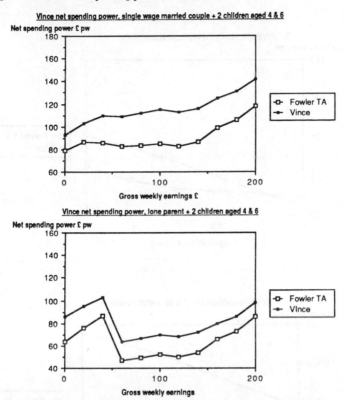

Source: Appendix 2. Work expense assumptions Chapter 11.

and to produce troughs in the Vince curves as well. Vince's marginal tax rate of 84 percent is too high to remedy the unemployment and poverty traps. The predicament of lone mothers is worst of all, because they probably have childcare costs and their earnings potential is lower. A lone mother in 1985-86 in the assumed circumstances would have been most unlikely to have earned sufficient to make work worthwhile under either system.

Figure 12.5 *disposable incomes of pensioners* shows a marked improvement in the pensioner poverty trap but surprising losses for low income single pensioners. Remember that with the existing system earnings above £75 disqualify from the basic pension, and capital above £6,000 disqualifies from income support and housing benefit. With the Vince system there would be no earnings limitation, but the capital rules are unclear. Married pensioners gain

183

Figure 12.5: Vince pensioner disposable incomes, March 1986

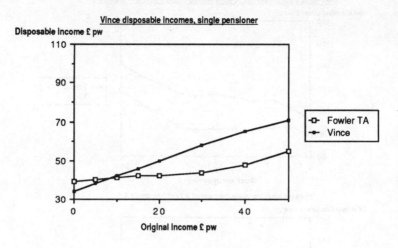

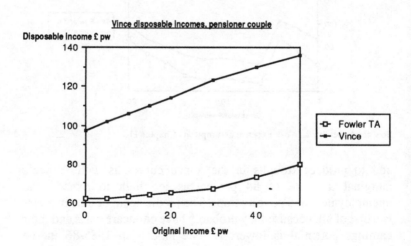

Source: Appendix 2.

significantly as a result of the move to marriage-neutral, non-earner credits, and also because of the householder credit, which seems to favour married pensioners disproportionately. Single pensioners lose, and with housing costs higher than those assumed in the graph, they would lose even more.

Gainers and losers: empirical analysis

In the UK, one of the earliest attempts to simulate the distributional and marginal tax rate effects of a major tax/benefit reform proposal concerned the Vince Tax-Credit scheme, and was produced by Professor A.B. Atkinson and Holly Sutherland at the London School of Economics in 1984 (Atkinson and Sutherland, 1984). Their analysis took a sub-sample of 3,535 tax units, representing the working population, from the 1980 Family Expenditure Survey.

Table 12.4: Estimated distribution of gains and losses, Liberal Tax-Credit scheme, working families only

| | Number of families 000s | | | | | | |
| | Lose: | | | Lose or Gain less than: | Gain: | | |
	£15-	£5-14	£1-4	£1	£1-4	£5-14	£15-
All families	991	2,174	2,536	1,802	3,591	3,130	510
(% of row)	(6.7)	(14.8)	(17.2)	(12.2)	(14.4)	(21.2)	(3.5)
Income in relation to SB scale rates							
below 160%	9	12	19	9	18	421	334
160-249%	0	24	167	249	959	2,055	149
250-399%	68	783	1,410	970	2,511	654	27
400% and above	913	1,356	940	575	102	0	0
Housing tenure							
Tenants	111	733	1,214	938	1,759	1,309	187
(% of row)	(1.8)	(11.7)	(19.4)	(15.0)	(28.1)	(20.9)	(3.0)
Owner-occupiers	880	1,441	1,322	864	1,832	1,821	323
(% of row)	(10.4)	(17.0)	(15.6)	(10.2)	(21.6)	(21.5)	(3.8)
Family type							
Single persons without children	82	413	1,123	1,126	2,390	415	9
(% of row)	(1.5)	(7.4)	(20.2)	(20.3)	(43.0)	(7.5)	(0.2)
Single parent families	4	69	96	46	35	62	15
(% of row)	(1.2)	(21.2)	(29.4)	(14.1)	(10.6)	(18.8)	(4.7)
Couples without children	56.1	1,135	806	278	332	660	25
(% of row)	(14.8)	(29.9)	(21.2)	(7.3)	(8.7)	(17.4)	(0.7)
Couples with children	345	556	511	352	834	1,993	460
(% of row)	(6.8)	(11.0)	(10.1)	(7.0)	(16.5)	(39.5)	(9.1)

Source: *A Tax Credit Scheme and Families in Work,* A.B. Atkinson and H. Sutherland. ESRC Programme on Taxation, Incentives and the Distribution of Income, Discussion Paper No. 54, London School of Economics, April 1984, Table 3.

It did not include people over retirement age, people who were self-employed or those who were out of work for whatever reason. The grossed-up number of units came to 14.7 million, which compares with an estimated total in 1980 of 20.3 million tax units where the head was under the minimum retirement age, and an overall total of 27.0 million. The Atkinson/Sutherland findings are summarised in Table 12.4, which is taken from their report.

The most striking feature is the "very considerable redistribution within the working population". Atkinson and Sutherland estimated that fewer than 2 million out of 14.7 million working tax units would have been within £1 a week of their 1980 net weekly incomes. One in four would have gained more than £5 a week and one in five would have lost more than £5 a week. Of those with incomes below 160 percent of their SB level, 90 percent would have gained at least £5 a week, and those losing £15 a week or more were mainly those with incomes equal to 400 percent or more of their SB levels. Families with children are among the principal gainers. Nearly half would have gained £5 or more. By contrast, and contrary to the implications in the model tables in Appendix 2, nearly half of couples without children would have lost more than £5 a week. Over 50 percent of lone parents would lose £1 or more, which can be explained by Vince's proposal that the children of lone parents living with another adult would not qualify for extra credits.

Marginal tax rates (MTRs)

For working families earning £35 or more Vince's combination of tax at 44 percent plus benefit withdrawal at 40 percent produces a maximum *marginal tax rate* (MTR) of 84 percent, which is an improvement by comparison with the pre- and post-Fowler systems, but is too high to remedy the poverty trap for people of working age. Nevertheless the different elements in the low income and householder credits combine to produce MTRs, especially for pensioners, that are more progressive than at first appears.

Table 12.5 shows the rates of benefit withdrawal plus income tax for people at the bottom of the income scale, and the higher rates of income tax for people with middle to high incomes. The new higher rate bands of income tax are intended to bring in more revenue than in 1985-86, but the extra could turn out to be less than expected, due to the independent taxation of husbands and wives. The new 44

Table 12.5: Liberal Tax-Credit proposals, effective marginal tax rates and thresholds, March 1986

	Income levels above which tax rates take effect £ per week	Tax and/or benefit withdrawal rate %
1. Benefit withdrawal + income tax		
(1) *Aged 65 or over*		
Non-householders	0.00	44
Householders:		
single	0.00	19
	34.40	44
	80.50	84
	102.00	44
married (both aged 65+)	0.00	14
	34.35	44
	80.50	84
	123.50	44
(2) *Age 18-64*		
Non-householders	0.00	84
	80.50	44
Householders:		
single (excluding lone parents)	0.00	59
	34.40	84
	102.00	44
married	0.00	54
	34.35	84
	123.50	44
	+ £11.50 per child	

	£ pa	pw	%
2. Higher rates of income tax			
All taxpayers (individual	18,400	354	50
assessment units)	21,400	412	55
	26,600	512	60
	34,500	663	65
	42,400	815	70

percent starting rate of tax represents a 14 per cent increase compared with income tax payable on earned incomes above the ceiling for NI contributions, and on unearned income including private and state earnings-related pensions. This change is important. It rationalises the existing system, but it produces losers.

How many families would be affected by the 84 percent MTR? The number of FIS families who in practice found themselves out of pocket as a result of earning more was always considerably lower than the number theoretically affected, because FIS was awarded for a year at a time. In 1985 it was about 70,000 (Hansard WA, 22

Oct 87). By contrast the marginal tax rates that Vince proposes are for real, because benefit entitlement is adjusted each time the families' incomes change.

Using TAXMOD, Atkinson and Sutherland concluded that if the Vince scheme had been operating in 1980 the percentage of tax units in the employed population facing actual (as opposed to theoretical) marginal tax rates of 75 percent or higher would have gone up from 0.2 to 5 percent, and the proportion of employed tax units with effective marginal tax rates of between 50 to 74 percent would have gone up from 3.4 to 5.6 percent. Those figures refer to £1 of additional earnings by the head of the tax unit. They imply that about 750,000 working households would have had marginal tax rates of 84 percent and a further 800,000 would have had marginal tax rates of 54 or 59 percent. Assuming £25 of additional earnings, the comparable figures are 74,000 and 1.3 million. The Atkinson and Sutherland figures are summarised in Table 12.6. In practice very much would depend on the unit of assessment, which Vince does not make clear.

Table 12.6: Marginal tax rates, effects of Liberal Tax-Credit proposals
Heads of tax units, working population only, 1980 figures

| Marginal tax rate % | Percentage of relevant tax units* | | | |
| | £1 extra earnings | | £25 extra earnings | |
	Actual	*Vince*	*Actual*	*Vince*
zero	0.2	0	0	0
1-19	0.3	0	0	0
20-29	0.1	0	0.1	0
30	10.1	0	0.1	0
31-39	80.6	0	83.6	0
40-49	5.2	89.4	5.2	90.8
50-74	3.4	5.6	0.2	8.6
75 and more	0.2	5.0	0.2	0.5

* Assuming basic rate tax at 44 per cent.

Source: *A Tax Credit Scheme and Families in Work,* A.B. Atkinson and H. Sutherland, 1984.

The Atkinson/Sutherland figures show the effects of the increased rate of income tax and abolition of wife's earned income tax allowance. What they do not show is the behavioural effects of the Vince scheme on participation in the labour market and on wage rates. Unfortunately no comparable estimates exist for the self-employed and non-working population. From Figure 12.3 it looks as though MTRs for most of the unemployed (but not single non-householders) would improve, but not enough to restore work incentives.

Summing up

The Liberal plan for reform of tax and social security is a partial BI scheme linked to residual income-tested and earnings-replacement benefits which rest uneasily together. The BI component of the scheme lends itself to integration, but the other components do not. The rates of BI selected are sufficient to produce a coherent strategy, but may not be sufficient to prevent poverty. The scheme is nevertheless a positive attempt to simplify and to improve access through partial integration. For the majority of the population equity between men and women, married and single would be greatly improved.

The advantage of the scheme is that it raises family living standards. The disadvantage is that the new income tax would cut in at 44 percent without reducing welfare dependency. In practice the tax rate might be nearer 50 percent than the 44 percent. The full potential advantages of integration are not allowed to come through because of retention of SERPS, mortgage interest tax relief and tax reliefs for private pensions. It looks as though the Liberals are trying to do too much.

Despite the moderate levels of most of the credits, the scale of income redistribution is so high that it would have to be introduced incrementally, requiring cross-party support over perhaps ten years. Here the complexity of the scheme could be a problem. The formulation of the different credits would be incomprehensible to the average voter. If some such scheme is to win support, the logic behind the credits needs to stand out. Voters need to be able to understand the ground rules and see at a glance how they themselves would be affected.

Table 12.7: Disposable incomes of selected model families, Liberal Tax-Credit proposals, detailed figures for Nov 85 to Mar 86, £ per week

Assumptions

All figures refer to the period November 1985 to March 1986. All families are tenants. Working age families live in council property, and pay the rents and rates used in the November 1985 DHSS Tax/Benefit Model Tables. Water rates, estimated by the DHSS to have been £1.65 a week on average, are not deducted. Families are assumed to take up entitlement to means-tested benefits in full. No allowance for any non-personal income tax reliefs, eg for private pensions. No allowance for cost of fares to work or childminding expenses. The personal credit is £23.95 for adults, £18.20 for juveniles aged 16-17, and £10.10 for children aged 0-15. Non-earner's credit is £56.15. Starting rate of the new income tax is 44 percent.

1. WORKING AGE HOUSEHOLDS

Table 1: Single non-householder aged 18-64

	£	£	£	£	£	£
Gross weekly earnings	0.00	40.00	80.00	120.00	160.00	200.00
+ Personal credit/PBI	—	23.95	23.95	23.95	23.95	23.95
+ Non-earner's credit	56.15	—	—	—	—	—
+ Low income credit	—	16.20	0.20	—	—	—
− Income tax	—	17.60	35.20	52.80	70.40	88.00
= Net & disposable incomes	56.15	62.55	68.95	91.15	113.55	135.95

Table 2: Single householder aged 18-64

	£	£	£	£	£	£
Gross weekly earnings	0.00	40.00	80.00	120.00	160.00	200.00
+ Personal credit/PBI	—	23.95	23.95	23.95	23.95	23.95
+ Non-earner's credit	56.15	—	—	—	—	—
+ Low income credit	—	16.20	0.20	—	—	—
+ Householder credit	—	8.60	8.60	—	—	—
− Income tax	—	17.60	35.20	52.80	70.40	88.00
= Net incomes	56.15	71.15	77.55	91.15	113.55	135.95
− Rent	13.80	13.80	13.80	13.80	13.80	13.80
− Rates	5.20	5.20	5.20	5.20	5.20	5.20
= Disposable incomes	37.15	52.15	58.55	72.15	94.55	116.95

Table 3: Single person + 2 children aged 4 and 6

	£	£	£	£	£	£
Gross weekly earnings	0.00	40.00	80.00	120.00	160.00	200.00
+ Personal credit/PBI	36.40	60.35	60.35	60.35	60.35	60.35
+ Non-earner's credit	56.15	—	—	—	—	—
+ Low income credit	—	16.20	0.20	—	—	—
+ Householder credit	16.10	26.40	26.40	10.60	—	—
− Income tax	—	17.60	35.20	52.80	70.40	88.00
= Net incomes	108.65	125.35	131.71	138.15	149.95	172.35
− Rent	16.50	16.50	16.50	16.50	16.50	16.50
− Rates	6.30	6.30	6.30	6.30	6.30	6.30
= Disposable incomes	85.85	102.55	108.95	115.35	127.15	149.55

Table 4: Married couple (single-wage)

	£	£	£	£	£	£
Gross weekly earnings	0.00	40.00	80.00	120.00	160.00	200.00
+ Personal credit/PBI	23.95	47.90	47.90	47.90	47.90	47.90
+ Non-earner's credit	56.15	—	—	—	—	—
+ Low income credit	—	16.20	0.20	—	—	—
+ Householder credit	6.90	17.20	17.20	1.40	—	—
− Income tax	—	17.60	35.20	52.80	70.40	88.00
= Net incomes	87.00	103.70	110.10	116.50	137.50	159.90
− Rent	13.80	13.80	13.80	13.80	13.80	13.80
− Rates	5.20	5.20	5.20	5.20	5.20	5.20
= Disposable incomes	68.00	84.70	91.10	97.50	118.50	140.90

Table 5: Married couple (two-wage, each spouse earns half)

	£	£	£	£	£	£
Joint weekly earnings	0.00	40.00	80.00	120.00	160.00	200.00
+ Personal credits	—	47.90	47.90	47.90	47.90	47.90
+ Non-earner's credit	112.30	—	—	—	—	—
+ Low income credit	—	48.40	32.40	16.40	0.40	—
+ Householder credit	—	5.00	8.60	8.60	8.60	0.80
− Income tax	—	17.60	35.20	52.80	70.40	88.00
= Net incomes	112.30	123.70	133.70	140.10	146.50	160.70
− Rent	13.80	13.80	13.80	13.80	13.80	13.80
− Rates	5.20	5.20	5.20	5.20	5.20	5.20
= Disposable incomes	93.30	104.70	114.70	121.10	127.50	141.70

Table 6: Married couple + 2 children aged 4 and 6 (single-wage)

	£	£	£	£	£	£
Gross weekly earnings	0.00	40.00	80.00	120.00	160.00	200.00
+ Personal credits	44.15	68.10	68.10	68.10	68.10	68.10
+ Non-earner's credit	56.15	—	—	—	—	—
+ Low income credit	—	16.20	0.20	—	—	—
+ Householder credit	16.10	26.40	26.40	10.60	—	—
− Income tax	—	17.60	35.20	52.80	70.40	88.00
= Net incomes	116.40	133.10	139.50	145.90	157.70	180.10
− Rent	16.50	16.50	16.50	16.50	16.50	16.50
− Rates	6.30	6.30	6.30	6.30	6.30	6.30
= Disposable incomes	93.60	110.30	116.70	123.10	134.90	157.30

Table 7: Married couple + 2 children aged 4 and 6 (two-wage, each spouse earns half)

	£	£	£	£	£	£
Joint weekly earnings	0.00	40.00	80.00	120.00	160.00	200.00
+ Personal credits	20.20	68.10	68.10	68.10	68.10	68.10
+ Non-earner's credits	112.30	—	—	—	—	—
+ Low income credit	—	48.40	32.40	16.40	0.40	—
+ Householder credit	9.20	14.20	17.80	17.80	17.80	10.00
− Income tax	—	17.60	35.20	52.80	70.40	88.00
= Net incomes	141.80	153.10	163.10	169.50	175.90	190.10
− Rent	16.50	16.50	16.50	16.50	16.50	16.50
− Rates	6.30	6.30	6.30	6.30	6.30	6.30
= Disposable incomes	119.00	130.30	140.30	146.70	153.10	167.30

2. RETIREMENT PENSIONERS

Table 8: Single retirement pensioner aged 65 or over

	£	£	£	£	£	£	£	£
Earnings/SERPS/private pension/								
investment income	0.00	5.00	10.00	20.00	30.00	40.00	50.00	100.00
+ Non-earner's credit	56.15	56.15	56.15	56.15	56.15	56.15	56.15	56.15
+ Low income credit	—	—	—	—	—	—	—	—
+ Householder credit	—	1.25	2.50	5.00	7.50	8.60	8.60	0.80
− Income tax	—	2.20	4.40	8.80	13.20	17.60	22.00	44.00
= Net incomes	56.15	60.20	62.35	72.35	80.45	87.15	92.75	112.95
− Rent	15.00	15.00	15.00	15.00	15.00	15.00	15.00	15.00
− Rates	7.00	7.00	7.00	7.00	7.00	7.00	7.00	7.00
= Disposable incomes	34.15	38.20	40.35	52.35	58.45	65.15	70.75	90.95

Table 9: Pensioner couple aged 65 or over

	£	£	£	£	£	£	£	£
Earnings/SERPS/private pension/								
investment income	0.00	5.00	10.00	20.00	30.00	40.00	50.00	100.00
+ Non-earner's credit	112.30	112.30	112.30	112.30	112.30	112.30	112.30	112.30
+ Low income credit	—	—	—	—	—	—	—	—
+ Householder credit	6.90	8.40	9.90	12.90	15.90	17.20	17.20	9.40
− Income tax	—	2.20	4.40	8.80	13.20	17.60	22.00	44.00
= Net incomes	119.20	123.50	127.80	136.40	145.00	151.90	157.50	177.70
− Rent	15.00	15.00	15.00	15.00	15.00	15.00	15.00	15.00
− Rates	7.00	7.00	7.00	7.00	7.00	7.00	7.00	7.00
= Disposable incomes	97.20	101.50	105.80	114.40	123.00	129.90	135.50	155.70

13

Patrick Minford's
"Efficient Relief of Poverty"

In evidence to the Meacher Sub-Committee enquiry already referred to, and in subsequent publications (Minford 1984; Minford *et al* 1983, 1985, 1986, 1987) Professor Patrick Minford and colleagues at Liverpool University have compiled proposals for privatisation of health, education and social insurance and for co-ordinated tax and benefit changes that include a conditional NIT for adults in full-time work and a partial BI (child benefit) for children. The proposals were intended more as a sketch than a blueprint, which makes a full appraisal difficult. They are nevertheless of great interest, partly because they are so different to previous NIT proposals, and partly because they show the sort of changes advocated by the New Right, although not everyone on the New Right would go along with all Minford's ideas, especially workfare.

Minford applies two different work tests, one for his NIT and another for the *subsistence income* (SI) that would replace income support. Minford's is the only hybrid scheme examined in this report with an income guarantee conditioned on work status, yet there are many precedents for this. Lady Rhys Williams's 1943 scheme included a work test, and Parker's *Basic Income 2000* could be made to include a work test, although her work test would apply only to housing benefit. Minford's is nevertheless the only scheme I have come across where the work test for the NIT refers categorically to paid work. His workfare includes community work, but not his NIT.

Minford's objective is "the efficient relief of poverty", defined as follows:

> ...to ensure that the poor have "good" education, "good" health care, and are at all stages of the life cycle supported

193

above "subsistence" income, while preserving incentives to obtain work and, once in work, to work for higher wages. (Minford 1984, page vii)

His starting point is the belief that public expenditure is too high. State production, state purchase and taxation should all be reduced, because they cause waste, and he cites the unemployment and poverty traps as examples of waste. Using techniques that are highly controversial (see for instance Nickell 1984), he then estimates that a 10 percent fall in benefit incomes measured in relation to incomes from paid work (*replacement ratios*) would reduce unemployment by half a million:

> Our estimates suggest that at rates of pay only 10 per cent below existing market rates, unemployment would effectively disappear. In other words, 2.25 million more jobs exist at rates of pay up to 10 per cent below the rates workers will not now willingly accept. These jobs are not taken (and in many cases potential employers do not even bother to advertise them because of the waste of time and money) because they are too low-paid relative to benefits. (Minford *et al.* 1985, page 88)

In order to cut unemployment and encourage lower paid work, Minford proposes a two-tier poverty standard, the SI and the *poverty threshold:*

> Our basic idea is simple. A "subsistence" income is defined for each type of family; this is a true minimum, and it is important that it exclude all items not necessary for survival, otherwise the whole system will become hopelessly expensive. Then there is a "poverty threshold" income defined in relation to social views of the income above which help would not be willingly given by society. It is also the threshold for ordinary income tax to start. Then the NIT does two things: it never allows income to drop below subsistence and, for incomes less than the poverty threshold, it supplements them by 70 percent of their difference from that threshold. (Minford *et al.* 1985, page 83)

The poverty threshold is the break-even point at which NIT is phased out, and people start to pay income tax. Below the threshold

NIT is payable, above the threshold income tax is payable, at a flat rate 25 percent. The NIT taper is 70 percent, but the SI taper is 100 percent.

At first glance the arithmetic of the scheme seems to imply that the SI as well as the poverty threshold would be politically determined, since the one should equal 70 percent of the other. But there are all sorts of complications. For instance, the NIT can only be claimed by people working for at least 30 hours a week (or 24 hours in the case of lone parents). At nil earnings SI (based on former supplementary benefit rates) is payable, but is capped at 70 percent of former disposable income. Additionally, the minimum NIT payment for working families with children is based on former total income support (TIS) at earnings of £60 a week in 1985-86, and can be higher than 70 percent of the poverty threshold.

The 70 percent benefit cap is intended to bring market pressures to bear on the unemployed, and to price unskilled labour back into work. The assumption is that paid work is potentially available for everyone who wants it, provided only that wages fall far enough. The 30 hour work rule is intended to prevent people becoming entitled to the NIT on account of a few hours' work. As a result, part-time work for less than 30 hours is not financially worthwhile. The financial inducements to do full-time paid work are bolstered by making payment of benefit (after six months) contingent on acceptance of a job from a "workfare pool". Those who do not participate lose benefit. This part of the proposal is similar to the Beveridge Plan, and raises similar administrative and policing problems.

Although nothing is said about income maintenance during sickness and invalidity, or for widows, the intention is that existing provisions should continue, but on a non-contributory basis. This proposal is surprising, given the danger that people who did not want to work would contrive to get themselves certified as unfit for work. In their 1984 White Paper on reform of personal taxation and social security, the Quebec Government noted that the rates of inability to work among recipients of social aid fell at age 30 from around 50 to around 30 percent. They also noted that the social aid entitlement was $149 a month on average for the under 30s if they were unemployed, compared with $409 if they could produce a medical certificate of inability to work. Over the age of 30 they all received $409 (Quebec Government 1984, page 176).

The NIT component of the Minford package, is illustrated in Figure 13.1. The tax break-even point A is the same as the tax

Table 13.1: Essential characteristics of Minford's scheme for the "efficient relief of poverty"

---

1. A negative income tax for adults in full-time work (defined as 30 hours a week or more), linked to greatly increased income tax thresholds.
2. Privatisation of National Insurance and the National Health Service, and replacement of NI contributions by statutory minimum contributions for private health and old age insurance.
3. Abolition of SERPS.
4. Privatisation of education and the equivalent of education vouchers as of right for every child.
5. Child benefit increased to allow for the cost of private health insurance and to include the equivalent of education vouchers.
6. Maximum subsistence income (SI) entitlement limited to 70 per cent of former income net of travel to work costs.
7. Compulsory *Workfare*, after about six months' unemployment.

---

threshold, so there looks to be no tax slippage. By lifting the lower paid out of income tax, Minford immediately reduces the scale of NIT provision that would be necessary. It is exactly the sort of change that is required. Retention of child benefit has a similar effect. Minford's NIT is not a guaranteed income in the sense used elsewhere in this report, because of the 30 hour work rule. It is

Figure 13.1: Minford's NIT

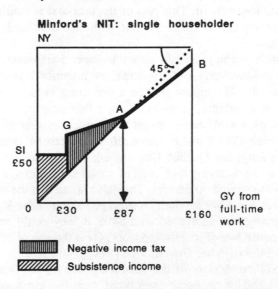

because the NIT is conditioned on work status that the horizontal axis in Figure 13.1 refers specifically to gross income in work, unlike all the other examples in our diagram series, which refer only to gross income. At this point no account is taken of Minford's statutory contributions for health and pensions.

It is not possible to specify the minimum guarantee level, which would depend on how little a person might earn in 30 hours. In countries with a national minimum wage this problem would not arise, but in the UK there is no minimum wage. One of Minford's objectives is to reduce labour costs, but there must nevertheless be a limit to the amounts by which the taxpayer should be expected to subsidise employers. Without a minimum wage employers might pay £15 for a 30 hour week, knowing that the wage-earner could top the wage up by 70 percent of the difference between £15 and the poverty threshold. Minford suggests a collusion clause, but that is unlikely to be enough.

In Figure 13.1 it is assumed that no one would earn less than £30 in 30 hours, so the GMI for a single person in paid work becomes £70. People not in paid work would have to depend on SI, and after six months they would have to work for it. Maximum SI for a single householder (including housing and before the cap) is £50.

Provision for children. The big attraction of the NIT is the increased tax thresholds, but for families with children there would still be tax slippage. Minford's NIT does not take account of the extra costs of children, and his £7.00 basic child benefit is well below subsistence, especially for older children. His NIT ceilings (and tax thresholds) are therefore at much lower *equivalent* income levels for families with children than for families without. Put another way, a GMI for a single person of £60.90 (or 70 percent of £87.00) compared with basic child benefit of £7.00 produces an implied equivalence ratio for children of all ages, by comparison with single householders, of only 1:9, which is far below most international estimates, with or without housing costs, and with or without taking into account economies of scale.

Minford tries to overcome this deficiency through his SI top-ups. The GMI for a lower paid couple with one child is £25 a week more than for a childless couple. A couple with two children receives a further £15, and so on. Unfortunately the withdrawal rate for these supplements is 100 percent. The reason for this is presumably to hold down the number of families subject to 70 percent marginal tax rates. Another solution would be to increase child benefit, and perhaps make it age-related, but this would add to the cost of the scheme. (Each £1 a week by which child benefit is increased costs approximately £550 million a year.) Yet another solution would be to make child benefit more generous and the adult tax thresholds somewhat lower. Although child benefit is expensive, raising child benefit is a more cost-effective way of combating child poverty than across the board increases in the adult tax allowances, since most tax units do not have children.

Having said this the figures in Appendix 2 do show some remarkable improvements in net incomes for families with children.

Need for family budget estimates. This brings us to a major weakness of the plan, namely the failure to attempt systematic assessment of "true subsistence" needs, or of the ratios between families of different sizes needed to produce approximate living standard equivalence, at either the poverty or subsistence level. Although it can be argued that, unlike Beveridge, none of the authors of the schemes in this report start from Family Budget estimates, Minford is the only author who, like Beveridge, is aiming at a "true minimum". It follows that in his case the need to get benefit rates right is crucially important, not just in order to be sure that poverty is being relieved, but also to be sure that the scheme is politically feasible. Minford's SI rates are based on former supplementary benefit, but they are subject to the 70 percent cap, and the amounts allowed for housing are based on average costs for the UK as a whole. These fixed amounts are shown in Table 13.2. Like Vince, Minford defends them on the grounds that housing, and housing costs, are a matter of personal choice.

Table 13.2: Minford's SI housing component, £ week 1985-86

| Family type | Weekly allowance for | |
	Rent £	Rates £
Single person	13.10	4.20
Married couple	14.20	4.75
MC + 1 child	15.25	5.25
MC + 2 chldren	16.30	5.80
MC + 3 children	16.80	6.30

Source: Liverpool Macroeconomic Research Ltd, Vol.5, No.4,
        December 1984, updated

Privatisation of social insurance, health and education. All employees' and self-employed NI contributions would be replaced by new, statutory minimum contributions for private health insurance and private pensions. These contributions would have to be paid whether or not the person was in employment. Credits for that purpose are added to the adult SI rates. Education too would be privatised, but the new education charge and the extra costs of health insurance incurred as a result of having children are both added to the basic child benefit. Entitlement to the NIT would be conditional on proof of adequate private insurance and payment of school fees.

Table 13.3: Minford's health, pension and education contributions, £ week, 1985-86

	Health £	Pension £	Education £	TOTAL (rounded) £
Single person	2.96	3.96	—	7.00
Married couple	5.92	7.92	—	14.00
Married couple + 1 child	8.08	7.92	14.13	30.00
Married couple + 2 children	9.56	7.92	28.26	46.00
Married couple + 3 children	11.02	7.92	42.39	61.00

Source: Minford 1985, Table 3.6. All figures increased by 5 percent.

Pensions. The ultimate objective is to transfer all pensions, including the state basic pension, into private schemes financed out of private contributions. SERPS would be abolished without delay, and the rest of the existing system would be phased out gradually, but existing rights would be protected.

The new pension contribution of £3.96 per person in 1985-86 is reckoned to be sufficient to buy a fully indexed retirement pension, from age 66, of £38.85 for a single person and double that (just under £78) for a married couple. At November 1985 prices the new statutory private pension (*sic*) would have been just under £39, compared with supplementary pension in November 1985 of £37.50. But supplementary pensioners were also entitled to housing costs in full, plus additional payments as necessary, whereas Minford's pensioners get no extras and would have to go on buying health insurance out of their £39.

Assuming that the actuarial estimates used by Minford are right, it follows that a statutory minimum contribution of £3.96 a week is nothing like enough to prevent poverty in old age. Minford leaves it to the individual to top up the statutory minimum pension contribution through voluntary savings. Each 40 pence contributed weekly over a 48 year period is reckoned to add around £4 to the weekly pension. Thus a weekly contribution of £6.00 would produce an indexed pension at age 66 of about £60 a week. If poverty in old age is to be avoided, a weekly contribution of £7.00 a week seems nearer the mark. This would produce a gross weekly pension of about £70.00 a week, assuming regular contributions from age 18 to age 66. This rate of contribution would have to be compulsory, and there would also need to be a system of credits during interruption of earnings on account of sickness or child-rearing. Despite the weight of argument in favour of abolishing SERPS, something secure needs to be put in its place.

Minford agrees that a contribution of about £7.00 a week is necessary in order to match existing provisions. A non-means-tested pension of £70 a week would be an improvement on existing provisions. But it would mean that the statutory weekly health and pension contribution for a married man would go up to £20. This would have a poll tax effect, and would reduce the gap between incomes in and out of work. It would also alter the programme's costings.

Health. The objective for health is a minimum standard of "comprehensive" health insurance for the whole population. In his 1984 *Economic Affairs* article Minford proposed that each insurance policy would specify a lower level of health expenditure below which no claim would be paid, or there could be a system of no claims bonuses. For serious illnesses all necessary expenditure above the lower level would be fully reimbursed. For illnesses of intermediate expense there would be a sliding scale and the insured person would be expected to pay something. In effect therefore the health insurance industry would pay medical bills only to the extent of the insured risk and the individual or family would have to pay the balance. In the second edition of *Unemployment Cause and Cure* Minford seems to be proposing full protection against medical costs, but his weekly contributions (at constant prices) remain unchanged. These contributions depend on family size, and there would be some economies of scale for large families. For a single adult the weekly premium is £2.96 and for a two child family it is £9.56. The parents would not be expected to pay the full amount, because a credit of nearly £4 would be incorporated in the new child benefit.

Figure 13.2: Minford's NIT and flat-rate health and pension contributions

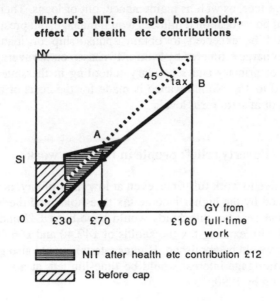

Minford's NIT: single householder, effect of health etc contributions

▦ NIT after health etc contribution £12

▨ SI before cap

Once again the cost estimates seem very low. In 1985-86 the average annual charge for all age groups of private insurers through BUPA, assuming the general (or lowest) scale, was £221 for a single adult. If we add to that figure Minford's estimate for the cost of family practitioner services, prescriptions and maternity, the annual charge per adult becomes £271, or £5.20 a week. Two years later, in 1987-88, average gross expenditure per person by the National Health Service was £377, or £7.25 a week. For a family of four it was £1,508, or £29 a week (Hansard WA 10 Feb 1988, c 280).

We seem to be reaching a statutory minimum contribution per adult of about £12 a week (£24 for a married couple), instead of Minford's estimated £7 (or £14 for a married couple). Add in the Government's proposed poll tax and the tax slippage becomes immense. By the 1990s a married man in inner London could find himself liable for tax of over £50 a week before he had earned a penny. Figure 13.2 illustrates the effects on Minford's conditional NIT of minimum contributions totalling £12.

Education. Schools and universities would be completely privatised. The estimated cost of minimum standard schooling, which would remain compulsory, is incorporated in the new child benefit. Students would be expected to pay sixth form, university and college fees, as well as maintenance, out of loans. There is no mention of how vocational trainees would manage, but presumably they would be expected to obtain sponsorship or loans. The education charge estimated by Minford is based on the average cost per child of primary and secondary schooling in the state sector from age 0 to 15 . No allowance is made for the costs of nursery education or at sixth form level.

Poverty relief: people in full-time work

The incentive to work full-time, even at low rates of pay, is greatly strengthened by the higher income tax thresholds and the NIT. In 1985-86 the new tax thresholds would have been £87 and £134, compared with existing tax thresholds of £42.40 and £66.44. Age allowance would be abolished. Higher rate tax would also go. Tax relief on mortgage interest would be time-limited, at a saving of £700 million by 1990.

Child benefit and one-parent benefit. Child benefit at £23 in 1985-86 comprises £7 basic, plus £16 credits for health insurance and education charge. One-parent benefit is also retained, and the November 1985 rate is £4.55. One-parent benefit is not payable to lone parents who are cohabiting with a man. Surprisingly, Minford allows cohabiting lone parents to retain the additional person allowance for income tax purposes. Unlike Vince and Parker, there is nothing in his proposals to tilt the tax/benefit balance more in favour of two-parent families, nor anything to encourage absent parents to pay maintenance.

The full-time work rule. As with FIS and family credit, Minford's NIT is restricted to people working full-time, or thereabouts. With an unconditional NIT, entitlement at nil earnings equals a fixed percentage of the guarantee, and is withdrawn as earnings approach the break-even point, at rates that depend on the taper. Making the NIT conditional produces weird effects. If Minford had not stipulated that the work must be full-time then one day's work for a wage of (say) £30 could net a married man his £30 wage *plus* 70 percent of the difference between £30 and the married man's poverty threshold, or £30 + 70% (£134-£30) = £102.80. On the other hand, because Minford stipulates that the work must be full-time, and because the SI involves a 100 percent taper, nobody in their right mind who was dependent on SI would choose to do paid work for less than 24 or 30 hours a week. Hence the need for workfare.

The NIT experiments in America suggested that an unconditional NIT would result in unacceptably high levels of withdrawal from the regular labour market. These conclusions are debatable (see Chapter 10), but widely accepted. Minford's proposals show that making the NIT conditional produces new problems and new anomalies.

Model families. Table 13.8 at the end of this chapter shows how Minford's NIT would operate. Once again the figures distinguish between net incomes (after tax and benefits) and disposable incomes (after payment of rents and rates as well). Because Minford does not relate his NIT to housing costs incurred, families with rents and rates higher than those assumed would have disposable incomes lower than those in the tables, and *vice versa.*

Table 13.4: Minford's SI scale rate minima, £ week March 1986

Family type	Weekly rate £	Housing component £
Single non-householder	25.30	—
Single householder	50.03	17.35
Single person + 2 children (1 under 5, 1/5-10)	89.45	22.05
Married couple	71.66	18.90
MC + 1 child under 5	87.20	20.50
MC + 2 children (1 under 5, 1/5-10)	101.47	22.05
MC + 3 children (1 under 5, 1/5-10, 1/11-15)	126.24	23.10

Breakdown of SI scale rate for couple + 2 children aged 4 and 6

	£
Adults	47.85
Children	20.20
Rent	16.30
Rates	5.75
Water rates	1.55
Heating for child under 5	2.20
Free school meals	2.60
Free welfare milk	1.67
Value of other passport benefits	3.35
Total SI scale rate	101.47

The subsistence income and the 70 percent cap

The SI scale rates are based on former SB scale rates, plus allowances for passport benefits, and with fixed additions for rent, rates and water rates. Minimum health, etc. contributions are credited. Table 13.4 sets out the SI rates applicable during the period November 1985 to March 1986. The rate for a lone parent is based on the November 1985 long-term SB rate. Also in Table 13.4 are the SI components for a couple with three children.

As explained, minimum net incomes from full-time working are not allowed to fall below total income support at a wage of £60 in November1985, assuming rents and rates as in the housing component of Table 13.4. This produces the GMIs in Table 13.5.

Table 13.5: Minford's GMIs for people in full-time work, £ week, March 1986

Family type	Minimum guarantee £
Single householder	62.68
Married couple	74.75
MC + 2 children aged 4 and 6	121.12
Single person + 2 children aged 4 and 6	124.17

The higher GMIs for families with children are necessary because basic child benefit is only £7. The effect is to produce the 100 percent MTRs at the bottom of the income distribution, shown in Figure 13.3.

The larger the family the higher the escape point from the 100 percent tax rate. For the two-child family shown in Figure 13.3 the GMI in 1985-86, assuming full-time work, would have been £121.12. The tax rate falls from 100 percent to 70 percent at earnings of £91 a week.

The 70 percent benefit cap. Income on SI for people not in full-time paid work is subject to a maximum replacement ratio override, or benefit ratio ceiling, equal to 70 percent of former net income from paid work, with the latter defined as gross earnings plus child benefit, plus NIT (or less income tax), and less work expenses.

Table 13.6 shows how the system would have worked for married couples with two small children, living in council accommodation and paying the average rents and rates reported to

Figure 13.3: Minford's poverty trap, families with children, March 1986

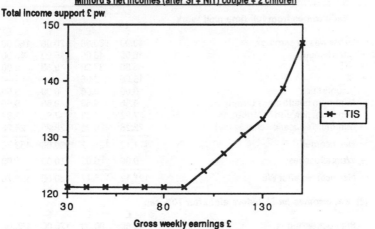

Minford's net incomes (after SI + NIT) couple + 2 children

Total income support £ pw

Gross weekly earnings £

the DHSS by the local authorities for the year 1985-86. The figures assume that the job paying only £40 a week involved no work expenses, that the job paying £80 a week involved work expenses of £5 and the jobs paying £120 and £160 a week involved work expenses of £10 and £15 a week respectively.

Section (1) of the table sets out the components of net income at different earnings levels. At earnings of £40 and £80 a week the families' NIT is topped up, bringing their net incomes before work expenses up to the £121 guaranteed floor. The family on £160 a week ends up less than £18 a week better off than the family on £40 a week.

Section (2) sets out net incomes on SI before and after the cap. The costs of the statutory health etc contributions are credited to people on SI. In each case net income from full SI is more than 70 percent of net income after work expenses shown in Section (1). So the cap takes effect.

Section (3) shows disposable incomes after applying the cap, and after paying the assumed rent, rates and water rates. Minimum health etc contributions are deducted as before. The family with previous earnings of £80 a week does worst because the job involved £5 a week in fares to work. If fares to work had been more than £5 a week, they would be even worse off.

Disposable income on Minford's capped SI turns out to be between £4 and £20 a week less than on SB, even assuming housing costs of only £24.45 a week. Families in London would have to use the housekeeping money to pay the rent.

Table 13.6: Minford's benefit cap: married man with two children aged 4 and 6, March 1986

(1) Net incomes from full-time paid work

	£	£	£	£
Gross weekly earnings	40.00	80.00	120.00	160.00
+ Child benefit	46.00	46.00	46.00	46.00
+ NIT	65.80	37.80	9.80	0.00
+ SI	15.06	3.06	—	—
− Income tax	0.00	0.00	0.00	6.50
− Minimum health contribution	9.56	9.56	9.56	9.56
− Minimum pension contribution	7.92	7.92	7.92	7.92
− Minimum education charge (av)	28.26	28.26	28.26	28.26
= Net incomes	121.12	121.12	130.06	153.76
− Work expenses	0.00	5.00	10.00	15.00
= Net incomes after WE	121.12	116.12	120.06	138.76

(2) Net incomes on SI, before and after 70% cap

	£	£	£	£
Previous earnings	40.00	80.00	120.00	160.00
SI scale rate for MC2 aged 4 and 6	101.47	101.47	101.47	101.47
+ Minimum health etc contributions (rounded)	46.00	46.00	46.00	46.00
− Minimum health etc contributions (")	46.00	46.00	46.00	46.00
= Maximum net income on SI	101.47	101.47	101.47	101.47
Maximum net incomes allowed after cap (70% net incomes after WE in section (1))	84.78	81.28	84.04	97.13
SI scale rate entitlement is therefore reduced by:	16.69	20.19	17.43	4.34
Net incomes on SI, after 70% cap are:	84.78	81.28	84.04	97.13

(3) Disposable incomes on SI, after 70% cap and housing costs

	£	£	£	£
Previous earnings	40.00	80.00	120.00	160.00
Capped SI scale rate entitlement	84.78	81.28	84.04	97.13
+ Minimum health etc contributions (rounded)	46.00	46.00	46.00	46.00
− Minimum health etc contributions (")	46.00	46.00	46.00	46.00
− Average local authority rent and rates	24.45	24.45	24.45	24.45
= Disposable incomes on capped SI	60.33	56.83	59.59	72.68
cf estimated disposable incomes on SB	77.00	77.00	77.00	77.00

There is little doubt that the cap would cause hardship. It is also questionable whether the labour market effects would be those intended. They might not be. Nobody who had previously been well paid would willingly take a lower paid job, in case he lost it and ended up on a lower rate of SI. Nobody would voluntarily take a lower paid job not close to home. Nor would any unemployed person with low housing costs voluntarily move to an area with higher housing costs (and perhaps more jobs), because they might end up falling foul of the cap. Workfare regulations would need to be draconian if reactions like these were to be prevented.

Workfare

The benefit cap is designed to bring market pressures to bear by making people take jobs at lower rates of pay than at present. Similar objectives are common to all the hybrid schemes in this report, but the other authors rely on increasing net incomes from lower paid work, whereas Minford is prepared to cut the dole as well:

> In principle, the state should only provide benefits where the unemployed can get no job, however unpleasant or low paid...It has been suggested that the state sets up "community work schemes" and that the unemployed be offered places on such schemes, benefit being conditional on acceptance of such places if offered. The problem with such ideas is that they are expensive to the state – involving supervision, equipment and other costs – and that the jobs involved have a very low value to society (otherwise they would already have been undertaken). However, as a last resort of benefit, they are of some use. Let us designate such a pool of jobs "workfare" jobs. It would then seem useful to include all existing jobs notified to job centres (often private sector but also public sector), in this pool; the "community" jobs would then be there as a last resort, in the total absence of normal jobs. (Minford *et al.* 1985, pages 48-49)

In America, where the term workfare originated, it is aimed primarily at lone mothers (AFDC) and unemployed fathers (AFDC-U), for the simple reason that there is no equivalent of income support (payable indefinitely) except for families with children. With workfare the mother's welfare cheque is divided by the hourly minimum wage, which then becomes the number of hours for which she is required to work. Despite use of the American terminology Minford's workfare is aimed at the unemployed – it does not include lone mothers. After about six months the unemployed person would be expected to work full-time for his or her benefit cheque. It is assumed that the costs (of administration, travel, and so forth) would be defrayed by the output of the workfarers. Minford's workfare is estimated to have no net cost, it could make a profit, which is surprising. In 1987 Government estimated that replacement of income support for 16-17 year olds by a comprehensive Youth Training Scheme would result in overall increased expenditure (House of Commons 1987).

How much would it cost?

Minford's is the only scheme in this report with costings that take into account the dynamic effects of change, yet there is much to be said for this approach. Minford is also the only author who

Table 13.7: Minford's budget for the year 1990 – 1984-85 prices

(1) *Direct expenditure savings*		(2) *Direct expenditure increases*	
	£ million		£ million
Health	6,000	Abolition of employees	
Education	16,000	NI contributions	9,700
Pensions	3,200	Raise tax thresholds	17,000
Unemployment benefits	1,000	Raise child benefits	9,800
Personal social services	600	70% NIT	500
Nationalised industries	2,000	Minus saving on tax	
Industry, etc	4,300	expenditures	−700
Housing	4,100		
Transport	500	Total	36,300
Agriculture	1,100		
Defence	2,000		
Environment	1,200		
Other programmes	1,000		
Total	43,000		

(3) *Indirect revenue effects*		(4) *Further recommended changes*	
	£ billion		£ billion
Rise in tax thresholds, child benefit, abolition of personal NICs	+2,900	Extra infrastructure spending	2,000
Unemployment benefit ceiling	+3,500	Abolition of employers' NIC	10,100
Abolition of employers' NIC's	+7,000	Abolition of higher rates of IT	4,000
Abolition of higher rates of IT and cut in standard rate to 25p	+1,400	Reduction of standard IT to 25%	5,500
Total	+14,800	Total	21,600

Source: Minford *et al.* 1985, Tables 3.8 – 3.11.

recommends large-scale expenditure cuts outside tax and social security, a move which would increase the political opposition to change, by adding to the numbers of losers, but which may well be necessary.

Writing in 1985, Minford took 1990 as his target year, and anticipated expenditure savings by then of £42.9 billion, against which his planned tax changes were expected to cost £36.3 billion. The figures are reproduced in Table 13.7. They give the appearance of optimism. For instance there seems to be a net savings on education expenditure of £7,000 million.

The net direct saving is £6.6 billion and the indirect savings, as a result of increased employment and output due to increased incentives, is £15 billion. These savings would be used to abolish employers' NI contributions, to increase infrastructure spending and to cut income tax rates. Roughly it is anticipated that there would be enough "spare" revenue to abolish employers' NI contribution, to cut the standard rate of income tax to 25 percent and to abolish the higher rate bands of income tax. This is a typical New Right strategy, aimed at overcoming poverty by encouraging economic growth. The annual rise in output by 1990 is expected to be 11 percent. The indirect effect is to increase revenues by £15 billion, and to reduce unemployment by about 2.5 million.

Administration

Minford says little about administration. The scheme has five main administrative components: the positive income tax, the negative income tax, the SI, the compulsory minimum health, pension and education contributions, and the compulsory workfare. The danger is that each component, but especially the last four, would nourish its own bureaucracy, and that each bureaucracy would proliferate according to the separate agendas, as Charles Murray might say (Murray 1987) of its officials. If this were to happen, new empires would replace existing ones and the dead hand of the State would remain.

Look again at the five elements:

(1) **The fully automated positive income tax,** with child PBIs credited presumably to the parents, and assessment units as at present. From the administrative point of view this looks straightforward. A flat rate 25 percent tax

would be easy to operate and would remove some of the anomalies that result from joint taxation of husband and wife. The number of taxpayers would be reduced, because of the increased tax thresholds.

(2) **A negative income tax,** theoretically integrated with the positive tax system, but this requires harmonisation of all regulations and procedures, which is impossible. Minford wants the benefit unit to be the same as the tax unit, but does not say whether cohabiting couples should count as one or two assessment units. At present they count as one unit for benefit purposes and two for tax. With an integrated system the unit must be the same for both. All NIT systems raise this sort of problem, but Minford's is more complicated than most, because of his 30 hour work obligation. All kinds of question come to mind. What would be the accounting period? How long would claimants need to wait before receiving their NIT? Would entitlement be cumulative and how would weeks of part-time working be calculated alongside other weeks of full-time working? Would the number of hours worked be cumulative or non-cumulative? Would some one who worked full-time for three months of the year be eligible for NIT, and for how long? What would happen to full-time workers during periods of short-time working? How would the self-employed be assessed? Would all members of the assessment unit have to work full-time, or would part-time work by one member disqualify the whole unit from entitlement to the NIT?

Entitlement to the NIT would also be conditional on proof of adequate private health and retirement insurance, and payment of school fees. How far back would this obligation go? Would people whose payments had lapsed get a second chance? Finally, what policing arrangements would be made to ensure that employers and employees did not collude to maximise benefit entitlement?

(3) **A capped subsistence income,** requiring detailed information not just of former earnings, but also of former work expenses. Income support is bad enough to administer, but the SI would be worse. In the case of married claimants two sets of earnings and of work

expenses would be required. Provided the accounting period was short this might be possible, but a year is much too long. People who are poor tend not to have the steady work and other records that the Minford scheme implies. They also tend to have debts. What would happen if capped SI claimants with high housing costs did not pay their rent arrears? Would they be put in gaol? Would the liability to maintain laws be the same as with income support, or would they go wider?

(4) **A workfare scheme,** requiring perhaps millions of job placements each year. It is not clear how the jobs would be created, how the people doing the jobs would move on into the regular labour market, or how the workfare obligation would be enforced. In America it was quickly found by scheme operators that refusal to pay a welfare cheque is extremely difficult, especially when mothers claim good reasons for not turning up, a sick child being one standard pretext. Would SI be stopped if the claimant did not turn up for work? Would the family be allowed to starve? Would the children be put into care? The closer one looks at large-scale workfare, the more it takes on the appearance of an empire builder's charter. An unconditional NIT, despite its limitations, might be the lesser of two evils.

(5) **Private health, etc. contributions,** without which there is no entitlement to the NIT, no entitlement to health care and no income security in old age. We must ask how payment of these contributions would be enforced, and what would happen to those who did not pay them? Would married and cohabiting couples be responsible for each other's pension contributions, as with poll tax? Would the same rules apply to homosexual couples? Would people who fell behind with their payments be left to starve in old age? Would they and their families be disqualified from health care? Would the children go without schooling? It is all too easy for intellectuals from comfortable backgrounds to assume that everyone finds it equally easy to find out about, understand and conform to bureaucratic regulations. But real life is different. In France for instance, where some family benefits are conditional on

211

turning up for medical examinations, or on living in accommodation that meets required standards, it has been found that the poorest families tend not to fulfil the conditions and to forfeit entitlement. Some are ignorant, some have problems they want to hide, and some are afraid of officialdom (Colin 1980, quoted in Wresinski 1987). Would Minford's system reach out to the very poor?

Who gains and who loses?

Due to the administrative complexity of the Minford proposals, the scale of change, and the large expenditure cuts in other programmes (especially education, health and housing) the model family analysis in Appendix 2 is only a very approximate guide, and no attempt has been made to use TAXMOD. Minford himself acknowledges that the proposed minimum statutory pension contribution of £3.96 would need to go up by £3 a week, and the proposed minimum health contribution also looks too low. From the information provided we cannot be sure how much extra money people would be expected to pay out of their own pockets on health care or education. Nor is there any information about the extra money that parents would be expected to pay to top up the minimum education charge, or for the costs of sixth form and further education.

From Appendix 2, it is nevertheless clear that the proposals constitute a double redistribution of income in favour of middle to high income groups and families without children. Whereas Vince tilted the net income curve in favour of people at the bottom of the income distribution, Minford tilts it in favour of the better off. On incomes above £100 a week there appear to be no losers, indeed most people in full-time paid work seem to be better off, although lower paid families with above average housing costs would not be. At the top of the earnings league the gains are very large, for instance at earnings of £52,000 a year, the gain would be about £11,000 a year.

The main losers are the unemployed, students, pensioners, and people on low incomes with high housing costs. The pension problem could be solved by putting up the minimum statutory pension contribution. Better health care could be provided in similar fashion. But this would exacerbate the poll tax effect of the

Figure 13.4: Minford net incomes, March 1986

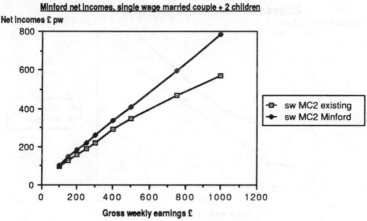

Minford net incomes, single wage married couple + 2 children

Source: Appendix 2

new flat rate contributions. It would also narrow the gap between incomes in and out of work, and more unemployed people would find their benefit incomes capped. The effect of the cap is to replace the supplementary benefit guarantee (supposedly based on minimum living costs) by a variable derived from an arbitrary ratio. There would no longer be a safety net in any meaningful sense of the word. Student grants would be replaced by loans. People with disabilities who were able to work full-time might gain from the NIT, but most people with disabilities cannot work full-time, and there is no proposal to increase public expenditure for people with disabilities.

Figure 13.4, *net incomes*, shows the proposed net income curve for single wage married couples with two children. Over the wide range of income shown, the curves do not vary significantly between the main family types, instead there is a consistent, significant shift in favour of single people, due mainly to the poll tax effect of the new health, etc. contributions. On earnings of £100 a week net income after those contributions (but before the NIT) goes up from £74 to £90 for a single person, and from £81 to £86 for a single wage married couple. So net income before the NIT is higher for a single person than a married couple. This is tax slippage by another name.

Minford's scheme is a useful way of illuminating the different effects on income distribution of different tax changes. His cuts in the standard rate of income tax help single people and the better off

Figure 13.5: Minford disposable incomes, March 1986

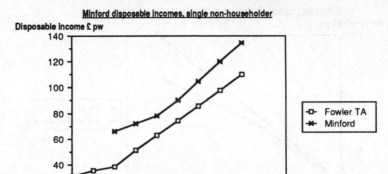

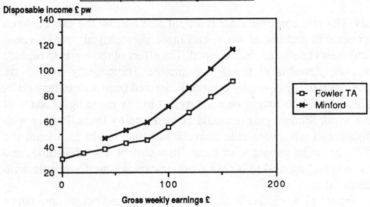

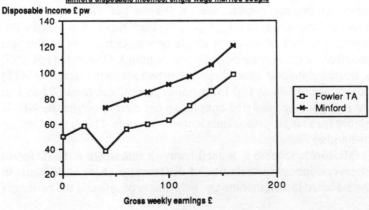

Minford disposable incomes, single wage married couple + 2 children aged 4 & 6

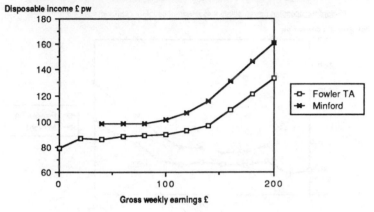

Minford disposable incomes, lone parent + 2 children aged 4 & 6

Source: Appendix 2

more than families and more than the lower paid. His increased tax allowances have the reverse effect, but part of the value of the increased tax allowance is offset by the new capitation charges.

Figure 13.5, *disposable incomes,* shows how Minford uses his NIT to boost the disposable incomes of the lower paid. All the householders are assumed to be tenants in low cost housing, and all are assumed to be in full-time work. If someone earned (say) £60 in two eight-hour days, there would be no NIT entitlement. This rule may look harmless, but it could exclude unemployed people trying to get back into the labour market. It could also exclude people with disabilities, trying to work part-time.

Figure 13.6: Minford net spending power, March 1986

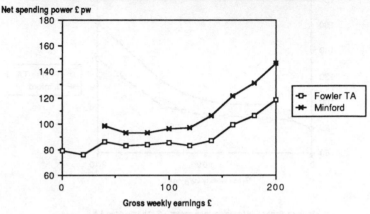

Source: Appendix 2. Work expense assumptions: Chapter 11.

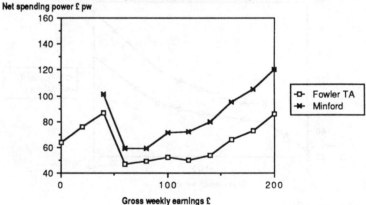

In each disposable income graph there is a gap where earnings are less than £40 a week. This is to emphasise the variable nature of Minford's SI guarantee, due to the cap, which overrides it. With this exception the figures suggest a remarkable improvement by comparison with Fowler TA. Disposable incomes go up and most marginal tax rates go down. But for some families with children the curve of disposable income is quite flat. Once again the income levels on the vertical axis vary between families with and without children, but scale is maintained.

Figure 13.7: Minford pensioner incomes, March 1986

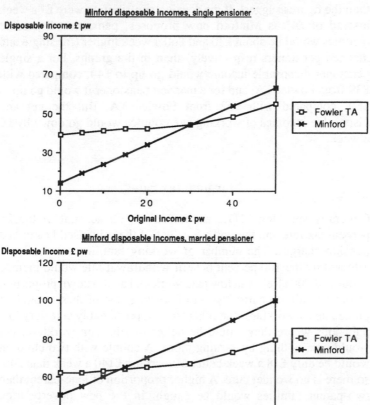

Minford disposable incomes, single pensioner

Disposable Income £ pw

Original Income £ pw

Minford disposable incomes, married pensioner

Disposable Income £ pw

Original Income £ pw

Source: Appendix 2.

Where the disposable income curve is flat, or almost flat, then the *net spending power* curve (after deduction of travel and childcare costs) is likely to develop troughs. In Figure 13.6 the same work expenses are assumed as before, and once again the disincentive to take lower paid work is very strong. For lone mothers the best bet is to stay on SI with maximum earnings disregard, topping their incomes up through the black economy.

Figure 13.7 shows the effect of the scheme on the *disposable incomes of pensioners* paying rent of £15 a week and rates of £7. Minford's pension is not payable until age 66, and is too low to prevent poverty. With housing costs higher than those assumed the losses would be still higher, but owner occupiers would do better than the figures suggest. If the pension contribution were £7 a week instead of £4, as Minford now proposes, pensioner disposable incomes would be about £30 and £60 a week higher (for single and married pensioners respectively) than in the graphs. For a single pensioner disposable income would go up to £44, compared with £39 from Fowler TA, and for a married pensioner it would go up to £80, compared with £62 from Fowler TA. But the net and disposable incomes of working age couples would go down by £6 a week.

Marginal tax rates

Generally speaking MTRs are improved, on account of the 25 percent tax rate and the poll tax effect of the privatised health and pension charges. The number of working families with children affected by the 100 percent benefit withdrawal rate would include about 150,000 already in low paid work and an unknown proportion of the 1.5 million currently out of work. Some of these would be picked up by workfare, and others would presumably take very low paid jobs where they would be better off than on workfare, but would gain nothing by earning more. A couple with two children would be only £18 a week better off earning £140 a week than £40, so there is no wonder cure. A higher proportion of lone-parent than two-parent families would be caught in the new poverty trap, because of their lower earnings potential.

Summing up

Minford's "Efficient Relief of Poverty" comprises a conditional NIT for people in full-time work, a capped subsistence income linked to compulsory workfare for the unemployed, and privatisation of pensions, health and education. Despite its attractions, most of all the big increases in disposable incomes from lower paid work, the scheme is unlikely to result in the efficient relief of poverty, for three main reasons:

(1) The conditional NIT would act as a disincentive to part-time working at a time when technological and social change is moving towards more, not less, part-time working.

(2) Some of the most difficult problems, for instance poverty due to disability and marriage break-up, are outside Minford's terms of reference.

(3) Minford creates his own Byzantium.

The results of a conditional NIT are unexpected and unsatisfactory. If part-time workers were allowed to claim it, there would be a disproportionate gain from part-time work. But by excluding them part-time work is no longer worthwhile. Either way the labour market effects are undesirable. Minford's conditional NIT runs counter to every other proposal in this report. The other authors tackle unemployment by making benefit entitlement regulations more responsive to labour market change. Minford makes them less responsive.

Minford reserves his carrots for the rich. For the poor he relies on the stick. Unfortunately he underestimates the difficulties of applying it without allowing some families to starve. One way to reduce waste is by getting the unemployed to accept lower wages, but two problems arise. The first is the problem of those who cannot do full-time or regular paid work, and who are therefore excluded from the NIT. The second is the problem of deciding how little constitutes "a true minimum". This is a key question, and Minford's minimum turns out to be bottomless.

The scheme does not appear to meet the criteria of even partial integration. The NIT does not replace all existing benefits, and administrative harmonisation is out of the question. In practice the scheme would probably involve an automated positive income tax alongside a series of extremely labour intensive, income support and job creation programmes – an extension, in other words, of the existing system. It is an open question whether the NIT could function without a minimum wage. Its main beneficiaries could be inefficient or unscrupulous employers.

Table 13.8: Disposable incomes of selected model families, Minford's "Efficient Relief of Poverty" proposals, detailed figures for Nov 85 to Mar 1986, £ per week

Assumptions

All figures refer to the period November 1985 to March 1986. All families are tenants. Working age families live in council property, and pay the rents and rates used in the November 1985 DHSS Tax/Benefit Model Tables. Water rates, estimated by the DHSS to have been £1.65 a week on average, are not deducted. Families are assumed to take up entitlement to means-tested benefits in full. No non-personal income tax reliefs. No allowance for cost of fares to work or childminding . Tax and poverty thresholds are £87 for single people, £134 for married couples and lone parents. Age allowance is abolished. Rate of income tax is 25 percent. NIT taper is 70 percent. NI contributions replaced by statutory minimum contributions for health and old age. Basic child benefit is £7.00 (November 1985 rate) plus credits for health & education charges £16.00, total £23.00. One parent benefit retained at £4.55 (November 1985 rate). *All earnings are for full-time work and none of the SI amounts are capped.*

Acronyms: NIT = negative income tax; SI = subsistence income; CC = contribution credit

1. WORKING AGE HOUSEHOLDS

Table 1: Single non-householder aged 18-65

	£	£	£	£	£	£
Gross weekly earnings	0.00	40.00	80.00	120.00	160.00	200.00
− Income tax	0.00	0.00	0.00	8.25	18.25	28.25
− Min. health contribution	2.96	2.96	2.96	2.96	2.96	2.96
− Min. pension contribution	3.96	3.96	3.96	3.96	3.96	3.96
= Net incomes before SI/NIT	−6.92	33.08	73.08	104.83	134.83	164.83
+ NIT	—	32.90	4.90	0.00	0.00	0.00
+ SI (before cap, & incl. CC)	32.22 max.	—	—	—	—	—
= Net & disposable incomes	25.30 max	65.98	77.98	104.83	134.83	164.83

Table 2: Single householder

	£	£	£	£	£	£
Gross weekly earnings	0.00	40.00	80.00	120.00	160.00	200.00
− Income tax	0.00	0.00	0.00	8.25	18.25	28.25
− Min. health contribution	2.96	2.96	2.96	2.96	2.96	2.96
− Min. pension contribution	3.96	3.96	3.96	3.96	3.96	3.96
= Net incomes before SI/NIT	−6.92	33.08	73.08	104.83	134.83	164.83
+ NIT	—	32.90	4.90	0.00	0.00	0.00
+ SI (before cap, & incl. CC)	56.92	—	—	—	—	—
= Net incomes after SI/NIT	50.03	65.98	77.98	104.83	134.83	164.83
− Rent	13.80	13.80	13.80	13.80	13.80	13.80
− Rates	5.20	5.20	5.20	5.20	5.20	5.20
= Disposable incomes	31.03 max	46.98	58.98	85.83	115.83	145.83

Table 3: Single person + 2 children aged 4 and 6

	£	£	£	£	£	£
Gross weekly earnings	0.00	40.00	80.00	120.00	160.00	200.00
+ Child benefit	46.00	46.00	46.00	46.00	46.00	46.00
+ One parent benefit	4.55	4.55	4.55	4.55	4.55	4.55
− Income tax	0.00	0.00	0.00	80.00	6.50	16.50
− Min. health contribution	6.60	6.60	6.60	6.60	6.60	6.60
− Min. pension contribution	3.96	3.96	3.96	3.96	3.96	3.96
− Min. education charge	28.26	28.26	28.26	28.26	28.26	28.26
= Net incomes before SI/NIT	11.73	51.73	91.73	131.73	165.23	195.23
+ NIT	—	65.80	37.80	9.80	0.00	0.00
+ SI (before cap, & Incl. CC)	77.72	6.64	—	—	—	—
= Net incomes after SI/NIT	89.45	124.17	129.53	141.52	165.23	195.23
− Rent	16.50	16.50	16.50	16.50	16.50	16.50
− Rates	6.30	6.30	6.30	6.30	6.30	6.30
= Disposable incomes	66.65 max	101.37	106.73	118.72	142.43	172.43

Table 4: Married couple (Single-wage)

	£	£	£	£	£	£
Gross weekly earnings	0.00	40.00	80.00	120.00	160.00	200.00
− Income tax	0.00	0.00	0.00	0.00	6.50	16.50
− Min. health contribution	5.92	6.92	6.92	6.92	6.92	6.92
− Min. pension contribution	7.92	7.92	7.92	7.92	7.92	7.92
= Net incomes before SI/NIT	13.84	26.16	66.16	106.16	139.66	169.66
+ NIT	—	65.80	37.80	9.80	0.00	0.00
+ SI (before cap, & Incl. CC)	85.50	—	—	—	—	—
= Net incomes after SI/NIT	71.66	91.96	103.96	115.96	139.66	169.66
− Rent	13.80	13.80	13.80	13.80	13.80	13.80
− Rates	5.20	5.20	5.20	5.20	5.20	5.20
= Disposable incomes	52.56 max	72.96	84.96	96.96	120.66	150.66

Table 5: Married couple (two-wage, each spouse earns half)

		£	£	£	£	£	£
Gross weekly earnings		—	—	80.00	120.00	160.00	200.00
− Income tax: Husband	0.00	0.00	0.00	8.25	18.25	28.25	
Wife	—	—	0.00	0.00	0.00	3.25	
− Min. health contribution		—	—	5.92	5.92	5.92	5.92
− Min. pension contribution		—	—	7.92	7.92	7.92	7.92
= Net incomes before SI/NIT		—	—	66.16	106.16	146.16	182.91
+ NIT		—	—	37.60	9.80	0.00	0.00
= Net incomes after NIT		—	—	103.96	115.96	145.16	182.91
− Rent		—	—	13.80	13.80	13.80	13.80
− Rates		—	—	5.20	5.20	5.20	5.20
= Disposable incomes		— max	—	84.96	96.96	127.16	163.91

Table 6: Married couple + 2 children aged 4 and 6 (single wage)

	£	£	£	£	£	£
Gross weekly earnings	0.00	40.00	80.00	120.00	160.00	200.00
+ Child benefit	46.00	46.00	46.00	46.00	46.00	46.00
− Income tax	0.00	0.00	0.00	0.00	6.50	16.50
− Min. health contribution	9.56	9.56	9.56	9.56	9.56	9.56
− Min. pension contribution	7.92	7.92	7.92	7.92	7.92	7.92
− Min. education charge (av)	28.26	28.26	28.26	28.26	28.26	28.26
= Net incomes before SI/NIT	0.26	40.26	80.26	120.26	153.76	183.76
+ NIT	—	80.86	40.86	9.80	0.00	0.00
+ SI (before cap, & incl. CC)	101.21	—	—	—	—	—
= Net incomes after SI/NIT	101.47	121.12	121.12	130.06	153.76	183.76
− Rent	16.50	16.50	16.50	16.50	16.50	16.50
− Rates	6.30	6.30	6.30	6.30	6.30	6.30
= Disposable incomes	78.67 max	98.32	98.32	107.26	130.96	160.96

Table 7: Married couple + two children aged 4 and 6 (two-wage, each spouse earns half)

	£	£	£	£	£	£
Gross weekly earnings	—	—	80.00	120.00	160.00	200.00
+ Child benefit	46.00	46.00	46.00	46.00	46.00	46.00
− Income tax: Husband	—	—	0.00	0.00	0.00	0.00
Wife	—	—	0.00	0.00	0.00	3.25
− Min. health contribution	—	—	9.56	9.56	9.56	9.56
− Min. pension contribution	—	—	7.92	7.92	7.92	7.92
Min. education charge	—	—	28.26	28.26	28.26	28.26
= Net incomes before SI/NIT	—	—	80.26	120.26	160.26	197.01
+ NIT	—	—	40.86	9.80	0.00	0.00
+ SI	—	—	—	—	—	—
= Net incomes after NIT/SI	—	—	121.12	130.06	160.26	197.01
− Rent	—	—	16.50	16.50	16.50	16.50
− Rates	—	—	6.30	6.30	6.30	6.30
= Disposable incomes	—	—	98.32	107.26	137.46	174.21

2. RETIREMENT PENSIONERS

Table 8: Single retirement pensioner aged 66

	£	£	£	£	£	£	£	£
Earnings/additional private pension/ investment income	0.00	5.00	10.00	20.00	30.00	40.00	50.00	100.00
+ Min private pension	38.85	38.85	38.85	38.85	38.85	38.85	38.85	38.85
− Income tax	0.00	0.00	0.00	0.00	0.00	0.00	0.00	0.00
Min health cont.	2.96	2.96	2.96	2.96	2.96	2.96	2.96	2.96
= Net incomes	35.89	40.89	45.89	55.89	65.89	75.89	85.43	122.93
− Rent	15.00	15.00	15.00	15.00	15.00	15.00	15.00	15.00
− Rates	7.00	7.00	7.00	7.00	7.00	7.00	7.00	7.00
= Disposable incomes	13.89	18.89	23.89	33.89	43.89	53.89	63.43	100.93

Table 9: Pensioner couple aged 66 or over

	£	£	£	£	£	£	£	£
Earnings/additional private pension/ investment income	0.00	5.00	10.00	20.00	30.00	40.00	50.00	100.00
+ Min private pension	77.70	77.70	77.70	77.70	77.70	77.70	77.70	77.70
− Income tax	0.00	0.00	0.00	0.00	0.00	0.00	0.00	0.00
Min health cont.	5.92	5.92	5.92	5.92	5.92	5.92	5.92	5.92
= Net incomes	71.78	76.78	81.78	91.78	101.78	111.78	121.78	160.91
− Rent	15.00	15.00	15.00	15.00	15.00	15.00	15.00	15.00
− Rates	7.00	7.00	7.00	7.00	7.00	7.00	7.00	7.00
= Disposable incomes	49.78	54.78	59.78	69.78	79.78	89.78	99.78	138.91

14

Basic Income Guarantee (BIG)

Unlike most proposals for integration of the tax and benefit systems, the Basic Income Guarantee (BIG) devised by Rhys Williams and Parker is an idea or concept rather than any particular scheme. The "BIG idea" rests on a view of society in which social welfare, social cohesion, economic revival and poverty prevention are interrelated and interdependent. The aim is poverty prevention not poverty relief, the emphasis is on individual freedom enhanced by sense of community, and the method is to replace existing cash benefits and income tax allowances by a mixture of age-related partial basic incomes (PBIs), selective but non-withdrawable PBI supplements, and a residual income-tested housing benefit.

Poverty prevention requires a life-cycle approach to income maintenance, an acceptance that during childhood we are all net beneficiaries, during working life most are net contributors (through unpaid as well as paid work), and during old age most again become net beneficiaries. BIG emphasises the value of unpaid work and questions traditional stereotyping, whereby a man who is not in paid work is assumed to be a loafer and a woman who is in paid work is thought to be shirking her family responsibilities.

All BIG schemes operate through two, clearly distinguishable components, first the centrally administered, fully integrated Transfer Income Account (TIA), responsible for the BIs and the new income tax or *BI contribution* (BIC), and second the locally administered *Cash and Care Departments* (C&C), responsible for housing benefit, emergency cash provision and certification of claims for disability BIs, as well as for counselling and other services at present the responsibility of local authority social services departments.

This is the standard framework, but there is no single BIG scheme. Flexibility is an important feature, because governments have different priorities, and a system that is to win all-party support cannot be rigid. In this chapter we shall discuss BIG strategy in general terms, followed by a short summary of one BIG option. Other options have been described in the evidence submitted by Sir Brandon Rhys Williams to the Meacher Committee (House of Commons 1983) and in Parker, 1984.

Helping people to become economically independent

All BIG schemes are devised as a base on which individuals can build, instead of a trap that turns them into paupers. All take citizenship or legal residence as the main basis of entitlement, and the individual as the main unit of assessment. All seek to reduce unemployment by setting people free to earn without loss of benefit, except as it is withdrawn through the income tax. All seek to strengthen the traditional, two-parent family, by removing the penalties for legal marriage and by increasing non means-tested child support. All seek to encourage voluntary saving and voluntary provision by reducing the number of people dependent on means-tested benefits.

All BIG schemes also seek to overcome the excessive costs associated with full BI. This they do by using carefully devised combinations of universal and selective benefits. When choosing benefit categories, two of the most important criteria are administrative simplicity and the avoidance of benefits that create their own demand. Age is the best category, since no one chooses to be born or to grow old. Disability is problematical but nonetheless essential. Selectivity does not have to be through income-testing or means-testing, a system of demogrants can be just as effective. With BIG schemes selectivity is sometimes through demogrants, sometimes through tests of income, and sometimes through tests of means (income and wealth). Although it is not possible to pay a full BI to all, every effort is made to ensure that incomes below the poverty line are free of tax. The avoidance of tax-induced poverty is a *sine qua non* of all BIG schemes.

No BIG scheme contains any NIT elements, for two reasons. The first is simplicity and ease of access and the second cost control. At first it was thought possible to operate the income-tested parts of a BIG scheme along NIT lines, but closer study showed this to be neither desirable nor feasible. As soon as people are subject to high benefit withdrawal rates the only way to keep control of expenditure is through specialist case officers and strict liability to maintain laws, hence the proposed Cash & Care departments, and the emphasis on keeping the need for income-tested benefits as low as possible.

Table 14.1: Essential characteristics of all BIG schemes

> 1. Citizenship-based partial basic incomes (PBIs), PBI supplements, and a Disability Costs Allowance replace all existing benefits except housing benefit and emergency provision, and all, or almost all, income tax reliefs.
> 2. All the BIs are fully integrated with a new, hypothecated income tax or BI contribution, administered by a new *Transfer Income Account*. Individual assessment units.
> 3. Residual, income-tested housing benefit and emergency cash support, administered through new, locally operated, *Cash and Care Departments*. Assessment unit is the family.
> 4. Abolition of NI contributions.
> 5. Abolition of all earnings restrictions.
> 6. Abolition of the cohabitation rule.
> 7. Starting rate of the new BI contribution is approximately equivalent to existing income tax plus contracted-in NI contribution.

Returning to our diagram series, we can compare BIG with the Vince proposals, and they start off looking similar. In Figure 14.1 the poverty line P for a single person is £60 a week. BIG aims at break-even points at the poverty line, whereas Vince's break-even point is below his (slightly lower) poverty line, and it is further below the poverty line for families with children than for single people.

Figure 14.1: BIG target system

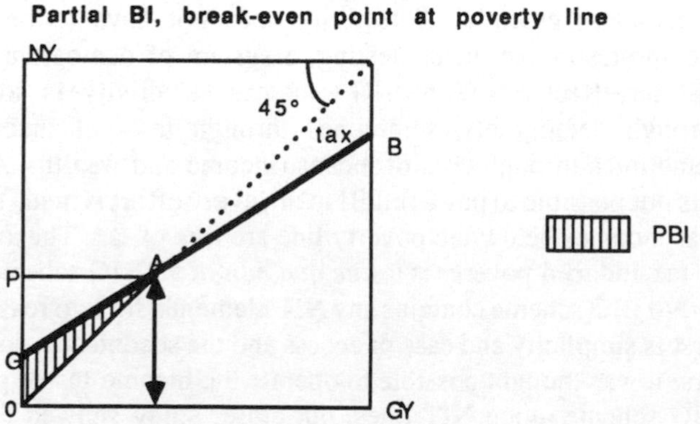

Partial BI, break-even point at poverty line

As before, the PBI is represented by the triangle OAG, and the question becomes how best to fill the GAP triangle without benefit over-spill to people with incomes above the poverty line, and without levying tax on incomes below the poverty line. At this stage BIG starts to diverge from the Vince scheme. Vince fills the GAP triangle using his withdrawable credits, whereas BIG includes non-withdrawable PBI supplements or demogrants as well as withdrawable housing benefit. At this stage there also start to be wide divergences between the different BIG schemes. The difficulty is to be able to fill the GAP triangle *and* keep the PBI at a level sufficient to be able to remove supplementary benefit.

A work test and a work guarantee? The PBIs and the PBI supplements are unconditional. This is essential if they are to be integrated with the new income tax. There is however no *a priori* reason why a BIG scheme should not include an obligation to work or train, coupled with a work guarantee, at local level. It is not an essential element, it would have to be judged on its merits, and if it were included, the benefits affected would be those administered at local level.

Two main administrative components, and a six-part benefit structure

As explained, all BIG schemes have two main administrative components, first the TIA operated by central government, and second the C&C departments operated by local government. The social security functions of the DHSS would be terminated, as would the income support functions of the Department of Education, the Department of Employment (MSC) and the Department of the Environment. The result would be a major rationalisation and a substantial cut in administrative costs. Although some former DHSS staff might be needed to help administer the new C&C departments, the total number of officials employed on income support would fall substantially. In theory the new C&C Departments could be the responsibility of the DHSS instead of the local authorities. In that case there is less local control. Either way the main regulations would need Parliamentary approval.

This two-tier provision, with its strong distinction between the fully integrated, fully automated, and fully individualised BI component, and the locally operated cash and care departments operated through old-style case-work, is an essential and distinctive characteristic of all BIG schemes. It is also one of the features that sets BIG schemes apart from negative income tax.

The benefits administered by the TIA and the C&C departments fall into six main categories, all of them financed by the new, hypothecated income tax:

Transfer Income Account

(1) Universal *partial basic incomes*
(2) Selective *PBI supplements*
(3) A *disability costs allowance* (DCA)

Cash and Care Departments

(4) Authorisation of disability supplements and DCA
(5) Income-tested *housing benefit*
(6) Residual income-tested (or means-tested) cash support in cases of emergency.

Transfer Income Account (TIA)

The TIA is responsible for the BIs and the new income tax that funds the whole system. The new tax does not have to be an income tax, it could be an expenditure tax or a value added tax, but all the schemes costed so far use a comprehensive income tax. Ideally this tax would be hypothecated and the TIA would be kept separate from all other government accounts.

The PBIs. Every legal resident would be entitled to an unconditional PBI, for which the unit of assessment is the individual. The system is sex and marriage neutral. The PBI for children is less than for adults, and the children's rates can be age-related. The PBI is tax-free and non-withdrawable. The test of need is applied through the tax payable on most other income. As with Vince, the PBIs replace the existing personal income tax allowances. For most adults they would operate like tax offsets. Tax would be assessed at the appropriate rate on all other income, and the amount of the BI would be deducted afterwards. For people on low incomes the PBIs convert automatically into cash.

Assuming PBIs high enough to permit abolition of supplementary benefit/income support (SB/IS) the net effect is like a huge increase in tax allowances, lifting the lower paid out of net

228

tax altogether. With tax at 40 percent, and a PBI of £24 a week the break-even point becomes £60. This equates to a tax allowance per person of £60 a week, compared with tax allowances in 1985-86 of £42.40 for a single person, £66.44 for a single-wage couple (or £33.22 per person), and £108.84 for a two-wage couple (or £54.50 per person).

It is reduced tax liability at the bottom of the earnings distribution that makes BIG schemes expensive. It is not because huge sums of money are being "given" away, but because huge sums of money are not being taken away, and because the tax penalties for marriage are removed. Income gains for the out-of-work population, by comparison with SB/IS, are small or non-existent, although with some BIG schemes benefits for the old, the disabled and carers are substantially increased. The increases are paid for by abolishing SERPS and private pension tax reliefs. For most out-of-work, able-bodied people of working age, who are restricted to the partial BI and housing benefit, the advantage of BIG is the replacement of dole money by an income guarantee on which they are free to build without bureaucratic interference.

PBI supplements. In addition to the flat rate PBIs, all BIG schemes include selective PBI supplements, targeted on people with above average living costs and/or limited earnings potential. In each case the PBI supplement is added to the PBI. All PBI supplements are tax-free and non-withdrawable. All BIG schemes pay PBI supplements during old age and disability, some include them for lone parents and some for carers. Some pay them (for limited periods) to widows, widowers and expectant mothers. The logic behind the supplements is to reduce the need for income-tested housing benefit, by giving extra help to people with low earnings potential or extra needs. Ideally the PBI plus supplement add up to a full BI, but this depends on how many of the non-personal tax reliefs are abolished, and whether or not SERPS is retained.

The main criterion for the *old age supplement* is age, although a minimum period of residence would be necessary to prevent an influx of elderly ex-patriates and other immigrants. Most costed BIG schemes take 65 as the age of entitlement to the old age supplement. It is much more difficult to find an acceptable criterion for the *disability supplement*, which is intended to help people below age 65 whose disabilities prevent them from earning, not those who have no intention of doing paid work. One solution is to restrict payment to people with disabilities "for whom no suitable paid work can be found", with the onus on the State to find or provide a suitable job, and on the disabled person to accept it (BIRG Bulletin No. 7).

Some BIG schemes include a *householder supplement*, but this produces administrative complications and would encourage household formation. In 1987 the Association of Metropolitan Authorities (AMA) recommended introduction of a *universal housing allowance* (UHA) of £10 a week as a replacement for mortgage interest tax relief (AMA 1987). In the United Kingdom there are approximately 21 million households, so a BI supplement of £10 a week would cost nearly £11,000 million a year, adding about 5 percentage points to the starting rate of the new income tax. The proposal begs the fundamental questions why people should receive a subsidy for living alone, and whether it would be beneficial in the long-term. Why should a benefit be ear-marked for housing? What makes housing so different to food, fuel or clothing?

There are no PBI supplements for the unemployed. It can be done, but it would reintroduce administrative complexity and an endogenous element (Smail 1985). Records would have to be kept of hours worked and earnings received, which could jeopardise abolition of the earnings rule. Most BIG schemes give priority to administrative simplicity and removal of all earnings rules, whilst making sure that the unemployed receive at least as much under the new system as under the old. The exception today would be single non-householders aged 25+, who gained about £8 a week in April 1988 as a result of the switch to IS.

Disability costs allowance (DCA). This is intended to ensure that the amounts received (or set against tax) provide the same, equivalent basic living standard for all, after taking into account the extra costs of disability. This is an objective of all BIG schemes. The DCA would be added to the PBI entitlement of children and old people as well as those with entitlement to the disability supplement. It has nothing to do with earnings replacement. It is concerned only with the extra costs of living incurred by people with disabilities. A person with a very severe disability might need a DCA of £100, in addition to the PBI and disability supplement. The combination of PBI, disability supplement, DCA and carer's supplement looks expensive, but costs less than hospitalisation.

Cash & Care Departments (C&C)

Amalgamation of cash *and* care responsibilities at local level would be controversial and is not an integral part of BIG proposals. It nevertheless has much to commend it, provided that an adequate income guarantee is introduced first.

The benefits operated by the C&C Departments, mainly housing benefit, are quite different to the BIs operated by the TIA. They are withdrawable, the assessment unit is the family, and they could be subject to a work test. In addition to cash help the C&C Departments would be responsible for care and counselling services to people who need more than just money, and for administrative support to the TIA. The administrative support would include investigation and certification of claims to the TIA for BI disability and carers' supplements, and for the DCA.

The BIG recommendation that old-style case-work be retained for all income-tested benefits is different to all the other proposals in this report, whose authors seem to think that income-tested benefits can be administered through the income tax system without public expenditure running out of control. With all BIG schemes the priority is to reduce drastically the numbers of people for whom individual case work is necessary, and then to move in with advice as well as cash help.

At present there is a strict division between DHSS officials, whose area of responsibility is cash, and social services staff, whose main job is care and counselling, but who are increasingly dragged into the cash nexus as welfare rights counsellors. So the taxpayer is financing two lots of officials, one to say "No", and the other to say "Try again, I'll show you how". This division of responsibility dates from the *Seebohm Report* (DHSS 1968) , and the resulting problems of liaison are well documented (Stevenson 1973; Jackson and Valencia 1979; Tester 1985; Leaper 1986). Professor Leaper has described the results of the post-Seebohm fragmentation in the following way:

> ...the needs and problems of people who seek state help, in cash *or* in kind, are seen by the beneficiaries themselves as one whole. The fragmentation of cash and care services between different agencies slots the citizen's requirements into administratively convenient categories, and produces a

network of financial assistance and social work services which are determined by influences other than a straight analysis of what clients actually need. (Leaper 1986(b))

Leaper argues strongly against continuance of the present functional separation of social work from income maintenance, but is nevertheless careful to insist that integration of the cash and care services must be preceded by thorough-going reform of the social security system, including the guarantee of a firm basis of non-means-tested cash for every citizen, and coordination of the laws of income maintenance with the laws of liability to maintain. Otherwise officials would continue to be overwhelmed by "increasing hordes" of people needing attention, and the taxpayer would go on paying fully trained social workers to act as welfare rights counsellors.

Authorisation of disability benefits. It is not possible for the disability supplements, the maternity supplement or the DCA to be automated in the same way as the other PBI supplements. Although they would be financed and paid out by the TIA, they would require prior authorisation through the C&C departments. This matter is discussed further in Chapter 20.

Housing benefit. All BIG schemes include an income-tested housing benefit. BIG is no panacea and nobody is claiming that housing benefit can provide a remedy for the "housing morass". BIG housing benefit is a palliative, nor is there anything sacrosanct about the housing benefit formula used for the BIG calculations in this report. Here the assessment unit is the same as in the existing system. So are the non-dependent deductions. At nil original income, and for householders with only their PBIs, housing benefit comprises rent, rates and water rates in full, plus a heating allowance and a householder element. Benefit is withdrawn by 50 percent of increases in net income. The long-term PBI supplements (but not the DCA) count £ for £ against housing benefit. The choice is between allowing pensioners more spending power and removing the pensioner poverty trap. Most BIG schemes give priority to the latter, but the details vary with each scheme.

The inclusion of a *heating allowance* is to draw attention to fuel poverty, especially where there is a communal heating system. Heating costs vary almost as much as housing costs, and there is a case for including at least a proportion of heating costs in the new housing benefit.

Inclusion of a *householder element* is to help make the system marriage neutral, and to cut public expenditure costs without leaving former SB/IS claimants worse off. In year one of a switch to BIG the proposed householder element is generally equal to the difference between the SB rate for a single householder (or the IS rate for single people aged 25+) and the PBI. Assuming a PBI in March 1986 of £24 the householder element becomes £29.50-£24.00 = £5.50 a week. By April 1988 the PBI is about £25.70, and the householder element becomes £33.40 – £25.70 = £7.70. The figures are approximate.

BIG housing benefit is income-tested, not means-tested. Wealth is excluded because a means test adds to administrative complexity and changes the nature of the benefit. Housing benefit is intended as temporary mechanism for topping up low incomes, not a last-ditch, long-term payment for people who have first got rid of their capital. Furthermore housing benefit is not just for help with the rent, it can include a rebate for local authority rates (or *community charge*). A tax rebate payable only after a test of means is effectively saying that people on low incomes are expected to sell their savings to pay their taxes.

With most BIG schemes mortgage interest is not payable with housing benefit, although it could be. The reason for excluding it is the unfairness of expecting taxpayers (often hard-pressed themselves) to help others acquire a capital asset. There are other ways to protect mortgagors. All new mortgagors could be required to take out insurance against loss of income as part of the contract (which is already possible, but expensive), or the TIA (through the C&C Departments) could pay the mortgage interest for a limited period, on a loan basis. The loan would be repayable when the property was sold, or on the death of the mortgagor, whichever was the sooner. An arrangement of this sort would prevent previously disinterested relatives from inheriting the full value of a property, the purchase of which had been partly financed by the taxpayer.

Emergency cash benefits. No system can cater for all the unexpected needs and circumstances of every citizen. C&C benefits are the final safety net. They should be designed and operated in such a way as to give local officials the ability to act quickly, and to use positive discretion in the interests of people who need extra cash in order to become financially independent. Some benefits might be on a loan basis, but not all. The C&C budget would not be cash-limited, a cash-limited emergency budget being a contradiction in terms. A cash limit used as a guideline could nevertheless be helpful. If expenditures exceeded targets in many areas during perhaps two consecutive years, this could be taken as a signal that the rest of the system was malfunctioning. In those circumstances the solution is not to sit back and watch the safety net choke up, but to remedy the faults in the main part of the system.

A comprehensive income tax or basic income contribution (BIC)

All BIG schemes abolish all employees' and self-employed NI contributions, which are subsumed in the new income tax. Most schemes also abolish the employers' NI contribution. Some replace it by a payroll tax and others by an increased tax on profits or a turnover tax. Once the principle of contributory benefits is abandoned the logic of involving employers in the income redistribution process wears thin.

Ideally all the transfer incomes referred to in the preceding section would be funded by a single hypothecated tax, which for the purposes of this report is assumed to be the BIC. The advantage of an income tax is that it stresses the link between money earned and money available for redistribution. It also forges a link between incomes at the bottom and living standards in general. Provided that all taxes on personal incomes were hypothecated to the TIA, the funds available for the BIs would move up in line with incomes generally, and the living standards of the poorest sections of the community would follow suit. Instead of indexation to either prices or earnings, each year a choice would have to be made between higher BIs or lower tax. During periods of low economic growth, sudden price rises, or demographic change, life could be tough. Although short-term deficits might be permissible, in the longer term the system must be self-financing. Experience after the oil price rises of the 1970s underlines the need for an income support system that can prevent poverty without requiring exponential rates of economic growth to sustain it.

Some BIG schemes include a tax on real capital gains (individualised and inflation-proofed) as part of the new comprehensive income tax. Some include an inheritance tax, with the individual as the assessment unit. These proposals are particularly relevant where the BIC is flat rate. All such taxes should be levied at the same rate.

All BIG schemes abolish all the personal income tax reliefs. All the BIG schemes devised by Rhys Williams and Parker would also phase out mortgage interest tax relief. The most radical BIG schemes aim at abolition of all income tax reliefs, and the relief for capital gains tax (after allowing for inflation). Other BIG schemes retain income tax reliefs for private pensions.

The success of any strategy for integration of the tax and benefit systems depends crucially on simplification. By removing as many as possible of the non-personal as well as the personal reliefs, thousands of millions of pounds can be made available for the BIs and the system can be automated with less fear of abuse. Unification of NI contribution with income tax intensifies the need to tackle the problem of the non-personal income tax reliefs, because the new, unified tax rate is bound to be higher than the old one, hence the value (and cost) of any remaining tax reliefs also goes up, perhaps by a third. This is one of the core issues discussed in Chapter 16.

Those BIG schemes that include abolition of pension tax reliefs are able to finance a PBI plus PBI supplement for pensioners of £60 a week (at 1985-86 prices and incomes). Those that do not have to rely on a much smaller basic pension, topped up by occupational pensions and/or housing benefit. The pensioner poverty trap remains.

The extent to which the tax base is thought to be reduced on account of mortgage interest and private pension tax reliefs is shown in Appendix 1, Table A.1.5. Of course no one is suggesting that the non-personal tax reliefs be abolished overnight. It would take years to phase them out. But the figures show the huge scale of hidden income redistribution that goes on at present, and the falsity of Government claims that resources are not available to lift the poor out of tax, or to raise the safety net to a more generally acceptable level.

BIG 1(a): High basic pension replaces SERPS and pension tax reliefs. Progressive income tax

Over the years Rhys Williams and Parker tried to distinguish between the main costed BIG options using a series of suffixes. Those with the suffix 1 aimed to abolish all income tax reliefs and used a graduated tax schedule. Those with the suffix 2 retained most private pension tax reliefs (the exception being tax-free lump sums) and used a flat rate tax. Here we will look briefly at BIG 1(a), costed for 1985-86. In practice BI upratings would take place each April, but in order to produce figures on a basis comparable to the system at that time (with benefit upratings in November), it is assumed that the BIs were all uprated by 5 percent (as for existing SB) in November 1985.

Table 14.2: BI amounts, BIG 1(a), Mar 86 rates

	Weekly rates £
1. BASIC INCOMES	
(1) *Partial basic incomes (PBIs)*	
Each adult, from age 16	24.00
Each child aged 0-15	17.15
(2) *PBI supplements*	
Each expectant mother (for 26 weeks)	17.15
Each widow/widower (for 26 weeks)	24.00
Each lone parent	10.00
Each person aged: 65-84	36.00
85 and over	41.00
Each person aged 16-64 with a disability that prevents or impedes paid work	36.00
(3) *Disability costs allowance*	variable

2. HOUSING BENEFIT

(1) *Householders in receipt of PBI only*
   At nil original income each working age householder receives rent, rates and water rates in full, plus:

householder allowance	£5.50
fuel allowance	£2.20
	£7.70

(2) *Householders in receipt of full BI*
(a) At nil original income a single householder receives rent, rates and water rates, less £20.30
(b) A married couple, each with full BI, receives rents, rates and water rates less £57.80
(c) A married couple, one with full BI one with PBI, as for (a).
(3) *Lone parents*
   At nil original income receive housing costs in full less £7.70
(4) *Taper is 50% of increases in net original income (excluding BIs)*

BIG 1(a) is a very simple, very radical option. Table 14.2 sets out the details. All the personal income tax reliefs, mortgage interest tax relief, as many as possible of the private pension tax reliefs, and all benefits except housing benefit and emergency relief are replaced by a standard adult PBI (from age 16) set at approximately half the SB scale rate for a married couple, a flat rate child PBI of £17.15, and PBI supplements for those with special needs.

The PBI plus old age/disability supplement equals £60, which is a full BI, as defined in Chapter 9. In order to ensure that no one pays net tax on earnings below the poverty level, the grossed up value of the PBI, assuming income tax at 40 percent, must not be less than the full BI. With a full BI of £60 and a 40 percent tax rate, the minimum PBI therefore becomes £24, compared with SB for a single non-householder in November 1985 of £23.60. From the costing figures it looks as though the scheme could be funded using a starting rate of tax of 38 percent, in which case a PBI of £24 produces a break-even point above £60, which is all to the good.

The £17.15 child BI is based on the value of SB for children aged 11-15, plus an allowance for free school meals. On an equivalent basis the BI for children under 11 should be about £13.90. The extra £3.25 takes into account the fact that families with younger children are more likely to be dependent on a single wage, or to have work-related childcare costs.

A full BI (PBI plus supplement) is payable to everyone once they reach age 65, and to people of working age who cannot do paid work on account of physical or mental disability. Smaller PBI supplements are payable, for six months only, to expectant mothers and to widows and widowers. The expectant mother's supplement is intended to cover the extra costs incurred, both for herself and the unborn baby. It is justified on grounds of preventive medicine. There is also a PBI supplement of £10 for all lone parents. Statutory sick pay (payable during the first twenty-six weeks of sickness) would continue as at present. It would be additional to the BIs, but taxable from the first £.

For able-bodied people of working age the PBIs are not enough to fill the GAP triangle in Figure 14.1. During short-term sickness there would be sick pay, otherwise they would have to rely on the PBI, income-tested housing benefit and their own earnings, all earnings restrictions having been removed. For people with disabilities at any age, and for everybody aged 65 or over BIG 1(a) fills the GAP triangle by means of the PBI supplements, with

Figure 14.2: BIG: PBI plus PBI supplement

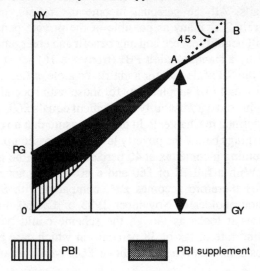

housing benefit as an added protection. Figure 14.2 shows the effects of the supplements. This is a full BI, so the tax break-even point A is well over to the right. For single pensioners it is £150 a week, so there is benefit spillage to people with incomes above the poverty line, but only a little more than with the existing system, due to the 40 percent tax rate and despite the greatly increased basic pension.

Some people may argue that the income tax rate for people receiving a PBI supplement should be higher than 40 percent, in order to reduce benefit slippage. But this is to misunderstand what is being proposed, for the £60 citizenship pension paid with BIG 1(a) replaces private pension tax reliefs as well as SERPS. The idea is to postpone the tax-free bonus until old age, not to make people pay tax twice over. The effect is a large-scale redistribution of income in favour of low income pensioners, and virtual eradication of the pensioner poverty trap. Saving for old age through whatever channels becomes worthwhile, not just for the rich, but also for the poor.

How much would it cost?

As explained, the tax rate necessary to finance BIG 1(a) depends crucially on how many of the non-personal income tax reliefs are

Basic Income Guarantee

Table 14.3: Rates of BI contribution, BIG 1(a), 1985-86

Taxable incomes bottom limit		Tax rate
£ pa	£ pw	%
0		38
8,890	171	45
17,780	342	50
26,670	513	55
35,560	684	60

retained. The costing details are in Table 14.5 at the end of this chapter. The lowest estimate is a starting rate of 35 percent, and the upper estimate is a starting rate of 44 percent. Assuming retention of about half the existing pension tax reliefs it becomes 38 percent. This compares with income tax and NI contribution (not contracted-out rate) in 1985-86 of 30 percent and 9 percent respectively, and is the tax rate used for the model family analysis in Appendix 2.

The BIG 1(a) tax rate is progressive. It goes up to 45 percent at average earnings, and by a further 5 percent at each multiple of average earnings thereafter, until the top rate of 60 percent is reached. The details are in Table 14.3. The reason for linking the higher-rate tax bands to average earnings is to keep tax liability in line with living standards generally. Although the progression looks steep, married couples benefit from independent assessment. The extra revenue from the higher rate tax bands is estimated to be £3,200 million, so the progressivity could be made less steep at no significant extra cost. Note that the figures in Table 14.3 refer to the taxpayer's own income, excluding the BI.

All the costing figures need to be treated with caution. The method used is once again the first of the three formulae in Appendix 1. TAXMOD was not used, because BIG 1(a) involves too many changes that do not show up in the Family Expenditure Survey. Of these the most important are the introduction of the disability costs allowance (and off-setting savings in personal social services), savings in tax expenditures, the phasing out of SERPS, and very significant savings in administration. Some of the tax expenditure savings (for instance on mortgage interest and superannuation reliefs) do show up through TAXMOD, but most do not. Assuming a new starting rate of tax at 38 percent, abolition of the superannuation tax reliefs is estimated to add around £2,000 million to tax revenues, but this is only one third of the extra £6,000 million expected if just half the pension tax reliefs could be phased out. Stage (3) of Table 14.5 shows anticipated savings on student grants, free school meals, administration, personal social services and agricultural subsidies totalling some £6,000 million, very little of which shows through in TAXMOD. Cuts in agricultural subsidies are included on the grounds that agricultural living standards would be protected through the BIs, on the same basis as everybody else.

No BIG scheme could be fully implemented before the year 2000, yet here we are trying to do costings on the basis of population, incomes and expenditures in 1985-86. One example of the problems involved is the treatment of SERPS. All BIG schemes abolish SERPS, which by the year 2003-4 will cost an estimated £5,300 million (at 1985 prices). It is not until the next century that the cost of SERPS really takes off (see Table 16.1), yet here the best we can do is to deduct the estimated costs in 2003-4 from the 1985-86 BIG budget, after allowing for the Government Actuary's estimated 1.5 percent real earnings growth per year between 1985 and the year 2000. This produces a (distinctly hypothetical) savings in 1985-86 of £4,000 million. The figure is included to emphasise the ever-increasing cost of SERPS, but it is most uncertain.

Who gains and who loses?

Measuring the redistributive effects of BIG 1(a) is as difficult as with Minford's scheme, because the scale of change is so large. TAXMOD records net income gains as a result of the BIs, and losses as a result of counting mortgage interest and superannuation contributions as taxable income, but it cannot show the effects of the Disability Costs Allowance, the removal of SERPS or the removal of tax reliefs on pension lump sums and employers' contributions. Nor can model family analysis. Assuming that half the private pension tax reliefs are removed, there is some £4,000 million worth of unidentified losses on this count alone. The DCA adds £4,000 million gross to the net incomes of people with disabilities, but more than £1,000 million of that is offset by savings on attendance and mobility allowance. Departmental savings on student grants, school meals and so forth would all affect personal incomes, but in ways that do not show up in TAXMOD.

Although precision is impossible, there is little doubt that abolition of pension tax reliefs would hit those on high incomes

Table 14.4: Distribution and cost of superannuation tax reliefs, 1987-88

Range of total income	No. of tax units receiving relief[1]	Average reduction in IT liability[2]		Tax expenditure cost in 1987-88
£	thousands	£ pw	£ pa	£ million
0 - 5,000	280	1.15	60	16.8
5,000 - 10,000	2,500	1.92	100	250.0
10,000 - 20,000	4,510	3.46	180	811.8
20,000 - 30,000	1,060	7.12	370	392.2
30,000 - 50,000	345	16.73	870	300.2
50,000 - 100,000	75	44.23	2,300	172.5
Over 100,000	10	123.08	6,400	64.0
				2,007.5

Notes: 1 For contributions to occupational pensions schemes or retirement annuity policies.

2 On account of individuals' contributions to occupational pensions schemes and retirement annuity policies.

Source: Hansard WA 18 December 1987, c 843.

hardest. Table 14.4 sets out estimates derived from a Written Parliamentary Answer.

Once again the figures refer only to superannuation contributions. They show that in 1987-88 most people contributing to occupational pensions or annuities saved an average of £3.50 a week in income tax, but those at the top saved an average of £123 a week. Allowing for the fact that Appendix 2 refers to 1985-86 incomes, net income losses as a result of BIG 1(a) could be £15 – £20 higher at the top of the income range shown than the published figures imply. Losses as a result of taxing pension lump sums and/or counting employers' contributions as a benefit in kind, remain unaccounted for, but could be higher still.

Model family analysis: net incomes, disposable incomes and net spending power. With BIG schemes net incomes are more important than disposable incomes, because fewer families would depend on means-tested benefits. BIG 1(a) is redistributive from rich to poor, those who stand to gain most being lower paid families with and without children, and low income pensioners. Losers include mortgagors with above average earnings, people with large amounts of private pension tax reliefs, and people with unearned income, on which the starting rate of tax goes up from 30 percent (in 1985-6) to 38 percent.

Figure 14.3: BIG 1(a) net incomes, March 1986

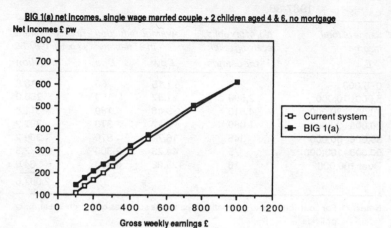

BIG 1(a) net incomes, single wage married couple + 2 children aged 4 & 6, no mortgage

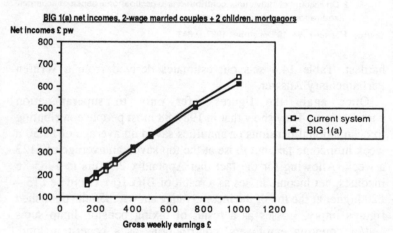

BIG 1(a) net incomes, 2-wage married couples + 2 children, mortgagors

Source: Appendix 2.

Figure 14.3, *net incomes*, shows gains and losses for a couple with two children, first non-mortgagors dependent on a single wage, and then two-wage with a mortgage. The first graph shows gains all the way up the line, but the second, which probably is more realistic, has a cross-over point at earnings just below £500. The cross-over point would be significantly lower if removal of pension tax reliefs were taken into account. For single-people with maximum mortgage tax relief the cross-over point is about £225, for single wage couples about £300 and for two-wage couples about £200. Again these points would be lower if the effects of removing pension tax reliefs were shown. The tax liability of two-wage couples would depend on the division of earnings between them, and the liability of each to higher rate tax.

Figure 14.4, *disposable incomes*, is subject to all the usual caveats. Most of the figures show marked improvements by comparison with the existing system, the exception being unemployed single non-householders aged 25+, who lose £7 a week. Fowler increased the amount for unemployed single non-householders aged 25+, but decreased it for the younger age-groups. BIG 1(a) takes the pre-Fowler rate for the age-group 18+, without the pre-Fowler non-householder's housing addition (*sic*). The extra £6 a week at nil earnings for married couples is due to the householder element in BIG 1(a) housing benefit, which puts married couples on an equivalent basis with single householders for

Figure 14.4: BIG 1(a) disposable incomes, March 1986

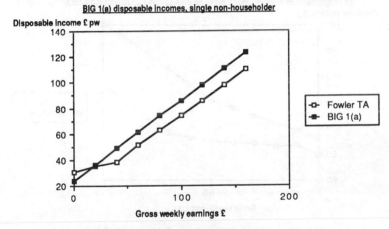

BIG 1(a) disposable incomes, single non-householder

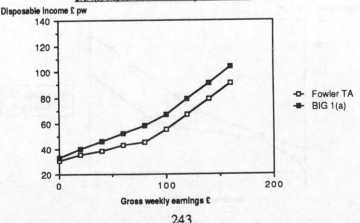

BIG 1(a) disposable incomes, single householder

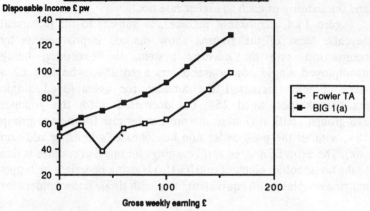

BIG 1(a) disposable incomes, single wage married couple

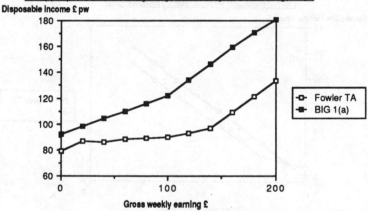

BIG 1(a) disposable incomes, single wage married couple + 2 children aged 4 & 6

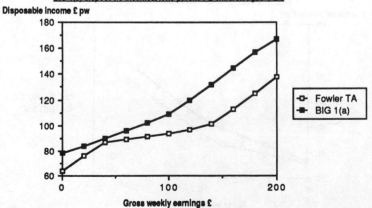

BIG 1(a) disposable incomes, lone parent + 2 children aged 4 & 6

the first time. Water rates and rates are paid in full at nil income with BIG 1(a), but not with income support. Lower paid families with children benefit greatly from the child PBIs, and their marginal tax rates are much improved.

Figure 14.5, *net spending power*, shows BIG 1(a) doing better than the existing system, and better than Vince or Minford, but still not well enough to restore work incentives at the bottom, especially for lone parents with childcare costs.

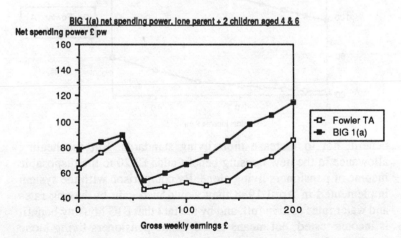

BIG 1(a) net spending power, single wage married couple + 2 children aged 4 & 6

BIG 1(a) net spending power, lone parent + 2 children aged 4 & 6

Source: Appendix 2.

Figure 14.6, *pensioner disposable incomes*, shows that BIG 1(a) uses the PBI supplement to lift low income pensioners off housing

Figure 14. 6: BIG 1(a) disposable incomes, low income pensioners, March 1986

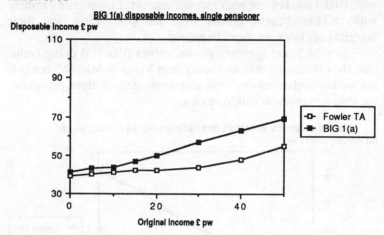

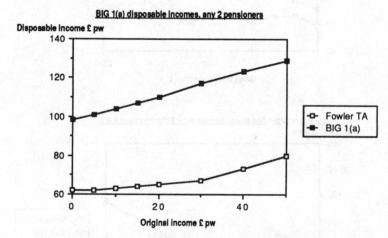

benefit, not to increase their living standards. But the heating allowance in the new housing benefit adds £2.20 to the disposable income of pensioners living alone. By comparison with the system implemented in April 1988 they would also gain by having rates and water rates paid in full, and by the fact that BIG housing benefit is income-tested, not means-tested. Some pensioners living alone would still require housing benefit, but very few in shared accommodation. BIG 1(a) makes a point of encouraging pensioners to make economies of scale by abolishing the cohabitation rule. All pensioners would be free to share accommodation with friends or relatives, without losing any of their BIs. The disposable income curve for married pensioners and for pensioners in shared accommodation is much more generous with BIG 1(a) than with the existing system. No pensioners in shared accommodation would need housing benefit, so for them the pensioner poverty trap would be ended.

When reading Figure 14.6, remember that the BIG 1(a) curve incorporates the BI old age supplement that replaces SERPS and half the private pension tax reliefs. It is therefore not strictly comparable with the Fowler TA curve, which does not include SERPS or private pensions. The £60 BI would have been sufficient to prevent most old age pensioners in 1985-86 from losing out, but pensioners whose fully matured SERPS entitlement would eventually be more than £22 a week (for single people at 1985-86 prices) or £59 (for married couples) would lose. Very few couples where the wife had not been in paid work, or had only worked part-time, would lose. Most would gain. Losers would include pensioner couples where each spouse had consistently earned near the upper earnings level for NI contribution[1]. It follows that if BIG 1(a) (or similar) were introduced, all further contributions to SERPS must be stopped as soon as possible, in order to prevent accrual of further rights. This subject is discussed in Chapters 16 and 20. Transitional protection would also be necessary to protect invalidity pensioners, who would forfeit the tax benefits that go with invalidity benefit.

Summing up

BIG 1(a) is in some ways similar to the Liberal Party Tax-Credit proposals, the main differences being the smaller reliance on income-tested benefits and the greater administrative simplicity, including the clear split between the centrally operated BIs, and the locally operated C&C benefits. Although all BIG schemes have the same philosophical starting point, there are considerable differences between them, which adds flexibility to the approach.

Like the Vince scheme, BIG 1(a) is based on the improbable assumption that the Inland Revenue could collect tax from the first £ of earnings, which would have to be changed. Income tax at 38-40 percent plus withdrawal of housing benefit at 50 percent of net original income produces a maximum marginal tax rate of 68-70 percent. This is much better than the existing system, and the numbers affected would also be much smaller. The lone-parent supplement would prevent lone parents from losing out under the scheme, but it would also prevent the system from being marriage neutral. Something more radical is needed if lone parents are to be helped to stand on their own feet without encouraging more of them. The solution advocated in *BI 2000* (Chapter 19) will be more childcare provision and income tax relief for work-related childcare costs. The details of administration are discussed further in Chapter 19.

Table 14.5: Costing BIG 1(a), 1985-86

BIG 1(a) is costed using formula 1 in Appendix 1, in six stages:

STAGE (1) Gross cost of BIG 1(a)

	1985-86 average weekly BI rate[1]	Population	Annual cost
	£	m	£m
1. BASIC INCOMES			
(1) Partial BIs			
Adult PBI	23.26	44.86	54,259
Child PBI	16.73	11.76	10,231
(2) PBI supplements			
Expectant mothers[2]	16.73	0.70	304
Widow/widowers[2]	23.26	0.30	181
Lone parents	9.69	1.00	504
Old age, aged 65-84	34.89	7.88	14,297
85 and over	39.89	0.68	1,411
Disability	34.89	1.0?	1,814
(3) Disability Costs Allowance	variable	N/A	4,000
			87,001
2. HOUSING BENEFIT			1,500[3]
3. OTHER C&C BENEFITS			200[4]
4. TIA ADMINISTRATION			500
TOTAL GROSS COSTS OF BIG 1(a)			89,201

NOTES:

1. These rates assume a 5% uprating in November 1985. 32 weeks are costed at the lower rate of BI and 20 weeks at the full rate shown in Table 14.2.
2. For 26 weeks only.
3. TAXMOD estimate.
4. Sources: Social Security Statistics 1986, Table 34.97; Hansard WA 10 May 1985 c 542.

STAGE (2): Cost of abolishing income tax, NI contributions and ACT, 1985-86

£64,707 million. (Appendix 1, Table A.1.4)

STAGE (3): Savings on existing public expenditure

	£ millions
Social security benefit excluding administration	40,969
Maintenance element of student grants	717
Free school meals	270
MSC grants and allowances	500
Cost of rate rebates	1,550
Costs of administration	2,758
Personal social services	500
Agricultural subsidies (CAP)	1,857
Estimated savings excluding SERPS	49,121
Allowance for abolition of SERPS	4,000
Total estimated savings	53,121

Basic Income Guarantee

STAGE (4): revenue from 8 percent employers' payroll tax

An 8 percent employers' payroll tax is estimated to bring in £12,630 million in 1985-86, which is approximately the same as revenue from employers' NI contributions (£12,337 million) and State Scheme premiums (£289 million) received in that year. The figures assume total wages and salaries in 1985-86 of £159,000 million (Inland Revenue estimate).

STAGE (5): Revenue from higher-rate tax

Assuming the higher rate tax bands in Table 14.3, the figure is estimated to be £3,200 million (Inland Revenue estimate).

STAGE (6): Starting rate of the new income tax or BI contribution

Using the tax base figure in Appendix 1, Table A.1.5, the starting rate of the new income tax is calculated as follows:

$$t = \frac{A + B - C - D - E - F}{G}$$

where:

A = cost of the BIs, housing benefit, residual C&C benefits and TIA administration.
B = cost of abolishing income tax, NI contributions and advance corporation tax (ACT).
C = savings on existing expenditure.
D = employers' new payroll tax.
E = revenue from higher rate income tax.
F = savings from abolition of life assurance income tax relief.
G = new income tax base.

For example:

$$t = \frac{89.2 + 64.71 - 53.12 - 12.63 - 3.2 - 0.6}{239} = \frac{84.36}{239} = 35.3\%$$

A new tax base of £239,000 million is the upper band in Table A.1.5. In practice the tax rate would depend on how many of the non-personal income tax reliefs were abolished. The following table shows rhe range:

Assumptions:	New IT base £ million	Starting rate of tax %
(1) All tax reliefs abolished	239	35.3
(2) As in (1), less reliefs for income of charities and for interest on British Government securities, where the owner is not ordinarily resident in the UK	237	35.6
(3) As in (2), less just under half of private pension reliefs, which are retained	222	38.0
(4) As in (3), less the balance of private pension reliefs, which remain as in 1985-86	206	41.0
(5) As in (4), less mortgage interest tax relief, which is also retained	191	44.2

250

Basic Income Guarantee

Table 14.6: Disposable incomes of selected model families, BIG 1(a), detailed figures for Nov 85 to Mar 86, £ per week

Assumptions

All figures refer to the period November 1985 to March 1986. All families are tenants. Working age families live in council property, and pay the rents and rates used in the November 1985 DHSS Tax/Benefit Model Tables. Water rates, estimated by the DHSS to have been £1.65 a week on average, are not deducted but are included in housing benefit. Families are assumed to take up entitlement to income-tested housing benefit in full. No allowance for cost of fares to work or childminding expenses. The PBI is £24 for adults from age 16, £17.15 for children. PBI supplements are £10 for each lone parent, and £36 for each person aged 65 or over, and each person with a disability that prevents or impedes paid work. Other PBI supplements (for instance the disability costs allowance) are not taken into account. Starting rate of the BIC is 38%. In the net income part of each table the words *married couple* can be replaced by *any two adults.*

Acronyms

PBI = partial basic income; BIC = basic income contribution; HB = housing benefit.

WORKING AGE HOUSEHOLDS

Table 1: Single non-householder aged 16-64

	£	£	£	£	£	£
Gross weekly earnings	0.00	40.00	80.00	120.00	160.00	200.00
+ PBI	24.00	24.00	24.00	24.00	24.00	24.00
− BIC	0.00	15.20	30.40	45.60	60.80	78.10
= Net & disposable incomes	24.00	48.80	73.60	98.40	123.20	145.90

Table 2: Single householder aged 18-64

	£	£	£	£	£	£
Gross weekly earnings	0.00	40.00	80.00	120.00	160.00	200.00
+ PBI	24.00	24.00	24.00	24.00	24.00	24.00
− BIC	0.00	15.20	30.40	45.60	60.80	78.10
= Net incomes before HB	24.00	48.80	73.60	98.40	123.20	145.90
+ Housing benefit	28.35	15.95	3.55	0.00	0.00	0.00
= Net incomes after HB	52.35	64.75	77.15	98.40	123.20	145.90
− Rent	13.80	13.80	13.80	13.80	13.80	13.80
− Rates	5.20	5.20	5.20	5.20	5.20	5.20
= Disposable incomes	33.35	45.75	58.15	79.40	104.20	126.90

Table 3: Single person + 2 children aged 4 and 6

	£	£	£	£	£	£
Gross weekly earnings	0.00	40.00	80.00	120.00	160.00	200.00
+ PBIs	68.30	68.30	68.30	68.30	68.30	68.30
− BIC	0.00	15.20	30.40	45.60	60.80	78.10
= Net incomes before HB	68.30	93.10	117.90	142.70	167.50	190.20
+ Housing benefit	32.15	19.75	7.35	0.00	0.00	0.00
= Net incomes after HB	100.45	112.85	125.25	142.70	167.50	190.20
− Rent	16.50	16.50	16.50	16.50	16.50	16.50
− Rates	6.30	6.30	6.30	6.30	6.30	6.30
= Disposable incomes	77.65	90.05	102.45	119.90	144.70	167.40

251

Table 4: Married couple (single-wage)

	£	£	£	£	£	£
Gross weekly earnings	0.00	40.00	80.00	120.00	160.00	200.00
+ PBIs	48.00	48.00	48.00	48.00	48.00	48.00
− BIC	0.00	15.20	30.40	45.60	60.80	78.10
= Net incomes before HB	48.00	72.80	97.60	122.40	147.20	169.90
+ Housing benefit	28.35	15.95	3.55	0.00	0.00	0.00
= Net incomes after HB	76.35	88.75	101.15	122.40	147.20	169.90
− Rent	13.80	13.80	13.80	13.80	13.80	13.80
− Rates	5.20	5.20	5.20	5.20	5.20	5.20
= Disposable incomes	57.35	69.75	82.15	103.40	128.20	150.90

Table 5: Married couple (two-wage, each spouse earns half)

	£	£	£	£	£	£
Gross weekly earnings	0.00	40.00	80.00	120.00	160.00	200.00
+ PBIs	48.00	48.00	48.00	48.00	48.00	48.00
− BIC	0.00	15.20	30.40	45.60	60.80	76.00
= Net incomes before HB	48.00	72.80	97.60	122.40	147.20	172.00
+ Housing Benefit	28.35	15.95	3.55	0.00	0.00	0.00
= Net incomes after HB	76.35	88.75	101.15	122.40	147.20	169.90
− Rent	13.80	13.80	13.80	13.80	13.80	13.80
− Rates	5.20	5.20	5.20	5.20	5.20	5.20
= Disposable incomes	57.35	69.75	82.15	103.40	128.20	153.00

Table 6: Married couple + children aged 4 and 6 (single-wage)

	£	£	£	£	£	£
Gross weekly earnings	0.00	40.00	80.00	120.00	160.00	200.00
+ PBI	82.30	82.30	82.30	82.30	82.30	82.30
− BIC	0.00	15.20	30.40	45.60	60.80	78.10
= Net incomes before HB	82.30	107.10	131.90	156.70	181.50	204.20
+ Housing benefit	32.15	19.75	7.35	0.00	0.00	0.00
= Net incomes after HB	114.45	126.85	139.25	156.70	181.50	204.20
− Rent	16.50	16.50	16.50	16.50	16.50	16.50
− Rates	6.30	6.30	6.30	6.30	6.30	6.30
= Disposable incomes	91.65	104.05	116.45	133.90	158.70	181.40

Table 7: Married couple + 2 children aged 4 and 6 (two-wage, each spouse earns half)

	£	£	£	£	£	£
Gross weekly earnings	0.00	40.00	80.00	120.00	160.00	200.00
+ PBIs	82.30	82.30	82.30	82.30	82.30	82.30
− BIC	0.00	15.20	30.40	45.60	60.80	76.00
= Net incomes before HB	82.30	107.10	131.90	156.70	181.50	204.20
+ Housing benefit	32.15	19.75	7.35	0.00	0.00	0.00
= Net incomes after HB	114.45	126.85	139.25	156.70	181.51	204.20
− Rent	16.50	16.50	16.50	16.50	16.50	16.50
− Rates	6.30	6.30	6.30	6.30	6.30	6.30
= Disposable incomes	91.65	104.05	116.45	133.90	158.70	183.50

Basic Income Guarantee

2. RETIREMENT AND INVALIDITY PENSIONERS

Table 8: Old age or invalidity pensioner, living alone

	£	£	£	£	£	£	£	£
Earnings/private pension/ investment income	0.00	5.00	10.00	20.00	30.00	40.00	50.00	100.00
+ BIs	60.00	60.00	60.00	60.00	60.00	60.00	60.00	60.00
− BIC	0.00	1.90	3.80	7.60	11.40	15.20	19.00	38.00
= Net incomes before HB	60.00	63.10	66.20	72.80	78.60	84.80	91.00	122.00
+ Housing benefit	3.35	1.80	0.25	0.00	0.00	0.00	0.00	0.00
= Net incomes after HB	63.35	64.95	66.45	72.40	78.60	84.80	91.00	122,00
− Rent	15.00	15.00	15.00	15.00	15.00	15.00	15.00	15.00
− Rates	7.00	7.00	7.00	7.00	7.00	7.00	7.00	7.00
= Disposable incomes	41.35	42.90	44.45	50.40	56.60	62.80	69.00	100.00

+ Disability costs allowance: variable

Table 9: Married pensioner/Any two pensioners sharing accommodation

	£	£	£	£	£	£	£	£
Earnings/private pension/ investment income	0.00	5.00	10.00	20.00	30.00	40.00	50.00	100.00
+ BIs	120.00	120.00	120.00	120.00	120.00	120.00	120.00	120.00
− BIC	0.00	1.90	3.80	7.60	11.40	15.20	19.00	38.00
= Net incomes	120.00	123.10	126.20	132.40	138.60	144.80	151.00	182.00
+ Housing benefit	0.00	0.00	0.00	0.00	0.00	0.00	0.00	0.00
− Rent	15.00	15.00	15.00	15.00	15.00	15.00	15.00	15.00
− Rates	7.00	7.00	7.00	7.00	7.00	7.00	7.00	7.00
= Disposable incomes	98.00	101.10	104.20	110.40	116.60	122.80	129.00	160.00

+ Disability costs allowance: variable

15

SDP Tax and Benefit proposals

Like the Liberals, Britain's Social Democrats (SDP) have been working for many years towards a scheme that would integrate personal taxation and cash benefits. The SDP have published three policy documents on the reform of tax and social security (SDP 1981, 1983 and 1986). All are transitional schemes, designed to be implemented within the life of a Parliament, and none sets out the target system. The SDP were always reluctant to accept Liberal tax credit policy, because of its 44 percent tax rate.

The 1986 policy document is the shortest and least clear. Following widespread criticism during Autumn 1986, modified proposals were included in the handbook for Alliance candidates at the 1987 General Election, but these were imprecise. In this chapter I shall stick to the 1986 scheme, since it helps to draw out the issues.

Despite considerable variation in the detail, each set of proposals is heavily influenced by the thinking of the Institute for Fiscal Studies (IFS), which is not surprising, given that Dick Taverne, who chaired the SDP tax reform/benefits working group, also founded the IFS. The IFS is well known for its full-blooded commitment to selectivity through income-testing, in particular its proposals to replace virtually all NI benefits, and child benefit, by income-tested *benefit credits*. (IFS 1984). The SDP take a similar line, but instead of benefit credit they have *basic benefit* (BB):

> It is...an inescapable dilemma that we either provide universal, non-selective benefits which cost so much, because they go to everyone including people not in need, that they can never be generous enough to *relieve* poverty – or we target benefits, which leads inevitably to high implied marginal tax rates, since the benefit is withdrawn as income

rises. *Our concern is the relief of poverty.* That is why we have chosen a withdrawal benefit. Only in this way can the benefit be made generous enough. (SDP 1986, page 3, my emphasis)

The emphasis is on avoidance of benefit leakage, and there is no mention of tax slippage, which turns out to be an integral part of the strategy. What is surprising is the large amount of benefit leakage allowed to remain, despite policy objectives to the contrary. Close analysis of the 1986 Policy Statement shows that it does not meet either of the integration criteria in Chapter 6. BI, even a partial BI through tax-free child benefit, is rejected. NIT is impossible, because the new income tax thresholds are too far below the new benefit ceilings.

The essential characteristics of the SDP scheme are set out in Table 15.1. The administration is complex, for instance the new non-contributory unemployment benefit would be assessed for individuals at existing rates but basic benefit would be assessed for families. Then each individual would receive his share of BB or unemployment benefit, whichever was the larger. The new, enhanced and taxable child benefit would normally be paid to the mother. Strictly speaking it would be paid to the member of a couple with the lower income, although how this would be applied is not specified.

Table 15.1: Essential characteristics of the SDP "Merging Tax and Benefits" proposals

> 1. Replacement of existing personal income tax allowances by a non-convertible tax credit equal to rather less than the existing value of single person's tax allowance, with the individual as the assessment unit.
> 2. This new tax credit is non-transferable between husbands and wives of working age, but fully transferable between pensioner spouses.
> 3. Replacement of SB/IS and FIS/FC by a NIT style basic benefit, with the family (not clearly defined) as the assessment unit, and with entitlement based on annual tax returns.
> 4. Child benefit retained and increased, but the extra becomes taxable as the income of the "caring" parent.
> 5. Housing benefit retained but linked to net instead of gross income.
> 6. Basis of entitlement for old age pensions becomes residence.
> 7. Basis of entitlement for unemployment benefit becomes a work test.
> 8. Unification of employees' NI contribution with income tax.
> 9. Starting rate of new IT is 39% (1985-86) for people of working age and 30% for pensioners. Progressive rates.

By increasing the basic pension and by keeping the tax rate for pensioners at 30 percent (compared with 39 percent for everyone else) the SDP contrives to raise the income break-even levels at which pensioners become net taxpayers, and to reduce selectivity for this age-group. On the other hand, by abolishing the married man's tax allowance and by making child benefit taxable on the income of the "caring" parent, break-even levels for working age families go down, resulting in net income losses and increased dependence on income-tested benefits.

The commitment to selectivity is thus itself selective, having as much to do with the debate between advocates and opponents of family income support, especially child benefit, as with the debate between universalists and selectivists. The SDP policy-makers (like the IFS) are on the side of those who regard wives and children as optional extras, whereas the Liberals, and other advocates of BI, look upon them as equal citizens. Family income support is a core issue, but it is first and foremost a political and social issue, not a technical one. The IFS and the SDP cause confusion by suggesting otherwise.

By making abolition of income tax relief for non-earning wives and abolition of tax-free child benefit their political starting point, the SDP end up with a system that would leave 20 percent of two-child families dependent on basic benefit, and subject to marginal tax rates of between 82 and 93.5 percent. This need not be so, as we have seen, and it would do great damage. For although only 20 percent of two-child families might be affected at any one time, far more would be affected over the life-cycle. The 20 percent statistic that comes out of the SDP model is no more than a snap-shot glimpse of a huge underclass of benefit recipients, forced into welfare dependency during childhood and child-rearing.

The SDP strategy is very different to that of the Liberal Party, so different that it is hard to see how they could be harmonised. The essence of the Liberal scheme (like BIG schemes) is to reduce dependence on means-tested and income-tested benefits by cutting net tax liability at the bottom of the income distribution. This is the main effect of Vince's personal credits and his non-earner credits for pensioners. Malign churning is reduced to a minimum. By contrast the essence of the SDP proposals (except for pensioners) is to increase dependence on income-tested benefits, by increasing tax liability at the bottom of the income distribution. Malign churning is institutionalised, and basic benefit (BB) is its instrument.

Another fundamental difference between the Liberal and SDP proposals is the assessment unit. Vince reduces the penalties for marriage by allotting the same personal credit to every adult between ages 18-64, regardless of marital status. The SDP increases the penalties for marriage during working life by taxing the incomes of married couples separately (as if there were no liability to maintain between spouses) then adding their incomes together if they claim BB.

BB would replace income support, family credit, free school meals and the extra income tax allowances currently available to married men and lone parents. In theory BB would be fully automated, but this seems likely to create administrative difficulties. In practice the SDP scheme would end up looking more like an extension of the existing tax and social security systems than even partial integration.

Adjusting the SDP figures to March 1986

As explained, all the figures in this part refer to the period between the November 1985 benefit uprating and the end of the 1985-86 tax year. A difficulty arises because the SDP figures apply to May 1986, when the SDP Policy Committee approved the October 1986 document. So we can use the SDP benefit rates, but must adjust their tax allowances to1985-86 levels. To do this I have converted the proposed, fixed-amount income tax allowance to 90 percent of single person's tax allowance in 1985-86 instead of 1986-87. I have also converted the proposed unified tax rate to 39 percent instead of 38 percent, since income tax in 1985-86 was 30 percent, not 29 percent, which is the figure referred to in the Policy Statement.

The effect of these two changes is to produce a weekly, non-convertible, tax credit for income tax purposes in 1985-86 of £14.89, instead of the figure of £15.35 implied in the policy document.

As Sutherland pointed out in her Discussion Paper on the SDP scheme, a number of features were not fully specified, resulting in doubts about key aspects (Sutherland 1986). Nothing, for instance, was said about *age allowance*. I have assumed it would continue, since there is not much point in increasing the basic pension and increasing income tax liability simultaneously. At 30 percent tax, the 1985-86 weekly value of a pensioner, fixed-amount tax

SDP Tax and Benefit proposals

Table 15.2: SDP income tax credits and tax rates, March 1986

1. *TAX CREDITS*

	Non-convertible tax credit £ pw	Tax rate %	Tax-free incomes £ pw
Each person up to age 65 (non-transferable)	14.89	39	38.18
Each person aged 65 or above (transferable)	15.52	30	51.73
Income limit for pensioner age allowance	169.23		

2. *INCOME TAX RATES AND BANDS*

Bands of taxable income £ pa	Tax rate %
0 – 16,200	38
16,201 – 19,200	40
19,201 – 24,400	45
24,401 – 32,300	50
32,301 – 40,200	55
over 40,200	60

allowance based on existing age allowance, and limited to pensioners with incomes below the annual, age allowance exemption limit of £8,800 becomes 30 percent of £51.73 = £15.52 per pensioner. To reach this figure I have also assumed that pensioner couples would get twice the single pensioner's amount, since the document is specific about transferability of the new tax allowance between pensioner spouses (SDP 1986, page 7).

The 1986 document makes no mention of higher rate tax. I have assumed no change to existing higher rate tax bands, although in practice it seems likely that the 40 percent rate band would be abolished, given that the new starting rate is 39 percent. The income tax reliefs and income tax rates used for all the calculations are summarised in Table 15.2. Remember that in each case the SDP would first apply the tax rate and then deduct the tax credit, whereas with the existing system the tax allowance is deducted from taxable income before applying the tax rate.

Tax slippage and benefit leakage

Returning to our diagram series, the figures show an amazing combination of increased tax slippage for working age families

Figure 15.1: SDP proposals, tax slippage
Working age households, March 1986

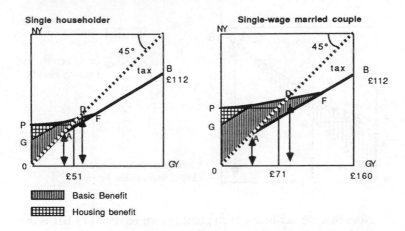

Single householder

Single-wage married couple

Basic Benefit

Housing benefit

alongside increased benefit leakage for pensioners. Look first at the working age population. Figure 15.1 shows how the SDP scheme would add to the size of the poverty gap by taxing married couples on incomes well below the SDP's own poverty lines. The figures assume housing costs of £19 a week. If housing costs were more than £19 a week, point D would move further to the right. The diagrams show a spurious NIT similar to the IFS version in Figure 8.6, although, if the figures referred to families with children, retention of child benefit by the SDP would show less dependence on income-tested benefits than the IFS prototype.

In both diagrams income after tax, but before BB and housing benefit, follows the line OAB. The poverty line is the BB guarantee (£32 for single people and £52 for married couples) plus £19 for housing. Although the 1986 document is scant on detail about housing benefit it is clear that housing costs would be met in full at nil income. Income tax cuts in at about three-quarters the poverty line for single people and at just over half the poverty line for single-wage married couples. The amounts of tax slippage are shown in the DAF triangles to the right of the 45° line. Despite the high benefit withdrawal rate the income level at which entitlement to income-tested benefits is phased out is over £120 a week for single-wage married couples, and £160 for couples with two children (not shown in the diagram). This is the area of income distribution where large numbers of tax units start to be concentrated.

259

Figure 15.2: SDP proposals, benefit leakage
Single pensioner households, March 1986

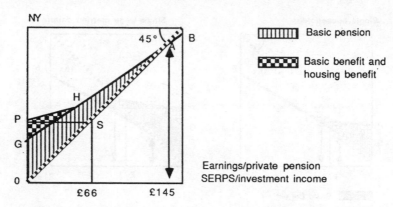

Note that the tax break-even point before payment of BB is the same for single people and single-wage couples, it is only the poverty levels that differ. If the married couple had children, point D would move still further up the 45° line. Note also that net income from weekly earnings of £160 is the same for married couples as for single people.

Now look at the effect of the SDP proposals on single retirement pensioners, assuming housing costs of £22 a week. Here there is a complete contrast. The break-even level is £145 a week. For married pensioners it is £251. Both these figures refer to original income, excluding the state basic pension. In Figure 15.2 the triangle PHG includes a small element of BB (£3.70 a week assuming no income other than the basic pension) but the amount is too small to show up.

Tax changes

The SDP propose four main changes to personal taxation: first the amalgamation of income tax with employees' NI contributions, second the replacement of tax allowances by fixed amount non-convertible tax credits, third the introduction of independent taxation of husband and wife, and fourth the taxation of child benefit.

Other important changes include the restriction of mortgage interest tax relief to 29 percent (30 percent in 1985-86), but there is no mention of any proposal to limit superannuation tax relief.

Investment income would be taxed at the same rate as earned income, which means an increase of 9 percentage points.

Amalgamation of income tax and NI contribution. Instead of two separate systems, there would be a single unified system, with the same threshold for everybody and one set of rates. NI contribution would be abolished and the starting rate of the new income tax (in 1985-86) would have been 39 percent. This compares with existing income tax at 30 percent, plus NI contribution at a starting rate (Class 1, not contracted-out) of 5 percent, and a standard rate of 9 percent. The change does not give the net income gains at the bottom which the SDP anticipated, because they did not take account of the reduced rates of NI contribution introduced in October 1985.

Replacement of tax allowances by fixed amount tax credits. As already explained, an income tax allowance is worth twice as much to people paying tax at 60 percent as to people paying tax at 30 percent. The SDP would remove this anomaly (and increase revenue) by applying the tax rates first and deducting a fixed amount tax credit afterwards. In March 1986 the new-style tax allowance would have been £1,985 a year, which is 90 percent of single person's tax allowance at that time. The reduction in the tax allowance is necessary in order to recoup the costs of abolishing the NI contribution, which is currently payable on all earnings once the NIC lower earnings level (LEL) is reached. An annual tax allowance of £1,985 produces a weekly tax credit, assuming 39 percent tax, of £14.89.

Progressive tax rates would be applied to the whole of taxable income, after which £14.89 would be deducted. It is important to remember that the SDP tax credit is not the same as the convertible tax credit or basic income proposed by Vince and Parker, because it does not convert into cash. Where the taxpayer has no income to set against it, or can only use part of it, it is wasted.

Independent taxation of husband and wife. Instead of single person's, married man's and wife's earned income tax allowances each person would be allowed to deduct £14.89 from their weekly tax bill, as explained above. Husbands and wives would be taxed independently. The investment income of the wife would no longer count as belonging to the husband, but working age spouses with no income would forfeit the value of their £14.89 tax credit, because it is neither convertible nor transferable to the other spouse. For pensioner couples the SDP partly overcome the problem by allowing them to set their tax allowances against the income of either spouse, but not for working age couples.

Two-wage couples would not forfeit the second tax allowance, provided each earned £38 or more, but they would lose the wife's earned income allowance. Lone parents would lose the additional personal allowance.

Taxation of child benefit. In the 1986 Policy Statement child benefit was to be increased to £11.50 per child per week, but taxed "as part of the income of the caring parent, which will normally mean the mother" (SDP 1986, page 3). The consequences of this proposal would have been so extraordinary, that it has since been amended. Even for two-child families it would have produced significant losses in net incomes. Families with four or more children would have had to pay tax on a non-earning mother's non-existent income, because child benefit for four children would have brought her income above the new tax threshold. Yet for single parents child benefit would not be taxable. The penalties for marriage would be reinforced.

Increased tax slippage

The result of these tax changes is the increased tax slippage for people of working age and the increased benefit leakage for

Table 15.3: SDP, proposed tax-free incomes[1], March 1986

Family type	Tax-free income, £ week	
	Existing system £	SDP proposals £
Single person	42.40	38.17
Single person + 2 children	82.99	61.17
Married couple, single-wage	64.44	36.17
Married couple, two-wage	106.84	76.34
Married couple, one-wage, one investment income	64.44	76.34
Married couple + 2 children, single-wage	78.44	61.17
Married couple + 2 children, two-wage	120.84	90.34
Married couple + 2 children, one-wage, one investment income	78.44	99.34

Note: 1. Tax-free income is defined as the amount of income that can be earned, plus child benefit and one parent benefit as appropriate, before liability to income tax commences.

pensioners illustrated in Figures 15.1 and 15.2. If the SDP proposals were put into effect the tax threshold for a single earner family would fall to its lowest level in relation to average earnings since the equivalent of married man's tax allowance was introduced in 1918. Table 15.3 shows that tax liability would depend more on the number of wage-earners in the family and on marital status, than on family size and the amount earned.

Families with children would suffer the worst tax slippage. At one time the SDP, like the IFS, wanted to make the whole of child benefit withdrawable. Although this proposal was dropped well before the 1986 document, much emphasis continued to be put on the wastefulness of a benefit that helps rich and poor alike, most of which allegedly goes to people "who are not in need". No estimates of needs and costs by family size were given to support this contention. Because child benefit would be taxable, the net value of child benefit would fall from £11.50 per child in small families to £9.90 per child in a five-child family. It is not clear whether this apparently anti-natalist proposal was intentional or an oversight.

Basic Benefit (BB)

Basic benefit is the centrepiece of the SDP strategy. It is intended to replace family income supplement/family credit, supplementary benefit/income support, free school meals and supplementary pension as well as the lost income tax allowances. The March 1986 BB entitlements, with supplementary benefit and Mr Fowler's illustrative income support rates for comparison, are set out in Table 15.4. The SDP rate of £32 for a single adult compares with supplementary benefit for a single householder of £29.50 plus water rates, which in 1985-86 averaged £1.65, so the gain is of little consequence.

From the figures in Table 15.4 we can deduce that the minimum income for a couple with three children, one of whom is over 11, would have been £95.50 a week in March 1986 under the SDP proposals, compared with £91.70 under Mr Fowler's income support. The gain is £3.80. One of the main differences between basic benefit and income support is that child benefit is added to BB, whereas with IS it counts as a resource and is deducted from the family's entitlement. Another is the inclusion of passport benefits with IS, which the SDP would abolish. Table 15.5 sets out the figures.

Table 15.4: SDP Basic Benefit rates, March 1986, £ week

Family type	Benefit entitlement SDP £	Fowler IS £
Single adult, age 18-24	32.00	24.00
Ditto, age 25-59	32.00	30.60
Ditto, age 60-79	+ 3.70[1]	40.60
Ditto, aged 80 +	+ 3.70[1]	42.85
Married/cohabiting couple, age 18-59	52.00	48.00
Ditto age 60-79	+ 5.75[2]	63.25
Ditto age 80 +	+ 5.75[2]	65.45
Supplements for families with children		
Family premium	17.00	5.75
Additional lone-parent premium	11.00	3.45
Each child aged under 11	0.00	10.10
Ditto 11-15	3.50	15.10
Ditto 16-17	3.50	18.20
Value of free school meals	0.00	2.06
Value of free welfare milk	0.00?	1.61
Heating addition for child under five	0.00?	2.20

Notes: 1. Plus non-contributory basic pension £41, total £44.70.

2. Plus non-contributory basic pension £63.25, total £69.00.

Sources: SDP 1986, pages 3 and 5.

DHSS December 1985, Technical Annex, pages 10-11.

For a family with two children the SDP figures in Table 15.5 look helpful. For a one-child family they would look even better, but for large families the gain fades away, because the SDP load £17 onto the first child instead of spreading benefit according to the number and age of the children. Thus a couple with four children aged 11, 13, 15 and 16 would receive £128.75 through income support, compared with £129 gross through basic benefit, before the SDP deduction of £3.44 income tax on child benefit for the fourth child, which brings its figure down to £125.56 net. Once again the SDP strategy seems like anti-natalism, although it could simply be a hand-down from family income supplement.

The advantages of lumping benefit onto the first child are questionable. In the UK it has been a feature of family income support since FIS was introduced in 1971, but elsewhere in Europe the opposite happens. Although some benefits for children are focused on families with one very young child, most are concentrated on large families and families with older children. This is thought to be good targeting, partly because it ties in with evidence that poverty correlates with large families, and partly because there

Table 15:5: SDP Basic Benefit compared with Income Support –
married couple + 2 children aged 6 and 12, £ week
March 1986

	Basic benefit £	Income support £
Child benefit	23.00	14.00
Parents	52.00	48.00
Family premium	17.00	5.75
Premium for each child aged over 11	3.50	
	95.50	
Income support for child under 11		3.10
Ditto for child over 11		8.10
Free school meals at £2.75	0.00	5.75
		84.70

are so many more one-child families, hence benefit loaded onto the
relatively better-off one-child families is an inefficient way of
using scarce resources. By lumping £17 onto the first child, the SDP
show that income-testing does not always result in good targeting.
Almost certainly it would be more cost effective to pay benefit
according to family size and the age of the children. Certainly it is
unsatisfactory to perpetuate the FIS benefit structure without a
thorough review.

BB is withdrawn as income rises, at a rate of 70 percent of
increases in net income, but there would be an initial weekly
income disregard of £15. In calculating the tables at the end of this
chapter I have assumed that *each* spouse with income is entitled to
this disregard, which applies to the lower paid as well as to the
unemployed. The capital disregard with supplementary benefit
would be replaced by the same income disregard of £15. Again it is
not clear whether each spouse can have £15 disregarded. When the
BB taper is added to 39 percent income tax, the wage earner is left
with just 18 pence out of each extra £ earned.

Housing benefit

It is not clear what the SDP propose to do about housing benefit.
Originally they planned to include a housing element in BB, but
later it was decided to keep housing benefit separate. From the
wording of the 1986 Policy Statement it seems that SDP housing
benefit would operate on the basis of the 1986 Social Security Act
(Fowler TA), except that rents and rates would be paid in full for

people with no income apart from BB. This is the assumption used for the tables in this chapter and in Part 4. Rent rebates and rate rebates are both calculated on a net income basis, with a 60 percent taper for rent rebates and a 20 percent taper for rate rebates. I have also assumed that the £15 earnings disregard per wage earner is for BB only.

Relief for mortgage interest would also be preserved. As a result of BB and the new formula for housing benefit, the SDP estimated that the housing benefit case load would drop by about one-third compared with 1985. For instance it would be rare for anyone in work to need housing assistance. This is due to the very high marginal tax rate (about 93.5 percent) imposed on people with housing benefit.

Lone parents

Lone parents would lose the additional personal allowance for tax purposes, instead they would have the same weekly tax discount of £14.89 as everybody else. According to the 1986 document they would also lose one-parent benefit, but this was subsequently reinstated. Child benefit for lone parents would not be taxable. In theory lone parents currently in receipt of SB would gain from the abolition of the SB earnings restrictions. But in practice, due to the high benefit withdrawal rate with BB, the existing situation would hardly change. Lone parents fortunate enough to have friends or relatives willing to provide free childcare might find paid work marginally worthwhile. But for the majority the system would remain a trap. Nothing is said about the cohabitation rule. Presumably it would continue.

Old age pensioners

The main beneficiaries from the scheme would be the elderly, especially those with an inadequate contribution record. The proposal to abolish contribution requirements for the basic state pension is a radical departure in the direction of a basic income for pensioners. But the rates of the new pension would still depend on marital status. A single pensioner would receive £40.60, and a married pensioner £65.45, the same as Mr Fowler's income support rates for pensioners in November 1985. This could produce problems since an increasing number of couples are building up entitlement to full Category A pension (worth £40.60) for each spouse. For them a non-contributory pension of £65.45 would be a loss, not a gain. Existing rights of wives to full pensions would nevertheless be preserved.

Although the SDP have no immediate proposals for the reform of SERPS, they emphasise that increases in the flat rate basic pension should be given higher priority. By linking BB and housing benefit to net income any future increases in basic pension would automatically reduce the number of pensioners in receipt of income-tested benefits.

The problem of tax break-even points remains. As already explained (Chapter 5, pages 65-67), the tax break-even point in 1987-88 was £100 for a couple with two children (taking income tax plus NI contribution into account), compared with £150 for a single pensioner. If the basic state pension is to be raised to the poverty line without producing massive benefit leakage to pensioners who do not need state assistance, either the pension has to be made withdrawable, which was the IFS solution, or the rate of income tax has to be increased substantially. The only other option I know of is the BIG 1(a) solution, which makes the enlarged basic pension tax-free as *quid pro quo* for abolition of private pension tax reliefs.

People with disabilities and carers

There is no mention of people with disabilities in the 1986 document, but in 1983 the SDP did recognise the case for introduction of a disability income payable irrespective of the cause of disability. At that time they postponed making any detailed recommendations on the grounds that the information was not available to cost it. Instead they proposed that £200 million extra should be used to extend *invalid care allowance* (ICA) to married women, to introduce a tapered disregard with invalidity benefit, to remove the age limit on entitlement to mobility allowance and other similar improvements.

How much would it cost?

The proposals are intended to be broadly self-financing in the sense that no increase in public borrowing or expenditure cuts elsewhere

Table 15:6: SDP tax/benefit reform budget, cost and savings

	£ billion
Costs of NI integration, abolition of MMA and new combined tax allowance of £2,100	+ 3.2
Phasing out of higher rate mortgage relief	+ 0.2
Replacing tax allowances by fixed amount credits	+ 0.4
Raising child benefit by £4.50 but making it taxable	− 1.2
Basic benefit	− 2.8
Carers' benefit	− 0.3
	− 0.5

Source: SDP 1986, Appendix A.

in the system are envisaged: "Better benefits for the poor will be paid for by tax increases on the best off" (SDP 1986, page 2).

A reasonable period would neverthless be allowed for adjustment. Table 15.6 sets out the costing figures in the 1986 Policy Statement.

For their detailed costings the SDP relied on the IFS Tax-Benefit Model. This model is conceptually similar to TAXMOD. It makes no allowances for behavioural or other changes as a result of the proposed reforms, nor can it measure changes that do not directly affect family incomes as reported in the Family Expenditure Survey. Given the large increase in the number of working families who would be subject to increased marginal tax rates if the SDP proposals were introduced, the first of these limitations is important. The second limitation matters less with the SDP scheme than with Patrick Minford's proposals or with *BIG* schemes, since the SDP keep employers' NI contributions and all the non-personal income tax reliefs except mortgage interest unchanged.

Administration

The Policy Statement has little to say about administration. On basic benefit all we have to go on is the following:

Basic benefit will be phased in through PAYE as part of a unified tax/benefit system. Entitlement will be on the basis of a very simple tax return and will be included in the personal coding, so that the determination of means will be the same for every person in the country, and payment of Basic Benefit with pay will be automatic. There will therefore be no stigma about means tests. The family element of Basic Benefit will however be paid direct to the caring parent through the Child

Benefit Order Book, together with Child Benefit. (SDP 1986, page 3)

It looks as though BB would depend on each person's *accumulated* income during the previous tax year, as reported in an annual tax return. The first problem is one of access. What happens to people in the meantime and how long would they have to wait for benefit? The second problem concerns cumulation and the accounting period. Would benefit entitlement be cumulative, like income tax liability, in which case would people be expected to pay back benefit "overpayments"? Or would tax liability be cumulative and benefit entitlement be non-cumulative, in which case how would the two be "merged"? Either way, what would be the accounting period? The third most obvious problem, and there are many more, concerns the unit of assessment. Is it really possible to operate a unified system where the assessment unit is the individual for tax purposes but the family (or household?) for benefit purposes? In 1983 the SDP said that the earnings of husband and wife, after being separately taxed, would be "automatically linked". This assumes that the Inland Revenue would have on record *all* income received by each spouse during the relevant accounting period, including income below the deduction card limit, for instance part-time earnings of less than £38 a week.

In practice none of this is realistic. The starting point for administration of any tax/benefit system is the need to pay benefit promptly, efficiently and humanely, *and* to avoid payment of benefit to those who do not need it. Selectivity can be through demogrants (children, the old, the sick, or people with disabilities) and it can be through income-testing or means-testing. Income-testing can be through the income tax or it can be through withdrawable benefits. Selectivity through demogrants and/or through the income tax is compatible with a fully automated tax/benefit system, but selectivity through withdrawable benefits is not, because it is impossible to police. Either it will be too severe, in which case claimants will be kept waiting, or it will be too lax, in which case expenditure will get out of control. Probably it will be a mixture both.

Marginal tax rates

For working families the starting rate of the new income tax would have been 39 percent in March 1986, and income tax plus

Table 15:7: SDP Basic Benefit, marginal tax rates, July 1986

Marginal rates %	HEADS				WIVES			
	%	Current CUMUL	%	SDP CUMUL	%	Current CUMUL	%	SDP CUMUL
0—	1.76	1.76	0.19	0.19	31.54	31.54	14.22	14.22
10—	0.06	1.82	0.03	0.22	1.08	32.62	0.24	14.46
20—	8.61	10.43	0.03	0.25	1.95	34.57	0.15	14.61
30—	81.30	91.72	86.91	87.16	58.45	93.02	82.54	97.16
40—	3.57	95.30	4.58	91.74	3.99	97.02	0.39	97.55
50—	1.58	96.87	2.07	93.81	0.88	97.90	0.74	98.29
60—	1.32	98.19	1.32	95.13	0.15	98.04	0.21	98.50
70—	1.81	100.00	4.87	100.00	1.96	100.00	1.50	100.00

Source: Sutherland 1986, Table 5.

withdrawal of BB would have produced an effective marginal tax rate of just under 82 percent, calculated as follows:

$$(0.39 + 0.7*(1 - 0.39))*100\% = 81.7\%$$

Additionally, for families (including most pensioners) affected by withdrawal of housing benefit as well as basic benefit, the effective marginal tax rate goes up to 93.5 percent. This is not specified in the text of the 1986 policy document, but is clear from the figures in Table 15.9, at the end of this chapter. Above the existing upper earnings level for NI contribution, the new income tax would continue at 39 percent, whereas in 1985-86 there was a drop from 39 per cent (income tax plus not contracted-out NI contributions) to 30 percent.

Model family analysis at the back of this chapter and in Appendix 2 shows how different families living in assumed circumstances would be affected. The question is how many families would be affected by increased marginal tax rates, and who would they be.

In December 1986, Holly Sutherland of ST/ICERD, London School of Economics, put the SDP proposals through TAXMOD (Sutherland 1986). All her figures refer to July 1986, and the analysis applied only to families with employed or self-employed heads.

Modelling the SDP proposal was impeded by a lack of administrative detail, for instance Sutherland had to assume that BB would be assessed on a non-cumulative, weekly or monthly basis, and that the laws of liability to maintain, including the cohabitation regulation, would remain unchanged. Another difficulty is that the FES incomes reflect the actual take-up of income-tested benefits (50 percent with FIS for example), whereas for basic benefit Sutherland assumed 100 percent take-up. Table 15.7, taken from Sutherland's paper, shows nearly 5 percent of working family heads with marginal tax rates of 70 percent or more, compared with just under 2 percent under the existing system.

The figures confirm the increased taxation of low incomes indicated in the model tables. Taking the bands of tax rates below 30 percent, the cumulative totals go down from 10.43 percent to 0.25 percent for heads and from 34.57 percent to 14.61 percent for wives. Those worst affected are working wives, of whom about 72 percent would experience an increase in their marginal tax rate if the proposals were put into effect. Additionally, married mothers with four or more children and not in paid work would face marginal tax rates of at least 38 percent, due to the taxation of child benefit as their income. These wives are not included in Table 15.7.

Who gains and who loses? Model family analysis

Figure 15.3 illustrates the effect of the SDP proposals on *net incomes* of single-wage married couples with two children. The shape of the net income curve is roughly similar for all working age families. At the bottom of the earnings distribution some families

Figure 15.3: SDP net incomes, March 1986

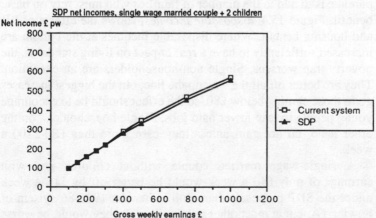

Source: Appendix 2.

lose and some gain, but at the top all seem to lose. The gains and losses are nevertheless quite small by comparison with the Vince and BIG proposals, which is not surprising, given that the SDP scheme was intended for immediate implementation.

On earnings below £300 a week single people gain £2 and single-wage couples with one to three children gain between £2 and £6. The couple in the graph gain £4 on earnings up to £250. Many people would lose. Single-wage couples without children lose around £5 a week on earnings up to £300. Some low income, two-wage couples with children also lose £5 a week or more. On earnings above £300 the losses become bigger, especially for mortgagors. Even single people lose if their earnings are above £300. Most lone-parents lose because the increased child benefit (which for them is tax-free) is not enough to offset loss of one-parent benefit and the additional personal allowance (for income tax).

Given the evidence that lower paid working families with children need extra help, and that all families with children have lost out in recent years, the additional support for single-wage families with children can be reckoned good targeting. But it is hard to understand why a single person on £150 a week should gain £2 whereas a two-wage couple with two small children and the same combined earnings should lose £5. Even for the single-wage family with children the gain is only £4, which is less in terms of equivalent incomes than the single person's £2.

The effect of the increased tax liability of single-wage couples without children, of two-wage couples with children and of lone parents, is to add to the number of families who must rely on basic benefit. Figure 15.4, *disposable incomes*, shows the effects of BB and housing benefit. Where disposable incomes at the bottom are increased sufficiently to have a real impact on living standards, the poverty trap worsens. Single non-householders are an exception. They are better off all the way up the line, but the biggest increases go to those earning below £80, so the effect should be to encourage young people to take lower paid jobs. Single householders, on the other hand, do not gain unless they earn more than £80-£100 a week.

A single-wage married couple without children and with earnings of only £40 a week would be better off by £18 a week under the SDP proposals than with either the 1985-86 system or Fowler TA, but at most other earnings levels they would be worse off. A single-wage couple with two small children, either

Figure 15.4: SDP disposable incomes, March 1986

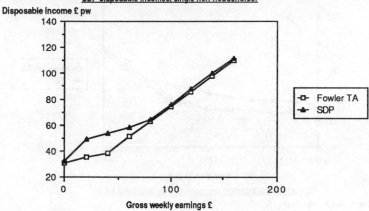

SDP disposable incomes, single non-householder

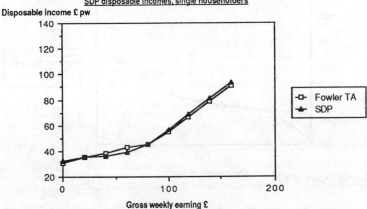

SDP disposable incomes, single householders

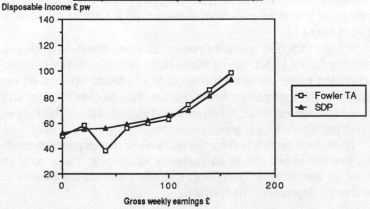

SDP disposable incomes, single wage married couple

273

SDP Tax and Benefit proposals

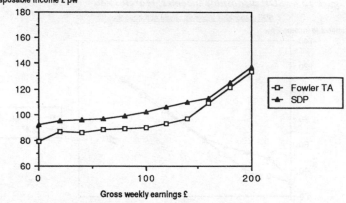

SDP disposable incomes, single wage married couple + 2 children aged 4 & 6

Disposable Income £ pw

Gross weekly earnings £

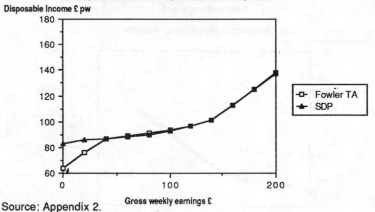

SDP disposable incomes, lone parent + 2 children aged 4 & 6

Disposable Income £ pw

Gross weekly earnings £

Source: Appendix 2.

unemployed or lower paid, would be significantly better off by comparison with Fowler TA, but the price of BB is a marginal tax rate so high that the gain from earning £140 a week as opposed to £40 is only £14.

Figure 15.5, *net spending power*, assumes travel-to-work and childcare costs as before and shows that a couple with two children where the father earns a £160 are only £11 better off than on the dole. For the lone parent the offer wage must be over £200, nearly twice average earnings for women in 1985-86, before the mother reaps any financial advantage.

From the figures one is forced to conclude that targeting through income-tested benefits is no guarantee of success. Those most in need do not necessarily do best, and when they do the penalty is increased dependence on welfare.

Figure 15.5: SDP net spending power, March 1986

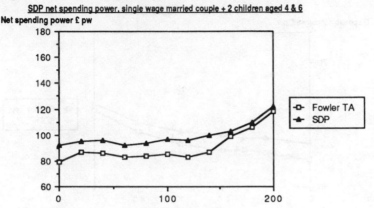

SDP net spending power, single wage married couple + 2 children aged 4 & 6

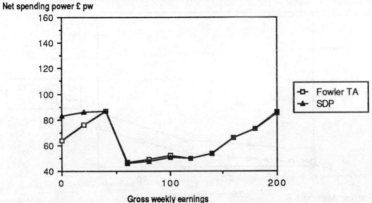

SDP net spending power, lone parent + 2 children aged 4 & 6

Source: Appendix 2.

Figure 15.6 summarises the effects of the SDP proposals on the *disposable incomes of retirement pensioners*. Although BB would be withdrawn very quickly, most pensioners in rented accommodation would be entitled to housing benefit. This is why the disposable income curves are so flat. Assuming rent of £15 a week and rates of £7, the levels of original income at which pensioners stand to gain by more than a few pence in the £ from their past savings would be £50 in the case of single people and £40 for couples.

Weekly gains for low income pensioners of £5-£7 a week are good news, but the minuscule advantages to pensioners with small occupational or earnings related pensions put a big question-mark over a system that first encourages people to save for their old age

Figure 15.6: SDP pensioner disposable incomes, March 1986

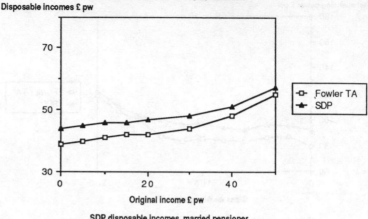

SDP disposable incomes, single pensioners

Disposable incomes £ pw

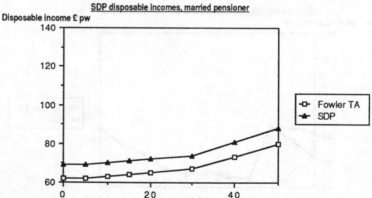

SDP disposable incomes, married pensioner

Disposable income £ pw

Source: Appendix 2.

(through income tax reliefs), and then prevents them from reaping the advantages.

Who gains and who loses? Empirical analysis

Empirical analysis, using TAXMOD, confirms these findings. In her Discussion Paper *Modelling the SDP Tax/Benefit Scheme*, Holly Sutherland emphasised the limitations of model family analysis, saying that "the gain/loss calculation depends crucially on the assumptions made about the hypothetical family", and that the number of assumptions that can be made although "not actually

Table 15:8: SDP "Merging Tax and Benefit" scheme, analysis of losers, families in paid work

	% losing	Average loss £ per week
Householder	76	5.05
Non-householder	21	1.02
Owner	82	6.62
Tenant	64	1.69
Married	81	5.84
Single	31	− 0.29
Children	70	3.78
No children	56	3.24
Wife works	95	8.18
Wife does not work (or no wife)	42	0.67
All	63	3.45

Source: *Modelling the SDP Tax/Benefit Scheme,* Table 4, Holly Sutherland 1986.

endless, it is very large" (Sutherland 1986, pages 13 and 14). Her findings illuminate but nevertheless confirm those presented above, and the fact that her figures refer to 1986-87 instead of 1985-86 makes little difference.

Putting the 15.5 million families with employed or self-employed heads through TAXMOD showed an average loss of £3.45 per week per family, with 63 percent of families losing as a result of the scheme. Although there were gainers and losers at every income level, most of the gainers were concentrated at the bottom, and most of the families losing large amounts were concentrated in the top income ranges. Yet there were also substantial numbers of losers in the middle and bottom ranges. Some of the losers were wage or salary earners exempt from NI contribution, or people with unearned income, whose tax rate would go up from 30 to 39 percent.

Table 15.8, taken from Sutherland's paper, summarises the average loss for the different family types in the sample and the proportion of the group that would lose from the SDP scheme. The findings highlight the immense variety of individual circumstances. The typical loser is a two-wage couple with children and a mortgage, but the same family could also gain, if they had low housing costs and a low income. The typical gainer is a single non-householder, but even some of them could lose, for instance if they were contracted out of SERPS or had substantial unearned income.

If the overall annual cost of the SDP scheme to working families

277

is £2.8 billion, as estimated by Sutherland , and since the scheme is designed to be revenue neutral, then it follows that nearly £3b is being transferred from earners to non-earners. Some of the non-earners who stand to gain would be out-of-work families of working age, for instance lone parents on supplementary benefit and most unemployed families with children. Sutherland's TAXMOD analysis did not include the out-of-work population, but it is clear that pensioners stand to gain from benefit increases and tax changes as well as from abolition of the contribution requirement. Although pensioners paying higher rate tax would lose out, the number affected would be very small. Single pensioners would need original incomes (excluding state basic pension) of more than £300 a week before they lost out, and married pensioners would need more than £400.

Summing up

The SDP Basic Benefit proposal does not constitute integration as defined in this report. It does not replace all other benefits, nor does it involve harmonisation of the administrative procedures below and above the break-even points. It is clearly a transitional scheme, hence the retention of unemployment benefit, and it would be helpful if the SDP were to publish the target system at which they are aiming.

Abolition of NI contribution and introduction of positional benefits like unemployment benefit and old age pension is close to the *Back to Beveridge* strategy referred to in Chapter 6, as is abolition of married man's tax allowance. Introduction of citizenship pensions is close to BI, but the heavy reliance on income-tested basic benefit for working age families is closer to IFS thinking.

The claim that selectivity through income-tested benefits is the best way to help "the poor" is not vindicated. Despite an overall redistribution of income from rich to poor and from the working to the out-of-work population, gains and losses tend to be haphazard, with some working age families on very low incomes among the losers.

Abolition of married man's tax allowance produces more tax slippage than the existing system. Basic benefit would top low incomes up again, but the overall result is to increase the number of families caught in the poverty trap. About 20 percent of families with two children would face marginal tax plus benefit withdrawal rates of 82 percent or more, and about 30 percent of the population would depend on basic benefit. Despite this there would still be hidden family poverty, because benefit is concentrated on families with one child, whereas the worst poverty tends to correlate with large families.

The SDP give the impression of being against the traditional, two-parent family. Husbands and wives would be assessed separately for tax but together for basic benefit, and the tax paid by single-wage couples would be the same as the tax paid by single people. The economic viability of the single-wage, two-parent family is undermined and the bias in favour of lone parenthood reinforced.

The reasons for treating working age families in this way are clearly political. The SDP realise the financial consequences of fully independent taxation, otherwise they would not recommend transferable income tax allowances between pensioner spouses:

We should recognise that the pension for a couple is in effect two persons' income. They should therefore have the option of splitting their income to obtain two persons' allowance and would not be worse off from abolition of the MMA. (SDP 1986, page 7)

Why is an old age pension two persons' income, but not a wage?

Table 15.9: Disposable incomes of selected model families, SDP Basic Benefit proposals, detailed figures for Nov 85 to Mar 86, £ per week

Assumptions

All figures refer to the period November 1985 to March 1986. All families are tenants. Working age families live in council property, and pay the rents and rates used in the November 1985 DHSS Tax/Benefit Model Tables. Water rates, estimated by the DHSS to have been £1.65 a week on average, are not included. Families are assumed to take up entitlement to means-tested benefits in full. No allowance is made for any non-personal income tax reliefs, eg for superannuation contributions. No allowance for cost of fares to work or childminding expenses unless specified. The weekly tax credit for people of working age is £14.89 and the starting rate of the new income tax is 39 %. Child benefit is £11.50, taxable on the income of the spouse/partner with the lowest income. Basic Benefit is £32 single with an £11 supplement for lone parents, £52 married, £17 supplement for families with children. The weekly tax credit for pensioners is £15.52 (up to age allowance upper limit of £169), and the tax rate is 30 per cent. Basic Benefit is £3.70 for single pensioners and £5.75 for pensioner couples, on top of non-withdrawable, non-contributory pension of £41 single and £63.23 married. BB taper is 70% of net income increases, after £15 disregard per wage earner. Housing benefit is rent and rates in full at nil original income. Tapers are 60% for rent and 20% for rates of increases in net income.

Acronyms: BB = basic benefit; B = housing benefit

WORKING AGE HOUSEHOLDS

Table 1: Single non-householder

	£	£	£	£	£	£
Gross weekly earnings	0.00	40.00	80.00	120.00	160.00	200.00
− Income tax	0.00	0.71	16.31	31.91	47.51	63.11
= Net income before Basic Benefit	0.00	39.29	63.69	88.09	112.49	136.89
+ Basic Benefit	32.00	15.00	0.00	0.00	0.00	0.00
= Net & disposable incomes	32.00	54.29	63.69	88.09	112.49	136.89

Table 2: Single householder

	£	£	£	£	£	£
Gross weekly earnings	0.00	40.00	80.00	120.00	160.00	200.00
− Income tax	0.00	0.71	16.31	31.91	47.51	63.11
= Net income before Basic Benefit	0.00	39.29	63.69	88.09	112.49	136.89
+ Basic Benefit	32.00	15.00	0.00	0.00	0.00	0.00
+ Housing Benefit	19.00	1.17	0.00	0.00	0.00	0.00
= Net incomes after BB & HB	51.00	55.46	63.69	88.09	112.49	136.89
− Rent	13.80	13.80	13.80	13.80	13.80	13.80
− Rates	5.20	5.20	5.20	5.20	5.20	5.20
= Disposable incomes	32.00	36.46	44.69	69.09	93.29	117.89

Table 3: Single person + 2 children aged 4 and 6

	£	£	£	£	£	£
Gross weekly earnings	0.00	40.00	80.00	120.00	160.00	200.00
+ Child benefit	23.00	23.00	23.00	23.00	23.00	23.00
− Income tax	0.00	0.71	16.31	31.91	47.51	63.11
= Net incomes before Basic Benefit	23.00	62.29	86.69	111.09	135.49	159.89
+ Basic Benefit	60.00	43.00	25.78	8.84	0.00	0.00
+ Housing Benefit	22.80	4.97	0.41	0.00	0.00	0.00
= Net incomes after BB & HB	105.80	110.26	112.88	119.93	135.49	159.89
− Rent	16.50	16.50	16.50	16.50	16.50	16.50
− Rates	6.30	6.30	6.30	6.30	6.30	6.30
= Disposable incomes	83.00	87.46	90.08	97.13	112.69	137.09

Table 4: Married couple (single-wage)

	£	£	£	£	£	£
Gross weekly earnings	0.00	40.00	80.00	120.00	160.00	200.00
− Income tax	0.00	0.71	16.31	31.91	47.51	63.11
= Net incomes before Basic Benefit	0.00	39.29	63.69	88.09	112.49	136.89
+ Basic Benefit	52.00	35.00	18.20	0.84	0.00	0.00
+ Housing Benefit	19.00	1.17	0.00	0.00	0.00	0.00
= Net incomes after BB & HB	71.00	75.46	81.89	88.93	112.49	136.89
− Rent	13.80	13.80	13.80	13.80	13.80	13.80
− Rates	5.20	5.20	5.20	5.20	5.20	5.20
= Disposable incomes	52.00	56.46	62.89	69.93	93.49	117.89

Table 5: Married couple (two-wage, each spouse earns half)

	£	£	£	£	£	£
Joint gross weekly earnings		40.00	80.00	120.00	160.00	200.00
− Income tax: Husband		0.00	0.71	8.51	16.31	24.11
Wife		0.00	0.71	8.51	16.31	24.11
= Net incomes before Basic Benefit		40.00	78.58	102.98	127.38	151.78
+ Basic Benefit		45.00	18.00	0.92	0.00	0.00
+ Housing Benefit		0.00	0.00	0.00	0.00	0.00
= Net incomes after BB & HB		85.00	96.58	103.90	127.38	151.78
− Rent		13.80	13.80	13.80	13.80	13.80
− Rates		5.20	5.20	5.20	5.20	5.20
= Disposable incomes		66.00	77.58	84.90	108.38	132.78

Table 6: Married couple + 2 children aged 4 and 6 (single-wage)

	£	£	£	£	£	£
Gross weekly earnings	0.00	40.00	80.00	120.00	160.00	200.00
+ Child benefit	23.00	23.00	23.00	23.00	23.00	23.00
− Income tax	0.00	0.71	16.31	31.91	47.51	63.11
= Net incomes before Basic Benefit	23.00	62.29	86.69	111.09	135.49	159.89
+ Basic Benefit	69.00	52.00	34.92	17.98	0.76	0.00
+ Housing Benefit	22.80	4.97	0.41	0.00	0.00	0.00
= Net incomes after BB & HB	114.80	119.26	122.02	129.07	136.25	159.89
− Rent	16.50	16.50	16.50	16.50	16.50	16.50
− Rates	6.30	6.30	6.30	6.30	6.30	6.30
= Disposable incomes	92.00	96.46	99.22	106.27	113.45	137.09

Table 7: Married couple + 2 children aged 4 and 6 (two-wage, each spouse earns half)

	£	£	£	£	£	£
Joint gross weekly earnings		40.00	80.00	120.00	160.00	200.00
+ Child benefit		23.00	23.00	23.00	23.00	23.00
− Income tax: Husband		0.00	0.71	8.51	16.31	24.11
Wife		1.88	9.68	17.48	25.28	33.08
= Net incomes before Basic Benefit		61.12	92.61	117.01	141.41	165.81
+ Basic Benefit		63.32	45.42	29.04	11.26	0.00
+ Housing Benefit		0.00	0.00	0.00	0.00	0.00
= Net incomes after BB & HB		124.44	137.03	146.05	152.67	165.81
− Rent		16.50	16.50	16.50	16.50	16.50
− Rates		6.30	6.30	6.30	6.30	6.30
= Disposable incomes		101.64	114.23	123.25	129.87	143.01

2. RETIREMENT PENSIONERS

Table 8: Single retirement pensioner

	£	£	£	£	£	£	£	£
Earnings/private pension/ SERPS/investment income	0.00	5.00	10.00	20.00	30.00	40.00	50.00	100.00
+ Citizen's basic pension	40.60	40.60	40.60	40.60	40.60	40.60	40.60	40.60
− Income tax	0.00	0.00	0.00	2.66	5.66	8.66	11.66	26.66
= Net incomes before Basic Benefit	40.60	45.60	50.60	57.94	64.94	71.94	78.94	113.94
+ Basic Benefit	3.70	0.20	0.00	0.00	0.00	0.00	0.00	0.00
+ Housing Benefit	22.00	20.90	16.96	11.09	5.49	1.48	0.07	0.00
= Net incomes after BB & HB	66.30	66.70	67.56	69.03	70.43	73.42	79.01	113.94
− Rent	15.00	15.00	15.00	15.00	15.00	15.00	15.00	15.00
− Rates	7.00	7.00	7.00	7.00	7.00	7.00	7.00	7.00
= Disposable incomes	44.30	44.70	45.56	47.03	48.43	51.42	57.01	91.94

Table 9: Pensioner couple

	£	£	£	£	£	£	£	£
Earnings/private pension/ SERPS/investment income	0.00	5.00	10.00	20.00	30.00	40.00	50.00	100.00
+ Citizen's basic pension	63.25	63.25	63.25	63.25	63.25	63.25	63.25	63.25
− Income tax	0.00	0.00	0.00	0.00	0.00	0.00	2.94	17.94
= Net incomes before Basic Benefit	63.25	68.25	73.25	83.25	93.25	103.25	110.31	145.31
+ Basic Benefit	5.75	2.25	0.00	0.00	0.00	0.00	0.00	0.00
+ Housing Benefit	22.00	20.90	18.54	10.60	2.60	0.15	0.00	0.00
= Net incomes after BB & HB	91.00	91.40	91.79	93.85	95.85	103.40	110.31	145.31
− Rent	15.00	15.00	15.00	15.00	15.00	15.00	15.00	15.00
− Rates	7.00	7.00	7.00	7.00	7.00	7.00	7.00	7.00
= Disposable incomes	69.00	69.40	69.79	71.85	73.85	81.40	88.31	123.31

Part 4

ASSESSMENT

16

Core Issues

Throughout this report there are certain core issues that form a backdrop to the debate. Some have roots that go far back in history and depend as much on gut feelings as on rational thought. Others are of recent origin and are technical as well as political. In this chapter we look briefly at six, and at the different approaches to each within the different reform strategies. The issues are: simplicity; the future of work; conditionality; family income support; tax expenditures; and pensioner incomes.

Simplicity

No reform proposal has a chance of being implemented unless it can win the hearts and minds of the electorate. To do that it must be easy to understand and easy to administer. Most would-be reformers accept the importance of simplicity, but tend to confuse administrative simplicity with automation. All the NIT-style proposals in the previous chapters rely heavily on computerisation, but computerisation on its own is no guarantee of success, which depends on the accuracy of the raw data, especially the details of income and family circumstances fed into the computers. Those details need constant checking, certainly where compliance costs are as high, as in most NIT schemes they would be. With pensioners the monthly turnover of new cases might be quite low, but for people of working age the number of new cases would far exceed the snap-shot estimates usually provided.

Chip technology can reduce the workload for officials operating withdrawable benefits, but it can never replace the experienced case officer. Real simplification requires low compliance costs, low

285

marginal tax rates and the minimum of restrictive legislation – a system in other words that can be automated without inviting fraud and abuse.

That is why all BIG schemes keep administration of the automated BIs completely separate from the withdrawable benefits. Where the system is automated the assessment unit never changes and the tax rate never goes above 60 percent. Some schemes (for instance *BI 2000*) have a flat rate tax, which makes administration of the Transfer Income Account even easier. For the withdrawable benefits all BIG schemes rely on old-style case-work. In the local authority Cash & Care departments, it would be part of the case-officer's job to find out why a person was poor, and to offer assistance that need not always be financial. Minford's approach is somewhat similar, but only for the unemployed, not for his NIT. This would have to be automated because of the numbers affected, and it would be very hard to police . Minford talks about a collusion clause but gives no details.

Where compliance costs are high, computerisation is an invitation to abuse. The higher the benefit withdrawal rate the greater the need to check that net benefit recipients are demonstrably poor, and, if they are, to help remedy the cause of their poverty. This itself is a costly process, which is one reason for keeping the number of people entitled to means-tested and income-tested benefits as low as possible. Insofar as some such benefits will always be necessary, personal involvement at local level must also remain, and is in the interest of claimants as well as taxpayers. Poverty prevention is about helping people to help themselves. Otherwise the system creates its own demand and will eventually wreck the economy. Insofar as Minford does face up to this problem, his remedy is very harsh. The Liberal and SDP proposals pay insufficient attention to cost control.

With all the early BIG schemes, and with the Liberal Tax Credit scheme, there also remains the impossible task of collecting tax on the first £ of income.

The future of work

The crunch issue is between those who think that full employment (defined as a full-time job for all who want it) is gone forever, and those who think it could return (without inflationary consequences) if only the tax and benefit systems were changed to make lower paid work worthwhile.

For those who take the first view, one solution is to widen our definition of work, by including unpaid and part-time paid work as well as full-time paid work, and simultaneously to replace the dole by an income guarantee based on need rather than labour market status. This is the approach taken by most advocates of integration, Minford is an exception. An unconditional BI or NIT raises the status of those who are excluded from the regular labour market, and it simultaneously promotes labour market flexibility by enabling the unemployed to take part-time or irregular work without forfeiting their right to income support.

The case for a new definition of work was well argued by Gabriel Fragnière (Director of the European Centre for Work and Society in Maastricht) in an essay in French, whose title can be translated as *Work and Employment in the Europe of Tomorrow* (Fragnière 1987). Fragnière traces the concept of work through history, and finds that it is only in industrial societies that work means paid employment. As a result of industrialisation not only has work come to mean paid employment, but the right to work has become the right to a wage. The wage has become more important than the work itself. The wage is calculated on the basis of hours worked, not the work done, and in a comparatively short space of time the whole of human life has become geared to hours of work, the working week, holidays and the age of retirement. If you are not part of this process you are excluded from mainstream society.

Fragnière proposes a definition of work that would encompass "any human activity which serves a social purpose". This definition is very close to the *unpaid* work to which reference is made throughout this report. Both need closer analysis, in order to exclude the daily tasks that people do for the benefit of themselves. Both are nevertheless making the same point, namely that human welfare is not derived solely, or even mainly, from the market.

Advocates of full BI would break the link between income and paid work entirely. Everybody would have enough money to live on, regardless of whether or not they bothered to earn it. This change is not intended to promote idleness. On the contrary, by enabling people to take jobs at wages that are below subsistence level a full BI in theory makes unskilled labour more competitive with machinery.

The late Keith Roberts argued the case for basic income as a remedy for unemployment in *Automation, Unemployment and the Distribution of Income* (Roberts 1982). Roberts was a distinguished physicist, who saw no reason why an economic system should not be designed like an engineer designs a machine. Starting from the observation that most tasks needed to keep the economic system running have always been of a routine nature, and are likely to remain so, he points out that most routine mechanical or intellectual tasks can now be automated. He then asks whether it is possible to design a version of the market economy that will function compassionately and efficiently, despite the large and increasing proportion of goods and services provided by automatic means (Roberts 1982, pages 10 and 14).

Roberts's solution, described as an alternative version of the market economy, was a National Dividend (ND) at subsistence level:

> Let us agree that the State continues to accept the responsibility for ensuring that everyone receives at least the level of income needed for basic subsistence. It is then suggested that the most logical arrangement would be to provide this basic income to all citizens in a uniform way by means of a standard payment to be called the National Dividend (ND), requiring no means test or other complex administration, and to allow the forces of the classical market to determine the equilibrium level of additional wages and other forms of income.(Roberts 1982, page 13)

Roberts's aim was to reduce unemployment by breaking the link between the minimum acceptable wage and the level of subsistence. The ND/BI would be payable on the basis of age alone. Lower paid jobs would become available because net income from work would always be worth more than the BI on its own. The disadvantage of a full BI, as we have seen, would be its cost. In his publications Roberts never put a figure on his BI, but when pressed to do so it was clear that he was thinking along the lines of what most people would call a partial BI.

At the other extreme from those who think human labour is about to be replaced by robots, are those, like Patrick Minford, for whom unemployment is the result of excessive trade union power and tax and social security systems that destroy work incentives:

> ...there are jobs at some rate of pay available for the unemployed to do. Our estimates suggest that at rates of pay only 10 per cent below existing market rates, unemployment would effectively disappear. In other words, 2.25 million

more jobs exist at rates of pay up to 10 per cent below the rates workers will not now willingly accept. These jobs are not taken...because they are too low-paid relative to benefits. (Minford *et al.* 1985, page 88)

To cut wages, says Minford, it is necessary to reduce the power of the unions, to increase the gap between incomes in and out of work (replacement ratios), and to make sure that no able-bodied person is allowed to claim benefit for more than a limited period (workfare). Unfortunately nobody can be sure how low wages would have to fall in order to make it worthwhile for employers to take on all the people who would like to work.

Advocates of partial BI fall between these two extremes. The Vince and Parker schemes, and to a lesser extent the SDP solution, all take a middle position. Vince and Parker are not prepared to cut the link between income and work entirely, but they are prepared to recognise the value to the community of unpaid work, and to reward it in money terms. This is the logic behind their PBIs for non-earning spouses, and the full BI for carers in Parker's *Basic Income 2000* (Chapter 19). Unlike full BI, a partial BI does not remove the incentive to do paid work, because it is not enough to live on and in any case the tax rate is much lower. On the contrary, a principle aim of the Vince and BIG schemes is to sharpen work incentives by providing a bridge between unemployment and full-time work, and by reducing replacement ratios. Employers are able to take on trainees at apprenticeship wages, instead of having to compete with income support grossed up for tax.

Advocates of partial BI start from the premise that governments should encourage labour market flexibility by protecting people from the worst effects of change, and should avoid tax and benefit systems based on the assumption either that full employment has gone forever, or that old-style labour markets can be restored by making the tax and benefit systems sufficiently draconian (Standing 1986). For many people, increased labour market flexibility is one of the chief attractions of BI. In times of slump people would tend to reduce the amount of paid work they did, and to withdraw from the labour market at an earlier age than in times of boom, but always they would be free to come back in, or to supplement their BIs by doing part-time or occasional work. And always it would be in the public interest for them to do so, for every £ of tax paid would reduce the amounts of net benefit paid out.

Advocates of partial BI emphasise the need to avoid tax and

benefit laws that in any way obstruct the workings of the labour market. Roberts was over-optimistic when he suggested BI would completely solve the problem of unemployment, but it would help. It would do so by setting unemployed people free to take whatever work was available, when it was available, without having to make the impossible choice between "claiming and earning", or reporting back to the social security and having their files snarled up for months. A partial BI would increase labour market flexibility without subjecting millions of people to the agonies of life on the dole, and it would do so at all stages of the adult life-cycle, from school-leavers, through prime age men and women, to the young elderly, many of whom would dearly love to build on their pensions by doing paid work if only they were allowed to do so.

Take the young first. For those who need to acquire skills, BI takes over from the ever-changing tangle of training allowances and student grants. It removes the discrimination almost unique to Britain between academic and vocational learning, with its built-in bias in favour of academic education, no matter how esoteric. At sixteen the choice between staying on at school or dropping out would cease to be slanted in favour of dropping out. School students would have the same PBI as school leavers. This investment in young people would be recouped in due course through the tax system, according to the earnings and taxable capacity of each.

It is often suggested that the best way to reduce unemployment is to share out existing jobs by cutting the working week and reducing the age of retirement. This approach wrongly assumes that there is a fixed pool of jobs, and it also takes for granted that there will never again be a labour shortage, although with an ageing population this could happen at any time. Given the near impossibility of raising the age of retirement once it had been lowered, or of increasing the working week once it had been re-duced, by far the wisest solution is one that allows the labour market to sort itself out.

As the population ages, and as the young old become less inclined to retire, the idea of a chronological retirement age becomes less and less acceptable. With BI, even a partial BI, the dream of a flexible retirement age comes closer to reality, and the idea of a statutory retirement age becomes obsolete. The ages at which people cease to do paid work become a matter of personal choice, taking into account the availability of paid work, the wages offered, the pensions on offer and family circumstances.

Conditionality

All the benefits referred to in this report are to some extent conditional. Even a full BI depends on age and proof of legal residence(however defined), and the BIG supplements are contingency based. All NIT schemes require details of income and family circumstances. Access is easier with BI than with NIT, but the criterion for receiving negative tax, or for receiving *net* BI, is need.

What makes Minford's NIT different to the North American NIT experiments and to previous NIT or partial NIT proposals in the UK (including the IFS proposals in 1984, the SDP proposals and Vince's low income and householder credits) is the full-time work condition. When Minford talks about need he means *demonstrable* need. He is not prepared to dispense largesse on grounds of low income alone, without finding out why the income is low. Nor is he prepared to extend his 30 hour a week work rule to include community work. It has to be work with a market value.

An opinion poll might well show a majority in favour of Minford's approach, although not his antipathy to community work. Paradoxically the same poll would probably also show a majority in favour of administrative simplicity and ease of access. And this is the heart of the problem, for the two are incompatible. As soon as the benefit condition is tied to demonstrable need the safety net becomes a tangle of red tape. There has to be compromise.

Even among advocates of a full BI there are some who include a full-time work condition. In *Something To Look Forward To*, Lady Rhys Williams made payment of benefit conditional on signature of a New Social Contract:

> The new relationship would be expressed by the actual signature of a contract between each individual man or woman of eighteen and over, and the State, whereby the State would acknowledge the duty to maintain the individual and his children at all times, and to ensure for them all the necessities of a healthy life. The individual, in his turn, would acknowledge it to be his duty to devote his best efforts to the production of the wealth whereby alone the welfare of the community can be maintained. (J. Rhys Williams 1943, page 145)

Lady Rhys Williams included conditionality because she recognised the strength of opposition to anything that might be said to encourage sloth. Payment of the Social Contract allowances was to be conditional on proof of gainful employment or registration for work. The administrative difficulties become painfully obvious as one reads through her book, and the scheme loses its appeal. The idea of submitting every person of working age who is not in paid work to an availability for work test is transparently impracticable. There would have to be exceptions, but who should they be? Mothers with young children? Fathers with young children? Mothers with older children? Baby-minding grandmothers? Vicars' wives? Voluntary workers? Part-time workers? Seasonal workers? The self-employed? The list is endless, and no matter how carefully the regulations were thought through, there would always be some people in genuine need who slipped through the safety net, and others (not in need) who clambered in.

Where in any case are the jobs to come from? If the State insists on all signatories to the Contract doing paid work, then the State must guarantee job availability. Lady Rhys Williams thought of this too, for she wondered what would happen if the available jobs were unsuitable, or in another part of the country? This is the road to direction of labour, which she abhorred, and in later life she tacitly dropped this part of her proposals.

With BI, the force of the argument for or against a test of demonstrable need becomes a trade-off between two variables: the amount of the guarantee and the costs of administering a work test. With a full BI of (say) £60 a week and a tax rate of 70 percent plus, direction of labour becomes inevitable. With a partial BI of £25 a week and a tax rate below 40 percent the costs of enforcing a work test (and of providing a work guarantee) would far outweigh the costs of supporting a tiny minority of "scroungers", who would probably find a way round the regulations anyway.

At first glance conditionality looks less difficult to operate with a NIT than with BI , because it is up to the needy individual to apply for the NIT, rather than the other way round. A conditional NIT nevertheless produces unexpected problems, as noted in Chapter 13. If it is not restricted to full-time work, part-time work becomes too attractive. If it is restricted to full-time work, part-time work is not at all attractive.

Any sort of work condition is inconsistent with the fully automated PBIs recommended by Vince and Parker. The BIG Transfer Income Account would grind to a halt if entitlement depended on the number of hours worked. Vince retains a work test for his non-earner and low income credits which would have to be administered separately from his personal credits. With BIG schemes, if there has to be a work test, then it must be at local level, administered on a case-officer basis by trained officials who know their communities. Given that the PBI is not enough to live on without income-tested housing benefit, there may be a case for a locally operated income and work guarantee. If the local authorities were able to guarantee sufficient work to lift claimants off housing benefit, then housing benefit could be made conditional. This proposal is a half-way house between Ashby's and Mitchell's guarantees of part-time work for all who want it (Ashby 1988 and Mitchell 1986), and Minford's compulsory workfare.

Family income support

Family income support can be defined as the sum of tax advantages and/or benefits to which married couples and families with children are entitled by comparison with single people and couples without children. In the UK this definition takes into account married man's income tax allowance (MMA) and child benefit as well as family credit and the larger income support entitlements of families with children by comparison with single people. Family income support includes tax reliefs and cash benefits for dependent spouses (spouse support) as well as benefits for children (child support). Family income support is on no account to be confused with poverty relief. Family income support is intended to reduce the gap in living standards between families with and without children at all income levels. Poverty relief helps only the poor.

During recent years family income support has become hopelessly confused with poverty relief. One reason for this is the growing incidence of child poverty (due to increased unemployment and family break-up), and a second reason is the emergence of poverty lobby organisations like the Child Poverty Action Group, who naturally concentrate their attentions on low income families. Those who dislike family income support in principle now find themselves able to argue against it on the grounds that taxpayer's money should be concentrated on "poor" families. They get no support from the poverty lobby, but they have managed to make their case look respectable to the media, and they are the darlings of a Government that puts cuts in the rate of income tax above increases in tax break-even points.

The switch from taxable family allowances and child tax relief to tax-free child benefit in 1979 added to the confusion. As already explained, child benefit is not a benefit in the conventional sense, but a convertible tax credit or BI for children. Most working families pay far more in tax than they receive in child benefit. All that child benefit does is to reduce their net tax bill by comparison with families at the same income levels who do not have children. It is the old principle of tax according to ability to pay, first introduced by William Pitt with the income tax in 1799.

In 1986, I summarised the issues as follows:

> The conflict of ideologies surrounding the family is nowhere more intense than in discussion of the tax and benefit treatment of dependent spouses (usually wives) and of dependent children. Although most people accept the need for some sort of social security safety net, and despite general agreement that family stability is a public good, there exists an apparently unbridgeable gap between those who would limit the safety net to poverty defined as destitution...and others who take a relative definition of poverty and a much broader approach to family income support, which they regard as investment in the future generation. (Parker 1986, page 70)

These differences of opinion are mostly ideological, and the ideological divide is nowhere more acute than in relation to child support. Those whose aim is poverty relief tend to be those who regard children as "an expensive hobby" (Meade 1978, page 15) which "parents have chosen to have" (IFS 1984, page 142). Those whose aim is poverty prevention take a wider view. They think of children as junior citizens, who did not choose to be born, and upon whom all our futures depend.

The case for providing child support at the same rate regardless of the income or other circumstances of the parents rests on a number of factors. These include administrative simplicity, the growing costs of children, the advantages of taking those costs out of the wage bargaining process, the disincentive and demoralising effects of child support targeted on the poorest families, and the destabilising effects on family life of child support that is restricted to families where the parents have split up or have never been married.

Some of the most important differences between the reform proposals discussed in this report concern family income support. At earnings of £150 a week, net income in 1985-86 for a single-wage, two-child couple would have been £175 pw with BIG 1(a), compared with £129 pw under the SDP proposals. Part of the gap is accounted for by BIG 1(a)'s £24 pw PBI for the non-earning spouse, and the rest by the much larger child benefit. These differences do not come about by chance.

All BIG schemes start from the premise that investment in families with children is investment in the future, and that spouses who work in the home deserve financial recognition. Vince takes a similar approach. In order to strengthen the traditional family the PBI for a married couple is twice that for a single person. Minford keeps MMA but is considerably less generous to spouses and children than either Vince or Parker. He is more generous than the SDP to dependent spouses, but he is less generous than any of the other schemes to children. The SDP abolish tax relief for dependent spouses, leaving single-wage couples with the same net income as single people. But they do increase child benefit, and for the unemployed and the lower paid they are more generous to children than any of the other schemes. The difficulty is that families do not apportion their budgets according to the benefit share of different family members. In terms of family income support (for spouses and children), BIG 1(a) is consistently the most generous, some would say too generous.

This is not so in regard to lone parents. Here there are complex problems, involving issues of parental responsibility and equity between one- and two-parent families, as well as the more obvious issues of adequacy and work incentives. Nobody wants to produce a proposal where low-income lone parents lose out. But it is hard to satisfy all the criteria. Vince helps some lone parents and also makes the system marriage neutral, by giving the same PBI to all adults regardless of marital status, but giving higher child credits to parents who are single householders. Minford (inadvertently) increases the penalties for marriage by introducing a NIT that is unrelated to household status, and by keeping one-parent benefit and the additional tax allowance for lone parents unchanged. BIG 1(a) includes a PBI supplement for lone parents, which breaks the BIG principle of marriage neutrality but may be a necessary compromise. As with the Vince scheme, non-householder lone parents would lose out. The SDP remove one-parent benefit (subsequently reinstated) and the additional personal allowance, but their basic benefit at nil earnings is very generous, as a result of which lone parents who are not in paid work are substantially better off than before, but those in work are worse off.

None of these solutions addresses the central problem facing lone parents, which is the combination of low earnings potential and high childcare costs. In *BI 2000* we will try a new approach, starting from the premise that the best way to help lone parents is by enabling them to get into the labour market.

When is a benefit a tax relief?

Income tax reliefs fall into two main categories, personal and non-personal. In Britain the main personal reliefs are single person's, married man's and wife's earned income allowances, to be replaced in April 1990 by a standard personal allowance and a married couple's allowance. Although the structure of the existing allowances is in need of reform, some such reliefs are essential to keep the lower paid out of tax, indeed the main reason for the poverty and unemployment traps is that they are too low. Here we are concerned with the non-personal reliefs, of which the most important are for mortgage interest and private pensions, including employers' and employees' contributions, self-employed retirement annuities and tax-free lump sums. These reliefs do rather little to prevent poverty, they have more to do with social engineering and with votes.

It is an inescapable fact of life that one person's tax relief is another person's tax increase. Very roughly, if the Chancellor forgoes £15,000 million of income tax in order to encourage people to buy houses and save for their old age, this adds nearly 10 percentage points to the standard rate of income tax or reduces the main personal allowances by some 60 percent. No matter how strong the case in favour of introducing or retaining any non-personal income tax relief, the question that has to be asked is who will pay for it, and the answer (in the main) is those who cannot afford to take advantage of it.

This is as true for the existing tax and benefit systems as for an integrated system. So long as the issues are fudged and so long as the Chancellor keeps introducing new reliefs, the chances of removing tax-induced poverty are minimal. In 1986-87 nearly three-quarters of the cost of mortgage interest tax relief went to

Table 16.1: Cost of mortgage interest tax relief

	Mortgage interest relief		
	Curent prices £m	1985-86 prices £m	as a % of IT and surtax receipts %
1960−61	70	540	2.7
1970−71	285	1,440	4.8
1980−81	1,960	2,720	8.1
1985−86	4,750	4,750	13.4

Source: Hansard WA 31 October 1986, c268.

people with gross incomes in excess of £10,000 (Hans WA, 18 Dec 1986, cc 740-742). In Table 14.4, taken from another Parliamentary answer, we already saw that the average reduction in income tax liability on account of employee's and self-employed contributions to private pension schemes was £60 a year for those earning less than £5,000 compared with £6,400 a year for those earning over £100,000.

The cost of tax expenditures on mortgage and private pension tax reliefs has grown faster than the income tax base, yet the attitude of Government is one of disinterest, since they start from the premise that tax reliefs are good and benefits bad. Table 16.1 shows that the cost of mortgage interest tax relief grew by a staggering 900 percent (at constant prices) between 1960 and 1985.

No comparable estimates are obtainable for private pension tax reliefs, but a Parliamentary Written Answer on 3 June 1986 sums up the official attitude. In reply to a question by Sir Brandon Rhys Williams MP, asking for estimates of the extra tax expenditure costs in the year 2000-01 as a result of pension changes in the 1986 Social Security Act, the Minister of State for Social Security said he did not know what they would be, nor whether they would offset the savings in SERPS. The information was not available and "could be produced only at disproportionate costs" (Hansard WA, 3 Jun 1986, c 532).

The cost of these tax expenditures varies inversely with the rate of income tax. With Minford's scheme the cost goes down, because the tax rate is reduced to 25 percent. But with most integration proposals the cost goes up, due to unification of NI contribution with income tax. With the Vince scheme income tax goes up to 44 percent, with BIG 1(a) to 38 percent and with the SDP scheme to 39 percent, so the revenue loss (by comparison with 1988-89) can go up by between 50 and 75 percent. Of the schemes discussed in this report BIG schemes are the only ones that phase out mortgage interest tax relief, BIG 1(a) and *BI 2000* are the only ones that seek to remove the private pension reliefs as well. Most authors try to limit the subsidies by restricting them to the pre-integration tax rate, but that ducks the issue.

In 1985-86, mortgage interest tax relief alone is estimated to have reduced the income tax base by around £15,000 million (Appendix 1, Table A.1.5), the starting rate of tax was 30 percent and the cost is officially estimated to have been £4,750 million. With a tax rate of 40 percent the cost goes up to a staggering £6,000 million, enough to finance a £4,000 million Disability Costs Allowance, and to increase child BIs by about £4 a week.

In 1985-86 the income tax base was further reduced by an estimated £31,000 million on account of private pension income tax reliefs. This figure includes employees' and employers' contributions to occupational pension schemes, self-employed retirement annuities and tax-free lump sums. Assuming a 40 percent rate of income tax, the revenue available for pensions would be reduced by up to £12,400 million. The figures are less certain than for mortgage interest tax relief, because little is known about the consequential changes on the income tax base if pension tax reliefs were withdrawn. We are nevertheless talking in terms of a sum of money theoretically sufficient to pay everybody aged 65 or over a BI old age supplement of £28 a week.

In the United States, President Reagan's tax cuts hinge on a radical scaling down of the non-personal income tax reliefs. The US now has minimum tax provisions which limit the total benefit that may be derived from tax preferences. But in Britain new tax reliefs are still being added. Each scheme starts off costing not very much, each is deceptively easy to justify, but each is another nail in the coffin of tax justice.

Pensioner incomes

All fully integrated tax/benefit systems abandon all contribution requirements and all earnings rules. The new pension would be based on citizenship or longstanding residence, and the amount recouped through tax or benefit withdrawal would depend on the pensioner's other income and the tax rate. In Britain removal of the contribution rule would alone be a major step forward. In 1986 about 1 million UK pensioners were receiving substandard NI basic pensions, due to inadequate contribution record (Hansard WA, 23 Jul 87, c 452).

Of our authors Minford is the only one who does not advocate a citizen's retirement pension. His is paid for by compulsory private insurance that looks perilously like a poll tax. Both the Vince and BIG pensions are non-contributory and fully individualised. The SDP pension would also be non-contributory, but the amount is less for married couples than for two single people living together, so the cohabitation rule remains. All the schemes remove all earnings rules.

The two main issues are expenditure priorities and indexation:

- Which is more important: SERPS or a bigger basic pension?
- How should pensions be uprated: in line with prices or earnings?

SERPS or a bigger basic pension? The first choice is between a citizen's pension at a rate sufficient to make income-tested supplements unnecessary, *or* a much smaller basic pension, plus an earnings-related pension and tax reliefs that encourage private pensions. Under present law, men aged 65 and women aged 60 who are fully paid-up contributors to the NI pension receive a basic NI pension of £41.15, plus an earnings-related component generally known as SERPS. Wives without their own insurance receive £24.75 through the insurance of their husbands. Low income pensioners may also be entitled to income support and housing benefit.

The UK basic NI pension is notoriously inadequate. It is less than the income support payable to those who have never contributed a penny to national insurance, moreover the means- tested benefits by which it is topped up are a chief cause of the pensioner poverty trap. In 1985-86 a single pensioner paying rent and rates of £22 was only £7 a week better off with a private pension of £40 a week than with no private pension at all, yet £40 a week was the amount of SERPS (at 1985 prices) payable in 1998 (when SERPS is fully matured) to a man whose earnings have been consistently at the average for full-time males throughout his working life.

SERPS is not targeted at those most in need. On the contrary, it uses taxpayer's money to carry the inequalities of working life into retirement. For most of the lower paid SERPS will turn out to be an illusion. Unless they are owner occupiers, it will serve merely to lift

Table 16.2: Projected expenditure on SERPS, November 1985 prices

	Years			
	1993-94	*2003-04*	*2013-14*	*2023-24*
Retirement pensions	1.1	4.2	7.5	10.3
Widows pensions	0.1	0.2	0.2	0.2
Invalidity pensions	0.4	0.9	1.0	1.1
Total	1.6	5.3	8.7	11.6

Source: *Report by the Government Actuary on the Financial Effects of the 1985 Social Security Bill,* Cmnd 9711, DHSS January 1986, Table 1.

them off entitlement to housing benefit. Although the 1986 Social Security Act cut down on the original SERPS scheme, the cost remains substantial. Table 16.2 shows how it will increase after the year 2000. This is SERPS as reformed by the 1986 Social Security Act, not the original scheme.

If small, voluntary savings are to be encouraged the first priority is a basic old age pension sufficient to lift pensioners off the need for means-tested supplementation. If this means getting rid of SERPS, then so be it. In countries where pensions have always been earnings-related the switch to a basic pension would be hard to accept, but in Britain it is part of the Beveridge tradition. In their Social Security Review Green Paper the Government tried to get rid of SERPS, but were forced to back down by the strength of the opposition. Yet the main reason for that opposition (insofar as the poverty lobby was concerned) was the failure to put anything in its place. Had Government suggested putting the money saved from SERPS into a bigger basic pension, the response would have been different.

All our schemes' authors either phase out SERPS or make noises in that direction. Minford abolishes it forthwith, and puts the expenditure savings into income tax cuts. BIG 1(a) puts the savings into much bigger basic pensions.

It would be wrong, nevertheless, to suppose that abolition of earnings related pensions and of all private pension tax reliefs is intrinsic to BI schemes, or even to all BIG schemes. Sir Brandon Rhys Williams wanted to replace SERPS by earnings-related, personal pensions funded through a 10 percent employers' payroll tax, and he would have retained all the private pension tax reliefs except the tax-free lump sums. In that case, at 1985-86 prices and

Table 16.3: Public expenditure savings on State basic pension, as a result of prices instead of earnings upratings, compared with savings on SERPS as a result of the 1986 Social Security Act

| | Projected savings £ billion at November 1985 prices | | | |
	1993-94	2003-04	2013-14	2023-24
	£ b.	£ b.	£ b.	£ b.
Retirement, widows and invalidity basic pensions, as a result of prices indexation	1.3	5.8	10.9	17.7
Earnings-related pensions, as a result of cuts in the 1986 SS Act	0.1	0.2	3.8	7.2

Source: Report by the Government Actuary on the Financial Effects of the 1985 Social Security Bill, Cmnd 9711, DHSS January 1986, Tables 1 and 2.

incomes, the partial BI plus BI old age supplement would have to remain at about the level of the present NI pension. The advantage is that the new pension would be non-contributory, and payable at the same rate to each man and woman aged 65 or more, regardless of marital status. Pensioner couples with no income other than the basic pension would gain about £20 a week, enough in many cases to lift them off housing benefit. But there would be far more pensioners (especially single pensioners) dependent on housing benefit than with BIG 1(a).

Indexation to prices or earnings. The second issue concerns benefit uprating. Given that some people depend on old age pension for thirty years or more, during which time prices and living standards can change unrecognisably, indexation to prices is not enough to prevent older age-groups from falling behind the living standards of the working population, and the newly retired. Nor is it enough to protect the living standards of invalidity pensioners, some of whom are in receipt of benefit for even longer periods.

During the next 30-40 years the government's main anticipated savings on pensions is due to indexation of the basic pension to prices instead of earnings. The figures are in Table 16.3. Unless the law is changed, the state basic pension will come to represent a smaller and smaller percentage of average earnings, and a smaller and smaller part of the pension package. By the year 2023-24, when this year's thirty-year-olds are nearing retirement, the basic pension could be worth only 10 percent of average earnings, compared with nearly 20 percent in November 1985. If this were to happen, the result would be a massive redistribution of income within the pensioner population, away from low income groups (especially those with a record of low or irregular earnings) in favour of middle to high income groups. The main beneficiaries would be couples where each spouse had a steady record of earnings near the upper earnings limit.

With the Vince scheme and with all BIG schemes, pensions are automatically linked to earnings through the income tax base. This is not the same as indexation, and if the tax base increased more slowly than prices it could produce difficulties. But it does mean that pensioner living standards would move in line with living standards generally. Minford's pension formula seems to lack any form of dynamisation. On reaching retirement age, and assuming that earnings had increased faster than prices during the forty year contribution period, the pension payable would be worth far less as a percentage of average earnings than when the first contribution was taken out. Once in payment the pension would be indexed to prices only. The SDP policy document does not mention benefit uprating.

17

Income redistribution

All the reform proposals in Part 3 would have substantial
redistributive effects. Until recently it was taken for granted that a
proposal involving too many losers was a political non-starter, but
events since 1979 have shown otherwise. Losses have become
acceptable, provided they are phased in carefully and provided the
groups affected are not too powerful.

Each proposal is intended to prevent, or relieve, poverty and to
improve work incentives. The Vince and BIG schemes are also
intended to strengthen the traditional family, by making the system
more marriage neutral. In this chapter we will start by comparing
the effects of each scheme on the disposable incomes of the model
families in Appendix 2. It is only a snap-shot glance, but it is well
worthwhile. Afterwards we will compare the ways in which income
would be redistributed vertically (from rich to poor, or poor to rich)
over a range of earnings between £5,200 and £52,000 a year.
Finally we will compare the effects on horizontal distribution
(between families of different composition), and on symmetry
between married and single. As before, all the figures refer to
1985-86, the post-April 1988 benefit system being represented by
the illustrative figures in the Technical Annex to Mr Fowler's 1985
Social Security White Paper (DHSS Dec 1985).

The scale of income redistribution is considerable, and some of
it is hard to quantify. Neither model family analysis nor TAXMOD
is able to show the effects of change on income redistribution
within the family. Nor can they show the wider effects of some of
the proposed changes, especially Minford's privatisation proposals
and BIG 1(a)'s proposal to phase out private pension tax reliefs. A
comparative assessment using TAXMOD is out of the question, and
once again it is necessary to stress the need for caution when

interpreting the results of model family analysis. Many of the gains as a result of Minford's proposals are more apparent than real, especially the gains at the bottom. And with BIG 1(a) some apparent gains would be offset by removal of pension tax reliefs and SERPS, and some losses are underestimated.

Remember also that the extent to which poverty is prevented (or relieved) depends as much on the administrative regulations and on the laws of liability to maintain as on the sums involved. From the arithmetic on its own, it is easy to form the impression that an automatic BI of £24 a week is worth the same as a conditional NIT or an income-tested basic benefit at the same rate, yet in practice the effects of each would be dissimilar. Arguably most people would prefer a slightly smaller BI that was automatic, to a more generous, family-based NIT that was conditional. Although some allowance can be made in the figures for alterations to the assessment unit, it is not possible to model the finer changes in liability to maintain, benefit conditionality, and so forth. Usually they are not even specified. The figures should therefore be regarded only as a guide, and we need to distinguish between minor discrepancies of £1-2 a week, and larger ones that result from major policy differences. Remember also that the SDP scheme is a stage one programme, whereas the others represent the final products.

Adequacy

As explained, the UK has no family budget standards to use as benchmarks for adequacy, which is sometimes taken to mean mere physical subsistence, but is more often assumed to include social as well as physical functioning, since the two are difficult to separate. So long, for example, as education remains compulsory, parents are bound to pay the costs of sending their children to school (transport, meals, uniform and so on), and in low income families this social need takes precedence over expenditure on food, clothing and a warm home. Likewise, since April 1988 all householders have to pay 20 percent of their local authority rates bill, no matter how poor they are, before they can start budgeting for other purchases.

Adequacy, like poverty, is essentially a relative concept. Beveridge, when referring to "*reasonable* human subsistence", argued that it was a matter of judgement, that estimates "change with time, and generally, in a progressive community, change upwards" (Beveridge 1942, para 27, my emphasis). And Beveridge's argument seems to be right, otherwise we would not be so startled at the idea of a state basic pension, uprated since 1948 in line with the retail prices index only, of less than £20 a week.

With no recognised standards to go by, the best we can do for present purposes is to compare disposable incomes under the different schemes, bearing in mind that Fowler TA is less generous than the system it replaced, which was itself barely adequate. When comparing the different schemes, remember again that benefit uprating policy can be as important as the amounts in year one. Existing benefits are indexed to prices. The Vince and BIG schemes are linked to earnings through the income tax base, but are not indexed to anything. Minford's pensions are indexed to prices only. The SDP do not mention benefit uprating.

Using model family analysis, the most important conclusion to emerge is the absence of any corollation between so-called "targeted" (ie means-tested) benefits and the success with which poverty is relieved or prevented. Means-tested benefits can be to the benefit of people on low incomes, but they need not be. Who gains and who loses depends on which groups are targeted, which groups pay the extra tax (or forfeit benefit) and the amounts involved – all of which has more to do with politics than mechanisms.

The safety net, working age families. The first test of any benefit system is the amount payable during interruption or loss or earnings. Are the systems that target through a means test really more generous, as is alleged, than systems that target through demogrants or contingency? Time and again, throughout the 1985 Social Security Review, Government repeated its commitment to transfer more resources to those in genuine need, but that promise was not delivered. At nil own income the only groups who have made worthwhile gains as a result of the Fowler reforms are single non-householders aged 25+ and some lone parents (Parker 1988). These changes do not show up in Figure 17.1, which takes Fowler TA as the reference point, but they are clearly visible in Appendix 2.

In Figure 17.1, Minford's safety net is invisible, because he has demolished it. Of the remaining schemes, Fowler is the least generous. The SDP and BIG 1(a) run neck and neck, but with older children the SDP would be the winner. Fowler TA income support rates for single non-householders were £19 for 16-17-year-olds, £25 for the 18-24 year age-group and £31 for over 25s. BIG 1(a)

Figure 17.1 : Comparative analysis, safety net at nil earnings

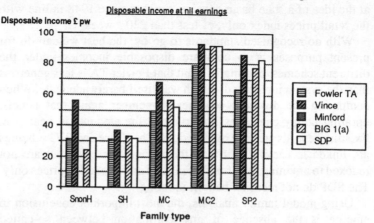

Disposable income at nil earnings

Disposable income £ pw

Legend: Fowler TA, Vince, Minford, BIG 1(a), SDP

Family type

Assumptions: S non H and SH are aged 25+ with Fowler TA, 18+ with Vince and SDP, 16+ with BIG 1(a).
Source: Appendix 2.

provides a guaranteed income of £24 a week from age 16, which is the same as previous supplementary benefit from age 18, without the non-householder's rent addition. Vince appears to be consistently the most generous, but the figures need to be treated with caution, because Vince's housing benefit is fixed, therefore with housing costs higher than those assumed his gains could turn to losses. Apart from Minford's disappearing subsistence income the most striking feature of the graph is Vince's £56 for single non-householders, which gives the appearance of bad targeting.

The lower paid. Figure 17.2, in five parts, compares the effects of each scheme on the disposable incomes of model families earning up to £120 a week, which in 1985-86 was roughly two-thirds of average earnings. The differences in disposable incomes between the different family types are unfortunately too great to be able to maintain scale without losing detail. The figures assume that earnings of £20 a week are for part-time work, otherwise the earnings are for work of 30 or more hours a week (24 hours in the case of lone parents), so they qualify for Fowler's family credit and Minford's NIT. Fewer than 30 percent of full-time workers earned less than £120 a week in April 1985, but of the 3 million who were unemployed a disproportionate number had low earnings potential, so the figures are relevant. Once again a blank has to be left for

Minford's disposable incomes at nil earnings and from part-time work, since both could be subject to his 70 percent cap. Part-time work does not qualify for Minford's NIT.

With the exception of Minford's NIT on earnings of £40 upwards, the withdrawable benefit systems look less generous than those based on demogrants, and Minford's gains would soon disappear if housing costs were higher than those assumed, or if his health and pension contributions were made more realistic.

At nil earnings BIG 1(a) produces a loss for single non-householders aged over 25 (by comparison with Fowler TA, but not pre-Fowler), but this loss is overtaken by gains as soon as earnings reach £20 a week. Vince and the SDP are more generous than BIG 1(a), but the incentive to earn is less. On earnings below £80 Vince is the most generous to single householders, but is overtaken thereafter by Minford and BIG 1(a). On earnings up to £80, the SDP scheme is less generous than Fowler TA. Subject to the *caveat* about Vince's fixed-amount housing credit, the married couple seems to do best from the Vince scheme. Fowler TA allows each spouse to earn £4 without loss of income support, but once the husband works full-time all they get is a greatly reduced housing benefit, hence the dip at earnings of £40 and the slow climb out of the unemployment trap. BIG 1(a) is less generous than Vince, but the poverty trap effect is less pronounced. Minford's guarantee does not start until work is for 30 hours or more and his 70 percent marginal tax rate continues until earnings reach £135. Apart from filling in the trough at earnings of £40, the SDP curve is little better than Fowler TA. Once earnings reach £110 their single wage married couple lose £5 a week (or more) throughout the income distribution.

All the schemes are more generous than Fowler to couples with children. Vince concentrates his help on families earning up to £140 a week, whereas BIG 1(a) has a greatly increased child benefit for all families. Minford cuts in with his beefed-up NIT once earnings are full-time, but the penalty is a 100 percent tax rate until earnings reach £100. On earnings up to £120 there is not much to choose between Minford and the SDP, but thereafter Minford forges ahead, because of his 25 percent tax rate. Vince, BIG 1(a) and the SDP are all more generous to lone parents at nil earnings and working part-time, than either Fowler or Minford. Vince is the most generous on earnings up to £100, but falls behind thereafter. The SDP concentrates help at the bottom, but once the lone parent is in full-time work the SDP solution is similar to Fowler's.

Figure 17.2 : Comparative analysis, safety net part-time and lower paid work

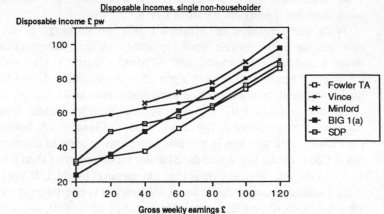

Disposable incomes, single non-householder

Assumption: age 25+ Fowler TA, 18+ Vince and SDP, 16+ BIG 1(a).

Disposable incomes, single householder

Assumption: Age 25+ Fowler TA, otherwise 18+.

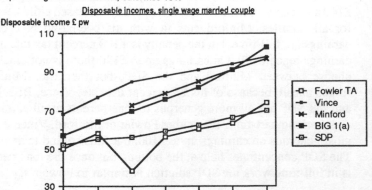

Disposable incomes, single wage married couple

Income redistribution

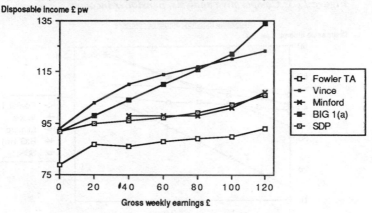

Disposable Incomes, single wage married couple + 2 children aged 4 & 6

Disposable Income £ pw

Legend:
- Fowler TA
- Vince
- Minford
- BIG 1(a)
- SDP

Gross weekly earnings £

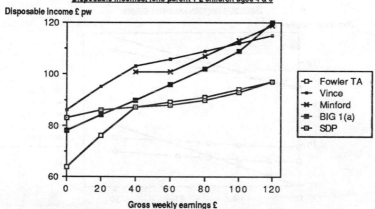

Disposable incomes, lone parent + 2 children aged 4 & 6

Disposable Income £ pw

Legend:
- Fowler TA
- Vince
- Minford
- BIG 1(a)
- SDP

Gross weekly earnings £

Source: Appendix 2.

Pensioners. The pensioner results in Figure 17.3 need to be set in the context of other changes affecting pensioners, for instance benefit uprating procedures, the age of entitlement to pension, the future of SERPS, the earnings rule, the cohabitation rule, and the tax treatment of private pensions. All the new schemes abolish the earnings rule, and hence the formal age of retirement. But the Vince and BIG 1(a) old age supplements are not payable until age 65, and Minford's pension is not payable until age 66. BIG 1(a) and Minford would stop the SERPS build-up forthwith. Vince and the SDP are more cautious, but stress the importance of the basic pension. Vince, BIG 1(a) and Minford all take the individual as the unit of assessment, and give twice as much to married pensioners

309

Figure 17.3: Comparative analysis, pensioner incomes

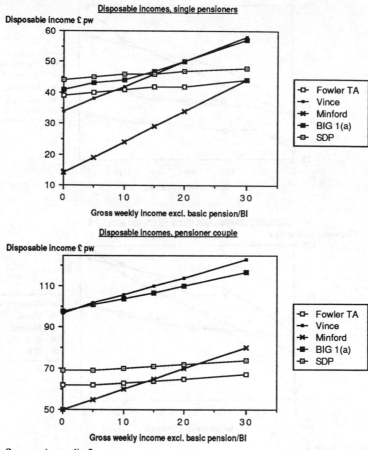

Source: Appendix 2.

A = Vertical redistribution of income

(or any two pensioners) as to single pensioners. This means that the cohabitation rule can be removed. BIG 1(a) is the only proposal that includes phasing out of private pension tax reliefs, from which it seems sensible to assume that private pension entitlements would be lower.

The Fowler reforms did nothing for low income pensioners. Either Mr Fowler did not include pensioners in his target or his aim was wrong. As we have seen (Chapter 4), the curve of disposable income became marginally less flat, but only by dint of cutting benefit entitlement at the bottom. The post-Fowler basic pension remains indexed to prices, and as SERPS builds up the living standards of pensioners who were previously lower paid will fall further and further behind living standards generally.

Figure 17.3 starts by showing the position of single pensioners living alone. The SDP scheme is the most generous to low income pensioners, and the SDP policy paper gave priority to further increases in basic pension. But the pensioner poverty trap gets worse. BIG 1(a) uses its £60 pension to lift pensioners off housing benefit. The disposable income gain at the bottom is only £2, but the pensioner poverty trap is greatly improved. Minford's private pension is indisputably inadequate, but his 25 percent tax rate would result in gains for pensioners with more than about £100 a week private pension. Unfortunately they are a tiny minority. Vince's pension formula requires adjustment, but the difficulty is probably a technical one.

The outstanding feature of the married pensioner graph is the huge scale of the increases provided by Vince and BIG 1(a). No BIG 1(a) pensioners in shared accommodation would get housing benefit, but surprisingly Vince's pensioner couple would still be eligible for withdrawable housing credit with a private pension of £100 a week. For Vince, BIG 1(a) and Minford the caption can read "any two pensioners sharing accommodation" , but the SDP retain the old distinctions based on marital status. The SDP disposable income curve runs parallel to that of Fowler, but is £7 more generous? Minford's pensioner couple does better than the single pensioner, and those at the top would make considerable gains.

Vertical redistribution of income

Figure 17.4 gives four examples of the vertical redistribution effects of our five systems, assuming earnings of £100 to £1,000 a week, and with net incomes defined as gross earnings less income tax and NI contribution (or Minford's health and pension charges), plus non-withdrawable benefits. No account is taken of withdrawable benefits (for instance Minford's NIT), because some of them depend on housing costs. The effects incurred would depend very much on whether or not the families were mortgagors (and the size of the mortgage), and on whether or not the married couples were both in paid work (and the proportion of combined earnings contributed by each spouse). For a more balanced picture it is advisable to refer to Table A.2.2 in Appendix 2, from which all the figures are taken.

Figure 17.4: Comparative analysis, vertical redistribution

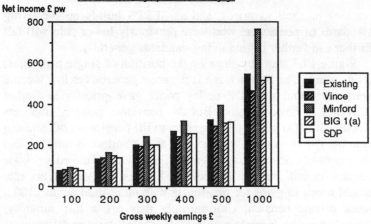

Net incomes, single person, no mortgage

Net income £ pw

Legend: Existing, Vince, Minford, BIG 1(a), SDP

Gross weekly earnings £

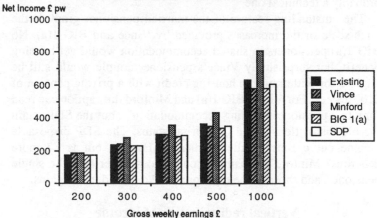

Net incomes, two-wage married couple, mortgagors

Net Income £ pw

Legend: Existing, Vince, Minford, BIG 1(a), SDP

Gross weekly earnings £

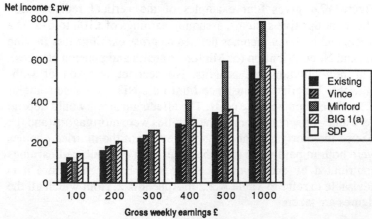

Net incomes, single wage married couple + 2 children, no mortgage

Net income £ pw

Legend: Existing, Vince, Minford, BIG 1(a), SDP

Gross weekly earnings £

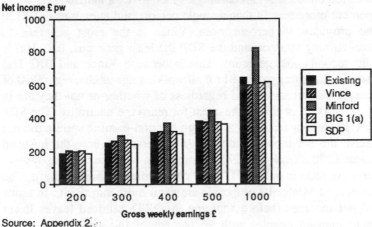

Net incomes, two-wage married couple + 2 children, mortgagors

Net income £ pw

Legend: Existing, Vince, Minford, BIG 1(a), SDP

Gross weekly earnings £

Source: Appendix 2.

Broadly speaking, Vince, BIG 1(a) and the SDP redistribute from rich to poor, whereas Minford redistributes from poor to rich. Vince appears to be the most redistributive from rich to poor, but this is because the figures do not show the effects of the BIG 1(a) proposal to abolish private pension tax reliefs. With BIG 1(a) a two-wage couple with joint earnings of £1,000 per week and maximum mortgage tax relief could lose £4,000 a year, depending on the value of their pension tax reliefs and the amount earned by each spouse. Figure 17.4 shows that large numbers of two-wage couples with mortgages would lose if either BIG 1(a) or the SDP proposals were implemented. Most single-wage couples with children and no mortgage with would gain from BIG 1(a), but the high earners would almost certainly have mortgages, in which case they would lose.

Horizontal redistribution of income

Family income support was one of the core issues discussed in Chapter 16, and the technicalities of each scheme were explained in Part 3. Here we will look at the effects of each scheme on the relative living standards of families of different composition. These are expressed in terms of ratios, with either the single person or the childless couple as the reference point. Table 17.1 distinguishes between spouse support, child support and family income support.

Spouse support is measured by comparing the ratios implied in the disposable and net incomes of single people and single-wage married couples. At nil earnings Vince gives a married couple 84 percent more benefit than a single person, and at earnings of £120 he provides 36 percent more. Vince is the most generous to non-earning spouses, and the SDP the least generous. BIG 1(a) is the second most generous. This is because Vince and BIG 1(a) provide the same partial BI for all working age adults, regardless of sex or marital status, and regardless of whether or not they are in paid work. It is part of the quest for marriage neutrality. The SDP tax single-wage couples as though the non-earning spouse did not exist, the net income ratio is 1.00. A couple where the husband earns £120 a week lose £9 by comparison with the existing system, and the ratio is only 1.01, even after adding in basic benefit. The effects of Minford's proposals are even more surprising. In terms of net incomes (before applying the NIT) Minford leaves lower paid married couples with 96 percent of the amount for single people. This is the poll tax effect of his health and pension contributions, already referred to. It is then offset by the NIT. Above the NIT ceiling Minford is only marginally more generous to non-earning spouses than the SDP.

Child support is measured by comparing the ratios implied in the disposable and net incomes of couples with and without children. Here the picture changes dramatically. All the couples are single-wage, and the children are aged 4 and 6, as before. If they were aged 11-15, the Fowler TA and SDP disposable income relativities would be higher, family credit and basic benefit being age-related. At nil earnings and at two-thirds average earnings the SDP is the most generous, otherwise BIG 1(a) is the most generous. Minford is consistently the least generous to children.

Family income support comprises spouse support and child support. It is measured by comparing the ratios implied in the disposable and net incomes of two-child couples and single people. At nil earnings the SDP is once again the most generous to families with children, otherwise BIG 1(a) is the most generous. Minford is consistently the least generous.

Some of the results in Table 17.1 are surprising. Minford keeps tax-free child benefit, but his scheme would nevertheless involve a double redistribution of income in favour of high income single people and two-wage couples without children. The SDP abolish tax relief for the non-earning spouse, and make child benefit

314

Table 17.1: Comparative analysis, family income support

(1) Spouse support

	Disposable income of sw MC as % of dis Y of SP		Net income of sw MC as % of net Y of SP			
	Gross weekly earnings		Gross weekly earnings			
	£0	£120	£100	£200	£300	£1,000
	%	%	%	%	%	%
Fowler TA	161	110	109	105	104	103
Vince	184	136	130	118	113	105
Minford	Variable	113	96	103	102	101
BIG 1(a)	173	130	131	116	112	105
SDP	163	101	100	100	100	100

(2) Child support

	Disposable income of sw MC2 as % of dis Y of sw MC		Net income of sw MC2 as % of net Y of sw MC			
	Gross weekly earnings		Gross weekly earnings			
	£0	£120	£100	£200	£300	£1,000
	%	%	%	%	%	%
Fowler TA	158	126	117	110	107	103
Vince	137	126	119	113	109	104
Minford	Variable	110	116	108	106	102
BIG 1(a)	161	130	131	120	115	107
SDP	177	151	130	117	112	104

(3) Family income support

	Disposable income of sw MC2 as % of dis Y of SP		Net income of sw MC2 as % of net Y of SP			
	Gross weekly earnings		Gross weekly earnings			
	£0	£120	£100	£200	£300	£1,000
	%	%	%	%	%	%
Fowler TA	255	139	128	116	111	105
Vince	251	171	155	132	123	109
Minford	Variable	124	111	112	108	102
BIG 1(a)	279	170	167	140	129	112
SDP	288	154	130	117	112	104

Source: Appendix 2.

taxable, but the relative living standards of lower paid families with children nevertheless go up. All the figures assume 100 percent take-up, although in practice take-up of the basic incomes would be much higher than take-up of Fowler's family credit, Minford's NIT or the SDP's basic benefit.

Income redistribution

Figure 17.5 : Comparative analysis, symmetry? Adults without children

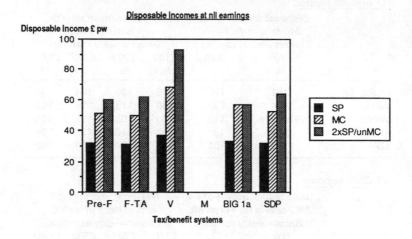

Source: Appendix 2.

Symmetry

One way to strengthen the traditional two-parent family is to make
the system more symmetrical between married and single. This was
discussed in Chapter 5 (see Table 5.3 and Figure 5.2), and it is a
primary objective of the Vince scheme and of all BIG schemes. In
a symmetrical benefit system the amount of benefit payable at nil
earnings would be the same for any two adults living in shared
accommodation, regardless of sex or marital status. The amount for
two people can be less than twice the amount for one person (if it
is thought right to take into account the economies of scale), or it
can be double the amount for one person. But it should not be less
for a married couple than for any other two people in similar
circumstances.

Figure 17.5 shows that BIG 1(a) is the only system that is
symmetrical between all non-earning adults. All the other systems
penalise marriage and heterosexual cohabitation. Vince makes the
existing situation worse, because of his very large non-earner credit
for single non-householders. Fowler TA has a similar effect. All the
figures assume that the single person is a householder and the two
single people are joint householders. Rent and rates are £19.00

The situation is even more problematical once children are
involved. Figure 17.6 compares disposable incomes at two-thirds

316

Figure 17.6: Comparative analysis, symmetry? Adults with children

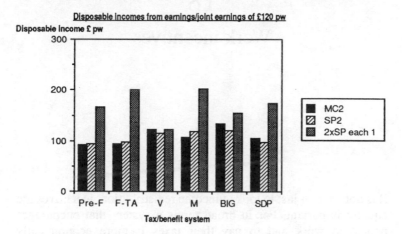

Source: Appendix 2.

average earnings for a single-wage married couple with two children, a lone parent with two children, and two lone parents each with one child. The children are aged 4 and 6, and housing costs are the same for each household. The two lone parents living together are assumed to be of the same sex, although for some of the systems it would make no difference.

Pre-Fowler, Fowler TA and Minford all give the lone parent (one adult and 2 children) a higher disposable income than the married couple (two adults and two children). Two lone parents living together are even more advantaged. This time it is Vince who comes nearest to marriage neutrality. He defines a lone parent as a single householder with a child, so his two lone parents sharing accommodation pay the same tax and receive the same BIs as the married couple. The disadvantage (apart from administrative problems) is the incentive to household formation. Fowler's emphasis on family credit (as opposed to housing benefit) has greatly increased the subsidy for lone parent households, and Minford's NIT is almost as bad. BIG 1(a) comes a little closer to marriage neutrality, but a penalty for marriage remains, in the form of the lone-parent supplement.

18

Work incentives

It is not enough just to look at income redistribution, incentives are equally important. For in broad terms a system that encourages people to work and to pay their taxes is more economically efficient, and more able to prevent poverty, than one which encourages idleness and tax avoidance. Economic efficiency defined in this way can be measured in terms of marginal and average tax rates, replacement ratios (out-of-work incomes as percentages of in-work incomes), and the income gains as a result of doing lower paid work, or earning more. The assumption is that low tax rates and low replacement ratios are more conducive to economic efficiency than high ones.

This is of course a very narrow definition. It disregards the economic advantages of improved living standards at the bottom – the savings, for instance, to the National Health Service as a result of better food and better housing, and the higher returns from education expenditure if all children get a good breakfast before going to school, and warmth and privacy for their homework. Lower tax rates are not necessarily better than higher tax rates, they are only a guide.

Marginal tax rates (MTRs)

In November 1985, the beginning of the period chosen for most of the comparisons in this study, there were about 22 million families under pension age in Great Britain only (DHSS May 1988). Of these an estimated 70,000 working families with children had marginal tax rates of 100 percent or more and 170,000 had marginal tax rates of between 70 and 100 percent. Since implementation of

Table 18.1: Poverty trap, number of working families affected, pre- and post-Fowler

Marginal tax rate % per £1 of extra gross earnings	Nov 85 000's	April 88 000's
1. Families with children		
Above 100	70	0
90 but less than 100	60	60
80 but less than 90	110	370
70 but less than 80	0	75
60 but less than 70	100	*
50 but less than 60	140	n.a.
	480	505
2. Families without children		
Above 100	0	0
90 but less than 100	0	10
80 but less than 90	50	10
70 but less than 80	0	20
60 but less than 70	60	0
50 but less than 60	90	0
	200	40
Totals with and without children	680	545

* Less than 5,000

Note: The April 88 figures assume income tax at 27% and IT allowances uprated in line with RPI.

Sources: Nov 85: Hansard WA 21 Oct 87, c 809.
Apr 88: Hansard WA 19 Nov 87, cc 647-648.

the Fowler reforms the number of working families with children whose marginal tax rates are above 100 percent is said to be nil, but the number with tax rates between 70 and 100 percent is expected to go up to more than half a million. The detailed figures are in Table 18.1. The figures refer to DHSS benefits only. No count is kept of families similarly affected by student grants, nor are there any similar figures for Northern Ireland. In all there must by 1988 be nearly 1 million UK working families (most of them with children) for whom the reward system has ceased to function normally. Additionally, those receiving out-of-work benefits face MTRs of at least 100 percent on earnings above the permitted disregards. In 1985 there were 3 million such families, described as unemployed, sick or disabled and a further 0.5 million lone parents receiving supplementary benefit (DHSS, May 1988).

Ideally each of the schemes under review would have been put through TAXMOD to find out the numbers and distribution of

319

Table 18.2: Comparative analysis, marginal tax rates

	Pre-Fowler 1985-86	Fowler TA	Vince	Minford	BIG 1(a)	SDP
	%	%	%	%	%	%
Starting rate of income tax +NIC, or new income tax	39	39	44	25*	38	39
Top rate of income tax	60	60	70	25	60	60
Income tax +NIC/new IT + withdrawable benefits, maximum rates	over 100	c98	84	100	68	94

Tax/benefit system

* Excluding health, etc. contributions.

families affected by high marginal tax rates. There would then have been further analysis to estimate the behavioural and other long-term effects. Unfortunately no such analyses have been possible. The figures in Table 18.1, together with the estimate of 3.5 million out-of-work, working age families in 1985, can nevertheless serve as a benchmark by which to judge the alternative systems.

Table 18.2 summarises the MTRs in each proposed system. Vince, BIG 1(a) and the SDP all unify income tax and NI contribution, so for the existing system we must include NI contribution with income tax. Minford reduces MTRs by replacing earnings-related NI contribution with flat rate health and pension charges, so comparisons are misleading. Minford apart, the effective starting rates of tax are all very similar. BIG 1(a) is the lowest by 1 percent, but that is on the assumption that half the private pension tax reliefs can be removed. Vince's 44 percent is significantly higher, and he also has the highest top rate of tax. All except Vince and Minford have a top rate of 60 percent. The tax plus benefit withdrawal rates shown are the highest for each scheme.

At the end of 1987 the April 1988 Fowler reforms were expected to leave 430,000 working families with children with MTRs of 80 percent or more. There has been no change to the MTRs of out-of-work families. Vince's 84 percent MTR would probably affect rather more working families, perhaps as many as 750,000, but for out-of-work families the 84 percent tax rate would be an improvement.

Minford's 100 percent MTR applies to families on his subsistence income, and to very low paid families with children. His NIT has a marginal tax rate of 70 percent. Apart from young single people, the working families most likely to be affected are single-wage couples with children and lone parents, perhaps 700,000 in all in 1985-86, of whom about 550,000 would have been subject to 70 percent MTRs and 150,000 to the 100 percent MTR. That is without taking into account the behavioural effects of Minford's workfare. In 1985 there were over 2 million unemployed families, many of whom would have been drawn into lower paid work by the threat of losing benefit. Half a million out-of-work lone parents would not be subject to workfare, but would face MTRs of 100 percent, as would 0.7 million sick or disabled, for whom there would be no change in existing provision.

It looks as though the total number of working age families facing MTRs of 70 percent or more would be about the same with Minford as post-Fowler, the difference being that the unemployed would be either in workfare programmes (100 percent MTRs) or in very low paid work (70 percent or 100 percent MTRs). Minford's workfare cuts the MTR during unemployment to zero, but once on workfare the MTR returns to 100 percent, and on lower paid work in the regular economy it is either 100 percent (for families with children), or 70 percent. So although he would succeed in forcing people into some sort of economic (or *quasi* economic) activity, he would not necessarily promote economic efficiency.

It is not known how many working families would be entitled to BIG 1(a) housing benefit and subject to a 68 percent MTR. If large numbers of unemployed people decided to top up their PBIs by doing part-time work (rather than none at all), the number of working families claiming housing benefit would go up, in which case the number of out-of-work claimants would go down. The number of pensioners (including people with disabilities) entitled to housing benefit would fall significantly, as a result of the £60 full BI and the disability costs allowance. Although the householder element in the BIG 1(a) housing benefit increases the value of housing benefit at nil earnings, and appears to widen the range of incomes over which it is withdrawn, the combined taper for rent and rate rebates has the opposite effect.

The SDP have estimated that 20 percent of families with two children would face MTRs of 82 percent. The total number of families with children affected in this way would be well over 1 million. About 30 percent of the population would be on basic benefit and subject to the 82 percent tax rate on earnings above the disregarded £15 a week.

Average tax rates (ATRs)

During recent years it has become fashionable to measure incentives in terms of MTRs, as though the average tax rate (ATR) played no part. In Chapter 8 we saw that the MTR is the amount lost out of each extra £ earned, whereas the ATR is the net amount paid out in income tax and NI contribution, as a percentage of total earnings. From the point of view of incentives, ATRs are at least as important as MTRs, because it is the ATR that determines take-home pay. Most people do not even know the meaning of the term marginal tax rate, let alone their own, but they do know how much is taken from them in tax out of the weekly wage packet. This depends on the tax allowance (or BI) as well as the tax rate, and for people on low incomes it depends more on the former than the latter.

Look now at Figure 18.1 and notice how Minford and both BIG options cut average tax rates at the bottom. This is the *only* way to remove the unemployment and poverty traps. Now compare the two BIG options. The first (with one asterisk) is the system outlined in Chapter 14. It keeps higher-rate tax. The second (with two asterisks) removes higher-rate tax. Both cut in with a marginal rate of 38 percent, which produces an ATR of 14 percent at earnings of £100, compared with 26 percent with the system in operation in 1985-86. Minford's ATR at £100 is only 10 percent, but would be much more if his health and pension contributions were more realistic.

Figure 18.1: Average tax rates, existing system ,Minford and BIG 1(a), 1985-86

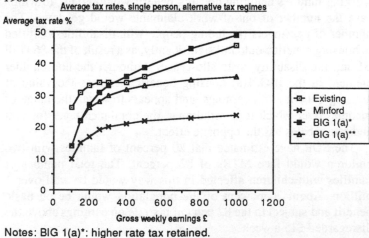

Notes: BIG 1(a)*: higher rate tax retained.
BIG 1(a)**: higher rate tax bands abolished.

With each increase in earnings the BIG 1(a)* average tax curve rises steadily, cutting through the flat line of the existing system between earnings of £200 and £400, and causing high earners to lose considerable amounts. If the figures took into account loss of mortgage interest and superannuation tax reliefs the BIG 1(a)* tax curve would be even more steeply progressive. Far from "giving benefit to the rich", as is sometimes alleged, a partial BI can be extremely redistributive from rich to poor – too redistributive for many.

BIG 1(a)** is a compromise solution. By removing higher-rate tax it can be made to mirror the shape of Minford's curve, albeit at higher marginal tax rates because it preserves the safety net. The cost in 1985-86 of making this change to original BIG 1(a) would have been just over £3,000 million, but the long-term cost (after taking into account behavioural change) would be much less. Nor need the gains to high earners be anything like so high as the diagram suggests. This would depend on how many non-personal tax reliefs were removed. A flat rate tax schedule offers an attractive *quid pro quo* for removal of those reliefs, and will be proposed as part of *Basic Income 2000*.

Turning back to the schemes outlined in Part 3, Figure 18.2 summarises the effects of each on the ATRs, at different earnings levels, of single people, single- and two-wage married couples and single-wage couples with two children. No account is taken of mortgage interest or superannuation tax reliefs, nor of withdrawable benefits. As before, this last exclusion is necessary because some of the withdrawable benefits depend on housing costs. It is also a useful way of showing why the withdrawable benefits become necessary.

For single people Minford's ATR is consistently the lowest. For the lower paid BIG 1(a)'s ATR is the second lowest, but at higher income levels the existing system is the second lowest. That is because all the new systems except Minford's are redistributing away from high income single people. Minford's ATR is also the lowest for two-wage couples without children, with the exception of the couple with only £100 between them, who forfeit part of their tax allowances. BIG 1(a) and Vince give net benefit to couples earning £100 a week, but the BIG 1(a) ATR is consistently the lower of the two. BIG 1(a)'s couple with two children receive net benefit on earnings up to £200 a week. This is well out of line with the other proposed systems, but it is very much in line with the situation in the early 1950s. Minford's couple with two children become net taxpayers at earnings of only £100.

Figure 18.2: *Comparative analysis, average tax rates*

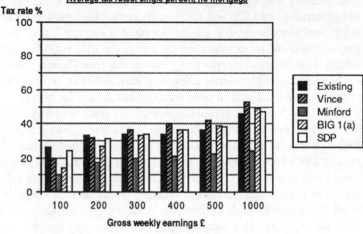

Average tax rates, single person, no mortgage

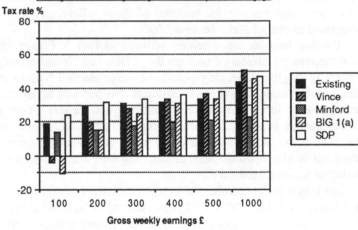

Average tax rates, single wage married couple, no mortgage

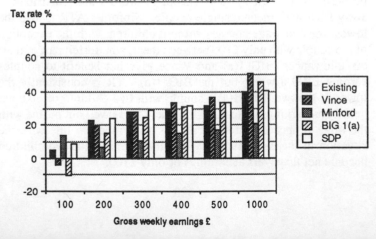

Average tax rates, two wage married couple, no mortgage

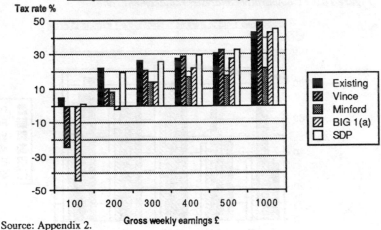

Source: Appendix 2.

Replacement ratios (RRs)

Replacement ratios measure the gap between incomes in and out of work. Minford, as we have seen, limits this gap to 70 percent of previous disposable income *less* work expenses. His 70 percent cap refers to previous earnings, but most unemployed people are more concerned with the gap between life on the dole and prospective earnings. For present purposes an RR is defined as disposable income on the dole in any given week, as a proportion of disposable income from a hypothetical job offer in the same week. For Figure 18.3 the offer wage is assumed to be £120 a week, or about two-thirds the average in 1985-86. For lone mothers the comparable figure is £80. This is low pay, but the aim of each scheme author is to encourage the unemployed to take lower paid jobs.

Figure 18.3 shows that it is possible to improve RRs without resorting to Minford's draconian cap, yet most of the proposed new systems remain perilously close to the 70 percent guideline, even before taking work expenses into account. BIG 1(a) tends to produce the lowest RRs, but not for lone parents. The SDP tend to have the highest RRs, and Fowler TA tends to be worse (or no better than) the system it replaced. The case for targeting through income-tested or means-tested benefits is wearing very thin.

An RR of more than 70 percent before work expenses is almost certainly too high to encourage lower paid work, and Minford's 70 percent cap does not necessarily serve any purpose, because it takes past work expenses into account. Prospective work expenses could

Figure 18.3 : Comparative analysis, replacement ratios

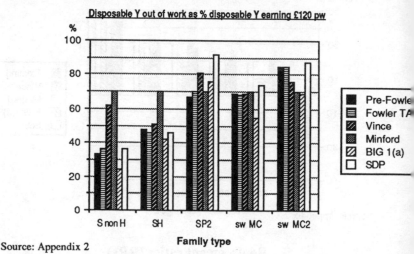

Source: Appendix 2

be much higher. A cap based on past earnings would encourage the unemployed to hang on until they could get the same wage and work expenses as before.

Disposable income gains as a result of working part-time

One of the main problems for unemployed people and lone parents is the earnings rule. In many areas the only paid work available is part-time and irregular, but the benefit regulations restrict unemployed claimants to earnings of £5 a week (non-cumulative). One of the purposes of the Vince, BIG and SDP schemes is to encourage unemployed people to work part-time by removing this restriction.

Figure 18.4 compares the gains in disposable income that unemployed people could have expected from each of the systems in 1985-86, if they had earned £20 a week from part-time work (ie less than 30 hours a week). With pre-Fowler and Fowler TA each spouse could earn £4 without loss of benefit, so the gain varies according to the number of earners. In the diagram the figures maximise disposable income by assuming that each spouse earned £4. Minford does not show up because he has a 100 percent withdrawal rate for part-time work, his NIT being restricted to people working 30 hours or more.

Figure 18.4: Comparative analysis, gains from part-time work

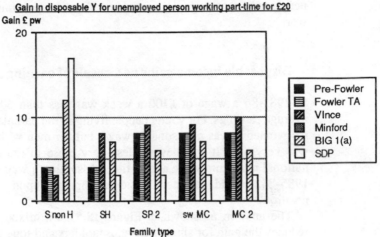

Gain in disposable Y for unemployed person working part-time for £20

Source: Appendix 2.

The figures are surprising. The breakthrough for part-time workers promised by BI enthusiasts turns out to be a delusion. With a full BI (not shown) the gain from earning £20 would be at most £6, because the tax rate on all other income has to be at least 70 percent. With a partial BI the effect is similar, because the income-related benefits that top up the PBI have to be withdrawn. If the new marginal tax plus benefit withdrawal rate is over 80 percent, the net gain for a single, unemployed person as a result of earning £20 is *less* from the new system than at present. And for married couples, assuming each earned the then £4 disregard, the new tax plus benefit withdrawal rate has to be less than 60 percent, in order to produce an improvement.

Now of course it is possible to qualify these findings. BIG 1(a) overcomes the problem for single non-householders, because they do not receive housing benefit. Work incentives for young unemployed people living in the parental home would improve greatly, and for single householders they would also be better. The SDP produce significant gains for single non-householders. It should also be said that unemployed people are most unlikely to be able to earn exactly £4 a week each on a regular basis, as the existing system requires. The whole idea is ridiculous. Thus in a sense the real advantage of a BI (or the SDP scheme) over the existing system is the freedom it would give to earn more than £4 when and if the work became available. Nevertheless, it is cloud cuckoo land to suppose that BI (either full or partial) would necessarily encourage the unemployed to take part-time or casual work.

Disposable income gains as a result of earning £100 pw

In 1985-86 a wage of £100 a week was less than 60 percent of average earnings. For young people living in the parental home and for women it was a reasonable wage, but for men with families it was very low. It was nevertheless very close to the target for a national minimum wage at that time. Assuming a wage of £100 in 1985-86, would the new systems improve upon the present position?

The answer, as shown in Figure 18.5, is a mixed bag. Vince reduces the gain for single non-householders and lone parents, but increases it significantly for couples with and without children. The SDP scheme tends to make the existing situation worse. Once again Minford has to be excluded because we do not know how much his unemployed families would receive. If the figures were available, Minford's NIT would almost certainly show a big improvement, but that is partly because he abolishes the safety net. BIG 1(a) is the only option that produces worthwhile improvements, and even BIG 1(a) does little for lone parents.

Figure 18.5: Comparative analysis, gains from lower paid, full-time work

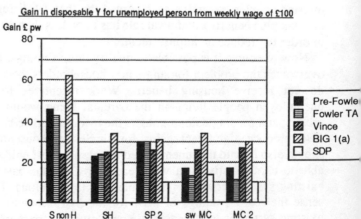

Gain in disposable Y for unemployed person from weekly wage of £100

Source: Appendix 2.

Figure 18.6: Comparative analysis, the poverty trap

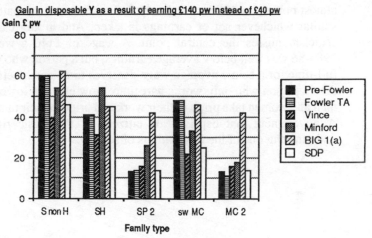

Source: Appendix 2.

The poverty trap

At the beginning of this chapter we compared marginal tax rates between the existing and proposed systems, but over-emphasis on marginal tax rates was criticised, on the grounds that most people do not know how much they lose out of each extra £ earned. What they do know, and what annoys them very much, is to get a pay rise, or work overtime, and find that they are little or no better off as a result. This is the poverty trap effect described earlier. In this final section we will take an extreme case by comparing disposable incomes from earnings £100 apart. What would have been the gain in 1985-86 from earning £140 a week, by comparison with £40? The results are shown in Figure 18.6, and once again they are unexpected.

Clearly, Mr Fowler's social security reforms did nothing for the poverty trap, as we have already seen. Even the £48 gain for the married couple is a fluke, for the £40 wage just happens to hit the trough of the unemployment trap. Vince tends to make the existing situation worse, or improves it only marginally. Minford makes it worse for single non-householders and single-wage couples, but otherwise improves it, although for couples with children the gain is too small to achieve anything. Overall BIG 1(a) looks the best, for it produces the biggest gains where they are most needed, ie for families with children. The SDP make the existing system worse.

329

Of course it may be said that the figures are unrealistic, since almost nobody in 1985 earned only £40 a week. But the pattern is similar whichever set of earnings is taken. And in any case the criticism misses the central point. A wage of £140 a week in 1985-86 was well below average earnings, but a person who works full-time for a below average wage deserves to be much better off than a person who only works part-time. How else can lower paid men and women take pride in their work and pride in their families? A government that deprives its citizens of this basic right is undermining one of the foundations of society.

Part 5

A STRATEGY FOR CHANGE

19

Basic Income 2000

Target system for the year 2000

By now it should be clear that even partial integration of the tax and benefit systems is not something than can be achieved within the life-time of a single Parliament. It would have to be done incrementally, for three main reasons. First is the need to phase in the redistributive changes slowly, in order to protect acquired rights and use economic growth as a means of softening the blow for losers. Second is the need to introduce civil service reorganisation in easy stages, relying on normal wastage rather than redundancies to achieve the bulk of the manpower savings. Third is the time needed for computerisation of the integrated part of the system. Exactly how much time is uncertain, but it is not something that can be rushed. Assuming that computerisation of PAYE and Schedule D is complete and "bedded down" by the early to mid 1990s, a further five years seems ample, moreover the decision to introduce independent taxation of husband and wife by the year 1990 is a move in the same direction.[1]

Given these limitations, the only way to achieve integration, even partial integration, is through political consensus. First the political parties would have to agree a target system, after which each must strive to move in the chosen direction. *BI 2000* is put forward as one such target system. It is a modified BIG scheme, aimed at the year 2000. As with all BIG schemes it is a strategy rather than a blueprint. The detail can and would be changed, what matters is the structure. This has been developed from BIG 1(a) during three years of study and consultation with people from many walks of life, including politicians, civil servants, academics, and representatives of business and the voluntary sector. BIG 1(a) was the only hybrid scheme examined in Part 3 that met the criteria of partial integration. Despite its limitations, it came out well from the comparative analysis in Chapters 17 and 18.

BI 2000 tackles poverty by strengthening the traditional two-parent family and replacing the dole with an income guarantee that is not conditional on not working. *BI 2000* is completely neutral between men and women, married and single. It protects lone parents, and helps them regain their financial independence, but it also protects the traditional family, by removing the subsidies for marriage break-up. It tackles unemployment by cutting unit labour costs (lifting the lower paid out of net tax, and abolishing all NI contributions), by encouraging the acquisition of new skills (income support during training), and by promoting labour market flexibility (minimum of red tape). Instead of the dole, people are set free to make their own decisions and to plan from a firm base.

Anatomy of *BI 2000*

This is set out in Figure 19.1. Notice the sharp distinction between basic incomes and replacement incomes. *BI 2000* is neither a socialist nor a libertarian dream, it is a compromise. Direct government involvement in cash support is limited to the safety net. The BIs, together with the Cash & Care (C&C) benefits, are intended to guarantee to each person living on these islands an approximately equivalent basic living standard, most of it as an automatic right of citizenship. Responsibility for the frills that make life more agreeable is put firmly back into the private sector, as Beveridge intended. Those desiring a given percentage of previous earnings during sickness, unemployment or old age would be expected to make the necessary provision through private insurance and/or collective agreements – without tax reliefs. Although *statutory sick pay* (SSP) is retained, in the long-term it is hoped to replace it by occupational sick pay at equivalent rates or better.

The role of the new C&C departments is of particular interest. Along with the BIs (but not without them) they could be the catalyst for increased voluntary action at community level. Greatly increased provision of child day-care facilities is an example. It would be up to the C&C departments to make their budget allocations for childcare go as far as possible, by involving their local communities on an unpaid as well as a paid basis. There is a crying need for well-run day nurseries in Britain, but there is no

Figure 19.1: Anatomy of Basic Income 2000

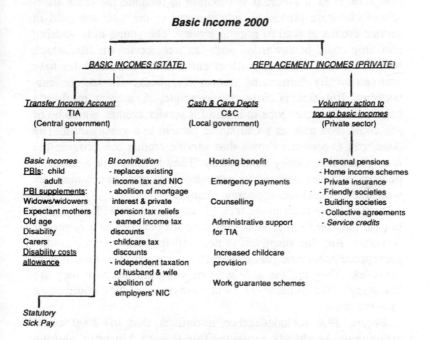

reason why all the staff should be enrolled on a paid basis, some could be voluntary workers. Nor is there any reason why private agencies should not be involved. Nor is there any reason why voluntary work need be limited to childcare provision. In the Netherlands midday school supervisors are not paid, the job is done by parents on a roster basis. The structure of *BI 2000* leaves ample scope for individuals, local communities, trade unions and employers to build on the basic provision using their own initiatives.

One way forward might be through the introduction of *service credits*, devised by Professor Edgar S. Cahn (Center on Aging, Florida International University) as a way of bridging the gap between the growing number of people "put on the scrap heap" of enforced inactivity and the growing pile of unmet social needs (Cahn 1986). By 1986 service credits had been created by law in three jurisdictions in the United States (District of Columbia, Florida and Missouri), and legislation was pending in seven other state legislatures. In those areas, service credits operate like a new currency, issued locally, tax exempt, guaranteed by local government and used as a form of payment for voluntary work.

The idea fits well with *BI 2000*. Service credits and BIs could complement each other. It is possible to imagine pre- and after-school childcare provision, where some of the staff are paid in service credits instead of regular money. The young-old, working part-time could be rewarded with tax-free service credits, which they could then use to pay others enrolled in the scheme for help with physically demanding chores like hedge-clipping or car-washing. But that is only one example. A student might do baby-sitting or other jobs in return for service credits, which he or she could then give as a Christmas present to a grandparent. The American experience shows that service credits can provide the intangibles that money cannot buy. They help restore a sense of purpose, and they help revive a sense of belonging in communities wracked by social and economic change.

Some people react to the idea of service credits with suspicion, in case they turn out to be a substitute for benefits, or a cover for workfare. But this suspicion is not well-founded. Service credits presuppose an income guarantee that is adequate, otherwise they do not work. They are the antithesis of workfare, because they are voluntary. If the voluntary element were removed they would cease to make sense.

Figure 19.4 includes other initiatives that *BI 2000* could encompass. As already explained this is not a blueprint, and the detail can be altered without changing the strategy.

Main differences between *BI 2000* and BIG 1(a)

With *BI 2000* the emphasis is more on work incentives (for rich and poor), and on cutting unit labour costs. In the analysis that follows all the figure-work is at 1985 prices, unless otherwise specified.

Earned-income tax discounts (TDs). In addition to the PBIs each person would be able to earn a small amount of money free of tax. The tax rate would be applied to all earnings and the TD would be deducted from the resulting tax bill. The effect is to reduce average tax rates (ATRs) at all levels of earnings, and marginal tax rates (MTRs) on part-time earnings. In Table 19.1 it is assumed that the TD is 40 percent of earnings up to a maximum of £8.00, which is equivalent to £20 a week free of tax. The figures are purely illustrative. On earnings below £20 a week the MTR is zero. On earnings above £20 the MTR becomes 40 percent, but because of

Table 19.1: Earned-income tax discounts

	£	£	£	£	£	£	£	£	£
Earnings	0.00	10.00	20.00	30.00	40.00	50.00	80.00	100.00	200.00
+ Partial BI	24.00	24.00	24.00	24.00	24.00	24.00	24.00	24.00	24.00
− Income tax	0.00	4.00	8.00	12.00	16.00	20.00	32.00	40.00	81.45
+ Tax discount	0.00	4.00	8.00	8.00	8.00	8.00	8.00	8.00	8.00
= Net incomes	24.00	34.00	44.00	50.00	56.00	62.00	80.00	92.00	150.55

the PBI the ATR is much lower, indeed there is no net tax payable on earnings below £80 a week, which becomes the tax break-even point. This compares with a tax break-even point of £60 a week with BIG 1(a) and £35.50 (the lower earnings limit for NI contributions) with the existing system.

Tax relief for work-related childminding costs. In addition to the earned-income TDs, *all* mothers and all *lone* fathers would be able to put their work-related childminding costs, up to a maximum of (say) £40 pw for the first child and rather less for subsequent children, against their income tax. Unlike the earned-income TD, the childcare TD would not be credited without proof of payment to a registered nursery or childminder. Tax relief for childminding costs is the minimum change necessary to enable lone parents to do paid work. Two-parent families are included, partly in order to preserve equity between one- and two-parent families, and partly because a second wage can make all the difference to family living standards. Although it is theoretically possible to limit this relief to younger children, the social costs of "latch key" children outweigh the financial savings.

A flat rate of income tax. Although not essential, a flat rate tax is included on grounds of administrative simplicity, increased incentives and to soften the blow for higher-rate taxpayers who lose their mortgage interest and pension tax reliefs.

Abolition of employers' NI contributions. The aim is to reduce unit labour costs. Once the link between income security and paid work is broken, it is hard to justify employers' payroll taxes. The costings assume that an amount equivalent to existing employers' NI contributions can be raised from the corporate sector through some other tax, for instance a turnover tax or an increased corporation tax. But the revenues from this tax would not go to the Transfer

Income Account, they would be used to finance general government spending.

Increased childcare provision. Tax relief for childminding costs serves no purpose if the mothers have nowhere safe to leave their children, yet this is an area where Britain lags far behind the rest of the European Community (Moss 1988; Cohen 1988). Table 19.2 sets out the most recent figures, taken from Bronwen Cohen's report for the European Commission's Childcare Network. In 1985 the total number of places provided by local authorities for under-fives in day nurseries was under 30,000, with the result that in most areas only children considered "at risk" have a chance of admission. *BI 2000* includes £500 million as part of the C&C budget for increased child day-care provision. This compares with expenditure in 1985-86 by the local authorities on schools for under-fives of £352 million. (Treasury, Jan 1987, Table 3.12).

Table 19.2: Non-parental childcare provision for under-fives, UK, 1985

Type of provision	No. of places	% of population aged 0-4 for whom this type of provision is available
LEA nursery class or school	338,541[1]	9.4
LEA primary school	295,202	8.2
LA day nursery	32,964	0.9
Registered childminder	144,908	4.0
Private and voluntary day nurseries	27,533	0.8
Private schools	35,000[1]	1.0
Playschools	468,945	13.0
Nannies, au pairs, etc	30,000	0.8
Relatives	Not known[2]	—
Non-registered childminders	16,000[3]	0.7

Notes: 1 Figures for LEA and private nursery schools, and for LEA primary schools refer to number of children attending, many of whom are part-time. Children attending LEA nursery schools are mostly aged 3 or more.
2 Estimated 47% of all working mothers use this form of childcare for under-fives.
3 Recent research suggests that 20% of childminders are not registered
Source: Based on Table 5.1 in Cohen 1988.

A full BI for carers. One of the most pressing questions of our time is how best to care for the growing number of people with very severe disabilities, some of whom belong to the new generation of very old people, and some of whom are younger people who, until the advent of modern medicine, would not have survived at all. If these people are to have a real choice between institutionalisation and being looked after at home, provision has to be made for those who care for them in the home. The cost to the taxpayer is insignificant compared with the costs of hospitalisation.

A lower rate of PBI for young people, aged 16-17. The full adult rate of PBI is not payable until age 18, instead of 16 with previous BIG schemes. The new rate of £21.50 is based on November 1985 supplementary benefit, plus an element for free school meals, plus 8 percent to allow for real earnings growth between 1985 and 2000. Every 16-17-year-old would be entitled to £21.50 (whether they stayed on at school, or took up vocational training or took a job), and the first £25 of earnings or training allowance would be tax-free. Those with disabilities would also be entitled to a disability costs allowance.

Why are earned-income tax reliefs necessary?

The earned-income tax discounts (TDs), the tax relief for childminding costs and the increased childcare provision, are justified on five main counts: administrative simplicity; poverty prevention; work incentives; reduced dependence on housing benefit; and equal opportunities.

Administrative simplicity. As already explained, the Inland Revenue would have the utmost difficulty in levying tax on all income other than the BIs. Far from being prepared to pay tax on the first £ of earnings, most people expect to be able to earn at least £25 a week without either paying tax or losing benefit. Likewise many householders expect to be able to employ people part-time, or on a casual basis, without having to bother about PAYE. If the Inland Revenue tried to tax all income except the BIs, much of it would simply go underground. Earned-income TDs provide a commonsense and relatively straightforward way out of this dilemma, since investment income can be taxed at source. The paper-boy can continue his round, the daily woman can carry on cleaning (in moderation) and the odd-job man remains largely unaffected. This proposal is nevertheless a major departure from social dividend tradition, and will be hotly disputed by BI purists.

Poverty prevention and the disutilities of work. A second reason for including the TDs is the need for a tax system that takes into

339

account the disutilities of work. Simplicity, though important, should not be allowed to crowd out tax justice, yet this is what is happening. The Inland Revenue rules out tax relief for fares to work, on the grounds that "people might choose to live long distances from their place of work", yet until 1973-74 wage and salary earners could at least claim a two-ninths earned-income relief. Since abolition of the investment income surcharge (in 1984-85) earned income is taxed more heavily than unearned income (being also subject to NI contribution), yet people in paid work need more not less net income than people not in paid work in order to reach approximate living standard equivalence. In Part 3 we saw the effects of fares to work and childcare costs on net spending power. Even without childcare costs a lower paid job was not worthwhile unless it was close to home, and none of the proposed new systems came anywhere near to making work worthwhile for lone parents. Earned-income tax reliefs could ease this problem.

Table 19.3: Effects of earned income TD on the net spending power of a single householder

(1) Without tax discount	£	£	£
Earnings	0.00	20.00	100.00
+ PBI	24.00	24.00	24.00
− BIC	0.00	8.00	40.00
+ Housing benefit	28.75[1]	22.75	0.00
− Housing costs	20.65[2]	20.65	20.65
− Work expenses	0.00	0.00	10.00
= Net spending power without TD	32.10	38.10	53.35
NSP gain		*6.00*	*21.25*
Marginal tax rate		*70%*	*79%*

(2) With tax discount	£	£	£
Earnings	0.00	20.00	100.00
+ PBI	24.00	24.00	24.00
− BIC	0.00	8.00	40.00
+ TD	0.00	8.00	8.00
+ Housing benefit[1]	28.75	18.75	0.00
− Housing costs[2]	20.65	20.65	20.65
− Work expenses	0.00	0.00	10.00
= Net spending power with TD	32.10	42.10	61.35
NSP gain		*10.00*	*29.25*
Marginal tax rate		*50%*	*71%*

Notes: 1. Rent and rates 19.00, water rates £1.65, householder addition £5.90, heating addition £2.20.
2. Rent, rates and water rates.

Work incentives. A BI system that taxed earned income from the first £ would be illogical as well as inoperable. To remove the earnings rule, in order to encourage the unemployed to do paid work, and simultaneously to remove the initial, tax-free tranche of income (thus discouraging paid work) would be self-defeating. This was clearly shown in Figure 18.4. In Britain, advocates of BI and NIT make wild claims that "the poverty and unemployment traps can be eliminated", without doing the arithmetic. Elsewhere in the EEC, where earned income tax relief *and* tax relief for work expenses are commonplace, the effect of a BI or NIT that made all other income taxable could be disastrous.

Table 19.3 shows the effect of an earned-income TD of £8 a week on net spending power and MTRs, assuming the same levels of earnings as in Figures 18.6 and 18.7, and a tax rate of 40 percent. The TD is equivalent to £20 a week tax-free. It is no breakthrough, but it is a move in the right direction.

Reduced dependence on housing benefit. As can be seen from Table 19.3, the TD also enables housing benefit to be withdrawn more quickly. Fewer people are subject to the 70 percent tax rate, and the housing benefit case load is diminished.

Equal opportunities. One of the criticisms directed against Vince's tax-credit proposals and previous BIG schemes has been the disincentive effects of increased marginal tax rates on working wives. No married woman on low earnings would lose out, and many would gain, but for those earning less than wife's earned income allowance (WEIA) the MTR shoots up from zero to around 40 per cent. One danger is that the Inland Revenue would be unable to lay its hands on the newly taxable earnings. Another, given that married women's affiliation to the labour market is less strong than men's, is the deterrent effect on women's participation in the labour market.

The second criticism raises two questions, first whether it really matters if some married women choose not to do paid work, and also whether the long-term effects would be the same as the short-term effects. The answer to the first question depends partly on whether one approves or disapproves of married women's participation in the labour market. But it also concerns family living standards, which would undoubtedly fall if large numbers of married women decided to give up paid work. The answer to the second question is more complicated. If sufficient married women

341

stopped doing paid work, women's rates of pay would tend to rise. At present there is little doubt that employers capitalise on the "preferential" tax status of married women by employing them part-time at very low rates of pay, on the pretext that what they earn is tax-free. If married women, like everyone else, became liable for tax on all their earnings, this argument would cease to apply. Some employers would be forced to put up pay, others would go out of business. In the first instance abolition of WEIA could be more effective than equal pay legislation as a means of bringing women's pay into line with men's, although the long-term effect of those increased wages could be to price unskilled female labour out of paid work, in much the same way as unskilled male labour has already been priced out.

The *BI 2000* solution is to meet the critics halfway by replacing WEIA with a standard, fixed-amount TD for men and women alike. The TD would soften the impact of removing WEIA and would also make the system symmetrical. Figure 5.1 brings out this point. Out of six alternative tax regimes, *BI 2000* is the only option that is completely symmetrical – not just between men and women, but also between earners and non-earners.

Filling the poverty gap

Figure 19.2 shows how the TD could help fill the gap between the PBIs and the poverty line. As before, the rate of the new income tax is assumed to be 40 percent. The TD is equal to 40 percent of earnings, and the maximum TD equals 40 percent of the difference between the poverty line (£60) and the PBI (£24), ie £14.40. Net income (line GCAB) starts off by running parallel to the 45° line, but when earnings reach £60 a week income tax cuts in at 40 percent. The effect of the TD is twofold. The size of the gap between the PBI and the poverty line is diminished, and the tax break-even point is pushed over to the right. Superficially it looks as though there is benefit leakage to people with gross incomes above the poverty line. But the overspill is an income tax relief, not a benefit.

Some people would also be entitled to housing benefit, represented in the second diagram by the triangle GCH, in which case net income increases more slowly. Net income including housing benefit follows the line HCAB. Housing benefit is extinguished once earnings reach £72, represented by point C. On

Figure 19.2: Basic Income 2000, effects of earned-income tax discount

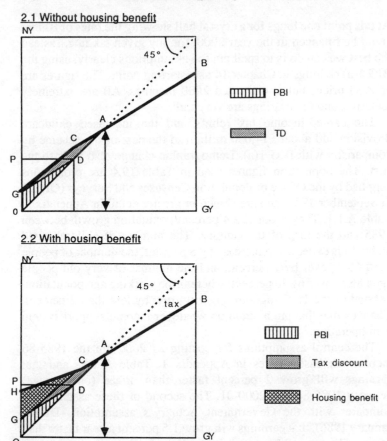

2.1 Without housing benefit

2.2 With housing benefit

earnings above £72 the marginal tax rate falls from 70 percent to 40 percent. Either way the tax break-even point is £96. With rent and rates less than those assumed, point C moves down to the left, and *vice versa.*

Despite its theoretical appeal, an earned-income TD on this scale would be very expensive (estimated gross cost in 1985-86 was £17,500 million), and could tilt the balance too much in favour of part-time work. A smaller TD enables the starting rate of tax to be lower and makes full-time work relatively more attractive. For our illustrative scheme, we shall assume a TD of £9.50 a week (equal to £25 a week tax-free).

BI 2000 tentative costings

At this point one longs for a crystal ball showing the rates of BI that could be financed in the year 2000, for any given tax rate. Instead the best we can do is to spell out the assumptions clearly, using the BIG 1(a) costings in Chapter 14 as a starting point. The figures are at 1985 prices but at estimated 2000 incomes. All are extremely tentative, and the costings are very tight.

The earned-income tax reliefs and the increased childcare provision add about £14,000 million to the cost of the scheme by comparison with BIG 1(a). Demographic change also adds to the cost. The population figures used in Table 19.4 are projections supplied by the Office of Population Censuses and Surveys (OPCS) in September 1987, and are shown in greater detail in Appendix 1, Table A.1.1. They produce a 4 percent population growth between 1985 and the turn of the century. The number of children aged under 16 is expected to increase by 8 percent, the number of people aged 65 or over by 7 percent, and the number of very old people aged 85 or over by 70 percent, whereas the working age population, defined as the 16-64 age-group, will grow by less than 2 percent. Changes like this put a strain on whatever income support system is in operation.

The central assumptions for costing *BI 2000* are the 1985-86 income tax base figures in Appendix 1, Table A.1.5., and that earnings will grow 2 percent faster than prices (on average) between 1985-86 and 2000-01. The second of these assumptions compares with the Government Actuary's assumption (DHSS, January 1986), that earnings will grow 1.5 percent a year faster than prices. The extra 0.5 percent is to allow for increased economic activity as a result of transitional change towards *BI 2000*. It produces a 35 percent increase in real earnings over the fifteen years between 1985-86 and 2000-01.

The other main assumptions are abolition of SERPS, unification of income tax and employees' NI contributions, and replacement of employers' NI contributions by an increased profits tax designed to yield approximately the same amount of revenue. The effects of other possible changes between now and the year 2000 are not included. Thus no account is taken of the effects of the community charge, or decontrol of rents.

The BIG 1(a) costings in Table 14.5, and the background statistics in Appendix 1, Table A.1.2, show that estimated savings on existing expenditure came to £53,121 million, compared with

Table 19.4: *Basic Income 2000*, gross costs at November 1985 prices and incomes

	Population m	Year 2000-01 weekly BI rate £	Annual cost £m
1. BASIC INCOMES			
(1) Partial BIs			
Adult PBI	44.71	26.00	60,448
Children/young people aged:			
0-10	8.91	15.00	6,950
11-15	3.80	18.50	3,656
16-17	1.43	21.50	1,599
(2) PBI supplements			
Expectant mothers[1]	0.83	15.00	324
Widows/widowers[1]	0.33	26.00	223
Age 65 or over	9.19	39.00	18.637
Disability	1.0?	39.00	2,028
Carers	0.5?	39.00	1,014
(3) Disability costs allowance	3.0?	variable	4,000
Total Cost of BIs			98,879
2. EARNED INCOME TAX RELIEFS			
(1) Earned income tax discounts		9.50	13,000
(2) Childcare tax discounts (upper limit per child)		15.40[2]	500
3. C & C BENEFITS			
(1) Residual housing benefit[3]			c500
(2) Emergency payments[4]			200
(3) Childcare provision[5]			500
Estimated programme cost, at 1985-86 prices			113,579

Notes: 1. For 26 weeks only.
2. Equivalent at 38% tax to £40.50 tax-free. £40.50 is average £30 child-minding charge in 1985-86 uprated by 35%, in line with average earnings.
3. Estimated from BIG 1(a).
4. £200 million for equivalent of single and additional needs payments. (Social Security Statistics 1986, Table 34.97, and Hansard WA 10 May 1985, c 542).
5. £500 million for pre-school and out-of-school provision.

£52,370 million extra costs on account of abolishing income tax, ACT and all NI contributions *except* the employer contributions. The difference is a net revenue gain of £750 million. On the assumption that tax forgone as a result of abolishing employer NI contributions can be fully recouped through increased profits or corporation tax and transferred to general government expenditure, there is no need to get embroiled in the complexities of the BIG 1(a) costing formula. Instead we can use the third formula in Appendix 1, where x is the cost of the BIs and the tax rate equals x divided by the new income tax base:

$$t = \frac{x}{\text{new IT base}}$$

Table 19.4 sets out the target BIs and earned-income TDs for the year 2000 on these assumptions. *BI 2000* contains a further hidden cost by comparison with BIG 1(a). The BIG 1(a) basic incomes were costed assuming a 5 percent benefit uprating in November 1985, which produced a significant expenditure saving over the year as a whole, but was in line with practice at that time. The *BI 2000* programme is costed using the same rates of BI throughout the financial year 2000-01, which makes it more expensive in accounting terms, but is in line with current practice. For this reason (as well as the increased dependency ratio and the extra costs of the earned-income TDs, the PBI supplement for carers and the increased childcare provision) the target PBIs are only 8 percent higher in real terms than the BIG 1(a) amounts in Chapter 14. This 8 percent compares with an estimated 35 percent increase in real earnings (and in the tax base) between 1985 and 2000.

Table 19.5: BI 2000, tax base and tax rates, year 2000, November 1985 prices

Assumptions	New IT base £ billion	Tax rate %
(1) Upper bound, all income tax reliefs abolished	323	35.3
(2) As for (1), less reliefs for income of charities and for interest on British Government securities where the owner is not ordinarily resident in the UK	320	35.6
(3) As in (2), less just under half of private pension reliefs, which are retained	300	38.0
(4) As in (3), less balance of private pension reliefs, which remain as in 1985-86	278	41.0
(5) As in (4), less mortgage interest tax relief, which remains as in 1985-86	258	44.2

The cost of housing benefit is extremely uncertain, since it would depend on how many lone parents and unemployed people could be got back into paid work.

On the assumptions in Table 19.4, the tax rate necessary to finance *BI 2000* works out at between 35 and 44 percent, depending on how many of the non-personal income tax reliefs can be phased out. The figure-work is in Table 19.5. The starting rate of tax could be reduced slightly if higher-rate tax were retained. Given the unlikelihood that all pension tax reliefs can be phased out by the year 2000, the most plausible figure is taken to be assumption (3), which produces an estimated tax rate of 38 percent. This estimate is very approximate.

A flat rate, unified BI contribution of 38 percent compares with Mr Lawson's new goal of a 20 percent starting rate of income tax, plus NI contribution at 9 percent, leaving most wage and salary earners paying 29 percent out of each extra £ earned, most pensioners and people with investment income paying 20 percent, and a few high-fliers paying 40 percent. Given the increasing cost of SERPS, NI contribution might well have to be raised, bringing the combined rate for most people by the year 2000 to over 30 percent.[2] Short of a miracle the *BI 2000* tax rate is almost bound to be higher, and this requires no apology, for it would be the result of three clear-cut policy decisions:

(1) To integrate NI contributions with income tax.
(2) To give priority to reducing average rather than marginal tax rates.
(3) To improve the safety net.

Administration

Administration of *BI 2000* would be split between the Transfer Income Account (TIA) and the new Cash and Care Departments (C&C), as for BIG 1(a).

Transfer Income Account (TIA)

The TIA is fully integrated (harmonisation of all administrative regulations) and fully automated. The emphasis is on simplicity, benefit categories that are exogenous, and ease of access. It follows that any sort of conditionality is out of the question. The assessment unit is the individual and the accounting period is the year. For the BIs, net tax liability/net benefit entitlement would be cumulative, but for the earned income tax reliefs it might have to be non-cumulative, on a monthly basis. This is to prevent people from compressing their paid work into a few months' tax-free bonanza.

The first question is how to get the BIs into the bank accounts (or pockets) of about 45 million adults, and the second is how to collect the tax that finances them. Several alternative methods have been investigated, but the simplest is thought to be as follows. The TIA would be responsible for assessing the age-related BI entitlements of every resident, and for collecting the tax necessary to finance them. The exception would be the disability and carer's supplements, and the DCA, for which the TIA would depend on information supplied by the C&C departments. The BIs would be credited by the TIA through the main settlement banks. Tax on investment income would be collected at source, as at present. Schedule D income tax (self-employed) would also be collected as at present. PAYE would continue to be collected through the employers. Final responsibility for the accuracy of the tax assessments would lie with the Inland Revenue, as agent of the TIA.

Delivery of the BIs. Each child would receive a TIA number as soon as the birth was registered, and that number would be his or hers for life. The nearest existing equivalent is the National Health Service or National Insurance number. The new TIA number would be sent to the settlement bank chosen by the child's parents, and the child BIs would be credited by the TIA each month accordingly. On reaching age 16 (or 18) young people would have the right to transfer their TIA numbers to the settlement bank of their choice.

It is sometimes suggested that each child and each adult should have his or her separate bank account, and that the BIs should be credited on a weekly basis. In practice both these proposals would add considerably to bank costs. Few banks would welcome accounts worth less than £100 a month and most banks would prefer monthly to weekly transmissions. The bankers' reasons for these preferences would be largely financial, but mandatory independent bank accounts for the entire population could also be regarded as an infringement of personal freedom. Many married couples prefer joint bank accounts and there is no good reason why the practice should be stopped.

On balance it therefore seems best to allow adults (whether married or single) to choose between separate and joint accounts, and to allow parents to choose whether their children should have their own accounts, or have the children's BIs credited to the bank account(s) of the parents. A refinement would be to require the child BI to be credited either to its own account, or to the account of the mother, except where the father had day to day responsibility for the child. A further refinement, in order to reduce bank costs, would be to stagger BI payments across the whole of each monthly period, perhaps in alphabetical order.

There remains the problem of how to reach the minority of people who do not have bank accounts. Although during the late 1970s the number of adults with a bank current account grew by 40 percent, this trend slackened off during the early 1980s. Information based on a survey carried out for the Inter-Bank Research Organisation (IBRO) in 1981 showed 75 percent of adults had some form of bank account, 65 percent had a bank current account, and over 50 percent had a building society account. Only 13 percent had no accounts at all (IBRO 1985). Some were married women whose husbands had bank accounts, others would be regarded by the banks as potential liabilities. But the figure also includes some of the poorest people, and it is important that they do not get left out. A series of options seems the most acceptable solution, of which one would be a GIRO account.

Processing the BIs. Each month the TIA would send to the bankers' automated clearing services (BACS) the BI information for every legal resident. This would be done using magnetic tapes or discs, or by on-line data transmission. BACS would process the information and pass it on to the appropriate settlement banks, who would credit their customers' accounts accordingly. There appear to be no major operational difficulties, except that of reaching out to the very small, but important, minority of people who do not have bank accounts of any sort. It could be that the introduction of a BI system would help to integrate these people into the community, by making it worth their while to open bank accounts. Nor should it be taken for granted that the existing tax and benefit systems are at present reaching out to these people.

Collection of the new income tax. Investment income would be taxed at source, as now, so the main problem concerns earned and self-employment income. Despite the earned-income TDs more people would be liable to income tax than at present, and the number of tax units would go up because of individual assessment. With flat rate tax and no mortgage or private pension tax reliefs, PAYE would nevertheless become much more straightforward than at present. The employer would deduct tax at the same flat rate for all, and the TIA would credit each wage earner with his/her earned income TD on receipt of the tax. Any remaining pension tax reliefs could become the responsibility of the pension funds, thus relieving employers of the complexity of code numbers. With Schedule D incomes, tax would be assessed on net profits, as at present, and the earned income TD credited against the tax due. With a non-cumulative TD and a monthly accounting period, there would have to be averaging for self-employed people.

Cash and Care benefits (C&C)

The C&C departments (either separate as at present, or amalgamated) would be responsible for assessment and payment of housing benefit and the emergency payments that constitute the final safety net. The scale of both would be much smaller than at present. The C&C departments would also send to the TIA the authorisations necessary for crediting of PBI disability and carers' supplements, and disability costs allowances – all under central government regulation. The role of the C&C departments is a crucial one. They are the safety valve for the whole system. They must keep in touch with the grassroots, encouraging local initiatives, making sure that individuals are helped to help themselves, and that expenditure on housing benefit does not get out of control.

Administration of disability benefits. The C&C departments would check all applications for disability and carers' supplements and for the disability costs allowance (DCA). Administration of these benefits is fraught with difficulties, some of which are not strictly within the scope of this enquiry, since they occur whether or not the tax and benefit systems are integrated. The DCA, for instance, requires a scale of allowances based on the extra costs incurred as a result of disability, and these do not always correlate with degree of disability. The issues were discussed in detail in 1986-87 by an expert working group under the auspices of the Basic Income Research Group, and the resulting discussion paper was published in 1988 (BIRG Disability Working Group 1988).

The most difficult issues concern the disability supplement. This is intended as a form of earnings replacement for those who are prevented from doing paid work, or who have difficulty in doing paid work on a full-time or regular basis. It is not intended for those who would not do paid work even if they were able-bodied. In some ways it resembles existing invalidity benefit, however, in keeping with the philosophy behind all BI schemes, it is also intended as a base on which people with disabilities can build by their own efforts, therefore it should carry the minimum of earnings restrictions.

The aim is a system that will take account of the extra difficulties experienced by people with disabilities in the job market, yet can remove entitlement to disability supplement when it is no longer needed, or if the claimant is not genuinely interested in doing paid work. One approach is to think of disability supplement in terms of an occupational handicap allowance, payable on production of a doctor's certificate to the effect that the claimant is unlikely to be able to earn on a normal, regular basis. Occupational handicap certificates could be made valid for up to a year at a time, but they would not be able to distinguish between those who genuinely wanted to work and those who did not. A refinement of this solution, closely related to the proposal put forward by Peter Mitchell for RADAR in 1986 (Mitchell 1986), would be to pay a disability supplement to anybody holding a valid occupational handicap certificate, subject to the proviso that they would forfeit the supplement if they refused *suitable* work or training. In that case, the onus would be on the C&C departments to make a suitable job or training offer. Payment of the supplement would be automatic until they did so. A system along these lines has many advantages, but the cost of the work/training guarantee would add considerably to the budgeted costs of *BI 2000*.

Payment of the carer's BI supplement would be primarily for "attendance", the carer being defined as the person with responsibility for the disabled person during most of each twenty-four hours. That should not prevent the carer from using the money to buy in care while s/he did paid work (or anything else) outside the home. Application for a carer's supplement would need to be endorsed by the family doctor and by the local C&C department, and would be subject to regular review.

Arguments for a locally applied work test. Many people who would otherwise support a switch to partial BIs have tremendous difficulty in accepting an income support system that has no strings attached. At some level and at some stage, they argue, there has to be a concerted effort to find out why a person is not self-supporting, and to make sure that s/he will become so. Although the BIs have to be unconditional, there is nothing in the structure of *BI 2000* to prevent inclusion of a work test at local level, in conjunction with housing benefit and/or C&C emergency payments. A good case can be made for linking housing benefit to some sort of work test, provided there is also a work or training guarantee. Instead of paying housing benefit automatically, claimants would be asked why they needed it, and if they were not earning, or only working part-time, they would be told to take full-time work or training, which would be provided. Some people, for instance full-time students or lone parents with young children, could be exempt, but generally speaking it could be taken for granted that a person's main source of income was through paid work.

In theory a work test would help to prevent expenditure from getting out of control and would be in the best interests of all concerned. In practice, as we saw in Chapter 16, it might turn out rather differently. Much would depend on whether or not there was a national minimum wage, on the level of the BIs and the tax rate. The decision whether or not to introduce a work test would be up to the government of the day.

Arguments for reviewing the liability to maintain laws. Another way to prevent C&C expenditure from getting out of control would be through stricter enforcement of and/or changes to the laws of liability to maintain. The *BI 2000* costings assume assessment units for the C&C benefits as at present, and no change to DHSS regulations regarding liability to maintain. Yet these are often quite astonishing. On the one hand a man and a woman who live together run the risk of being counted as "husband and wife", with a mutual obligation to maintain, whether or not they think of their relationship in that way. On the other hand the DHSS has invented a new definition of marriage, whereby a "married couple means a man and woman who are married to each other and are members of the same household" (House of Commons, Jan 1986, Part 2, Clause 19). This is another way of saying that the taxpayer moves in if the marriage breaks down. In similar fashion a person responsible for a child counts as a single parent provided s/he does not have a partner, which is DHSS-speak for letting the absent parent off the hook, but making any new spouse/partner responsible for somebody else's child.

With *BI 2000* the main problem area would be housing benefit, which can all too easily become a mechanism for encouraging household formation by people who otherwise could not afford to live alone. As envisaged, *BI 2000* would exclude young people aged 16-17 from entitlement to housing benefit, unless they could show good reason for not living in the parental home. Another way to tighten up housing benefit regulations would be to count parents as part of the assessment unit of claimants under 21 years of age. This raises awkward questions, for instance whether parents should have the right to refuse to pay, on the grounds that the offspring could live in the parental home, but those questions need to be addressed. Similarly, in the case of lone parents, or separated spouses, it is difficult to see why taxpayers should automatically foot the bill for housing benefit, without first enquiring if the absent parent/spouse is able to do so.

Changes like these may seem draconian, and would doubtless be greeted with howls of anguish. But they could be the only way to prevent the same ever-increasing dependence on C&C benefits that has characterised means-tested benefits in Britain since 1948. Britain has some of the most generous liability to maintain regulations in Western Europe, and they require investigation.

Who would gain and who would lose?

Extreme care is necessary when referring to the model tables at the end of this chapter and in Appendix 2. They are included for illustrative purposes only, and are not comparable with the other proposed systems, since they assume a 35 percent increase in the income tax base, and an 8 percent increase in the real value of the BIs. Nor is it possible to estimate the effects of *BI 2000* on the incomes of actual families by putting it through TAXMOD.

The philosophy behind *BI 2000* is to create wealth in order to prevent poverty (not as an end in itself), and to attack poverty at its roots rather than symptomatically. In each case the PBI supplements are added to the PBIs, and the effects on the most disadvantaged families would be dramatic. For example a disability costs allowance (DCA) would be added to the PBI of anyone, at any age, whose disabilities resulted in living costs beyond a recognised

353

minimum. A family with a severely disabled child would receive a DCA and a carer's supplement. A family looking after a severely disabled elderly person would also receive a carer's supplement, and the elderly person would receive a DCA as well as the PBI and old age supplement. During pregnancy every mother would receive the equivalent of a child PBI during the last six months of pregnancy. If she was disabled, she would also receive a DCA. Statutory sick pay would be in addition to the PBI, although it would be taxable. Housing benefit would be as for BIG 1(a), but the new householder element has been increased faster than inflation.

By comparison with the existing system, *BI 2000* is revolutionary. Many of the implied gains (as a result for instance of the DCA, the childcare tax reliefs, the improved childcare facilities, the abolition of earnings rules, the freedom to train or study without loss of benefit, or even the greater emphasis on maintenance payments) do not show through in either model family analysis or TAXMOD. We can include an estimate for childcare tax reliefs in model family analysis, but the costs of childcare cannot be identified by TAXMOD in the Family Expenditure Survey. Under present law maintenance payments are deducted £ for £ for income support, with *BI 2000* they would not be.

There are losses too which cannot be identified. The net income gains to pensioners, especially married pensioners, look impressive, but for some people those gains would be offset by reduced SERPS entitlement. The removal of half the private pension tax reliefs would be bound to affect the pattern of savings, and could result in an overall reduction in savings for old age.[3] Much would depend on which reliefs were removed and which retained. The assumption that half the existing pension tax reliefs can be phased out by the end of the century adds an estimated £22,000 million to the tax base in year 2000 (worth about £8,000 million in extra revenue at 38 percent tax), but there is no way of estimating the distribution of gains and losses. TAXMOD can calculate the effects of removing superannuation and retirement annuity tax reliefs, but that only accounts for about £2,000 million of the extra revenue, and in any case those are perhaps the pension tax reliefs that should stay. Neither TAXMOD nor model family analysis can show the redistributive effects of removing tax-free pension lump sums nor the effects of making employers' contributions taxable. At the bottom of the income distribution the losses are offset by the PBIs and PBI supplements, and at the top they can be softened by removal of all higher-rate tax, but adjustments would still be necessary to prevent unacceptable losses for people in the middle.

Generally speaking *BI 2000* would be redistributive from rich to poor, from those without in favour of those with dependent children, and from the able-bodied in favour of people with disabilities. But it would be less redistributive than BIG 1(a), due to removal of higher-rate tax, the introduction of age-related child BIs, and the earned-income tax reliefs. These would be of particular benefit to the lower paid, but would reduce the amounts available for the out of work by about £14,000 million.

From the figures in Appendix 2 it is clear that the formula would not be to everybody's taste. At nil earnings the families with younger children do noticeably less well with *BI 2000* than with most of the other proposals. Childcare tax reliefs and increased childcare provision would help mothers who work outside the home, but the poorest families are often those with very young children where the mother cannot go out to work. That is why some people prefer flat-rate child PBIs and some would go even further, by having a PBI supplement for children under five. The danger is that non-earning, low income lone parents, including some widowed mothers, would otherwise find themselves worse off than before.

Finally, the reader needs to remember that the costings in this chapter were extremely tentative. The amounts available for the BIs in the year 2000 would in practice depend crucially on the effects of transitional change towards the target system between now and then. It is to the early phases of transition that we must now turn.

Table 19.6: Disposable incomes of selected model families, *Basic Income 2000*, projected amounts for the year 2000 at November 1985 prices, £ per week

Assumptions
All figures are at November 1985 prices, but refer to the financial year 2000-01, costed on the basis of OPCS population projections and estimated real earnings growth between 1985-86 and 2000-01 of 35% (average 2% pa), but no other changes. All families are tenants. Working age families live in council property, and pay the rents and rates used in the November1985 DHSS Tax/Benefit Model Tables. As in Chapters 12 - 15, water rates (estimated by the DHSS to have been £1.65 a week) are credited as part of *BI 2000* housing benefit but are not deducted with housing costs. Families are assumed to take up entitlement to housing benefit in full. The PBIs are £26 for adults from age 18, £15 for children aged 0-10, £18.50 for children aged 11-15, and £21.50 for age 16-17. The PBI supplement for pensioners is £39, producing a full BI of £65. BI contribution is at a flat rate of 38%. Earned income tax discount is £9.50. Childminding expenses assumed to be £40.50 for the child aged 4 and £10 for the child aged 6 in Tables 3 and 7. No allowance for fares to work except in Tables 3 and 7.

Basic Income 2000

Housing benefit formula: (1) At nil original income, householders with PBI only get rent and rates in full + water rates £1.65 + householder supplement £8.30. (2) At nil original income, householders in receipt of full BI get: (a) single householder or couple where only one is in receipt of full BI: rent, rates and water rates in full, less £22.80. (b) Couple where both are in receipt of full BI: rent, rates and water rates in full, less £62.80. Taper is combined 50 percent of net income. Childcare TD is not reckonable.

Earnings levels: In November 1985 average earnings of full-time men and women was about £180 a week. By the year 2000, assuming a 2% average annual growth rate in real earnings, that figure becomes £240 at November 1985 prices. Hence the new earnings column of £240.

1. WORKING AGE HOUSEHOLDS

Table 1: Single non-householder aged 18 to 64

	£	£	£	£	£	£	£
Gross weekly earnings	0.00	40.00	80.00	120.00	160.00	200.00	240.00
+ PBI	26.00	26.00	26.00	26.00	26.00	26.00	26.00
− BI contribution	0.00	15.20	30.40	45.60	60.80	76.00	91.20
+ Earned-income TD	0.00	9.50	9.50	9.50	9.50	9.50	9.50
= Net and disposable incomes	26.00	60.30	85.10	109.90	134.70	159.50	184.30

Table 2: Single householder aged 18 to 64

	£	£	£	£	£	£	£
Gross weekly earnings	0.00	40.00	80.00	120.00	160.00	200.00	240.00
+ PBI	26.00	26.00	26.00	26.00	26.00	26.00	26.00
− BI contribution	0.00	15.20	30.40	45.60	60.80	76.00	91.20
+ Earned income TD	0.00	9.50	9.50	9.50	9.50	9.50	9.50
= Net incomes	26.00	60.30	85.10	109.90	134.70	159.50	184.30
+ Housing benefit	28.95	11.80	0.00	0.00	0.00	0.00	0.00
− Rent	13.80	13.80	13.80	13.80	13.80	13.80	13.80
− Rates	5.20	5.20	5.20	5.20	5.20	5.20	5.20
= Disposable incomes	35.95	53.10	66.10	90.90	115.70	140.50	165.30

Table 3: Single person + 2 children aged 4 and 6

	£	£	£	£	£	£	£
Gross weekly earnings	0.00	40.00	80.00	120.00	160.00	200.00	240.00
+ PBIs	56.00	56.00	56.00	56.00	56.00	56.00	56.00
− BI contribution	0.00	15.20	30.40	45.60	60.80	76.00	91.20
+ Earned income TD	0.00	9.50	9.50	9.50	9.50	9.50	9.50
+ Childcare TD	0.00	7.60	19.19	19.19	19.19	19.19	19.19
= Net incomes	56.00	97.90	134.29	159.09	183.89	208.69	233.49
+ Housing benefit	32.75	15.60	3.20	0.00	0.00	0.00	0.00
− Rent	16.50	16.50	16.50	16.50	16.50	16.50	16.50
− Rates	6.30	6.30	6.30	6.30	6.30	6.30	6.30
= Disposable incomes	65.95	90.70	114.69	136.29	161.09	185.89	210.69
− Childcare costs	0.00	20.00	50.50	50.50	50.50	50.50	50.50
− Travel to work costs	0.00	0.00	5.00	10.00	10.00	15.00	15.00
= Net spending power	65.95	70.70	59.19	75.75	100.59	120.39	145.19

Assumptions: Childcare costs of £20 a week on earnings of £40, otherwise of £50.50 a week (£40.50 for the 4 year old and £10 for the 6 year old).

Table 4: Married couple/any two adults (single-wage)

	£	£	£	£	£	£	£
Gross weekly earnings	0.00	40.00	80.00	120.00	160.00	200.00	240.00
+ PBIs	52.00	52.00	52.00	52.00	52.00	52.00	52.00
− BI contribution	0.00	15.20	30.40	45.60	60.80	76.00	91.20
+ Earned income TD	0.00	9.50	9.50	9.50	9.50	9.50	9.50
= Net incomes	52.00	86.30	111.10	135.90	160.70	200.70	210.30
+ Housing benefit	28.95	11.80	0.00	0.00	0.00	0.00	0.00
− Rent	13.80	13.80	13.80	13.80	13.80	13.80	13.80
− Rates	5.20	5.20	5.20	5.20	5.20	5.20	5.20
= Disposable incomes	61.95	79.10	91.10	116.90	141.70	181.70	191.30

Table 5: Married couple/any two adults (two-wage, each person earns half)

	£	£	£	£	£	£	£
Gross weekly earnings	0.00	40.00	80.00	120.00	160.00	200.00	240.00
+ PBIs	52.00	52.00	52.00	52.00	52.00	52.00	52.00
− BI contribution	0.00	15.20	30.40	45.60	60.80	76.00	91.20
+ Earned income TD	0.00	19.00	19.00	19.00	19.00	19.00	19.00
= Net incomes	52.00	95.80	120.60	145.40	170.20	195.00	219.80
+ Housing benefit	28.95	7.05	0.00	0.00	0.00	0.00	0.00
− Rent	13.80	13.80	13.80	13.80	13.80	13.80	13.80
− Rates	5.20	5.20	5.20	5.20	5.20	5.20	5.20
= Disposable incomes	61.95	83.85	101.60	126.40	151.20	176.00	200.80

Table 6: Married couple/any two adults + 2 children aged 4 and 6 (single-wage)

	£	£	£	£	£	£	£
Gross weekly earnings	0.00	40.00	80.00	120.00	160.00	200.00	240.00
+ PBIs	82.00	82.00	82.00	82.00	82.00	82.00	82.00
− BI contribution	0.00	15.20	30.40	45.60	60.80	76.00	91.20
+ Earned income TD	0.00	9.50	9.50	9.50	9.50	9.50	9.50
= Net incomes	82.00	116.30	141.10	165.90	190.70	215.50	240.30
+ Housing benefit	32.75	15.60	3.20	0.00	0.00	0.00	0.00
− Rent	16.50	16.50	16.50	16.50	16.50	16.50	16.50
− Rates	6.30	6.30	6.30	6.30	6.30	6.30	6.30
= Disposable incomes	91.95	109.10	121.50	143.10	167.90	192.70	217.50

Table 7: Married couple/any two adults + 2 children aged 4 and 6 (two-wage, each adult earns half)

	£	£	£	£	£	£	£
Gross weekly earnings	0.00	40.00	80.00	120.00	160.00	200.00	240.00
+ PBIs	82.00	82.00	82.00	82.00	82.00	82.00	82.00
− BI contribution	0.00	15.20	30.40	45.60	60.80	76.00	91.20
+ Earned income TD	0.00	19.00	19.00	19.00	19.00	19.00	19.00
+ Childcare TD	0.00	0.00	0.00	7.60	7.60	15.20	15.20
= Net incomes	82.00	125.80	150.60	183.00	207.80	240.20	265.00
+ Housing benefit	32.75	10.85	0.00	0.00	0.00	0.00	0.00
− Rent	16.50	16.50	16.50	16.50	16.50	16.50	16.50
− Rates	6.30	6.30	6.30	6.30	6.30	6.30	6.30
= Disposable incomes	91.95	113.85	127.80	160.20	185.00	217.40	242.20
− Assumed childcare costs	0.00	0.00	0.00	20.00	20.00	40.00	40.00
− Assumed travel costs	0.00	0.00	0.00	10.00	10.00	10.00	20.00
= Net spending power	91.95	113.85	127.80	130.20	155.00	167.40	182.20

2. OLD AGE PENSIONERS

Table 8: Single person aged 65 or over
(a) No earned income

	£	£	£	£	£	£	£	£
Private pension/ investment income	0.00	5.00	10.00	20.00	30.00	40.00	50.00	100.00
+ PBI	26.00	26.00	26.00	26.00	26.00	26.00	26.00	26.00
+ PBI old age supplement	39.00	39.00	39.00	39.00	39.00	39.00	39.00	39.00
− BI contribution	0.00	1.90	3.80	7.60	11.40	15.20	19.00	38.00
= Net incomes	65.00	68.10	71.20	77.40	83.60	89.80	96.00	127.00
+ Housing benefit	0.85	0.00	0.00	0.00	0.00	0.00	0.00	0.00
− Rent	15.00	15.00	15.00	15.00	15.00	15.00	15.00	15.00
− Rates	7.00	7.00	7.00	7.00	7.00	7.00	7.00	7.00
= Disposable incomes	43.85	46.10	49.20	55.40	61.60	67.80	74.00	105.00

(b) No unearned income (except the BIs)

	£	£	£	£	£	£	£	£
Earnings	0.00	5.00	10.00	20.00	30.00	40.00	50.00	100.00
+ PBI	26.00	26.00	26.00	26.00	26.00	26.00	26.00	26.00
+ PBI old age supplement	39.00	39.00	39.00	39.00	39.00	39.00	39.00	39.00
− BI contribution	0.00	1.90	3.80	7.60	11.40	15.20	19.00	38.00
+ Earned income TD	0.00	1.90	3.80	7.60	9.50	9.50	9.50	9.50
= Net incomes	65.00	70.00	75.00	85.00	93.10	99.30	105.50	136.50
+ Housing benefit	0.00	0.00	0.00	0.00	0.00	0.00	0.00	0.00
− Rent	15.00	15.00	15.00	15.00	15.00	15.00	15.00	15.00
− Rates	7.00	7.00	7.00	7.00	7.00	7.00	7.00	7.00
= Disposable incomes	43.00	48.00	53.00	63.00	71.10	77.30	83.50	114.50

Table 9: Pensioner couple/any two people aged 65 or over

	£	£	£	£	£	£	£	£
Private pension/ investment income	0.00	5.00	10.00	20.00	30.00	40.00	50.00	100.00
+ PBIs	52.00	52.00	52.00	52.00	52.00	52.00	52.00	52.00
+ PBI supplements	78.00	78.00	78.00	78.00	78.00	78.00	78.00	78.00
− BI contribution	0.00	1.90	3.80	7.60	11.40	15.20	19.00	38.00
= Net incomes	130.00	133.10	136.20	142.40	148.60	154.80	161.00	192.00
+ Housing benefit	0.00	0.00	0.00	0.00	0.00	0.00	0.00	0.00
− Rent	15.00	15.00	15.00	15.00	15.00	15.00	15.00	15.00
− Rates	7.00	7.00	7.00	7.00	7.00	7.00	7.00	7.00
= Disposable incomes	108.00	111.10	114.20	120.40	126.60	132.80	139.00	170.00

Note: If either pensioner has earned income, there is a tax discount of 38% of earnings, maximum £9.50 each.

20

Getting from here to there:
BIG PHASES 1 and 2

Having accepted that integration (even partial integration) would have to be introduced incrementally, and assuming agreement between the political parties that something close to *BI 2000* should be the target system, then everything would depend on political consensus, because every change must move in the chosen direction. Above all there must be no changes in the wrong direction. The Secretary of State for Social Services must stop widening the gap between benefits paid to single people and married couples, and the Chancellor must stop creating new income tax reliefs.

By the year 2000 the following major changes should be completed:

Abolished:
1. All NI contributions.
2. All NI benefits, including SERPS.
3. Income support and family credit.
4. All earnings rules.
5. All the personal income tax reliefs.
6. As many as possible non-personal income tax reliefs.

Introduced:
1. Transfer Income Account
1.1 Individual assessment units.
1.2 PBIs, PBI supplements and disability costs allowance (DCA).
1.3 A comprehensive income tax or BI contribution (BIC).
1.4 Earned-income tax discounts (TDs).
1.5 Work-related childcare TDs.

1.6 Any remaining non-personal tax reliefs become fixed amount TDs.

2. *Local authority cash and care departments*
2.1 New, income-tested housing benefit.
2.2 Means-tested emergency benefits/loans.
2.3 Greatly increased childcare provision.

3. *A new corporate tax replaces employer NI contributions*

Optional:
1. Hypothecation of the new income tax to the TIA.
2. Flat rate income tax or BI contribution.
3. Amalgamation of local authority Cash and Care departments.
4. New liability to maintain laws.
5. Housing benefit becomes conditional, and is linked to an income and work guarantee.

These changes would have a major impact on income distribution, between families and within families. The question becomes how best to move towards the target system with minimal upheaval, yet reaping the benefits as soon as possible. The proposals that follow show how the early period of transition might be approached. Phase 1 was costed using TAXMOD, at projected October 1988 incomes. It was designed as a revenue neutral alternative to the 1988 Budget, although it could not be implemented before the Inland Revenue are able to handle independent taxation of husband and wife, in April 1990. Phase 2, which unifies NI contribution with income tax and abolishes the contributory principle, has not been costed. It is more complicated, but should follow as soon as possible, in order to maintain the impetus of reform and reap maximum benefit from behavioural change.

There is, of course, nothing sacrosanct about the *BIG PHASE 1* described in this chapter.The detail can be altered almost endlessly, without undermining the basic strategy, and without losing revenue neutrality. But always there is a price to pay, and always the room for manoeuvre is rather narrow. The starting rate of income tax can be 25 percent, provided the PBIs are £10 instead of £10.50. The top rate of tax can be 40 percent, provided the income level at which it becomes payable is reduced, or the child PBIs are smaller. Mortgage interest and private pension tax reliefs do not have to be restricted to basic rate tax, but in that case something else has to give. Every change has a distributional impact, and most distributional changes have an impact on incentives. The *BIG PHASE 1* described here is one particular balancing act between a range of criteria. It tries to give priority to incentives, at every income level, but it is not immutable.

BIG PHASE 1

The main changes are summarised in Table 20.1. The objectives are threefold: to prepare the way for future change, to reduce dependence on *income support* and *family credit*, and to make the tax and benefit systems more symmetrical.

Table 20.1: *BIG PHASE 1*, main changes, 1988-89 prices and incomes

1. Replacement of personal income tax allowances by PBIs of £10.50 per person pw.
2. All NI benefits reduced by £10.50 pw, PBIs count as a resource for income support. Residual NI benefits and IS become tax-free.
3. Independent taxation of husband and wife.
4. First £20 pw of earned income becomes tax-free.
5. Standard rate of income tax becomes 27 percent.
6. Top rate of income tax becomes 45 percent.
7. All non-personal income tax reliefs restricted to 27 percent.
8. Child benefit becomes child PBI and goes up to £10.50 pw.
9. Work-related childcare costs up to £2,000 pa become tax-free.
10. Increased public expenditure on child day-care.
11. One-parent benefit restricted to lone parents with a child under five.
12. Standard rate of Class 1 NI contribution becomes 9%. No contracting-out.
13. PBI supplements of £4 pw for each person aged 65 or over, for people with disabilities, and for carers.
14. Consequential adjustments to age allowance. Married pensioners can choose joint taxation.
15. Abolition of earnings rule for pensioners.

BIG PHASE 1: first objective
To prepare the way for future change

Tax reliefs. Right from the start, it has to be made clear that the days of tax-free mortgages and tax-free private pensions are numbered. By the turn of the century, if we are to move in the direction of *BI 2000*, savings for house purchase and old age should be competing on equal terms with savings for industry. The pension funds, like the monasteries and the mediaeval barons, must forfeit their privileges. Mortgagors need to be warned that all mortgage interest tax relief will be phased out by the year 2000. By keeping the ceiling for tax relief at its present limit of £30,000, its cost can be contained. It can be diminished forthwith by restricting the relief to a fixed 27 percent of eligible interest, and it can be phased out by making further, annual reductions until there is none left.

Phasing out pension tax reliefs is more difficult. One difficulty is their diversity and the comparative ease with which one can be substituted for another. If they are phased out in a piecemeal way, people will rearrange their affairs and the overall cost will go on rising. The first step, as with mortgage interest, is to limit tax relief for employees' superannuation and self-employed annuities to 27 percent of eligible contributions. Additionally, an across the board strategy is needed that will protect accrued rights, yet prevent the growth of new ones. This could be along the lines set out by Philip Chappell and Nigel Vinson on a number of occasions (Chappell and Vinson 1983 and 1985; Chappell 1988) and summarised below:

- All employees' and self-employed contributions become tax deductible.
- All employers' contributions are taxed as a benefit in kind.
- Even the promise of a future pension is taxed as a benefit in kind, and the pay of the civil service and armed forces is adjusted accordingly.
- All existing private sector schemes are closed off and their members given the right to take their assessed share out of the fund.
- Tax relief for employers' new schemes is restricted to a nominal amount of perhaps £250 per employee.
- All lump sum commutations become taxable as income.
- No exemption from capital gains tax on new funds.

Retirement age. Assuming agreement that a full BI will not be payable before age 65 (except for people with disabilities and carers), transitional arrangements would be necessary to protect women in the 60-65 age-group already drawing a full retirement pension, and others below age 60 with sufficient contributions to entitle them to one. This would be a relatively simple matter of excluding women in the 60-65 age-group from the PBI old age supplement and closing off all further contributions, thus leaving a dwindling number with acquired rights to Category A and small amounts of earnings-related pension. Phase 1 reduces Category A pension by the amount of the PBI, and each subsequent PBI increase (above the rate of inflation) would be similarly deducted.

State earnings-related pension. The build-up of SERPS would have to stop. Existing entitlements must be honoured, but no new entitlements allowed to accrue. As the PBI old-age and disability supplements build up, pensioners would have the choice of drawing either their SERPS entitlement or the PBI supplement, but not both. Pending unification of NI contribution with the new income tax, which is left to Phase 2, immediate action is also necessary to prepare for the unified tax rate, and to stop the flow of new savings into SERPS by those who currently pay NI contribution at the contracted-out rate. It is proposed that the standard rate of Class 1 NI contribution be made 9 percent for all employees, and the right to contract-out be stopped forthwith. Any future payments by contracted-out contributors would be on a voluntary and non-statutory basis.

The extra revenue in 1988-89 as a result of this change is nearly £2,000 million, which is sufficient to finance old age, disability and carers' PBI supplements of about £4 a week.

BIG PHASE 1: second objective
To reduce dependence on income support and family credit

Reduced dependence on income support is given top priority, because of the way IS excludes unemployed people and lone parents from the labour market. In 1985 about 40 percent of families with four or more children were out of work (Appendix 5, Table A.5.2.), which cannot be right. The long-term aim is to let everyone earn as much as they can without forfeiting their right to basic income protection, and without disobeying the law. If the earnings rules with existing benefits were made more generous, as is sometimes suggested, this would merely add to the number of people out of work. But if existing benefits, together with their attendant earnings rules, can be phased out, there is a new ball game.

Family credit is the second target, because of its poverty trap effects. In a free and prosperous society there is no justification for turning parents into paupers. *BIG PHASE 1* starts the liberation process. Using TAXMOD, it is estimated that the number of working families with children subject to marginal tax rates of more than 70 percent would go down by at least a fifth.

The essence of the proposal is very simple and was put forward by Sir Brandon Rhys Williams MP in the House of Commons on several occasions (eg House of Commons, 2 Nov 1987, cc. 688-697), although he did not quote any figures, and might not have approved all the changes recommended here. Every man, woman and child would receive a small automatic credit or PBI, which would replace all existing personal tax allowances and child benefit. For those in paid work the PBI would be an offset against tax, for those receiving NI benefits or IS it would be an offset against benefit entitlement. Additionally the first tranche of earnings would be tax-free. The effect is to give each unemployed person or lone parent a choice between remaining on IS , with all its rules and regulations, or using the new PBIs and earned-income tax reliefs as stepping stones to financial independence. Figure 20.1, which assumes PBIs of £10.50, shows how IS becomes a much smaller part of the total benefit package. There is no change to overall entitlement, but with *BIG PHASE 1* only half of it carries an earnings rule.

Figure 20.1: BIG PHASE 1, options for the unemployed
PBIs as a proportion of income support, 1988-89

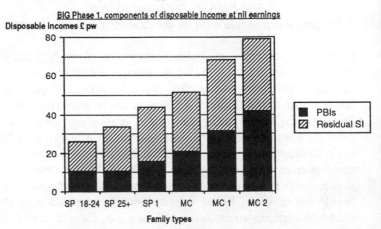

Assumptions: SP 1 includes one-parent benefit, child under 5.
        MC 1 and MC 2 children are under 11.
Source: Appendix 2.

If it had been possible to implement *BIG PHASE 1* in April 1988, a couple with two small children would now start from an unconditional, guaranteed weekly income of £42 compared with £79 on IS. If the father lost his job they would have a choice. Either they could stick with their PBIs (plus housing benefit and residual family credit), in which case they would be free to earn as much as possible, and the first £20 pw earned by each spouse would be tax-free; or they could top up their PBIs with IS, in which case their earnings would be restricted to £5 per spouse, and the husband would be subject to an availability for work test. A lone mother with a child under five would start from a guaranteed income of £25.90, compared with £54 on IS. If she chose not to take IS and found a job that necessitated day-care for her child, she would be able to earn £58.50 before becoming liable to any income tax.

BIG PHASE 1: third objective
To make the tax and benefit systems more symmetrical

The decision to recognise the existence of married women in the tax system is a major step forward, but the structure of allowances put forward in the 1988 Budget is anything but symmetrical. Taking the

Figure 20.2: Symmetry, BIG PHASE 1

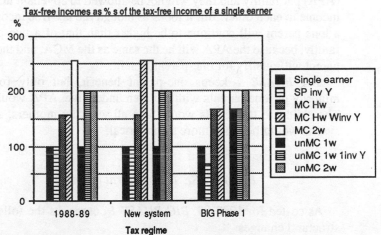

Acronyms: SP = single person, inv Y = investment income, MC = married couple, H = husband, W = wife, w = waged, 2w = two-wage, 1w = one-wage, unMC = unmarried couple.
Source: Appendix 2.

365

single earner without children as the reference point, Figure 20.2 compares the relativities implied in the tax-free incomes of various households, mostly two-adult, and all without children. As we saw in Chapter 5, the only arithmetical difference between Mr Lawson's new system and the existing system is that a married couple where the wife has investment income will get 257 percent of the allowance of a single person, instead of 157 percent. The married couple's allowance (MCA) will put married couples at an advantage compared with single people and unmarried couples, whether their incomes are earned or unearned. By 1990, when the new system is introduced, the Secretary of State for the Environment will hold married and unmarried (heterosexual) couples "jointly and severally liable" for each other's poll tax, and the Secretary of State for Social Services will continue to impose a mutual liability to maintain. But for income tax purposes the unmarried couples will count as separate units, and will be ineligible for MCA. This is blatantly unfair.

By contrast *BIG PHASE 1* proposes tax-free incomes for adults without children that are completely symmetrical between men and women, married and single, earners and non-earners.

The position of families with children in Mr Lawson's new system was not clear at the time of writing. Unmarried couples with children will be restricted to one additional personal allowance (APA) per family and they will not be allowed to covenant tax-free income to each other. But it looks as though the tax-free income of a lone parent will continue to be higher than that of a two-parent family, because the APA will be the same as the MCA, and the lone parent will qualify for one-parent benefit.

BIG PHASE 1 keeps one-parent benefit, but only for the minority of lone parents with children under five. APA would go. The childcare tax reliefs would help all working mothers, so the system would be much more symmetrical.

BIG PHASE 1: Structural changes

As costed for 1988-89, *BIG PHASE 1* comprises the following structural changes:

A universal PBI of £10.50. Instead of single person's and married man's tax allowances each person receives a non-contributory, non-withdrawable, tax-free PBI of £10.50 a week. There is no earnings restriction, and the assessment unit is the individual. The PBIs are deducted £ for £ from NI benefits and count as a resource for income support. The one exception is the main rate of invalid care allowance, to which the PBI is additional. This is in preparation for the carer's PBI supplement. Category A pension is reduced from £41.15 to £30.65 and Category B pension is reduced from £24.75 to £14.25. NI unemployment benefit becomes £22.25, and the amount for a dependent adult becomes £9.70. Income support becomes £8.90 for a 16-17-year-old, £15.55 for a single person aged 18-24, £22.90 from age 25, and £30.45 for a married couple. None of the premiums is affected.

The flat rate component of all residual NI benefits and income support (after deduction of the PBIs), but not any earnings-related element, becomes tax-free. This is a consequential change, to prevent unintended losses and to ensure that people do not have to pay tax on their benefits. It does not produce net income gains by comparison with the existing system, but it is easier to understand. No tax refunds could be claimed because all the income tax allowances would have been converted into PBIs.

Independent taxation of husband and wife. Each person is credited with his or her PBI. Husbands and wives are taxed separately on all their incomes. Residual Category B pension counts as the wife's income, but pensioner couples would be able to choose joint taxation. This is necessary to prevent losses where one spouse has less taxable income than the amount of the new age allowance.

Earned-income and childcare tax discounts. Instead of wife's earned-income allowance, everyone (including old age pensioners) can earn £20 pw free of tax. Unlike the PBIs, the earned-income TD does not convert into cash. It is non-transferable between husband and wife and non-cumulative. This is to prevent people from concentrating their earnings into a few weeks or months of each tax year. Self-employed people would be allowed to average their profits. Additionally, lone parents and second-earner parents would be able to put up to £38.50 pw for the first child and up to £23.10 pw for each successive child against income tax, on proof of payment to a registered nursery or childminder. All the reliefs are fixed amount TDs. The earned-income TD is worth £5.40 pw and the childcare TDs are worth a maximum of £10.40 for first children and £6.24 for successive children.

Child benefit becomes child basic income, and goes up from £7.25 to £10.50. As a result of this change, IS rates can be reduced to 25 pence for children aged 0-11, £5.60 for children aged 11-15, and £8.90 for 16-17-year-olds. Free school meals and welfare milk are unaffected. The difference between existing child benefit at £7.25 and the new child PBI at £10.50 is also deducted £ for £ from FC entitlement.

One-parent benefit is restricted to parents with children aged under five. The purpose is to improve symmetry between married and single. In 1988 one-parent benefit was £4.90 per family. The loss to parents with children over five is offset by the new childcare tax reliefs and increased childcare provision. In 1985 an estimated 69 percent of families receiving one-parent benefit had no child under age five, and nearly all of those who did have children under five were one-child families, where the benefit helps most (DHSS 1986 (C), Table 31.40).

£4 pw PBI supplements, paid for by abolition of Class 1 contracted-out NI contribution. The standard rate of NI contribution for all Class 1 contributors becomes 9 percent. The PBI supplements financed by this change would be non-contributory and without earnings restrictions. They would be payable, in addition to the PBIs and residual NI benefits, to each person aged 65 or over in receipt of NI pension or income support with pensioner premium; to each person in receipt of NI invalidity benefit, or income support with disability premium (but not their spouses or children); to each person receiving severe disability allowance; and to each person receiving invalid care allowance. They would count as a resource for income support and housing benefit.

Mortgage interest and superannuation income tax reliefs restricted to 27 percent. The purpose, as explained, is to prepare for abolition of the non-personal tax reliefs.

Abolition of the pensioner earnings rule. Retirement pension becomes old age pension. Women from age 60 and men from age 65 are free to earn as much as they like without loss of pension.

Age allowance (AA) is increased to £1,040 per person per year (£20 pw), and the upper limit comes down to £8,460 (£163 pw). The changes here are complicated but almost entirely consequential. The new AA equals the difference between existing AA for a single pensioner and existing Category A pension. The upper limit is reduced because the basic pension has become tax-free. As before the new upper limit is the same for married and single, but the AA for couples takes longer to phase out than for singles, since it is twice as big. For low income single pensioners the total amount of tax-free income remains unchanged, but for those with incomes above the new AA upper limit the amount of tax-free income is reduced by £8.95 (ie the difference between existing single person's tax allowance and Category A pension). For married pensioners the new AA becomes twice the amount for single people, ie £40. In cases where one spouse has no income, and either is aged 65 or more, the couple can choose joint taxation. Low income single pensioners neither lose nor gain as a result of the change, married couples with income below the AA upper limit gain slightly, but pensioners with income above the AA upper limit pay slightly more tax than at present.

Strictly speaking the AA upper limit should be reduced by a further £208 pa (£4 pw) to offset the new £4 PBI supplement. This would enable the £4 supplement to be withdrawn through the tax system from better-off pensioners. By the year 2000, assuming that the target PBI plus PBI supplement of £65 pw had been reached, AA should have been phased out. A refinement is to extend the equivalent of AA (during the transition period) to people with disabilities. Neither of these changes was included in the costings. The first would reduce the overall net cost of the scheme, the second would increase it.

BIG PHASE 1 : How much would it cost?

Tax cuts in the 1988 Budget cost £6,000 million in terms of revenue forgone. The starting rate of income tax was reduced from 27 to 25 percent, at a full-year cost of £3,000 million, and the top rate was cut from 60 to 40 percent, at a full-year cost of £2,000 million. Income tax allowances were raised by twice the rate of inflation (approximately in line with earnings growth) at a full-year cost of £1,000 million, but child benefit was frozen, in order to save £220 million. Removal of the higher-rate tax bands was linked to far-reaching reform of capital taxation, and is expected to pay for itself in increased revenues before the end of this Parliament.

Were it not for the two-year delay necessary to introduce independent taxation of husband and wife, *BIG PHASE 1* could have been introduced in April 1988 on a revenue neutral basis, provided that the starting rate of income tax had been held at 27 percent, the top rate of tax had been reduced to 45 percent instead of 40 percent, and tax relief for mortgage interest and superannuation had been restricted to 27 percent.

All the proposals except items 8-10 in Table 20.2 have been costed using TAXMOD. Each change or group of changes was fed in and the computer was asked to calculate the net cost or gain to the revenue as a result of that change, as well as the cumulative effects of all the changes. Increases in the thresholds for higher-rate tax are in order to prevent people at the cross-over points from being worse off. No account is taken in the costings of the behavioural effects of change, which are likely to be considerable. The black hole in this government's economic strategy has always been its indifference to incentives at the bottom. Instead of using his £6,000 million tax rebate to lift the lower paid out of tax and give them back their independence, Mr Lawson concentrated once again on the better off.

The figures in Table 20.2 assume no change to any of the other Budget proposals. There is an estimated revenue gain of £803 million before allowing for the childcare tax reliefs and the increased childcare provision. Of this £803 million, perhaps £300 million should be allocated to increased pre-school and after-school provision, and £500 million to the new tax relief. The behavioural effects of these changes would be at least as beneficial in budgeting terms (benefit savings plus increased tax revenues) as the cuts in higher-rate tax. The existence of childcare tax relief would encourage employers to set up workplace nurseries, which have become fewer in number since the 1986 tax changes counted them as a benefit in kind (Cohen 1988, page 95). More mothers would be able to afford to work, and more jobs would be created.

BIG PHASE 1 : Who gains and who loses?

Model family analysis. The most significant changes concern net incomes and net spending power. The PBIs increase net incomes at the bottom, and this increase is used to start the process of lifting the lower paid off the need for family credit and housing benefit.

Table 20.2: Big Phase 1 costings

	Estimated revenue loss (−), or gain (+), projected Oct 88 incomes	
	£ million itemised	£ million cumulative
1. Partial basic incomes (PBIs) of £10.50 pw/£546 pa for each adult, from age 18, replace all the personal IT allowances (including age allowance). The PBIs are deducted £ for £ from existing NI benefits and count as a resource for IS. Residual NI benefits and IS become tax-free IVB taxable like other benefits. Abolition of pensioner earnings rule. Starting rate of tax is 27%. Tax rate is 40% on incomes (excluding BIs) above £21,905 pa/£421.25 pw. Tax rate is 45% on incomes (excluding BIs) above £24,405 pa/£469.33 pw.		+10,047
2. Independent taxation of husband and wife.	−420	+9,627
3. New age allowance of £1,040 pa/£20 pw per person, with upper limit £8,460 pa/£162.70 pw. Married couples (either aged 65+) can choose joint taxation.	−1,082	+8,545
4. First £20 pw of earned income becomes tax-free. Fixed amount tax discount of £5.40 pw.	−6,466	+2,079
5. Child benefit becomes child PBI and goes up to £10.50. The extra £3.25 is deducted £ for £ from family credit and counts as a resource for IS. Net cost.	−1,793	+286
6. Mortgage interest and superannuation IT reliefs restricted to 27%.	+397	+683
7. Abolition of contracted-out NI contribution.	+1,914	+2,597
8. PBI supplement of about £4 for each person aged 65+ in receipt of NI retirement pension or IS with pensioner premium, each IVB claimant, each SDA claimant and each ICA claimant. Net cost.	−1,914	+683
9. One-parent benefit restricted to children under 5.	+120	+803
10. Work-related childcare tax reliefs and increased childcare provision.	−803	NIL
Overall Gross Revenue Gain/Loss		NIL

Sources: TAXMOD, London School of Economics. Except items 8, 9 and 10.
Item 8: Estimated on the basis of population breakdown in Appendix 1, Table A.1.1, and Treasury Jan 1988.
Table 15.6, less reduced expenditure on IS and housing benefit.
Item 9: Assuming that about 65% of families drawing OPB have no children aged under five (DHSS 1986 (C), Table 31.40). Also Treasury Jan 1988, Tables 15.1 and 18.12.

Acronyms: IS = income support. IT = income tax. IVB = invalidity benefit. SDA = severe disability allowance. ICA = invalid care allowance.

371

Disposable incomes remain unchanged, but the means-tested component is reduced, so fewer people are caught in the poverty trap. The childcare tax reliefs add to net incomes and net spending power, because the extra net income on this account is excluded from the family credit and housing benefit formulae. The idea is to encourage out-of-work families (especially lone parents with older children) into the regular labour market. Fewer families would be caught in the unemployment trap.

Tables 20.3 and 20.4 use model family analysis (TAXEXP) to illustrate the scale and pattern of change involved. Table 20.3 shows families with below average earnings and no mortgages. Table 20.4 starts at about three-quarters average earnings and ends up at just under five times average earnings. All the families have mortgages, at the amounts shown in the footnote. In practice many of them would also be paying superannuation contributions, but the figures do not show the effects of restricting superannuation tax relief to 27 percent. So on earnings above £400 a week the net income losses by comparison with 1988-89 would be larger than shown.

The first thing to notice is the very small scale of change at the bottom of the earnings distribution as a result of Mr Lawson's "humdinger" budget. It is astonishing that so much tax could be forgone to so little effect. For most families the gain was between £3 and £4 pw, although some two-wage couples did rather better. For people earning £50 pw there was no gain at all. On earnings above £400 pw (£21,000 pa) the gains go above £5. On earnings of £1,000 pw (£52,000 pa) single people gained £75 pw. *BIG PHASE 1* would have distributed the gains more evenly across the population, with a bias in favour of working families with children. Those at the top would still have made the biggest gains, but some lower paid families with children would have gained over £20.

By comparison with 1987-88 net incomes *BIG PHASE 1* produces gains for almost everybody, which is not surprising given the huge scale of Mr Lawson's tax cuts. By comparison with 1988-89 people in the middle of the earnings distribution would lose. The cross-over points, from gain to loss and then back to gain, vary between the different family types. Two-earner couples without children lose most, but two-earner couples with children tend to gain, partly because of the PBIs, but mainly because of the childcare tax reliefs. A family with two small children where the father earns £150 pw (above the ceiling for family credit) gains £10 by comparison with the existing system. Yet the notion that child

Table 20.3: BIG Phase 1 (BPI), net incomes of non-mortgagors earning up to £200pw, 1988 prices and incomes

| | Net incomes from gross weekly earnings of: | | | |
	£50	£100	£150	£200
1. Single person				
1987-88	47	77	109	141
1988-89	48	81	112	145
1988-89 (BP1)	50	82	112	144
2. Single-wage MC				
1987-88	48	84	116	148
1988-89	48	88	119	152
1988-89 (BP1)	60	92	122	154
3. Two-wage MC				
1987-89	—	95	130	160
1988-89	—	95	135	168
1988-89 (BP1)	—	100	132	164
4. Single-wage MC + 2 children				
1987-88	62	98	130	162
1988-89	62	102	133	166
1988-89 (BP1)	81	113	143	175
5. Two-wage MC + 2 children				
1987-88	—	110	145	175
1988-89	—	110	150	183
1988-89, BP1 (no childcare costs)	—	121	153	185
1988-89, BP1 (max. childcare tax relief)	—	129	170	202
6. SP + 2 children under five				
1987-88	67	103	135	167
1988-89	67	107	138	171
1988-89, BP1 (no childcare costs)	76	108	138	170
1988-89, BP1 (max. childcare tax relief)	84	124	154	186
7. SP + 2 children over five				
1987-88	67	103	135	167
1988-89	67	107	138	171
1988-89, BP1 (no childcare costs)	71	103	133	165
1988-89, BP1 (max childcare tax relief)	79	119	149	181

Assumptions: In the case of two-wage married couples the combined earnings come to the totals shown. On combined earnings of £100, each spouse earns £50, on combined earnings of £150-£500 the wife earns £100, and on combined earnings above £500 the wife earns £200.

Acronym: BPI = BIG Phase 1.

benefit is poor targeting is shown to be false. For despite the extra child support the same family earning £500 a week would be £7 a week worse off than at present.

The beneficial effects of the childcare tax reliefs are clearly visible, although at £50 pw the mother pays too little tax to be able to benefit in full. A lone mother with two children under five and a

Table 20.4: BIG Phase 1 (BPI) net incomes of mortgagors earning between £200 and £1,000pw, 1988 prices and incomes

	Net incomes from gross weekly earnings of:					
	£150	£200	£300	£400	£500	£1000
1. Single person						
1987-88	119	156	221	294	360	596
1988-89	121	159	225	300	371	671
1988-89 (BP1)	122	159	223	296	357	632
2. Single-wage MC						
1987-88	126	163	228	301	370	612
1988-89	128	166	232	307	382	683
1988-89 (BP1)	133	170	234	307	368	643
3. Two-wage MC						
1987-88	—	176	240	304	377	652
1988-89	—	183	247	313	387	696
1988-89 (BP1)	—	179	241	305	378	666
4. Single-wage MC + 2 children						
1987-88	140	178	242	315	385	627
1988-89	143	181	247	321	396	697
1988-89 (BP1)	154	191	255	328	389	664
5. Two-wage MC + 2 children						
1987-88	—	190	254	319	392	667
1988-89	—	197	261	327	402	710
1988-89 BP1	—	200	262	326	399	687
(no childcare costs)						
1988-89 BP1	—	217	279	343	416	704
(max. childcare TD)						
6. SP + 2 children under five						
1987-88	145	177	—	—	—	—
1988-89	147	180	—	—	—	—
1988-89 BP1	148	180	—	—	—	—
(no childcare costs)						
1988-89 BP1	165	197	—	—	—	—
(max. childcare TD)						
7. SP + 2 children over five						
1987-88	145	177	—	—	—	—
1988-89	147	180	—	—	—	—
1988-89 BP1	143	175	—	—	—	—
(no childcare costs)						
1988-89 BP1	160	192	—	—	—	—
(max. childcare TD)						

Assumptions: Mortgage is assumed to be £20,000 at earnings of £150 and for the lone parent at earnings of £150 and £200. Otherwise mortgage is assumed to be £30,000. Interest rate 10%. Distribution of earnings for two-wage couples, as in Table 20.3.

Acronym: BP1 = BIG Phase 1

wage of £100 would be £17 pw better off than at present, and most of the extra would not count against family credit. Provided that good childcare facilities can be made available, the incentive for lone parents to take work in the regular labour market would be greatly increased.

Without the £4 PBI supplement, few pensioners would notice much change in their net or disposable incomes by comparison with 1987-88, although married pensioners would benefit from the move to a marriage-neutral age allowance (AA) of £20 per pensioner, and most would welcome removal of the earnings rule. Women aged 60 to 65 would not get the £4 supplement. On the other hand they would be free to earn as much as they liked without loss of pension, and the first £20 earned would be tax-free. All would pay 2 pence more in the £ income tax by comparison with 1988-89. For people aged 65 or over the net effect of the PBIs, PBI supplement and AA changes, by comparison with 1988-89, is to leave single pensioners with up to £20 pw private pension/investment income £4 pw better off, and pensioner couples with up to £40 a week £8 pw better off. Once tax becomes payable the £4 supplement is gradually recouped, through the extra 2p on income tax. Those with incomes above the new AA pay would be paying more net tax than at present. Pensioners with no income of their own would neither lose nor gain, because the £4 would be used to lift them off income support. Table 20.5 sets out some illustrative figures.

Table 20.5: BIG PHASE 1: Pensioner net incomes, 1988-89 prices and incomes

	Existing system £ pw	BIG PHASE 1 £ pw
(1) *Single pensioner aged 65+*		
NI Category A pension	41.15	30.65
+ PBI	—	10.50
+ PBI Supplement	—	4.00
− Private pension	30.00	30.00
− Income tax	2.50	2.70
= Net income	68.65	72.45
(2) *Pensioner couple aged 65+*		
NI Category A + B pension	65.90	44.90
+ PBIs	—	1.00
+ PBI supplements	—	8.00
+ Private pension	40.00	40.00
= Income tax	2.27	0.00
= Net income	103.63	113.90

Actual family analysis. TAXMOD is less useful for measuring the redistributive effects of *BIG PHASE 1* than for the costings. This is because it cannot pick up the effects of the childcare tax reliefs, the increased childcare provision, the loss of one-parent benefit to families with children over five, nor the distribution of the £4 old-age supplements. Some of the reasons for this are explained in Appendix 1. TAXMOD shows a revenue gain of £683 million, which it translates into an average weekly loss of 44 pence per family. In fact there is no overall gain or loss. The whole of the £683 million goes to families with children, although the benefits from increased childcare provision would be indirect. This does not mean to say that all families with children would gain. Lone parents with children over five, and who did not benefit from the new childcare provisions, would lose. Within the overall income distribution there is also a transfer of £1,914 million away from future earnings-related pensions in favour of increased flat-rate provision now (£4 pw each) for people aged 65+, disability pensioners and carers. This is not essential. It is included here on the assumption that the agreed target system is *Basic Income 2000*.

Reference to the individual cases that TAXMOD prints out is most useful. It highlights the problem of invalidity pensioners, some of whom stand to lose significantly from the changes to their tax status. The £4 PBI supplement would not be enough to offset all the losses that would result as a result of putting invalidity benefit on the same basis as other benefits for tax purposes. Those affected would be invalidity pensioners with occupational pensions or investment income, and/or with spouses who were earning. There is an urgent need to rationalise the tax treatment of disability benefits. One way would be to extend the new age allowance to all invalidity pensioners, including those claiming severe disablement allowance or invalid care allowance.

TAXMOD also shows some unemployed families with small amounts of unearned income losing out. Most people aged less than 65 and wholly dependent on unearned income would lose out. If this were considered undesirable, one solution would be to allow everyone (at any age and whether or not disabled) a small amount of unearned income (perhaps £1,000 a year) tax-free. If the tax-free amount were in the form of an exemption (like age allowance) the cost need not be excessive, and it would help to encourage savings. But it is not part of the package described here.

BIG PHASE 2

The phase one changes could be introduced in a single Budget. The second phase is more complicated, with threefold changes: unification of NI contribution with income tax; abolition of the contributory principle; and reform of housing benefit.

These changes would require major new legislation, and the proposals that follow are intended only as a guide. They have not been costed, nor has it been possible to work out the distributional effects. The aim is to carry change further in the direction of *BI 2000*, with minimum delay and disruption.

BIG PHASE 2: *Unification of NI contribution with income tax*

Abolition of NI contribution is a pre-condition of integration, but it has far-reaching implications. The new income tax would subsume NI contribution, therefore the new marginal rate of income tax would have to go up, and would be the same for earned and unearned income. For most people in paid work the new rate would make little difference, since it would replace NI contribution. But for people who currently pay reduced rates of NI contribution, or with earnings above the upper earnings level (UEL) for NI contribution, unification would almost certainly result in higher tax bills. People with unearned income (from investments and/or occupational pensions), would also pay at a higher starting rate of tax.

Increased tax liability for those with earnings above the UEL is not hard to justify, on the contrary it is much easier to justify than the existing system, which taxes the lower paid at higher marginal rates than the well-to-do (Figure 5.1). Nor, in theory, is it hard to justify a system that taxes unearned income at the same rate as (or higher than) earned income. But in practice it would be very difficult to introduce a system that appeared to penalise people on small unearned incomes. This reinforces the case for an investment-income tax exemption. Another solution is to distinguish once again between marginal and average tax rates, and to protect low income pensioners by increasing the PBI old age and disability supplements. Using TAXMOD at October 1987 incomes, it has been provisionally estimated that a unified tax rate of 35 percent coupled with a £3 a week PBI supplement for people aged 65+ and invalidity pensioners would have been approximately revenue neutral, and would have left pensioners with up to £33 per person per week of own income (including SERPS) no worse off.

BIG PHASE 2: *Abolition of the contributory principle*

The second major implication of abolishing the NI contribution is that benefit entitlement ceases to depend on contribution record. Instead it depends on different mixtures of contingency, citizenship (or legal residence over a required period), and need.

Abolition of the contributory principle would be an immense step towards poverty prevention among the elderly and those with disabilities. But it is bound to cost money, and would take several years to phase in. On reaching age 65 (if that were the agreed age) every citizen would be entitled to the same PBI supplement, regardless of their contribution record. Likewise every person with a disability who was unable to do paid work would be entitled to the same disability supplement, whether or not they had contributed to national insurance. The aim, by the year 2000, is a PBI of at least £28 and a PBI supplement of £42, *at April 1988 prices*. Phase 1 produces a PBI supplement of £4 and Phase 2 should produce at least a further £3. But that is nowhere like enough. If progress is to be made, all the extra revenue as a result of restricting the private pension tax reliefs would need to be put into these supplements, not into reducing the marginal tax rate.

What would happen to unemployment benefit? *BI 2000* does not include a supplement for the unemployed, the idea being to replace the dole by a guaranteed income that is at least as high as IS, but does not inhibit initiative, or encourage families to split up. Paying people so long as they do not do paid work or training is the antithesis of *BI 2000*, so old-style unemployment benefit has to go. That does not imply that people who are unable to find paid work would be left with nothing to live on. Some would get more than at present. But it does follow that until such time as the PBIs are equal to half the married couple's IS scale rate (see next section), unemployed people must be permitted to choose between topping up their PBI with residual IS (if no work at all is available), or topping it up with part-time earnings plus family credit and housing benefit.

In terms of disposable incomes, most unemployed people would be largely unaffected by this change, but some would lose. A spouse or partner who became unemployed would lose the independent right to NI benefit, instead their benefit would depend on the income of the other spouse or partner. The way to overcome this problem is by increasing the PBIs, to which each person has an independent right, as fast as possible. It follows that any savings in benefit expenditures as a result of *BIG PHASE 1*, and any savings in tax expenditures as a result of further restrictions in mortgage tax relief, should be used to increase the PBIs, not to reduce the marginal tax rate.

BIG PHASE 2: Housing benefit reform

All BIG schemes reduce costs and remove the penalties for marriage in the existing system, by incorporating the householder element implied in most UK benefit structures within the new housing benefit. At April 1988 benefit rates, the IS scale rate for each person aged 18 or over would be standardised at £25.75, which is half the rate for a married couple. Deduct £10.50 for the PBI, and residual IS becomes £15.25. The difference of £7.65 between IS at £33.40 for a single person aged 25+ and half the married couple's rate becomes the householder element in the new housing benefit (as with BIG 1(a)).

This change removes the marriage/cohabitation penalty in the IS scale rates and reintroduces the traditional recognition of householder costs, which disappeared as part of the Fowler social security changes. It also reinforces the incentive to take paid work illustrated in Figure 20.1, because a further £7.65 is taken out of IS and reappears as a new band across the middle of each column, to which no earnings restrictions apply.

The new housing benefit would be income-tested, not means-tested. At nil income rent and water rates (but not mortgage interest) would be paid in full (subject to local ceilings), plus the householder element and 80 percent of rates or community charge. With each increase in net income, housing benefit would be withdrawn, preferably using a combined taper, which would speed up withdrawal of rate rebate. Those who would lose from this change are non-householders, especially those aged 25+ (who gained from the Fowler changes). Those who would gain are married couples and families with children.

BIG PHASE 2 would reinforce the impact of *BIG PHASE 1*. Marginal tax rates (excluding benefit withdrawal) would go up for some people, but average tax rates would come down. The lower paid would start to be lifted out of net tax, as a result of which the number of people caught in the poverty and unemployment traps would go down. Tax and benefits would move closer to marriage neutrality, and income support (with its horrendous taboo on paid work or training) would become a diminishing part of the total benefit package. Some people will throw up their hands in horror at the thought of yet another reform of housing benefit. But we are talking about the year 1991 or 1992. The housing benefit system introduced in April 1988 is unlikely to be in a happy state by then.

Conclusion: The obstacles are political

Income tax, NI contribution and benefits should be reformed together. Instead the integration debate is being stifled.

This enquiry started by drawing attention to the inadequacies of an income redistribution system that has its roots in the distant past. Mr Norman Fowler set out to improve the social security part of it, but did not succeed. His terms of reference were too narrow, his objectives were incompatible, and in any event the DHSS case-load depends too much on policies elsewhere in the system, especially taxation. The first and overriding precondition for successful reform of social security is to lift the lower paid, and people on small incomes generally, out of liability to tax. This requirement is steadfastly ignored.

In a first leader on 25th June 1986, *The Times* said:

> There is only one way to tackle reform in the late 1980's, and that is to oblige both the Treasury and the Department of Health and Social Security to see income taxation, employment tax (national insurance) and benefits as different parts of one single financial relationship with the state. This joint treatment would lead logically to the universal application of certain principles (such as equal treatment of the sexes)...The natural development of an integrated tax and social security system would also oblige government to confront contradictions. Instead, the Prime Minister has preferred to preserve them, clinging to an outmoded distinction between tax and national insurance on the one hand, and national insurance benefits and other "non-contributory" ones on the other. This has drastically impeded proper reform.

Why the intransigence? If the findings of this enquiry are correct, the Prime Minister was right not to jump on the full integration bandwagon, but wrong to try to stifle the debate.

Full integration is not feasible.
A partial BI is economically and technically feasible, but
only provided it is unconditional.
For this reason it may not yet be politically feasible.

Full integration is neither feasible nor desirable, and a negative
income tax is not integration at all, it is much more like an
uncontrollable extension of the existing system. Part of the Prime
Minister's seeming intransigence may stem from a confusion
between negative income tax and basic income, and from failure to
distinguish between full integration (abolition of all other benefits)
and partial integration, with income guarantees below subsistence
level and one part of the benefit system still run along conventional
lines. Like NIT, a full BI can be ruled out, but a partial BI is both
economically and technically feasible, and could be integrated with
the tax system. That was Lord Cockfield's conclusion in 1972, and
events since then have strengthened his case. Even so there is one
vital proviso. If integration is to function smoothly the BI has to be
unconditional, otherwise the new system becomes as inoperable as
the old. That is the nub of the problem, and that, almost certainly,
is why the Prime Minister does not like it.

The introduction of an unconditional BI, no matter how small,
would be revolutionary. The idea that able-bodied men and women
should get anything without working for it (or being prepared to
work for it) in the paid labour market, is not part of the protestant
work-ethic, and would be regarded by many as encouraging sloth.
The fact that the existing system already pays people for not
working, and actively discourages them from taking paid work or
training, is either overlooked or becomes the justification for
workfare. Before BI can become politically feasible, attitudes will
have to change.

The protestant work-ethic requires modification.
Government should be encouraging debate, not stifling it.

There is no *a priori* reason why a work-ethic that developed in
response to the early stages of industrialisation should have
perpetual validity. The technological, economic and sociological
revolution that has swept through Europe since World War 2 must
ultimately cause people to question the continuing relevance of a
work-ethic that puts so little value on unpaid work. Voters may not

understand the complexities of tax and benefit regulations, but they are not blind. Everywhere they see the paradox of high unemployment in the regular labour market, alongside a growing pile of unmet needs outside it, litter in the streets, families broken up, old people pushed into institutions and communities destroyed. A small, unconditional income guarantee of £10.50 a week, gradually increasing to £25 or £26, could help right the balance. The most likely alternative is workfare, or some other form of State compulsion. Workfare has theoretical appeal for many, but the administrative difficulties (and costs) are enormous. The advantage of an unconditional partial BI, with perhaps a work test and work guarantee linked to housing benefit at local level, is that the scale of the latter would be comparatively small, and more easily containable.

The speed with which an unconditional partial BI can become politically acceptable depends very much on government. So long as the power of the executive is used to manipulate public opinion in favour of the means test, the electorate will remain confused. But if government were to stop being doctrinaire and open up the debate, there could be progress.

Two nations or one nation?

As the century draws to its close there are two visions. The first vision rests on a view of society in which the devil takes the hindmost. Self-interest is the guiding force, wealth creation becomes an end in itself, there is one set of laws for the poor (including perhaps half the nation's children) and another for everyone else. The second vision tries to blend self-interest with sense of community. It stems from the one-nation or solidarity view of society. Wealth creation is encouraged as a means of preventing poverty (not for ostentatious self-indulgence), everyone is subject to the same ground-rules, taxes may be higher (initially), but there is no discrimination and no underclass, low income families are lifted out of tax, and benefit becomes a springboard to economic independence, instead of a trap.

In Britain it is the first vision that currently predominates. Many of the ideas now on offer have been imported from the United States of America, where extreme wealth and extreme poverty live side by side in shameless abandon. With luck the more extreme versions of this trend will turn out to be a temporary aberration, for the second vision is much more in line with British (and European) values.

Partial integration is economically and technically feasible, and in my view it is also desirable. If at this moment in time it is not politically feasible, that is because the full effects of current tax and benefit policies have yet to work their way through. "It will never happen", said one Government adviser, with categorical assurance. Let him bide his time. I put more reliance in the words of Barbara Wootton, herself a staunch supporter of basic income and life-long champion of the impossible:

> The limits of the possible constantly shift, and those who ignore them are apt to win in the end. Again and again, I have had the satisfaction of seeing the laughable idealism of one generation evolve into the accepted common-place of the next. (Wootton 1967, page 279)

Appendix 1:
Costing basic income

This appendix explains and compares two different methods of costing basic income. The first method, which will be called the *NA/SPI method*, uses a mixture of national accounts statistics, the Inland Revenue *Survey of Personal Incomes* and the Family Expenditure Survey (FES).The second method, which will be called the *FES* method, relies on computer models of the tax and benefit systems based on data from the Family Expenditure Survey. The Institute for Fiscal Studies (IFS) has been using one such model since the early 1980s. Similar work started at the London School of Economics in 1981 as part of the ESRC Programme on Taxation, Incentives and the Distribution of Income. The first LSE model for use on a micro-computer was designed in 1983, written by Atkinson and Sutherland and called TAXMOD. It is the model used for this enquiry, and the version used here was completed in spring 1988. Tax-benefit models are described in Atkinson and Sutherland 1988, and a short account by Sutherland is included in this appendix. It is emphasised that neither the NA/SPI method nor the FES method takes into account the behavioural effects of change.

NATIONAL ACCOUNTS STATISTICS/SPI METHOD

In 1972 Professor Meade presented his now famous paper *Poverty in the Welfare State*, (Meade 1972), in which he estimated that an unmodified social dividend scheme, with dividends/BIs equal to 1970 supplementary benefit (including average rents), would require a proportional tax on all other income of 53%.

The Meade costing formula had four main elements:

A   Cost of social dividends/basic incomes/tax credits
B   Savings on existing expenditure
C   Cost of abolishing income tax and employees' National
     Insurance contribution
D   New income tax base

The calculation of the required tax rate went as follows:

$$t = \frac{A - B + C}{D}$$

Putting figures to elements A, B and C presents no great difficulty. A is a function of the BIs, B and C can be obtained from the annual Public Expenditure White Papers, from Inland Revenue Statistics and (for points of detail) from Hansard Written Answers. The main problem concerns the new income tax (IT) base. Meade estimated the IT base by adding together the following components of personal sector incomes, taken from the annual *National Income and Expenditure (Blue Book)*: wages and salaries, pay in cash of HM Forces, income from self-employment, rent and net interest, pensions and other benefits from life assurance.

Similar techniques were used by Parker for the Basic Income Guarantee costings submitted by Sir Brandon Rhys Williams MP in evidence to the Meacher Committee Enquiry (Rhys Williams, 1982); and by Philip Vince for the Liberal Party (Vince, 1983).

In 1984 Professor A.B. Atkinson wrote a detailed critique of the Parker and Vince costings, and concluded that the tax rate necessary was probably at least 4 percentage points higher than those assumed and perhaps 10 percentage points higher (Atkinson, Apr 1984). The main reason for the discrepancies was the new income tax base. Atkinson pointed out that the Blue Book estimates differed significantly from the income actually taxed at that time, as recorded in the Inland Revenue *Survey of Personal Incomes* (SPI). He found it hard to reconcile the two estimates and concluded that the Blue Book:

> does not seem...a satisfactory basis for estimating the size of the tax base under a social dividend or tax credit scheme,

and that:

it seems preferable to work "constructively" from the existing tax base, considering the way in which it would be extended. (Atkinson Apr 1984, page 22)

All subsequent BIG costings (including those in Parker 1984) have used tax base figures that build up from the SPI, specifying the estimated amounts by which each of the main non-personal income tax reliefs reduces the existing tax base. The figures, which were calculated by the Inland Revenue for Sir Brandon Rhys Williams MP, rely mainly on data from the Survey of Personal Incomes, but also include data from the FES and the Blue Book (Table A.1.5).

In the same 1984 paper, Atkinson also drew attention to the dangers of assuming that the income tax base would automatically be increased by the full amount of the non-personal income tax reliefs withdrawn under any scheme:

Under the Parker scheme the tax base would be extended in a number of ways. It is not however clear that all of these would lead to additional revenue on the scale indicated by the present magnitude of the different items. There are certain areas where changes in behaviour seem inevitable. In particular, the extension of the tax base to include employee pension contributions is likely to lead to a switch to non-contributory schemes. (Atkinson Apr 1984, page 22)

Atkinson quoted evidence submitted by Richard Hemming to the Meacher Committee that:

there is no Inland Revenue requirement that employees contribute to exempt approved schemes: only employers must contribute. The most likely outcome is that most schemes would become non-contributory. Employers would make what were previously employees' contributions. (Hemming, House of Commons 1983, 20-11, App. 32, para 4)

This criticism is important, because extension of the tax base by removal of some or all of the non-personal income tax reliefs is central to many BI proposals. If the reliefs cannot be removed piecemeal, the answer may be to remove them *en masse*. Moreover, since the obstacles are mainly political, it seems right to show their estimated costs in full, not a watered down version of them that implicitly assumes they are beyond the pale. In 1985-86 the income tax base is estimated to have been reduced by around £30,000 million on account of private pension tax reliefs, without taking into account the reliefs on civil service and armed forces non-contributory pensions. The method used to calculate the income tax base is shown in Table A.1.4, below. Following Atkinson (Apr. 1984), a distinction is drawn between lower- and upper-bound estimates.

Costing formulae

Using the NA/SPI method, there are three formulae for costing BI:

Formula 1. This is the Meade formula. To find the rate of tax on all income except the BIs, add together the costs of the proposed BIs, and the costs of abolishing existing income tax, Advance Corporation Tax and NI contributions (IT, ACT & NIC); deduct the anticipated savings on existing public expenditure (S); divide the balance by the estimated new income tax (IT) base, and multiply by 100. Note that ACT is included because it will be replaced by the new income tax, not because there is any intention of removing liability to tax on investment income:

$$\text{Tax rate} = \frac{\text{BI} + \text{IT, ACT \& NIC} - \text{S}}{\text{New IT base}} \times 100$$

Formula 2. Formula 1 calculates the rate of tax necessary to fund the basic incomes and to maintain the existing level of public expenditure on programmes other than income support, without any other tax changes. Under the existing system there is no *a priori* reason why the revenues from IT and NI contributions should exactly equal public spending on income support, indeed it would be extraordinary if they were to do so. Put this way the Formula 1 can be simplified as follows:

$$t = \frac{x + y}{\text{new IT base}}$$

where x is the cost of the BIs (including administration) and y is the amount of revenue currently raised by income tax for purposes other than income support.

Formula 3. If it were decided to introduce a BI system, it would make sense to hypothecate all the revenues from the new income tax (or BI contribution) to the Transfer Income Account (TIA). In Chapter 20 (*Basic Income 2000*) the revenues from the new corporate tax that would replace employer' NI contributions are assumed to be approximately equal to "y" in Formula 2, and are used for general government spending, not the TIA. Thus the formula for a fully hypothecated TIA becomes:

$$t = \frac{x}{\text{new IT base}}$$

where x is the cost of the BIs, including administration.

In Chapters 9 and 14 the costings use modified versions of Formula 1, and the outcome depends crucially on the assumptions made about savings on existing expenditure and the size of the new IT base. In Chapter 20 the costings use Formula 3, and the outcome depends on the IT base.

It is sometimes assumed that the IT base is equal to income-based Gross Domestic Product (GDP), or even National Income, but this is incorrect. GDP includes employer NI contributions, trading profits of companies, the trading surplus of public corporations, etc. as well as income from employment, self-employment and rent. In 1985-86 GDP was about £360,000 million (Treasury, Mar 1986, Table 2.5), whereas the maximum IT base, even assuming abolition of every personal and non-personal IT relief (including employers' contributions to private pensions) has been estimated by the Inland Revenue at perhaps £239,000 million. The IT base would be even lower during the initial stages of a transition to BI, while the non-personal income tax reliefs were being phased out, or if some of the non-personal IT reliefs were retained permanently.

A full list of all the allowances and reliefs that can in theory be set against income tax is included in Appendix 4. Even assuming that it were politically possible for government to abolish all these reliefs, some of the losers would require compensation, for instance through higher rates of interest. In his Discussion Paper (Atkinson, Apr 1984) Professor Atkinson noted that it would be especially difficult to tax the incomes of charities, and the interest on British Government securities where the owner is not ordinarily resident in the UK. These tax reliefs are therefore shown separately in all the costings.

389

Appendix 1: Costing Basic Income

It is emphasised that most of the figures used for costing BIG 1(a) and *BI 2000* were obtained during 1986. By now some of the figures will have been revised, but the differences should not alter the validity of the overall conclusions, which in any case are extremely tentative. Between them the formulae have four main components: the cost of the BIs, the cost of abolishing existing income tax and NI contribution, the likely savings on existing expenditure and the income tax base. Other components, for instance revenue from higher-rate tax or from employers' payroll taxes, are relatively straightforward.

Main components

(1) Cost of the basic incomes, population figures

The cost of the BIs varies according to each scheme. But the gross cost of each scheme starts off by multiplying the proposed rates of

Table A.1.1: UK population statistics

Age-group	Mid-1985 estimates		Projections for year 2000
0-4		3,610,400	3,997,000
5-10		4,093,700	4,916,000
11-15		4,058,200	3,800,000
Total children		11,762,300	12,713,000
16-17		1,800,700	1,434,000
18-59		31,351.700	32,693,000
60-64		3,145,600[1]	2,829,000[2]
Of which, 63-64	1,303,000		1,097,000
65 and over		8,557,600	9,190,000
Of which:			
65-69	2,540,000		2,520,000
70-79	4,226,100		4,264,000
80-84	1,108,000		1,244,000
85 and over	683,500		1,162,000
Total Population		56,617,900	58,859,000
Of which:			
total adults		44,855,600	46,146,000
total children		11,762,300	12,713,000

Notes:
1. Men: 1,494,300; women: 1,651,300.
2. Men: 1,378,000; women: 1,451,000.
Source: OPCS Sep 1987.

390

BI by the number of people in each population sub-group or demogrant, and then adding them together. The population figures used are in Table A.1.1.

(2) Cost of abolishing income tax, ACT and NI contributions

Table A.1.2: Receipts from IT, ACT and NICs

	1985-86 £m
Income tax	36,492
Employers' NICs	12,337
Employees' NICs	11,045
Self-employed NICs	700
Voluntary Class III	30
State scheme premiums	289
Advance corporation tax	3,814
Total	64,707

Source: Hansard WA 11 Jun 1986, c 197.

(3) Savings in existing expenditure

Savings in existing expenditure falls into two categories, first the savings on social security and other cash benefits (including administration) that would almost certainly be abolished as result of a move to BI, and second a grey area of possible additional savings that would depend on the government of the day.

All the figures assume that all existing DHSS benefits would be abolished, including housing benefit and supplementary benefit. Improved disability incomes and the reduced need for welfare rights counselling would undoubtedly result in savings by social services departments. If everybody were guaranteed enough to live on, the case for agricultural subsidies also wears very thin. A BI (even a partial BI) at European Community level could be linked to phasing out of the Common Agricultural Policy. In the UK introduction of a full BI for elderly people could be linked to a gradual phasing out of public sector pensions. In 1985-86 the MSC spent over £2,000 million on employment and training measures of one sort or another. With BI some or all of these measures might cease to be necessary. Finally, there is the savings due to behavioural effects, especially the effects on economic activity and family life.

These are controversial changes. For the costing calculations in Chapters 9, 14 and 19 the upper-bound, and more controversial, figures are used to estimate the cost of full BI, and the lower-bound figures are used for partial BI, unless otherwise specified. Thus the £500 million saving on MSC grants and allowances is no more than the saving as a result of reducing existing entitlements by the amount of the PBIs. Savings on child dependency additions have not been taken into account. The savings of £717 million on student grants and allowances assumes that the existing student support system would be abolished. With full BI this would clearly be the case. With BIG schemes the saving on student maintenance is partly offset by increased entitlement to housing beneft. Ideally there should also be either loans or grants to cover the costs of books, equipment, etc.

The administrative costs of BI depend on the particular scheme chosen, and on the extent to which means-tested benefits are retained. They are shown separately. Disability supplements and the DCA would clearly involve administrative expense, which would fall on the C&C Departments and would partly offset savings elsewhere. Overall expenditure on personal social services is assumed to fall by £500m (lower bound) and £1,000m (upper bound). The figures are most uncertain. Cost of the new housing benefit, including administration, is shown separately, as are the administrative costs of the TIA.

Allowance should also be made for the savings on state earnings-related pension (SERPS), which would be abolished with most BI schemes. The figure of £4,000m used in Table A.1.3. is based on the Government Actuary's estimated expenditure of £5,300 million (at November 1985 prices) in the year 2003-04. For 1985-86 the figure has been discounted by 1.5% per year for assumed, real earnings growth over 18 years. From the year 2003-04 onwards the cost of SERPS is expected to increase substantially, but the figures do not take this into account.

Note that with all BIG schemes statutory sick pay is assumed to remain unchanged, at a cost of £560 in 1985-86 (Hansard WA 13 May 1987, c 231). This is the amount rebated by Government to the employers in 1985-86 and is classified as *negative income*.

Table A.1.3: Savings on existing public expenditure

| | 1985-86 | |
	Lower bound £m	Upper bound £m
Social security benefits (UK), excluding administration[1]	40,969	
Maintenance element of student grants[2]	707*	
Free school meals[3]	270*	
MSC grants and allowances (+N.Ireland equivalent)[4]	500	1,156
Cost of rate rebates[5]	1,550	
Costs of administration: DHSS benefits, income tax, MSC grants and allowances, housing benefit[6]	2,758*	3,057
Personal social services[7]	500?	1,000?
Estimated savings	47,264?	48,719?
Possible additional savings:		
State earnings related pension[8]		4,000
Agricultural subsidies (CAP)[9]		1,857
Public sector pensions, savings assuming tax rate of 70%[10]		4,082
MSC expenditure on employment and training measures, excluding the £1,156m shown above[11]		1,000
Statutory sick pay (SSP)		560
Possible total savings, upper bound		60,218?

1. Public Expenditure White Paper (PEWP) 1987, Cm 6.11, Table 2.11.
2. Hansard WAs: 3 June 86 cc 478-9 (England/Wales)
   4 June 86 c 582 (N. Ireland)
   19 Jan 87 c 397 (Scotland).
3. For pupils only. Hansard WA 3 Jun 86, c 434, updated.
4. Hansard WA 19 Jan 87, c 405, assuming PBI is deducted from allowances payable with: adult training, YTS, Community Industry, Enterprise Allowance Scheme and Employment Rehabilitation. Hansard WA 4 Jun 86, c 583 (N.Ireland), re-calculated at 1985 prices. The figure of £1,156m is an estimate of the amounts that could be saved by full BI, not the total amounts on grants and allowances currently expended.
5. Hansard WA 3 Jun 86, c 432.
6. See Table A.1.4, administration costs.
7. PEWP 1987, Cm 56.11 Table 3.14. GB only. Total net expenditure on personal social services was £2,491m. The savings are to take account of the proposed DCA and BIs for carers.
8. SERPS is projected to cost £5.3 billion by the year 2003-04, at November 1985 prices (DHSS Jan 1986, Tables 1 and 2).
9. PEWP 1987, Cm 56-11, Table 3.4.
10. Hansard WA 23 Jul 86, cc 316-319, made up as follows:

	£m
Civil service	1,232
Local government	1,165
Teachers	1,193
NHS	821
Police	343
Fire	88
Armed Forces	865
Overseas	124
	5,831

11. Letter from Department of Employment to Sir Brandon Rhys Williams MP, 5 June 1986.
* Provisional

Table A.1.4: Administration costs

	1985-86 £ million UK
(a) Social Security benefits	1,828
(b) Housing benefit[1]	137
(c) Income tax[2]	793
Saving on administration: lower bound	2,758
(d) MSC and N. Ireland: equivalent schemes[3]	299
Saving on administration: possible higher bound	3,057

1. Item (b) represents the cost to local authorities of administering housing benefit. The cost to central Government of administration of this benefit cannot be identified separately, and is included in item (a).
2. The cost to central Government of the collection of income tax.
3. The cost of administering all MSC programmes in GB except the Skills Training Agency and Professional and Executive Recruitment and the costs of administering the N. Ireland schemes equivalent to those administered by the MSC.

Source: Hansard WA, 3 Jun 86, cc 431-3. Item (a) updated from PEWP Cm. 56-11. Table 2.11.

(4) The new income tax base

All the figures in Table A.1.5. assume abolition of all the personal income tax reliefs. The figures in Section 1 also assume abolition of all the non-personal income tax reliefs. The resulting tax base figure of £239,000 million is the upper-bound tax base for 1985-86. In Section 2 some of the non-personal tax reliefs are itemised. In Section 2(a) retention of reliefs for charities and for British government securities where the owner is not ordinarily resident in the UK reduces the tax base to £237,000 million. This is taken to be the highest realistic tax base figure. In Section 2(b) the private pension tax reliefs are also retained, reducing the tax base by a further £31,000 million, to £206,000 million. And in Section 2(c) mortgage interest tax relief is also retained, resulting in a tax base of £191,000 million. The figures throughout this section are cumulative.

The costings for partial BIs in Chapters 14 and 19 specify the tax base used. The residual cost of life assurance tax relief at 15%, which in 1985-86 came to about £640 million, is included in the numerator. The continuing cost of tax relief for life assurance, which was "abolished" in the 1984 Budget, underlines the length of time necessary to phase out acquired rights.

Appendix 1: Costing Basic Income

Table A.1.5: New income tax base

	1985-86[1] £ billion
Section 1: all reliefs abolished	
Total income covered by SPI[2]	214
+ pay below deduction card limit	1
+ NIRP not covered by SPI	7
+ NSB exempt income	1
+ Employees' contributions to occupational pension schemes[3]	4
+ Employers' contributions to occupational pension schemes[4]	14
+ Building Society deposit interest not covered by SPI, up to	5
+ Income (including lump sums) for life assurance and superannuation schemes not subject to tax (including some taxable income not covered by SPI)[5], possibly	12
	258
Less NIRP and taxable social security benefits	19
= BI tax base, upper bound	239
Section 2: LESS any tax reliefs retained:	
(a): charity, etc. reliefs retained	
− income of charities and scientific research organisations[6]	1
− exemption of interest on British Government securities, where the owner is not ordinarily resident in the UK[6]	1
= BI tax base, first lower bound	237
(b): private pension reliefs retained	
− self-employed retirement annuities	1
− employees' contributions to occupational pension schemes	4
− employers' contributions to occupational pension schemes	14
− income (including lump sums) for life assurance etc, possibly	12
= BI income tax base, second lower bound	206
(c): mortgage interest relief retained	
− mortgage interest	15
= BI income tax base, third lower bound	191

Notes:
1. Projected from 1983-84, therefore provisional.
2. These include: wages and salaries: £159b.
               self-employment income: £19b.
3. Not included in SPI, because when employers hand over PAYE the tax is calculated on a net of occupational pension contribution basis. The figures are taken from CSO occupational pension scheme statistics.
4. Information is taken from individual items in the Blue Book.
5. Treated as a benefit in kind. Blue Book updated by Monthly Digest of Statistics, Dec 1986, Table 1.4.
6. Estimate only. Inland Revenue Statistics 1986, Table 1.5, grossed up.

Source: Inland Revenue Jun 1986.

FES METHOD, USING TAXMOD
by Holly Sutherland

This is the technique used for costing *BIG PHASE 1* in Chapter 20. The general principle behind this method is to calculate the net effect of a policy change on the income of each family in the population. The sum of these effects gives the total net revenue cost or gain of the policy change. In order to calculate the effect on an individual family, each component of the personal tax and benefit systems is worked out, including those parts which interact. Using gross earnings, investment income, housing costs and so on of the individual family as inputs, final net income is calculated, first for the base or current system and then for the policy change under consideration. The changes in net income, and the changes in each component of net income (eg income tax, child benefit) for each family are added up, and the sum of all the changes in net income equals the net change in government revenue. Thus a gain in net income for an individual family is a net loss to the government, and *vice versa*. Changes in the amounts of particular benefits received by families are also added up, giving the gross cost of each of these to the government. Similarly, changes in the amounts of income tax or NI contributions paid by individuals add up to changes in tax revenues.

Of course, information in the required detail is not available for the whole population, and calculations on this scale would in any case not be feasible. What is needed is a sample of families that is manageably small but adequately representative of the whole population. All the significant, possible variations in family composition (by tenure, age, income level, sources of income, region etc.) must be represented, and they must be represented in proportion to their actual occurrence in the population.

The accuracy of the technique for costing purposes depends on the quality of the data chosen to represent the population, the precision with which the component parts of the tax-benefit system are modelled, and the validity of the assumptions adopted about how the system actually operates, for example how the take-up of means-tested benefits is modelled, or how the model accounts for tax avoidance.

TAXMOD is a user-friendly computer model, written for IBM-PCs and compatibles. Details of TAXMOD are available in Atkinson and Sutherland (1988, Chapter 3). TAXMOD uses all 5,824 FES family units interviewed between April and November

1982. The FES is designed to be representative of the whole UK household population, but for two reasons some adjustments are necessary. Firstly, there is evidence that certain types of household (for example the very rich, the very poor and older people) are less likely to respond than others. Secondly, there have been changes since 1982, particularly in family composition and housing tenure. Adjustments are made to correct for both these problems simultaneously, by attaching differential weights to each observation, depending on its characteristics. This method is described in Chapter 8 of Atkinson and Sutherland (1988). Income variables and housing costs have also been updated from their 1982 values to 1988-89 levels, in line with inflation.

Although the FES provides a rich source of data on income and family circumstances, it was not designed with tax-benefit models in mind. When modelling the current system, approximations have to be made and estimates rather than actual values used. For example, although the amount of NI contribution paid by an individual is recorded, there is no mention of whether or not the individual is contracted out of SERPS, or paying at the married women's lower rate. This information has to be approximated by working backwards through the rules governing NI contribution assessment, using earnings and NI contribution payments as inputs. Although the results of this technique are broadly in line with official sources, they may not be correct in individual cases.

Trying to model a new system can present additional difficulties where the administrative details are different. For a BI scheme the definition of income (for tax, BIs and means-tested benefits) is clearly crucial. TAXMOD uses definitions of taxable and non-taxable income appropriate to the current system, but for a BI scheme these might not be the same. The introduction of new benefits, for instance the PBI supplements contingent on certain types of disability in BIG 1(a) and *BI 2000* cannot be modelled accurately, because the only data available from the FES on disability concerns receipt of benefits currently available to the disabled. Nor is there any information in the FES about childcare costs. Any modelling of a childcare tax discount would have to use estimated costs, based on family composition, hours of work and numbers and ages of children. This is unlikely to be accurate, therefore the TD in BIG PHASE 1 was not modelled.

In large part, the programme calculates taxes and benefits, rather than using the values reported in the FES. This is because we wish to make a comparison with a policy alternative, where the amounts must of necessity be calculated. The calculation involves a number of assumptions, for instance that all income (other than under-stated self-employment income) is declared to the authorities, and that income is received at the same rate throughout the tax year. Wherever possible we have however used the data on actual benefit receipt. For example, the amount of NI retirement pension is based on the observed amount, including additional pension, increments for deferred retirement, incomplete contribution records, etc. TAXMOD also allows for non-take-up of certain means-tested benefits. This is allocated at random, with the probability designed to secure the observed, proportionate take-up, allowing for different take-up rates for pensioners and taking some account of the interaction between the take-up of different benefits.

Finally, it should be stressed that the model takes no account of behavioural change. It assumes that gross incomes are the same before and after a policy change. This is not too much of a problem when modelling the effects of a marginal change, or the first-round effects of a major change. However, for schemes that are specifically designed to induce a change in behaviour, for instance to encourage more part-time working, there are difficulties in modelling the final effect.

NA/SPI AND TAXMOD COSTING METHODS COMPARED

Each method has its advantages, disadvantages and limitations. Ideally both would be used, but in practice it is more realistic to use whichever is more suitable for the required purpose. The FES method, assuming a well-constructed model, is by far the best for measuring transitional change (like *BIG PHASE 1*) but can be misleading if used to cost major reform packages like Minford's NIT, BIG 1(a) or *BI 2000*. This is because it cannot estimate the effects of changes that do not directly alter the net incomes of the families in the survey, or that are inaccessible through the survey. In 1985 the IFS checked on the 1982-83 BIG 1(a) costings in Parker (1984), using their own model, and concluded that BIG 1(a) had a net cost of £10,000 million (Dilnot 1985). Careful analysis showed that some of the apparent deficit was due to errors or misunderstandings, and the balance could be accounted for by the fact that the IFS tax-benefit model took no account of abolition of the pension tax reliefs, nor of savings in administration, nor of the extra revenue as a result of replacing employers' NI contribution by a 10 percent payroll tax (Parker 1985).

(1) Expenditure savings outside the personal sector. TAXMOD cannot pick up the effects of administrative savings following a switch to BI. Using national accounts statistics the estimated gross savings in administration in 1985-86 were between £2,700 million and £3,400 million, depending on which BI scheme was chosen, and the net savings were an estimated £1,700 million. The likely savings in personal social services are not known, but £500 million is allowed for in Table A.1.2. Other operational savings are not known.

(2) Effects of abolishing income tax reliefs. Although TAXMOD takes into account the effects on net incomes of abolishing mortgage interest and superannuation tax reliefs, it cannot measure the net income effects of taxing pension lump sums, investment income of pension funds or employer contributions to private pensions. The upper-bound increase in the tax base on account of those changes was £26,000 million in 1985-86, which implies extra revenue at 38 percent tax of £9,800 million. Even assuming that only half the tax reliefs were removed, the extra revenue would still have been nearly £5,000 million. The total, together with items under (1) above, is over £7,000 million.

(3) Changes to employers' NI contributions. Some BIG schemes, including BIG 1(a), replace employer NI contributions by a 10% payroll tax. The revenue does not necessarily equate to existing employer NI contributions, but neither the excess or shortfall would show up in a tax-benefit model. In 1985-86 total wages and salaries were about £159,000 million (Table A.1.5), so a 10% payroll tax would have produced £15,900 million compared with employers' NIC of £12,337 million (Table A.1.2).

(4) Exclusion of certain benefits from TAXMOD. Some benefits that would be abolished with BI may not be included in all tax-benefit models. TAXMOD, for instance, does not include supplementary benefit single payments. Additional requirements and benefits in kind through personal social services may also be excluded. Most BI schemes abolish student maintenance grants, but the only students who show up in the FES are those living in private households.

399

In conclusion the reader should be warned that neither method, used jointly or apart, can overcome the difficulty of trying to use data from a year in the past to measure the effects of major tax and benefit changes in a year in the future. In practice BI would be introduced incrementally. And for the measurement of incremental change a well-constructed tax-benefit model is undoubtedly the best method currently available.

Appendix 2:
Redistributive effects of integration:
model family analysis

Each year the DHSS publishes its own *Tax/Benefit Model Tables*, which show the financial position of working age single people and married couples with up to four children, both in and out of paid work, based on a series of clearly defined assumptions, and with earnings below the upper earnings limit for NI contribution. All the working families in the DHSS model are single-wage and all are assumed to live in council property appropriate to the family's size, and to pay the estimated average rents and rates charged by the local authorities during the financial year to which the figures refer. All those in paid work in 1985-86 were assumed to pay £5.95 a week in fares to work, with no allowance for childminding costs.

This Appendix uses a similar computer model, written by Professor A.B. Atkinson, Holly Sutherland and Brian Warren at the London School of Economics (TAXEXP) to show the effects on net and disposable incomes in 1985-86 of each of the reform options discussed in this study, and to compare them with the system then in force and with the system introduced in April 1988. TAXEXP enables the user to make a wide range of housing assumptions and there is virtually no upper limit to the level of earnings for which tax calculations can be made. It is also possible to take account of mortgage interest tax relief, and to include one- and two-wage couples.

Note that *BI 2000* is shown separately. Although the figures are at November 1985 prices, *BI 2000* refers to the year 2000 and is costed on a different tax base (see Chapter 19).

Appendix 2: Redistributive effects of integration

Systems compared

(1) *Pre-Fowler:* the system in force in November 1985.

(2) *Fowler TA:* the illustrative figures in the Technical Annex to the Social Security Review White Paper (DHSS, Dec 1985). No allowance is made for the 20% contribution to local authority rates because the Technical Annex did not specify the compensatory amount with IS.

(3) *Full basic income:* illustrative system with 70% tax rate.

(4) *Vince:* Liberal Party's 1983 Tax Credit proposals.

(5) *Minford:* Professor Patrick Minford's conditional NIT.

(6) *BIG 1(a):* A Rhys Williams and Parker illustrative BIG option.

(7) *SDP:* Social Democrats' 1986 *Merging Tax and Benefits* plan.

(8) *BI 2000:* Parker's modified BIG scheme, aimed at the year 2000.

Income levels

All the figures are in £ per week and are valid for the period November 1985 to March 1986. One of the difficulties when constructing tax/benefit model tables is to select the levels of gross earnings at which to start and finish. The levels chosen here may be compared with average weekly earnings as reported in the April 1985 and 1986 *New Earnings Surveys*, as shown below.

	April 1985 £	April 1986 £
Full-time manual men	163.6	174.4
Full-time non-manual men	225.0	244.9
Full-time men, all occupations	192.4	207.5
Full-time manual women	101.3	107.5
Full-time non-manual women	133.8	145.7
Full-time women, all occupations	126.4	137.2
Full-time males and females on adult rates	171.0	184.7

Source: Department of Employment Gazette June 1987, Table 5.6.

Appendix 2: Redistributive effects of integration

Disposable incomes

Disposable incomes show the amounts of money people have to spend each week, after paying income tax, NI contribution, rent and rates, and after receiving all benefits to which there is entitlement. The assumptions made in the tables are as follows:

- All householders are tenants, paying the rents and rates shown below.
- Water rates are £1.65 for all households, and disposable income is before payment of water rates, which are added to SB, but are not added to IS.
- At nil earnings benefit is SB or equivalent, at £20 the work is assumed to be part-time, otherwise full-time work is assumed.
- No allowance is made for SB additional payments, but the £2.20 SB heating addition is included for children under five.
- The families have no capital, and no other income.
- All means-tested benefits are taken up in full.
- Value of passport benefits is:
  adults: £0.75 with SB and FIS, and with IS and FC.
  children over five: free school meals £2.06 (with SB, FIS and IS).
  children under five: free welfare milk and vitamins £1.61 (with SB, FIS and IS).
- No entitlement to free school meals above the FIS entitlement ceilings.
- All earners are contracted in to SERPS.
- Fares to work are not deducted, but *BI 2000* makes childcare costs tax deductible up to a maximum of £40.50 per child. For the single mother with two children, childcare costs are assumed to be nil at earnings of £20 a week, £20 at earnings of £40 and £60 a week, otherwise £50.50, that is £40.50 for the child aged 4 and £10 for the child aged 6.
- Rents and rates:
  working age: families without children: rent £13.80, rates £5.20,
                 families with children: rent £16.50, rates £6.30.
  pensioners: rent £15, rates £7.

Net incomes

These are defined as gross weekly earnings, plus non-withdrawable benefits, less income tax and NI contribution (or equivalent). Child benefit is included, as are basic incomes. FIS, family credit and housing benefit are excluded. So are Vince's withdrawable benefits, Minford's NIT, Parker's housing benefit and the SDP basic benefit. The exclusions are necessary in order to avoid assumptions about housing costs with pre- and post-Fowler systems and with BIG schemes, and to put the figures on a comparable basis. The assumptions are as follows:

For people of working age net incomes are shown with and without
mortgages. The former are shown in italics in the second line for each
system. The interest rate is assumed to be 10%. On earnings of £100 a
week there is no mortgage. On earnings of £150 a week the mortgage
is assumed to be £20,000 and the gross weekly mortgage interest
payable is £38. At all other income levels the mortgage is assumed to
be £30,000 or more (ie at or above the upper limit for mortgage
interest tax relief), and the weekly interest is £58.

In the case of two-wage married couples, the combined wages come
to the gross earning shown. On combined earnings of £150-£500 the
wife earns £100. On combined earnings of £750 and £1,000 the wife
earns £200.

All the families are contracted into SERPS.

No allowance is made for superannuation tax reliefs. This means that
tax liability for all the systems except full BI, BIG 1(a) and *BI 2000* is
unrealistically high, especially for high earners (see Chapter 16).

Pensioner net incomes are defined as basic NI pension (or
equivalent), plus income from SERPS or additional pension/
private pension/annuities/investment income, less income tax.
Where the new system abolishes the pensioner earnings rule, other
income can include earnings.

Family types

Working age

(1) Single non-householder
(2) Single householder
(3) Single person with two children under five
(4) One-wage married couple
(5) Two-wage married couple (net incomes only)
(6) One-wage married couple + 2 children under five
(7) Two-wage married couple + 2 children under five (net
    incomes only)

Pensioners

(8) Single pensioner
(9) Pensioner couple

With full basic income and with the BI components of the Vince
and BIG schemes, the term "married couple" can be replaced by *any
two adults*.

Table A.2.1: Disposable incomes, working-age families, November 1985 to March 1986

	Disposable incomes from gross weekly earnings of:										
	£ 0	£ 20	£ 40	£ 60	£ 80	£ 100	£ 120	£ 140	£ 160	£ 180	£ 200
1. Single non-householder											
Pre-Fowler											
Age 16-17	19	23									
18-20	24	28	38	51	63	74	86	98	110	123	135
21-24	28	32									
25 and over	28	32									
Fowler TA											
Age 16-17	19	23									
18-24	25	29	38	51	63	74	86	98	110	123	135
25 and over	31	35									
Full Basic Income	60	66	72	78	84	90	96	102	108	114	120
Liberal	56	59	63	66	69	80	91	102	114	125	136
Minford	V**	V**	66	72	78	90	105	120	135	150	165
BIG 1(a)	24	36	49	61	74	86	98	111	123	136	146
SDP	32	49	54	58	64	76	88	100	112	125	137
BIG 2000	26	46	60	73	85	97	110	122	135	147	159
2. Single householder											
Pre-Fowler											
Age 16-17	32	36									
18-24	32	36	38	45	49	55	67	79	91	104	116
25 and over	32	36									
Fowler TA											
Age 16-17	19	23									
18-24	25	29									
25 and over	31	35	38	43	45	55	67	79	91	104	115
Full Basic Income	41	47	53	59	65	71	77	83	89	95	101
Liberal	37	45	52	55	59	62	72	83	95	106	117
Minford	V**	V**	47	53	59	71	86	101	116	131	146
BIG 1(a)	33	40	46	52	58	67	79	91	104	116	127
SDP	32	35	36	39	45	57	69	81	93	106	118
BI 2000	36	46	53	59	66	79	91	103	116	128	141
3. Single person + 2 children aged 4 and 6											
Pre-Fowler	58	70	88	98	99	96	93	101	113	125	138
	66*	78*									
Fowler TA	64	76	87	89	91	94	97	101	113	125	138
Full Basic Income	83	88	94	100	106	112	118	124	130	136	142
Liberal	86	95	103	106	109	112	115	119	127	138	150
Minford	V**	V**	101	101	107	113	119	127	142	157	172
BIG 1(a)	78	84	90	96	102	109	120	132	145	157	167
SDP	83	86	87	88	90	93	97	101	113	125	137
BI 2000 incl. childcare TD	66	76	91	97	115	124	136	149	161	173	186

Table A.2.1 (continued).

	Disposable incomes from gross weekly earnings of:										
	£ 0	£ 20	£ 40	£ 60	£ 80	£ 100	£ 120	£ 140	£ 160	£ 180	£ 200
4. Married couple (one-wage)											
Pre-Fowler	51	55/59	38	56	65	68	74	86	99	111	123
Fowler TA	50	54/58	38	56	60	63	74	86	99	111	123
Full Basic Income	101	107	113	119	125	131	137	143	149	155	161
Liberal	68	77	85	88	91	94	98	107	119	130	141
Minford	V**	V**	73	79	85	91	97	106	121	136	151
BIG 1(a)	57	64	70	76	82	91	103	116	128	141	151
SDP	52	55	56	59	62	66	70	81	93	106	118
BI 2000	62	72	79	85	91	104	117	129	143	154	167
5. Married couple + 2 children aged 4 and 6 (one-wage)											
Pre-Fowler	77	81/85	84	96	97	94	91	97	109	121	123
Fowler TA	79	83/87	86	88	89	90	93	97	109	121	133
Full Basic Income	142	148	154	160	166	172	178	184	190	196	202
Liberal	93	103	110	114	117	120	123	126	135	146	157
Minford	V**	V**	98	98	98	101	107	116	131	146	161
BIG 1(a)	92	98	104	110	116	122	134	146	159	171	181
181 SDP	92	95	96	97	99	102	106	110	113	125	137
BI 2000	92	102	109	115	122	131	143	156	168	180	193

* Long-term SB rates, after one year on benefit

V** = variable, depending on effects of Minford's benefit cap

Table A.2.2: Net Incomes, Working-Age Families, excluding withdrawable benefits

	Net incomes from gross weekly earnings of:								
	£ 100	£ 150	£ 200	£ 250	£ 300	£ 400	£ 500	£ 750	£ 1000
1. Single person									
Existing	74	104	135	165	199	264	320	441	544
	116	*152*	*183*	*216*	*286*	*346*	*473*	*579*	
Fowler TA	No change to existing								
Full basic income	90 ditto	105	120	135	150	180	210	285	360
Liberal	80	108	136	164	192	241	291	387	465
	125	*161*	*189*	*217*	*273*	*323*	*425*	*506*	
Minford	90	127	165	202	240	315	390	577	765
	137	*179*	*217*	*254*	*329*	*404*	*591*	*779*	
BIG 1(a)	86 ditto	117	146	173	201	254	304	413	513
SDP	76	106	137	167	198	256	310	429	530
	118	*154*	*185*	*215*	*274*	*328*	*446*	*547*	
BI 2000	98 ditto	129	160	191	222	284	346	501	656
2. Single person + 2 children aged 4 and 6									
Existing	99	130	160	191	225	292	349	473	577
	141	*178*	*208*	*242*	*312*	*375*	*505*	*612*	
Fowler TA	No change to existing								
Full basic income	135 ditto	150	165	180	195	225	255	330	405
Liberal	116	144	172	200	228	277	327	423	501
	161	*197*	*225*	*253*	*309*	*359*	*461*	*542*	
Minford	112	158	195	233	270	345	420	608	795
	162	*208*	*247*	*285*	*360*	*435*	*622*	*810*	
BIG 1(a)	130 ditto	161	190	218	245	299	348	508	558
SDP	99	129	160	190	221	279	333	452	553
	141	*177*	*208*	*238*	*297*	*351*	*469*	*570*	
BI 2000	147 ditto	178	209	240	271	333	395	550	705

Table A.2.2 (continued).

	Net incomes from gross weekly earnings of:								
	£ 100	£ 150	£ 200	£ 250	£ 300	£ 400	£ 500	£ 750	£ 1000
3. Married couple (one-wage)									
Existing	81	111	142	172	206	274	331	454	559
		123	*159*	*190*	*223*	*293*	*357*	*486*	*593*
Fowler TA	No change to existing								
Full basic income	150 ditto	165	180	195	210	240	270	345	420
Liberal	104	132	160	188	216	265	315	411	489
		149	*185*	*213*	*241*	*297*	*347*	*449*	*530*
Minford	86	132	170	207	245	320	395	582	770
		136	*184*	*222*	*259*	*334*	*409*	*597*	*784*
BIG 1(a)	110 ditto	141	170	197	225	278	328	441	537
SDP	76	106	137	167	198	256	310	429	530
		118	*154*	*185*	*215*	*274*	*328*	*446*	*547*
BI 2000	124 ditto	155	186	217	248	310	372	475	682

	Net incomes from gross weekly earnings of:								
	£ 100	£ 150	£ 200	£ 250	£ 300	£ 400	£ 500	£ 750	£ 1000
4. Married couple (two-wage)									
Existing	95	126	155	185	216	280	341	480	598
		138	*172*	*202*	*233*	*297*	*365*	*508*	*630*
Fowler TA	No change to existing								
Full basic income	150 ditto	165	180	195	210	240	270	345	420
Liberal	104	132	160	188	216	272	328	504	540
		149	*185*	*213*	*241*	*297*	*353*	*481*	*578*
Minford	86	136	186	229	266	341	416	604	791
		136	*186*	*236*	*281*	*356*	*431*	*618*	*806*
BIG 1(a)	110 ditto	141	172	203	232	287	340	473	579
SDP	91	121	152	182	213	274	332	472	587
		123	*169*	*200*	*230*	*291*	*350*	*490*	*604*
BI 2000	133 ditto	164	195	176	257	319	381	536	691

Table A.2.2 (continued).

	Net incomes from gross weekly earnings of:								
	£ 100	£ 150	£ 200	£ 250	£ 300	£ 400	£ 500	£ 750	£ 1000
5. Married couple + 2 children (one-wage)									
Existing	95	125	156	186	220	288	345	468	573
		137	*173*	*204*	*237*	*307*	*371*	*500*	*607*
Fowler TA	No change to existing								
Full basic income	195 ditto	210	225	240	255	285	315	390	465
Liberal	124	152	180	208	236	285	335	431	509
		168	*205*	*233*	*261*	*317*	*367*	*469*	*550*
Minford	100	146	184	221	259	334	409	596	784
		150	*198*	*236*	*273*	*348*	*423*	*611*	*798*
BIG 1(a)	144 ditto	175	204	232	259	313	362	472	572
SDP	99	129	160	190	221	279	333	452	553
	ditto	*141*	*177*	*208*	*238*	*297*	*351*	*469*	*570*
BI 2000	154 ditto	185	216	247	278	340	402	557	712

	£ 100	£ 150	£ 200	£ 250	£ 300	£ 400	£ 500	£ 750	£ 1000
6. Married couple + 2 children (two-wage)									
Existing	109	140	169	199	230	294	355	494	612
		152	*186*	*216*	*247*	*311*	*379*	*522*	*644*
Fowler TA	No change to existing								
Full basic income	195 ditto	210	225	240	255	285	315	390	465
Liberal	124	152	180	208	236	292	348	524	560
		169	*205*	*233*	*261*	*317*	*373*	*501*	*598*
Minford	100	150	200	243	281	356	431	618	806
		150	*200*	*243*	*295*	*270*	*445*	*632*	*820*
BIG 1(a)	144 ditto	175	206	237	266	321	374	507	614
SDP	105	135	166	196	227	288	347	486	601
		147	*183*	*214*	*244*	*305*	*364*	*504*	*618*
BI 2000 incl. childcare TD	163 ditto	202	240	271	306	368	430	585	740

Table A.2.3: Pensioners, disposable incomes

	Disposable incomes, assuming weekly incomes other than state basic pension/Bls/minimum pensions, of:								
	£ 0	£ 5	£ 10	£ 15	£ 20	£ 30	£ 40	£ 50	£ 100
1. Single pensioner (householder)									
Existing	41	41	41	42	43	46	48	55	90
Fowler TA	39	40	41	42	42	44	48	55	90
Full basic income	38	40	41	43	44	47	50	53	68
Liberal	34	38	42	46	50	58	65	71	91
Minford	14	19	24	29	34	44	54	63	101
BIG 1(a)	41	43	44	47	50	57	63	69	100
SDP	44	45	46	46	47	48	51	57	91
BI 2000	44	46	49	52	55	62	68	74	105
2. Married pensioner (householder)									
Existing	64	64	64	65	68	71	73	80	115
Fowler TA	62	62	63	64	65	67	73	80	115
Full basic income	98	100	101	103	104	107	110	113	128
Liberal	97	102	106	110	114	123	130	136	156
Minford	50	55	60	65	70	80	90	100	139
BIG 1(a)	98	101	104	107	110	117	123	129	160
SDP	69	69	70	71	72	74	81	88	123
BI 2000	108	111	114	118	120	127	132	139	170

Table A.2.4: Pensioners, net incomes

	Net incomes, assuming original incomes (all unearned) other than state basic pension/Bls/minimum pensions, of:						
	£ 50	£ 100	£ 150	£ 200	£ 300	£ 400	£ 500
1. Single pensioner							
Existing	77	112	145	180	250	310	363
Fowler TA	77	112	145	180	250	310	363
Full basic income	75	90	105	120	150	180	210
Liberal	93	113	140	168	224	277	323
Minford	85	123	160	198	273	348	423
BIG 1(a)	91	122	153	182	237	290	339
SDP	79	114	148	183	250	307	359
BI 2000	96	127	158	189	251	313	373
2. Married pensioner*							
Existing	102	137	168	203	273	333	387
Fowler TA	102	137	168	203	273	333	387
Full basic income	135	150	165	185	210	240	270
Liberal	158	178	196	224	280	333	379
Minford	122	161	218	255	330	405	480
BIG 1(a)	151	182	213	242	297	350	399
SDP	110	145	179	214	279	335	385
BI 2000	161	192	223	254	316	378	438

* Assumption: All the original income belongs to the husband.

Appendix 3:
Estimated costs of UK personal income tax allowances and reliefs

| | £ million estimated cost | | % increase |
	1985-86	1987-88	
Married man's allowance	12,900	13,250	3
Single person's allowance	7,550	8,050	7
Wife's earned income allowance	3,450	3,600	4
Husband and wife election for separate taxation of wife's earnings	210	390	86
Age allowance	425	450	6
Additional personal allowance for one-parent family	150	170	13
Widow's bereavement allowance	50	30	
Blind person's allowance	3	5	
Dependent relative allowance	12	10	
Housekeeper allowance	under 1	under 1	
Son's or daughter's services allowance	under 1	under 1	
Relief for:			
Employee's contributions to occupational pension schemes	1,400	1,600	14
Employer's contribution to occupational pension schemes	2,200*	2,900*	32
Investment income of occupational pension schemes	3,500	4,100	17
Lump sum payments to pensioners	1,000	1,200	20
Retirement annuity premiums	325	450	38
Life assurance premiums (contract made before 14 March 1984)	640	520	−19
Qualifying interest on loans for purchase or improvement of owner-occupied, etc. property	4,750	4,750	0
Approved profit-sharing schemes	60*	75*	
Approved savings-linked share option schemes	5*	45*	
Approved share option schemes	under 1*	200*	
Instalment relief on share options exercised outside approved schemes	10*	2*	
Personal equity plans	—	10*	
Business Expansion Scheme	75*	80*	
Profit-related pay	—	under 1	
Expenditure on property managed as one estate	2*	2*	
Foreign pensions: 10% deduction	3	5*	
Foreign emoluments (non-domiciled employee of foreign employer)	65*	25*	
Schedule E Work expenses allowed as deduction	400	320	
Half of Class 4 National Insurance Contributions	—	70	

| | £ million estimated cost | | % |
	1985-86	1987-88	
Exemption of:			
First £70 of National Savings Bank, ordinary account interest	20*	15*	
Interest on National Savings Certificates	450*	410*	
Premium Bond prizes	40*	40*	
SAYE	25*	25*	
British Savings Bonds bonuses	under 1	under 1	
Income of charities and scientific research associations	300	390	
Charitable donations under the payroll giving scheme	—	1	
British government securities where owner not normally resident in UK	280	390	
Foreign service allowance paid to Crown Servants abroad	45	50	
Statutory redundancy payments	150*	—	
Payments under job release scheme	5*	1*	
Student maintenance awards	30*	40*	
NI child dependency additions	20	15*	
Sickness benefit	75	40	
Invalidity and severe disablement allowances	135	160*	
Industrial disablement allowances	25*	80	
Allowances to rehabilitees	under 1	under 1	
Attendance allowance	50	45*	
Mobility allowance	20*	35*	
Maternity benefits/allowance	50*	10*	
Family income supplement	25*	30*	
Supplementary benefits	65*	110*	
£10 Christmas bonus	9	10*	
War disablement benefits	30*	90*	
War widow's pension	20*	20*	
Children's allowance to Forces' widows	under 1	under 1	
Pensions and annuities paid to holders of the Victoria Cross and certain other gallantry awards	under 1	under 1	
Option to tax woodland under Schedule B instead of Schedule D	10*	10*	
Farming etc average profits	10*	10*	

* This figure is particularly tentative and subject to a wide margin of error.

Sources: 1985-86: *Public Expenditure White Paper,* Cmnd 9702-11, Table 2.24, HM Treasury, January 1986.
1987-88: *Public Expenditure White Paper,* Cm 288-1, Table 6.5, HM Treasury, January 1988.

The original sources include numerous, explanatory footnotes.

Appendix 4:
Income distribution, GB 1985:
families with dependent children
and retirement pensioners

Families with dependent children

Tables A.4.1 and A.4.2 show the numbers of working and out-of-work families with children, at different income levels and according to the number of wage earners and the number of

Table A.4.1: Number of working families with children at various income levels – Great Britain 1985, thousands

Gross weekly income excluding state benefits £	Total families	Lone parent	Two parent	One wage	Two wage	No. of dependent children 1	2	3	4+
Under 80	90	10	70	70	10	40	40	10	*
80-89	20	*	20	20	*	20	10	*	*
90-99	50	10	40	40	10	40	10	*	*
100-109	100	10	90	70	30	40	40	20	*
110-119	130	10	120	80	40	60	50	10	10
120-129	130	20	110	100	30	70	60	10	*
130-139	170	30	140	130	40	80	70	10	10
140-149	150	10	140	100	60	70	60	10	10
150-159	260	10	240	170	90	130	100	30	*
160-169	190	10	170	100	90	90	80	20	*
170-179	230	10	220	110	120	120	90	20	*
180-189	200	10	190	120	80	90	80	20	10
190-199	250	10	240	130	110	.120	100	20	10
200-219	480	10	470	220	260	170	230	60	20
220-239	440	10	430	170	270	170	180	70	30
240-259	370	10	360	120	250	130	160	60	20
260-279	360	*	360	110	250	130	170	40	10
280-299	290	10	280	100	190	110	130	30	10
300 and over	1,480	10	1,470	480	1,010	550	700	170	60
TOTAL	5,390	220	5,180	2,460	2,940	2,230	2,340	610	200

Source: Hansard WA, 21 Jan 1988, cc 836-840.

Table A.4.2: Number of out-of-work families of working age at various income levels: Great Britain 1985, thousands

| | Gross weekly income including state benefits | | | | | | | |
	£0-50	£50-69	£70-89	£90-109	£110-129	£130-149	£150+	Total
Total	90	180	410	370	170	80	150	1,450
Lone parent	70	150	220	150	60	20	30	690
Two parent	20	30	200	230	110	60	110	760
No. of children								
One	80	130	220	90	30	20	50	630
Two	10	40	160	170	60	20	60	510
Three	*	10	30	80	30	20	20	180
Four+	*	*	*	30	50	30	10	130
NI benefits received								
None (a)	30	20	30	60	30	10	90	260
(b)	60	130	330	230	100	40	10	890
UB (a)	*	10	10	20	*	*	*	50
(b)	*	*	20	20	10	*	*	60
SB/SSP (a)	*	*	*	*	*	*	*	10
(b)	*	*	*	10	*	*	*	10
IVB (a)	*	10	10	20	20	20	20	80
(b)	*	*	*	*	*	*	*	10
Other (a)	*	10	*	20	20	20	10	60
(b)	*	*	10	*	*	*	*	20

* Less than 5,000
(a) Without supplementary benefit
(b) With supplementary benefit

Acronyms: UB = unemployment benefit; SB = supplementary benefit; SSP = statutory sick pay; IVB = invalidity benefit; Other = includes industrial disablement, maternity and widows benefit.

Source: Hansard WA 21 Jan 1988, cc 836-840.

Note: The figures in both tables are rounded to the nearest 10,000. Therefore the rows and columns may not sum to the totals shown.

children. The figures are derived from the 1985 *Family Expenditure Survey* and are subject to sampling error. All figures are rounded to the nearest 10,000, so the rows and columns may not sum exactly to the totals shown. In Table A.4.1. gross weekly income means the income reported in 1985, without any updating. A working family is defined as one where at least one parent is in full-time employment or self-employment and includes families where the head has been sick or unemployed for less than three months. In such cases the income shown is the income when the head was in work. A two-wage family is defined as one where the second wage exceeds £4 a week. In Table A.4.2. gross weekly income includes housing benefit. An out-of-work family is defined as one where neither parent is in full-time employment or self-employment, but excludes families where the head has been sick or unemployed for less than three months.

Retirement pensioners

The following table, based on the 1985 Family Expenditure Survey, shows the number of pensioners with income excluding state retirement pension of any category or supplementary pension, at the levels specified. Pensioners are here defined as the individuals in a tax unit which receives some form of retirement pension. The figures refer to single pensioners or married couples where the husband is over 65.

Table A.4.3: Number of retirement pensioners at various income levels: Great Britain 1985, thousands

Gross income excluding state pension (£ pw at 1985 prices)	Single pensioners	Married couples
Less than £5	430	110
5-10	440	130
10-15	410	190
15-20	590	210
20-30	1,070	460
30-40	320	240
40-50	170	180
50-60	100	140
60-70	70	80
70-80	90	90
80-90	50	70
90-100	50	40
100-150	160	240
150-200	50	100
200-250	20	50
250-300	10	70
300-350	—*	20
350-400	—*	10
400-450	—*	10
450-500	—*	—*
Over 500	—*	10
Total	4,030	2,450

* Less than 10,000 cases

Source: Hansard WA, 14 Jul 1987, cc 451-452.

Glossary of acronyms
and technical terms

AA: Age allowance (income tax).

AFDC: Aid to families with dependent children (US).

AFDC-U: Aid to families with dependent children, unemployed fathers (US).

APA: Additional personal allowance (income tax, lone parents).

ATR: Average tax rate.

BB: Basic benefit. New income-tested benefit proposed by the SDP.

BI: Basic income.

BI 2000: *Basic Income 2000*. A modified BIG scheme targeted at the year 2000.

BIC: Basic income contribution. Replaces income tax and NI contributions with BIG schemes.

BIG: Basic Income Guarantee. Partial integration strategies devised by Parker and B. Rhys Williams.

BIG PHASE 1: Stage one of a transition to *BI 2000*.

BIRG: Basic Income Research Group.

CB: Child benefit. A tax-free, universal benefit or BI payable for children.

DCA: Disability costs allowance.

DHSS: Department of Health and Social Security. (Now called DSS: Department of Social Security.)

Dinkys: Double income no kids yet.

Disposable income: Net income minus rent and local authority domestic rates plus any income-tested or means-tested benefits to which there may be entitlement (*see* net income and NSP).

FAST: Forecasting and Assessment in the fields of Science and Technology (EEC Commission).

FC: Family credit. A new means-tested benefit for lower paid families with children, which replaced FIS in April 1988.

FES: Family Expenditure Survey.

FIS: Family income supplement. Former income-tested benefit for lower paid families with children, replaced by FC in April 1988.

GDP: Gross Domestic Product.

GMI: Guaranteed minimum income.

Glossary of acronyms and technical terms

GY: Gross income.

Hansard WA: Parliamentary/Hansard Written Answer.

HB: Housing benefit.

ICA: Invalid care allowance.

Income-tested benefit: A benefit payable if the claimant's income is below the income levels specified in government regulation.

IS: Income support. Britain's safety net of last resort, restricted to people who are out-of-work but available for work, unless they are not required to work (eg retirement and invalidity pensioners and lone parents). Replaced former SB in April 1988. Means-tested.

IT: Income tax.

IVB: National insurance invalidity benefit.

LEL: Lower earnings limit, ie the earnings level at which NI contribution becomes payable.

MC: Married couple.

MC2: Married couple with two children.

MCA: Married couples' allowance (for income tax, after April 1990).

Means-tested benefit: A benefit payable after a test of wealth (£8,000 of income-producing assets in 1988) as well as income.

MITR: Mortgage interest tax relief.

MMA: Married man's allowance (for income tax).

MSC: Manpower Services Commision.

MTR: Marginal tax rate.

Net income: Gross income (earned and/or unearned) minus income tax and NI contribution, plus any non means-tested / income-tested benefits to which there may be entitlement, eg child benefit or NI pension (*see* disposable income and NSP.

NI: National insurance.

NIT: Negative income tax.

NSP: Net spending power, ie disposable income minus travel to work and/or work-related childcare costs (*see* disposable income).

NY: Net income.

pa: Per annum.

PBI: Partial basic income.

pw: Per week.

RR: Replacement ratio, ie out-of-work/benefit income as a proportion of in-work income.

SB: Supplementary benefit (a means-tested benefit restricted to people who were out of work, replaced in April 1988 by IS).

SDA: Severe disability allowance.

SERPS: State Earnings Related Pension.

SH: Single householder.

SI: Subsistence income proposed as replacement for SB by Minford.

SIME/DIME: Seattle-Denver Income Maintenance Experiment, the last and longest of the US negative income tax experiments.

SP: Single person.

SP2: Single person/lone parent + 2 children.

SPA: Single person's allowance (income tax).

SPI: Survey of Personal Incomes (Inland Revenue).

SSP: Statutory sick pay. Minimum, flat-rate, occupational sick pay, payable during first 26 weeks of sickness instead of NI sickness benefit. Employers' costs refunded by Government.

SSR: 1985 Social Security Review.

ST/ICERD: Suntory Toyota International Centre for Economics and Related Disciplines, London School of Economics.

TAXEXP: A computer model of the tax and benefit systems, written by Professor A.B. Atkinson, Holly Sutherland and Brian Warren at the London School of Economics, which allows the user to calculate the net and disposable incomes of model families over a wide range of gross earnings, under the existing tax/benefit system and assuming policy changes.

TAXMOD: A computer model of the tax and benefit systems, based on the 1982 Family Expenditure Survey, and written by Professor A.B. Atkinson and Holly Sutherland at the London School of Economics, as part of the ESRC Programme on Taxation, Incentives and Distribution of Income.

TC: Tax credit.

TD: Tax discount.

TIS: Total income support.

UB: National Insurance unemployment benefit.

UEL: Upper earnings limit, ie the earnings level above which NI contribution ceases to be payable.

UnMC: Unmarried couple.

1w: One-wage (in reference to married couple).

2w: Two-wage (in reference to married couple).

WE: Work expenses.

WEIA: Wife's earned income allowance (income tax).

Y: Income

Notes

Chapter 2 - Flaws in the Beveridge Plan

1. Compare German social assistance/*Sozialhilfe*, which covers the whole population and gives more benefit to people in paid work or training than to non-workers.

Chapter 4 - 1948-88: Genesis of an underclass

1. The term "underclass" is used throughout this report to refer to individuals and families who have lost their economic independence, because they are subject to the rules and regulations applied with state benefits, especially means-tested benefits.
2. See also the Memorandum of Evidence prepared by Professors A.B. Atkinson, M.A. King and N.H. Stern for the House of Commons, Treasury and Civil Service Select Committee *Enquiry into the Structure of Personal Income Taxation and Income Support* (House of Commons, May 1983, Appendices).
3. This is one reason why *Low Income Families* has been discontinued.
4. The Minister's estimate was 1.3 million, but this was in November 1987, before the April 1988 announcement that poll tax rebates will be withdrawn using a taper of 15 percent instead of 20 percent.

Chapter 6 - Forwards or backwards?

1. Not the fixed amount tax credit, or tax discount, referred to in some OECD publications and by the Institute for Fiscal Studies (Dilnot, Kay and Morris 1984), but the convertible tax credits proposed in the 1972 *Proposals for a Tax-Credit System* (Treasury and DHSS 1972). See Chapter 8, pages 102-103

Chapter 9 - Basic Income

1. Forecasting and Assessment in the fields of Science and Technology.
2. Jacques Duboin's writing, now out of print, included: *La grande révolution qui vient* (1934); *En route vers l'abondance* (1935); and *Libération* (1936). A monthly journal, *La grande relève des hommes par la science*, continues to be published by his daughter.

Chapter 10 - Negative Income Tax

1. *Double income, no kids yet.* For loans taken out after 1 August 1988, tax relief has been limited to the interest on £30,000 per residence, regardless of the number of borrowers.

Chapter 14 - Basic Income Guarantee

1. For projected SERPS amounts in selected years between 1983 and 2008, see Hansard Written Answer, 28 January 1986, c 509.

Chapter 19 - Basic Income 2000

1. A good account of the technical background to computerisation was provided by Mr S.C.T. Matheson, Board of Inland Revenue, in evidence to the Meacher Committee (House of Commons 1983, Minutes of Evidence, 10 November 1982). The Inland Revenue remit for computerisation of PAYE included a stipulation "not to close up options for perhaps far-reaching change in the future" (para 1043). Once computerisation of the existing income tax system is complete, it should therefore be comparatively straightforward to adapt it to an integrated tax and benefit system. It is also technically possible to start planning for a new, integrated requirement before implementation of the existing requirement. What is inadvisable is to make changes to the existing requirement during the critical period of final design and testing.

2. The lower and higher earnings levels for NI contribution are uprated each year in line with increases in the basic NI pension. Since the pension is indexed to prices, not earnings, and since earnings tend to increase faster than prices, this has a fiscal drag effect similar to the indexation of the personal income tax allowances to prices instead of earnings. Each year more of the lower paid have to pay NIC and income tax. Despite the resulting buoyancy of NI contributions, it seems likely that the NI contribution will have to be increased once SERPs matures in 1998.

3. That is why some BIG schemes retain private pension tax reliefs. BIG 2(a), for instance, keeps all pension tax reliefs and replaces employers' NI contributions by a 10 percent payroll tax, all of which goes towards personal pensions.

Chapter 20 - Getting from here to there

1. A tax exemption is less expensive in terms of revenue forgone than a tax allowance, because above the exemption limit tax is payable on *all* income. The lower earnings limit for NI contribution is a tax exemption. On earnings up to the LEL no NI contribution is payable, but once the LEL is reached NI contribution is payable on all earnings, from the first £. Age allowance (with income tax) is another example of a tax exemption. In 1987-88 it cost only £450 million. The disadvantage of tax exemption systems is that they create disincentives at the point of entry into tax. These can be modified by the use of vanishing exemptions. The disincentive effect would in any case be much smaller with investment income than with earnings.

References and bibliography

Abbott, E. and Bompass, K., *The Woman Citizen and Social Security: A Criticism of the Proposals in the Beveridge Report as they Affect Women*, Women's Freedom League, 1943.

Adam Smith Institute, *Social Security Policy*, Omega Report, ASI, 1984.

Anderson, M., *Welfare: The Political Economy of Welfare Reform in the United States*, Hoover Institution, Stanford University, 1978.

Ashby, P., *Social Security after Beveridge – What Next?*, National Council for Voluntary Organisations, 1984.

Ashby, P., *Towards an Income and Work Guarantee*, BIRG Bulletin No.7, BIRG, 102 Pepys Rd, London SE14 5SG. Spring 1988.

Association of Metropolitan Authorities, *A New Deal for Home Owners and Tenants. A Proposal for a Housing Allowance Scheme*, AMA, 1987.

Atkinson, A.B., *Review of the UK Social Security System, Evidence to the National Consumer Council*, March 1984.

Atkinson, A.B., *The Costs of Social Dividend and Tax Credit Schemes*, ESRC Programme on Taxation, Incentives and the Distribution of Income, Discussion Paper No. 63, London School of Economics, April 1984.

Atkinson, A.B., *A Guide to the Reform of Social Security*, New Society, 13 December 1984.

Atkinson, A.B., *Social Insurance and Income Maintenance*, Welfare State Programme Discussion Paper No. 11, ST/ICERD, London School of Economics, October 1986.

Atkinson, A.B., Maynard, A., and Trinder, C., *National Assistance and Low Incomes in 1950*, in Social Policy and Administration, 1981.

Atkinson, A.B., and Sutherland H., *A Tax Credit Scheme and Families in Work*, ESRC Programme on Taxation, Incentives and the Distribution of Income, Discussion Paper No. 54, London School of Economics, April 1984.

Atkinson , A.B., and Sutherland, H. (Ed), *Tax Benefit Models*, ST/ICERD Occasional Paper No. 10, London School of Economics, 1988.

Australian Government Commission of Inquiry into Poverty, *Poverty in Australia: First Main Report*, Canberra, AGPS, 1975.

Barr, N., *Strategies for Income Support: A Simple Taxonomy*, Welfare State Programme, Research Note No. 3, ST/ICERD, London School of Economics, January 1987.

Basic Income Research Group (BIRG), BIRG Bulletins Nos. 3-7 , BIRG, 102 Pepys Road, London SE14 5SG, 1985-88.

Beveridge, Sir W., *Social Insurance and Allied Services*, Cmd 6406, HMSO, 1942.

Beveridge, Sir W., *Full Employment in a Free Society*, George Allen & Unwin, 1944.

Beveridge, Lord, *Voluntary Action*, George Allen & Unwin, 1948.

References and bibliography

BIRG Disability Working Group, *Implications of Basic Income for People with Disabilities*, BIRG Bulletin No. 7, 102 Pepys Rd, London SE14 5SG, April 1988.

Bresson, Y., and Guilhaume, P., *Le Participat: Réconciler l'Économique et le Social*, Chotard et Associés Éditeurs, 68 rue J.-J. Rousseau, 75001 Paris, 1986.

Brittan, S., Economic Viewpoint: Capitalism and the Under Class, *Financial Times*, 1 October 1987.

Burton, J., *Would Workfare Work?* Occasional Papers in Employment Studies No. 9, Employment Research Centre, University of Buckingham, 1987.

Cahn, E.S., *Service Credits: A New Currency for the Welfare State*, Welfare State Programme Discussion Paper No. 8, ST/ICERD, London School of Economics, July 1986.

Cahn, E.S., *Service Credits: A New Currency*, BIRG Bulletin No. 6, BIRG, 102 Pepys Rd, London SE14 5SG, Autumn 1986.

Canadian Government, *Report of the Royal Commission on the Economic Union and Development Prospects for Canada (The Macdonald Report)*, Canadian Government Publishing Centre, Supply and Services Canada, Ottawa, Ontario KIA 0S9, 1985.

Cantillon, B., and Deleeck, H., *Prestations non contributives et revenu minimum garanti*, European Institute of Social Security Yearbook 1985.

Chappell, P., *Back to Basics*, BIRG Bulletin No. 7, BIRG, 102 Pepys Rd, London SE14 5SG, Spring 1988.

Chappell, P., and Vinson, N., *Personal and Portable Pensions – For All*, Centre for Policy Studies, 1983.

Chappell, P., and Vinson, N., *Owners All – Personal Investment Pools*, Centre for Policy Studies, 1985.

Christopher, A., Polanyi, G., Seldon, A., and Shenfield, B., *Policy for Poverty*, Institute for Economic Affairs, 1970.

Christophersen, G., *Final Report of the Seattle-Denver Income Maintenance Experiment, Volume 2: Administration*, Mathematica Policy Research, May 1983.

Clark, C., *Poverty before Politics*, Institute for Economic Affairs, 1977.

Cohen, B., *Caring for Children: Services and Policies for Childcare and Equal Opportunities in the United Kingdom*, Report for the European Commission's Childcare Network, Commission of the European Communities, 8 Storeys Gate, London SW1, 1988.

Colin, C., *Maternité et Extrême Pauvreté*, University of Nancy, 1980.

Comité Européen des Assurances, *The Future of Pension Systems in Europe*, CEA Booklets, Nb4, 1986.

CSO, *Social Trends No. 4*, HMSO, 1973.

CSO, *Social Trends No. 6*, HMSO, 1975.

CSO, *Social Trends No. 8*, HMSO, 1977.

CSO, *Social Trends No. 13*, HMSO, 1983.

CSO, *Social Trends No. 15*, HMSO, 1985.

Davies, S., *Beveridge Revisited: New Foundations for Tomorrow's Welfare*, Centre for Policy Studies, 1986.

Desai, M., *Drawing the Line: on Defining the Poverty Threshold*, in *Excluding the Poor*, Ed Peter Golding, Child Poverty Action Group, 1986.

DHSS, *Report of the Committee on Local Authority and Allied Personal Social Services (Seebohm Report)*, HMSO, 1968.

DHSS, *Separated Wives and Supplementary Benefit*, Hazel Houghton, Social Research Branch, 1973.

DHSS, *Report of the Committee on One-Parent Families (Finer Report)*, Cmnd 5629, HMSO, July 1974.

DHSS, *Reform of Social Security*, Green Paper, Cmnd 9517-9519, HMSO, June 1985.

DHSS, *Tax Benefit Model Tables: The Financial Position of Hypothetical Families where the Head is Working or Unemployed*, November 1985.

DHSS, *Reform of Social Security: Programme for Action* , White Paper, Cmnd 9691, December 1985.

DHSS, *Social Security Bill 1986: Report by the Government Actuary on the Financial Effects of the Bill on the National Insurance Fund*, Cmnd 9711, HMSO, January 1986.

DHSS, *Low Income Families – 1983*, July 1986.

DHSS, *Social Security Statistics 1986*, HMSO 1986.

DHSS, *Abstract of Statistics for Index of Retail Prices, Average Earnings, Social Security Benefits and Contributions*, Branch HQ SR8A, August 1986 and 1987.

DHSS, *Low Income Statistics: Report of a Technical Review* , March 1988.

DHSS, *Low Income Families – 1985*, May 1988.

DHSS, *Households Below Average Income: A Statistical Analysis 1981-85*, May 1988.

Dilnot, A.W., *Basic Income Guarantee*, Analysis Using IFS Tax-Benefit Model, Institute for Fiscal Studies (IFS), 1985.

Dilnot, A.W., Kay, J.A., and Morris C.N., *The Reform of Social Security*, Institute for Fiscal Studies (IFS), 1984.

Disability Alliance, *Poverty and Disability: Breaking the Link*, DA, 1987.

Disability Income Group, *DIG's National Disability Income*, DIG, Millmead Business Centre, Millmead Road, London N17 9QU, 1987.

Douglas, C.H., *Credit Power and Democracy* , 1922.

Douglas, C.H., *Economic Democracy*, 1920, Bloomfield Books, 1974.

Eakins, P. (Ed), *The Living Economy: A New Economics in the Making*, Routledge & Kegan Paul, 1986.

Edwards, M. A., *The Income Unit in the Australian Tax and Social Security Systems*, Institute of Family Studies, 766 Elizabeth Street, Melbourne, 3000 Australia, 1984.

Esam, P., Good, R., and Middleton, R., *Who's to Benefit? A Radical Review of the Social Security System*, Verso, 1985.

Euzéby, C., *A Minimum Guaranteed Income: Experiments and Proposals*, International Labour Review, Vol. 126, No. 3, May-June 1987.

Finer, M. and McGregor, O.R., *The History of the Obligation to Maintain*, Report of the Committee on One-Parent Families, Cmnd 5629-1, HMSO, 1974.

References and bibliography

Fisher, H.A.L., *A History of Europe*, Edward Arnold & Co., 1936.

Fragnière, G., *Le Travail et l'Emploi dans la Sociétée Européenne de Demain* , Essay Work and Social Change no. 20, European Centre for Work and Society, *NEWS* No. 14, August 1987.

Friedman, M., *The Case for the Negative Income Tax*, in Republican Papers, Ed M. Laird, Anchor Books, N.Y, 1966.

Friedman, M., *Negative Income Tax 1* and *Negative Income Tax 11*, Newsweek, 16 September and 7 October 1968.

Friedman, M. and R., *Capitalism and Freedom*, University of Chicago Press,1962.

Friedman, M. and R., *Free to Choose*, Pelican, 1981.

Gilder, G., *Wealth and Poverty*, Basic Books Inc., New York, 1981; Buchan & Enright, London, 1982.

Goodwin, R.E., and Le Grand, J., *The Middle Class Infiltration of the Welfare State: Some Evidence from Australia*, Welfare State Discussion Paper No. 10, ST/ICERD, London School of Economics, 1986.

Green, C., *Negative Taxes and the Poverty Problem*, Brookings Institution, 1967.

Hemming, R., *The Tax Treatment of Occupational Pension Schemes*, Memorandum to House of Commons May 1983, 20-11, Appendix 32, para 4.

House of Commons, *Select Committee on Tax-Credit*, Report, Evidence and Appendices, June 1973.

House of Commons, *Enquiry into the Structure of Personal Income Taxation and Income Support*, Third Special Report from the Treasury and Civil Service Committee, Session 1982-83, May 1983.

House of Commons, *Social Security Bill 1986 (Bill 59)*, HMSO, January 1986.

House of Commons, *Social Security Bill 1987, Explanatory and Financial Memorandum*, 1987.

House of Commons Debates, *Family Allowances Bill Second Reading*, Hansard, 8 March 1945; *Social Security Bill 1987, Second Reading*, Hansard, 2 November 1987.

Howell, Rt Hon. D., *Blind Victory: A Study in Income, Wealth and Power*, Hamish Hamilton, 1986.

Howell, R.H., *Why Unemployment?* Adam Smith Institute, London, 1985.

Inland Revenue, *Inland Revenue Statistics 1980*, Section 2A: *Tax Thresholds*, HMSO, 1980.

Inter-Bank Research Organisation (IBRO), *Research Brief October 1985*, IBRO, 32 City Rd, London EC1, 1985.

Institute of Fiscal Studies (IFS) 1984 and 1985 (*see*, Dilnot, A.W.)

Jackson, H.P., and Valencia, B.H., *Financial Aid through Social Work*, Routledge & Kegan Paul, 1979.

Jordan, B., *The State: Authority and Autonomy*, Basil Blackwell, 1985.

Jordan, B., *Rethinking Welfare*, Basil Blackwell, 1987.

La Révue Nouvelle, *L'Allocation Universelle*, Rue des Moucherons 3/5, 1000 Bruxelles, Belgium, No. 4/April 1985.

Leach, D., and Wagstaff, H., *Future Employment and Technological Change*, Kogan Page, 1986.

References and bibliography

Leaper, R.A.B., *Cash and Caring,* BIRG Bulletin No. 5, BIRG, 102 Pepys Rd, London SE14 5SG, Spring 1986.
Lister, R., *There is an Alternative. Reforming Social Security,* Child Poverty Action Group, 1-5 Bath St, London EC1, 1987.
Liverpool Macroeconomic Research Limited, *Quarterly Economic Bulletin,* Research Group in Macroeconomics.
Mair, P.B., *Shared Enthusiasm : The Story of Lord and Lady Beveridge* , Ascent Books Ltd, 1982.
McClements, L.D., *The Economics of Social Security,* Heinemann, 1978.
Meacher Committee Report, see House of Commons, May 1983.
Meade, J.E., *Planning and the Price Mechanism,* George Allen & Unwin, 1948.
Meade, J.E., *Poverty in the Welfare State,* Oxford Economic Papers, Vol. 24, No. 3, Clarendon Press, Oxford, November 1972.
Meade, J.E., *The Structure and Reform of Direct Taxation,* IFS, 1978.
Meyer, N.I., (a) *Gradual Implementation of a Basic Income in Denmark;* (b) *Alternative National Budget for Denmark including a Basic Income,* Papers presented at First International Conference on Basic Income at Louvain-la-Neuve, Belgium, 1986.
Meyer, N.I., Petersen, K.H., and Sorensen, V., *Revolt from the Center,* 1978 in Danish, Marion Boyars, London 1981.
Minford, P., *State Expenditure: A Study in Waste,* Supplement to Economic Affairs, Vol. 4, No. 3, April-June 1984.
Minford, P., Davies, D., Peel, M., and Sprague, A., *Unemployment: Cause and Cure,* Martin Robertson 1983; Basil Blackwell 1985.
Minford, P., and Davis, J., *Germany and the European Disease,* Symposium on Unemployment in Europe, Récherches Économiques de Louvain, Vol. 52, Nos 3-4, 1986.
Minford, P., Peel, M., and Ashton, P., *The Housing Morass,* Institute for Economic Affairs, 1987.
Mitchell, P., *Constructing a National Disability Income. A Discussion Document,* RADAR, 25 Mortimer St, London W1, 1986.
Montreal Diet Dispensary, *Budgeting for Basic Needs and Budgeting for Minimum Adequate Standard of Living,* MDD, 1984.
Morley-Fletcher, E., *Per una Storia dell Idea de "Minimo Sociale Garantito"* in *Rivista Trimestrale No. 64-66,* Rome, October 1980-March 1981.
Moss, P., *Childcare and Equality of Opportunity,* Consolidated Report to the European Commission, 8 Storeys Gate, London SW1, 1988.
Murray, C., *Losing Ground,* Basic Books Inc., New York, 1984; Buchan & Enright, London 1982.
Murray, C., *A Radical Perspective,* paper at Centre for Policy Studies conference The Welfare Challenge, March 1987.
National Consumer Council, *Of Benefit to All,* NCC, 1984.
Netherlands Scientific Council for Government Policy, *Safeguarding Social Security,* The Hague, 1985.
Nickell, S., Review Article, Economic Journal, Vol. 94, Dec. 1984.
Nottage, R., and Rhodes, G., *Pensions: A Plan for the Future,* Anglo-German Foundation, London, 1986.
Nozick, R., *Anarchy, State and Utopia,* Basil Blackwell, Oxford, 1974.

References and bibliography

OECD, *Negative Income Tax*, 1974.

OPCS, *General Household Survey 1983*, HMSO, 1985.

Opielka, M., and Vobruba, G., *Das Garantierte Grundeseinkommen: Entwicklung und Perspektiven einer Forderung*, Fischer Taschenbuch Verlag GmbH, Frankfurt/ Main, May 1986.

Owen, S., *Childminding Costs*, BIRG Bulletin No. 6, November 1986.

Pahl, J., *Patterns of Money Management within Marriage*, Journal of Social Policy, 1980.

Pahl, J., *The Allocation of Money and the Structuring of Inequality within Marriage*, Sociological Review, May 1983.

Pahl, J., *The Allocation of Money within the Household*, in *State, Law and the Family*, Ed. M. Freeman, London, Tavistock, 1984.

Pahl, J., *Social Security, Taxation and Family Financial Arrangements*, BIRG Bulletin No. 5, BIRG, 102 Pepys Rd, London SE14 5SG, 1986.

Parker, H., *Action on Welfare*, Social Affairs Unit, 9 Chesterfield St, London W1, 1984.

Parker, H., *The Debate about Costings*, BIRG Bulletin, BIRG, 102 Pepys Rd, London SE14 5SG, 1985.

Parker, H., *Family Income Support: Government Subversion of the Traditional Family*, in *Family Portraits*, Ed. Anderson, D.C., and Dawson, G., Social Affairs Unit, 9 Chesterfield St, London W1, 1986.

Parker, H., *Effects of Mr John Moore's April 1988 Benefit Changes on the Disposable Incomes and Work Incentives of Low Income, Working Age Families*, Welfare State Programme Research Note No. 10, ST/ICERD, London School of Economics, January 1988.

Prest, A., and Barr, N., *Public Finance*, Weidenfeld and Nicolson, 1986.

Quebec Government, Ministry of Finance, *White Paper on the Personal Tax and Transfer Systems*, Ministère des Communications, Direction de la Commercialisation, C.P. 1005 Quebec, (Quebec) G1K 7B5, 1984.

Roberts, K., *Automation, Unemployment and the Distribution of Income*, European Centre for Work and Society, Maastricht, 1982.

Rothbard, M., *For a New Liberty: The Libertarian Manifesto*, Collier Macmillan, 1978.

Rhys Williams, B., *The New Social Contract*, Conservative Political Centre, 1967.

Rhys Williams, B., *Redistributing Income in a Free Society*, Economic Age, Vol. 1, No. 6, 1969.

Rhys Williams, B., *From Status to Contract in Social Reform*, paper delivered at Institute for Fiscal Studies conference at the London School of Economics, May 1972.

Rhys Williams, B., *Proposals for a Basic Income Guarantee*, evidence submitted to the Treasury and Civil Service Committee, 21 July 1982, House of Commons, May 1983.

Rhys Williams, J., *Something To Look Forward To*, Macdonald, 1943.

Rhys Williams, J., *Taxation and Incentive*, William Hodge, 1953.

Rhys Williams, J., *A New Look at Britain's Economic Policy*, Ed. Susan Glyn, Penguin, 1965.

Salter, T.A., *Defined Contributions and Defined Benefits: Some Thoughts on the Future of Pension Plan Design*, 17th Annual IBIS Conference, Cascais, Portugal, May 1987.

Schulte, B., *The Future of Social Security in the European Community: Community Actions*, Trans European Policy Studies Association, Château du Pont d'Oye, Habay-la-Neuve, Belgium, September 1985.

SDP, *Attacking Poverty*, Green Paper No. 11, 1981.

SDP, *Poverty, Taxation and Social Security*, SDP Policy Document No. 8, 1983.

SDP, *Merging Tax and Benefits, Attacking Poverty*, SDP, Cowley Street, London SWI, 1986.

SIME/DIME Distribution Centre, *Final Report of the Seattle Denver Income Maintenance Experiment*, Department of Health & Human Services, ASPE, Humphrey Building, Room 410E, 200 Independence Avenue, SW, Washington, DC, 20201,1984.

Smail, R., *A Two-Tier Basic Income and a National Minimum Wage*, BIRG Bulletin No. 4, BIRG 102 Pepys Rd, London SE14 5SG, 1985.

Smith, A., *The Wealth of Nations*, first published 1776, Everyman Edition, 1947.

Social Planning Council of Metropolitan Toronto, *Guides fo Family Budgeting*, SPC, 1984.

Spahn, H.-P., and Vobruba, G., *Das Beschäftigungsproblem: Die Ökonomische Sonderstellung des Arbeitsmarktes und die Grensen der Wirtschaftspolitik*, International Institute of Management, IIM, Wissenschaftszentrum Berlin, Platz der Luftbrücke 1-3, 1000 Berlin 42, October 1986.

SRI International, *Final Report of the Seattle-Denver Income Maintenance Experiment, Volume 1, Design and Results*, May 1983.

Standing, G., *Unemployment and Labour Market Flexibility: the United Kingdom*, ILO, Geneva, 1986.

Stevenson, O., *Claimant or Client?* Allen & Unwin, 1973.

Sutherland, H., *Modelling the SDP Tax/Benefit Scheme*, ESRC Discussion Paper No. 101, ST/ICERD, London School of Economics, December 1986.

Tachibanaki, T., *Non-Wage Labour Costs: Their Rationale and Economic Effects*, Discussion Paper No. 19, Welfare State Programme, ST/ICERD, London School of Economics, July 1987.

Tester, S., *Cash and Care*, Bedford Square Press, 1985.

Theobald, R., (ed) *The Guaranteed Income: Next Step in Economic Evolution?* Doubleday and Company, Garden City, New York, 1965.

Titmuss, R.M., *The Social Division of Welfare*, in *Essays on the Welfare State*, Allen & Unwin, London 1958.

Tobin, J., *Improving the Economic Status of the Negro*, Daedalus, Fall 1965.

Torry, M., *Basic Income for All: A Christian Social Policy*, Grove Ethical Studies No. 68, Grove Books Ltd, Bramcote, Nottingham NG9 3DS, 1988.

Toynbee Hall, *After Beveridge*, Proceedings of a Conference held at Toynbee Hall, June 1985.

Treasury, *The Reform of Personal Taxation, Green Paper*, Cmnd 9756, HMSO, March 1986.

Treasury, *Budget Statement & Budget Report*, HMSO, March 1986.

Treasury, *Public Expenditure White Paper*, Cm 56, HMSO, January 1987.

References and bibliography

Treasury, *Public Expenditure White Paper*, Cm 288, HMSO, January 1988.

Treasury and DHSS, *Proposals for a Tax-Credit System*, Green Paper, HMSO, October 1972.

US Department of Health and Human Services, Office of Income Security Policy, Office of the Assistant Secretary for Planning and Evaluation, *Overview of the Seattle-Denver Income Maintenance Experiment Final Report*, U.S. Government Printing Office, 1983.

Van der Werf, D., *Summary of Five Scenarios for Work in Europe*, FAST Forecasting and Assessment in Science and Technology, Directorate General for Science, Research and Development, Commission of the European Communities, 200 rue de la Loi, B-1049, Brussels, April 1987.

Van Neuss, R., Fragnière, G., and Delforge, C., *Les sept pilliers de la civilisation du travail*, Scholtens Boek BY, PO Box 101, NL – 6120 AS Sittard, 1987.

Van Parys, P., *La préhistoire du débat: L'ombre de Speenhamland*, in *La Revue Nouvelle*, rue des Moucherons 3/5, 1000 Bruxelles, April 1985.

Van Slooten, R., and Coverdale, A.G., *The Characteristics of Low Income Households*, in Social Trends No. 8, HMSO, 1977.

Vince, P., *...To Each According...Tax Credit – Liberal Plan for Tax and Social Security*, Women's Liberal Federation, 1983.

Vince, P., *Basic Incomes: Some Practical Considerations*, BIRG Bulletin No. 5, BIRG, 102 Pepys Rd, London SE14 5SG, 1986.

Vobruba, G., *History and Present Position of Discussion of Guaranteed Basic Income*, in *The Guaranteed Basic Income and the Future of Social Security*, Green-Alternative Link (GRAEL), European Parliament, 79 rue Belliard, 1040 Brussels, June 1986.

Walter, J.A., *Basic Income: Escape from the Poverty Trap*, Marion Boyars, 1988.

Whiteford, P., *Work Incentive Experiments in the United States and Canada*, Research Paper No. 12, Research and Statistics Branch, Development Division, Department of Social Security, Canberra, 1981.

Whiteford, P., *A Family's Needs; Equivalence Scales, Poverty and Social Security*, Research Paper No. 27, Development Division, Department of Social Security of the Government of Australia, Canberra 1985.

Williams, S., *Exclusion: the Hidden Face of Poverty*, in *Excluding the Poor*, Ed. Peter Golding, Child Poverty Action Group, 1986.

Wootton, B., *In a World I Never Made*, George Allen & Unwin, 1967.

Wootton, B., *Reflections on the Welfare State*, in *Approaches to Welfare*, Eds Philip Bean and Stewart MacPherson, Routledge & Kegan Paul, 1983.

Wresinski, M.J., *Grande pauvreté et précarité économique et sociale*, Report presented by Father Joseph Wresinski of ATD Fourth World to the Conseil Économique et Social, *Journal officiel de la République Française*, sittings of the 10 and 11 February 1987.

Index

Index

Index

Index